MUSLIM RAP, HALAL SOAPS, AND REVOLUTIONARY THEATER

Artistic Developments in the Muslim World

EDITED BY KARIN VAN

UNIVERSITY OF TEXAS PRESS ◆ *Austin*

Requests for permission to reproduce material from this work should be sent to:
    Permissions
    University of Texas Press
    P.O. Box 7819
    Austin, TX 78713-7819
utpress.utexas.edu/about/book-permissions

♾ The paper used in this book meets the minimum requirements of ANSI/NISO
Z39.48-1992 (R1997) (Permanence of Paper).

LIBRARY OF CONGRESS CATALOGING-IN-PUBLICATION DATA

Muslim rap, halal soaps, and revolutionary theater : artistic developments in the
Muslim world / edited by Karin van Nieuwkerk. — 1st ed.
    p.   cm.
    Includes bibliographical references and index.
    ISBN 978-0-292-74768-5
    1. Popular culture—Islamic countries.   2. Arts—Islamic countries.   3. Islam
and art.   4. Islamic civilization—Western influences.   5. Muslims—Non-Muslim
countries—Social conditions—21st century.   I. Nieuwkerk, Karin van, 1960–
    DS35.62.M885   2011
    700.88'297—dc23

2011021616

First paperback printing, 2012

CONTENTS

ACKNOWLEDGMENTS

I WISH TO THANK SEVERAL PEOPLE who advised, criticized and helped during the process of finishing the book *Muslim Rap, Halal Soaps, and Revolutionary Theater: Artistic Developments in the Muslim World*. First of all I would like to thank ESF (the European Science Foundation) for financing the exploratory workshop "Islamization of the Cultural Sphere? Critical Perspectives on Islam and Performing Arts in Western Europe and the Middle East," which was held in Amsterdam in 2008. I would also like to thank the KNAW (Royal Netherlands Academy of Arts and Sciences) for additional funding of this workshop. Moreover, I would like to show my appreciation for the peer reviewers and editors of the University of Texas Press for their helpful comments. Finally, I would like to thank my partner Hans Stukart for his continuous support and his willingness to help me out in many practical matters related to this book.

MUSLIM RAP, HALAL SOAPS, AND
REVOLUTIONARY THEATER

ARTISTIC DEVELOPMENTS IN THE MUSLIM CULTURAL SPHERE: ETHICS, AESTHETICS, AND THE PERFORMING ARTS

KARIN VAN NIEUWKERK

GREEN POP, CLEAN CINEMA, HALAL SONGS, Islamic soaps, Muslim rap and hip-hop, Islamist fantasy serials, postrevolutionary Islamic "Dance-Theatre," Suficized music, as well as heavy metal against Islam, are just a few of the performing arts that will be presented here. This book will trace Islamic discourses on performing arts and give insight into several genres of religious and nonreligious productions that manifest Islam in its various forms. It will foreground case studies from Germany, France, Turkey, Egypt, Syria, Lebanon, Iran, Canada, and the USA. The book will analyze the way piety movements and politically engaged Islamists, Islamic states as well as moderate believers, have both rejected and embraced popular culture and performing arts as potential sites to propagate their religio-ethical normative projects.

This book is the result of the European Science Foundation exploratory workshop "Islamization of the Cultural Sphere? Critical Perspectives on Islam and Performing Arts in Western Europe and the Middle East," which was held in Amsterdam in 2008. The workshop consisted of scholars from diverse disciplines such as Islamic Studies, ethnomusicology, anthropology, sociology, cultural studies, and political science. The aim of the workshop was to show the multiplicity of voices, discourses, and practices in Muslim communities with regard to Islam and performing arts.

After the Danish cartoon affair in 2006, the general discourse with regard to freedom of speech and expression of culture in Islam has been put in a negative light. There were also several incidents involving secular Western art productions that were felt to hurt religious sensibilities of Muslims and were eventually withdrawn from production, such as the German *Idomeneo* and the Dutch opera production *Aisha*. These cases have received media attention to such an extent that the representations of Islam and performing arts as incompatible and the lack of creative freedom as marking the difference between Muslims and non-Muslims are firmly established. As Michael

Frishkopf (this volume) argues, the diasporic Muslim community of Canada also seizes upon expressive forms such as music and musical ritual practices to express Muslim difference within Canadian society. Stating that "music is forbidden in Islam" becomes a productive marker of difference. Artists have at times suffered where Islamists have risen to power, as is documented by the website of the anti-music-censorship organization Freemuse. Heavy metal musicians thus protest the Islamization of the public sphere in Turkey (Pierre Hecker, this volume), and Los Angeles exile musicians from Iran attempt to subvert and counter the Islamic Republic of Iran with their sensuous and cosmopolitan musical productions (Farzaneh Hemmasi, this volume). At present, though, the tide within Islamist movements is changing and some strands of Islamists and piety movements embrace art and popular culture. Pious forms of art are created that cater to religious sensibilities and can be used to promote Islamic messages and lifestyles. This development is carefully monitored by states that fear the rise of Islamism. The relationship between Islam and the performing arts has thus become an arena of contest of great relevance to many actors.

Studying the contestations with regard to Islam and performing arts is important for several reasons. First, as illustrated above, popular culture and arts are vital instruments for cultural politics, whether for states or countermovements. Second, the analysis of Islam and performing arts sheds light on the development within Islamist movements toward a post-Islamist, liberal public sphere, as well as the influences of (religious) markets and globalization. Third, studying performing arts productions can add to our understanding of the character and scope of the Muslim cultural sphere. Where, how, and why have popular culture and performing arts been turned into a religious mission? Finally, a focus on Islam and performing arts opens up the study of the sensitive relationship among gender, religion, and the body. It is particularly the strong emotive and sensory power of performing arts and sonic forms that makes them such a sensitive matter in the eyes of religious authorities. The study of Islam and performing arts calls for a careful examination of religious sensibilities and the development of Islamic ethics and aesthetics catering to pious subjectivities. Can we see the development of a new Islamic aesthetics? How are religious ethics embodied in pious productions?

In this introduction the main trends indicated by the contributions will be drawn together. In the first section the importance of art for Muslim cultural politics will be highlighted. In the next section the subversive potentials of (pious) productions will be examined. In the third section the different ways the global and Muslim cultural spheres have intersected and developed toward specific cultural forms will be highlighted. The emerging market for pious popular culture will be sketched as well. Finally, the religious missions of Islamist groups, states, and power holders will be analyzed. This section will particularly highlight the emergent religious sensibilities among Muslim audiences, the pious body on stage, and the conversion of Islamic ethics into aesthetics.

PERFORMING ARTS, CULTURAL POLITICS, AND THE MUSLIM CULTURAL SPHERE

"Performance Studies" is an emergent field of scholarly research drawing on a wide range of disciplines including social science, cultural studies, history, and gender studies. Performance is a broad concept too and can, according to Schechner, be perceived as a wide spectrum of actions extending from ritual, play, popular entertainment, and performing arts to everyday performances and the enactment of social, professional, or gender roles (2002, 2). What counts as "performance" and as "art" is historically and culturally variable. For that reason an open concept of performance and art is needed. Popular culture and popular art are also difficult to separate (Fabian 1998, 96), as are art and vocation or crafts (Fabian 1998, 17; Van Nieuwkerk 1995). Defining performance as a broad spectrum of practices avoids reinstating unproductive distinctions between low culture and high culture or marking off performing arts from popular culture. The tendency over the past century has, according to Schechner, been to dissolve boundaries separating "performing" from "not-performing" and "art" from "not-art" (2002, 30).

Many phenomena can be studied "as performance." Events can be staged as performance for the political effects they create. Most of this volume's contributors document events that are—also according to conventional usage—"a performance." We will particularly focus on performativity rather than simply performance—that is, what performances accomplish or "show doing." As Schechner holds, "The 'working' is as important, maybe more so, than the 'work'" (1987, 8).

Popular culture and performing arts are vital in the identity construction of individuals and communities. Art is generally an instrument for cultural politics. Popular culture, entertainment, and performing arts are specific targets for the cultural politics of competing groups because they are very influential in people's daily lives and lifestyles. Due to the important role played by popular and performing arts in cultural politics as well as in processes of identification, they are crucial arenas of contest.

Several contributors give insight into the emergent Muslim cultural sphere, or *saha Islamiyya* (Harb 2006; Joseph Alagha, this volume; Karin van Nieuwkerk, this volume). By the cultural sphere we mean the debates and contestations by different actors within the public sphere regarding cultural expressions. The notion of a "cultural sphere" is thus not used to separate or distinguish it from the "public sphere," but to highlight and focus on specific deliberations within the public sphere—that is, discussions within the cultural field or on artistic expressions. In the Muslim world we can discern an increasing influence of religiously inflected voices and visions within the cultural sphere, and for that reason it is important to study this Muslim cultural sphere. The most important debates and developments within the Muslim cultural sphere, as well as the cultural politics of states and groups impeding or facilitating its development, emerging from this volume's chapters will be discussed below.

The place of religion in the cultural sphere is highly contested in the West. Yet also in many Muslim countries in the Middle East and beyond, the cultural field is one of the last bastions of secularized elites. In Muslim-minority countries any manifestation of Islamism, especially in regard to art and expressive freedom, is carefully watched and interpreted as a sign of (a lack of) integration and citizenship. A discourse on the incompatibility of values between "us" and "them" has gained strong ground in many European countries. As Frishkopf (this volume) shows, the tendency toward "schismogenesis" is also strong among the Muslim immigrant community in Canada. As a result of the Canadian multicultural politics of "tolerance of intolerance" and a policy that is tolerant of non-Muslims but not at all tolerant of Muslim internal differences, little space is provided for ritual and aesthetic diversity. The ethnically diverse and geographically widespread Muslim population that is also skewed toward high educational levels and elite professions tends to follow reformist ideological powers and external global authorities as representing "true Islam." The Canadian diaspora includes few aesthetic specialists who could counter the reformist attempts to unify the diaspora through ritual conformity. In postrevolutionary Iran, on the other hand, the establishment of an Islamic public sphere was a fact. Yet it still was a real challenge to develop a cultural realm compatible with the country's religious sensibilities, as initially most forms of art were banned.

Expressive culture is not only a contested matter between states and Islamist groups, but also within Islamist movements. Opinions differ among hard-liners, moderates, and liberals as to what forms of music and instruments are allowed (Otterbeck 2008; Alagha, this volume; Frishkopf, this volume). These contestations exist up till today in Muslim-minority and -majority contexts. In the Canadian multicultural context, a distinctively modernist Islamic reformism has gained prominence that insists on a rationalized ritual unity and purity; other contexts show more cultural and ritual diversity among Muslims. Several case studies show an opening up within the Islamist movements with regard to art and entertainment. A new generation of religious scholars and preachers has developed discourses that stress the importance of the arts for the development of nations. Art is to embody the socioreligious body politic. Instead of leaving art to the secular cultural field and closing their eyes to "immoral" or "lowbrow" productions, Islamists feel the need to produce alternatives. These alternatives have to be in accordance with the religious sensibilities of pious audiences and spectators and be religiously "correct." Alternatives are not only available from regional cultural centers, but globally accessible, especially since the spread of satellite and other new technologies. Global musical youth cultures are attracting many fans among Muslim youth as well. Instead of banning artistic expression, Islamists have started to use art as a source for mobilization of youth (Boubekeur 2007). Nooshin (2005) shows that the Iranian state felt forced to counter the flood of exile pop music from Los Angeles by producing alternative forms of art and entertainment. Islamists are only the most recent groups to instrumentalize art for their ideological purposes; so did Nasser (Abu Lughod 2005) and the Pahlavi government (Zeinab Stellar, this volume). Yet the specific project of Islamists and their special way of using art for missionary purposes, as will be highlighted in some of the contributions, are not yet well studied. How to develop pleasant forms of pious arts that combine morals, messages, and merriment has become a major challenge (Van Nieuwkerk, this volume).

Of critical importance to performance studies are issues of embodiment, action, agency, the body, and sensory experience (Kirshenblatt-Gimblett 2004). The focality of the body, sound, and affect, and the aesthetic habitus more generally, are also the issues that make performing arts so crucial for cultural politics. Sonic forms are powerful forces in naturalizing embodied affective social identities, and as Frishkopf argues, maybe even more powerful because they lie outside the discursive realm. Dance in particular is a sensitive arena of bodily discourse (Desmond 1993–1994). The body, the pious body included, is highly gendered and an important matter of concern to religious authorities. The disciplining of the body according to religio-moral scripts, and controlling the way bodies embody piety, make pious productions central issues for cultural politics, a subject upon which I will elaborate in the last section.

What these artistic fields share and what makes them interesting for comparative purposes are the notion of "subverting power relations" attached to popular culture and performing arts (Fabian 1990, 1998; Carlson 2004). After the postrevolutionary state of Iran restricted music and dance, exiles in the USA took these up as constitutive elements of their oppositional version of Iranian culture, which they then circulated globally via a transnational alternative public sphere (Hemmasi, this volume). Turkish metalheads have used music to subvert the perceived encroaching Islamization of the Turkish public sphere (Hecker, this volume). Yet what about the possible counterpublic character of the Islamist public sphere itself (Hirschkind 2006)? To what extent can we regard the pious productions as subversive, and if they are, what are they subverting? So it is interesting to examine the extent to which notions of the subversiveness of popular art and performing arts also hold for pious performing productions. This implies carefully scrutinizing the various historical contexts in which different publics can be considered a counterpublic. I will turn to these questions now.

POWER, SUBVERSION, AND THE COUNTERPUBLIC

Do performances sustain, reproduce, challenge, subvert, or critique ideologies and regimes of power (Schechner 2002, 19)? Some theorists view performance as reinforcing cultural givens, others see it as potentially subversive, while still others see it working under some circumstances in one way and in some the other (Carlson 2004, 20). Play and popular culture have been particularly analyzed for their rebellious potential. Fabian warns against the political naïveté of some approaches toward performance within the social sciences and points at the possibility that colonial rulers encourage performances as entertainment—that is, as a way to co-opt or channel social protest (1990, 17). In *Moments of Freedom*, Fabian (1998) examines the concept of popular culture for the spaces of freedom and creativity it might provide. Popular culture can create sites for individual or collective freedom but is not in itself liberating (1998, 19–21). "If freedom is conceived not just as free will plus the absence of domination and constraints, but as the potential to transform one's thoughts, emotions, and experiences into creations that can be communicated and shared . . . then it follows that there can never be freedom as a state of grace, permanent and continuous. . . . Freedom . . . comes in moments" (1998, 20–21).

To perceive the relationship between dominant power and popular culture and art in terms of conformity versus resistance is thus far too simple. As Fabian holds, "The issue of power and resistance in studies of popular culture . . . cannot be reduced to determining whether or not, or when and where, expressions of popular culture qualify as acts of resistance; what we need to understand is how popular culture creates power to resist power" (1998, 69). He also draws attention to the "power from within"—that is, the possibility that processes and forms of domination that popular culture opposes also work within popular culture. Power is constantly established, negated, and reestablished. "It is not its being power free that distinguishes popular culture . . . but its working against the accumulation and concentration of power, which, when institutionalized, cannot do without victims" (Fabian 1998, 133). Fabian's theory sensitizes us to oversimplified approaches of conformity versus resistance and opens our eyes to power structures within popular art.

Several studies have pointed at the use by young Muslims of music—for instance rai, rap, hip-hop, and heavy metal—as a way to protest against forms of discrimination and stigmatization of Muslims in Europe (Thomas Solomon, this volume; Gazzah 2008). Music is also used to protest the lack of democracy in countries such as Egypt, Morocco, and Pakistan (LeVine 2008). Musicians can also oppose a perceived Islamization of the cultural sphere in Muslim-majority countries (Hecker, this volume; Hemmasi, this volume). Boubekeur (2007) shows how young Muslims in France and elsewhere search for a "cool Islam," expressed in different forms including music, as a way to fight public discourses that stigmatize Islam or present it as an archaic religion. Yet they also want to get rid of the radical Islamist rhetorics of the old generation of political mobilizers.

Solomon (this volume) compares the way Turkish youth express forms of protest by way of rap in the diaspora in Germany and in the Turkish homeland. Islam arises as one theme in rap and is imagined in rather different ways in the two contexts. For these diasporic Turkish youth, Islam is not a doctrinal religious body of knowledge and practices, but an identity. It is "Muslim-ness" rather than Islam. The rappers construct an emotional way of bonding with religion. In the diaspora, they are confronted with negative stereotypes and can revalorize the symbol of Islam. They turn it into a sign of pride and call for a shared cultural or ethnic identity. In Turkey, rappers can use religious discourse as political oratory to challenge the secular state. Rappers in both contexts express oppositional identities in which Islam is a diverse set of discourses and practices that can be employed in various ways to create Muslim subjectivities.

Hecker (this volume) discusses the way heavy metal musicians contest the Islamization of the public sphere in Turkey. Metalheads are accused of moral, sexual, and religious subversiveness and are called Satanists. They distance themselves from religious practice and transgress verbal, gender, and physical boundaries by blasphemy and bodily display, for instance, by wearing long hair. Interestingly, metalheads use anti-Christian symbols to rebel, like the inverted cross, instead of anti-Islamic symbols. This is not only due to fear of repercussions, or a possible lack of anti-Islamic symbols, but also relates to the global flow of symbols belonging to metalhead culture and lifestyle.

Hemmasi (this volume) offers insight into the Iranian exile popular music and entertainment industry in Los Angeles as a transnational alternative means of expression that emerged in response to the Iranian Revolution. The postrevolutionary state established a religious public sphere within the country in which "impious" performing arts were banned. Initially, this included popular music, which impelled the mass exodus of most of the country's popular music industry to Southern California, where a new Iranian music industry began. As a result of the state's restriction of popular music and dance in the aftermath of the revolution, these cultural forms became important in émigré culture. These productions, ironically, returned from exile locations to Iran by means of new media technologies and attracted a large fan base in Iran.

What counts as the public sphere to be countered can thus be radically different. For Turkish metalheads it is the growing Islamist presence; for some Turkish rap groups it is the domination of secular Kemalism. Many performers in Egypt working in the field of pious art productions go against the grain of the officially secular state. Yet, matters are more complex as regards what can be considered counterpublic in Egypt. Due to the ambiguous policies of the Egyptian state toward Islamists and the partial co-opting of moderates and al-Azhar conservative religious authorities, as well as the influence of Islamist groups within the huge state bureaucracy, the state and counterpublic are not clearly demarcated (Van Nieuwkerk 2008). The Iranian case also points at the possibilities of reversal. Once in power, the new power becomes institutionalized and enforces its own regimes of power, of which, in this case, the victims appear to be the players in the cultural field. So, singing religious songs within the initially restrictive climate of postrevolutionary Iran can be a moment of freedom (as well as an expression of faith) (Bayat 2007), whereas chanting similar songs in Egypt can express an identity oppositional to the secular field of art.

Protest can take many artistic forms. Heavy metal, rap, and hip-hop are global protest genres. Often the text is the main vehicle for expressing oppositional identity, sometimes rather straightforwardly (Solomon, this volume), sometimes by subtly changing existing texts into morally upright ones, as by the Egyptian "*halal* song movement" (Van Nieuwkerk, this volume). Humor is an important tool for commenting on structures of domination; the growing amount of Muslim stand-up comedy, particularly in the UK and the USA, constitutes an important field for further study. Dutch-Moroccan rappers often choose a stage name that mocks stereotypes about them in Dutch society. Ali B., for instance, intentionally chose his stage name in reference to the way Dutch media speak about criminal suspects by reporting their first name and last initial. In this way, the popular rapper mocks the stereotype holding that many Dutch-Moroccan boys are criminals (Gazzah 2008, 205). Also bodily forms and stances, such as maintaining a certain ethical comportment, refusing certain "immoral" acts on screen and stage, and insisting on veiling, subvert secular artistic normative structures (Van Nieuwkerk, this volume).

In accordance with Fabian's insights, pious art does not simply resist structures of power; it also has its own structures of control and domination. In an inspiring article, the sociologist Asef Bayat wonders why puritan Islamists express hostility toward fun and joy (2007, 433). He argues that "anti-fun-damentalism" is not restricted to Islamists or even to religious fundamentalists, but extends to all rigid one-dimensional discourses and authorities. According to Bayat, purists do not reject pleasure as long as it is rationalized and controlled (2007, 437). It is particularly the spontaneous, uncontrolled character of fun and relaxation that worries the puritans, because it not only disrupts the moral order, but, more importantly, the doctrinal paradigm on which their power and authority is based. Stellar (this volume) details how in postrevolutionary Iran, theatrical dance was transformed into a rationalized and controlled form, which was reintroduced as a new mode of theatrical performance. The Lebanese Hizbullah only permits art if it is purposeful and there is an advantage (*maslaha*) behind it that outweighs the disadvantage (*mafsada*) (Alagha, this volume). Van Nieuwkerk (this volume) analyzes Egyptian moderate Islamist discourse, which aims to strike a balance between piety and pleasure, morals and messages, by insisting on the purposefulness of art. New regimes of power are established, particularly with regard to gender and the body (see below).

Interesting in this regard is Hirschkind's notion of the counterpublic (2006). He analyzes the Islamic missionary movement, or *da'wah* movement, as a counterpublic. He does not use the notion, as does Fraser (1990), in the sense that the counterpublic is autonomous and sovereign with respect to the state. In his study of the Islamic cassette media, Hirschkind shows that this Islamic soundscape combines ethical exercise, political debate, and popular entertainment. The cultivation of religious sensibilities is a form of political contestation through creating a separate moral space. He thus shifts the attention from Habermas's idea of political deliberation as a rational, disembodied form of reasoning to the ethical values and religious sensibilities of social and political life (2006, 30–31). Hirschkind emphasizes the different sensorium and moral dispositions underlying the discursive practices of the oppositional *da'wah* movement as forming an ethical counterworld, rather than the independent character or content of its deliberations (2006, 105–143). Hirschkind particularly elaborates his arguments with regard to the aural—preaching or listening to cassette sermons—as the medium for contestation.

So, by extension, we could analyze pious art productions as potentially subverting secular artistic norms—and installing new disciplinary forms—by creating a separate moral space and creating art in accordance with religious sensibilities. In the last section I will come back to religious sensibilities and aesthetic forms. But first I will discuss the emergence of different forms of a Muslim cultural sphere in the countries under study.

THE POST-ISLAMIST CULTURAL SPHERE

The emergence of pious performing arts calls for a careful contextualizing and historicizing. In some cases, as in Canada (Frishkopf, this volume), ritual and cultural diversity is hindered by several internal and external circumstances leading to a closed, uniform cultural sphere marked by an absence of musical ritual practices. In other cases, an opening up of the Muslim cultural sphere is visible. Some interesting parallel developments toward a diversification of the Muslim cultural sphere are apparent from the presented case studies.

First, there appears to be emerging a more liberal attitude toward art among several groups of Islamists and politically engaged Muslims. At present, young generations of Islamists have created their own niches of pious art and diversion. Several terms are *en vogue* to express the current liberal climate: "cool Islam," (Boubekeur 2007), "air-conditioned Islam," or "casual Islam" (Tammam and Haenni 2003), as well as "fifteen-minute Islam," "Islam lite," or "market Islam."[1] All these notions share a conception of Islamist currents that are open, up-to-date, liberal, and "easy" in character, as opposed to the former heavy, strict, and closed forms of Islamist movements. A notion that is theoretically more sophisticated in denoting the present developments is "post-Islamism" (Roy 2004; Bayat 2002, 2005; Kepel 2000). Bayat and Kepel define post-Islamism as the turn of moderate Islamist movements away from violence or rigid doctrinal views toward a fusion of religion with democracy. Post-Islamism does not mean the end of Islamism, but a reformulation of Islamist discourse from within the Islamist movement aiming to reconcile "religiosity and rights, faith and freedom" (Bayat 2005, 5). Roy links post-Islamism to the individualization and privatization of Islam (2004, 97–99). Post-Islamism is not directed at reconstructing the state, but at the Islamization of individual practices. This view emphasizes the turn from "religion" into "religiosity"—that is, stressing the virtuous self as the core of faith—and focuses on the development of new forms of piety. The turn from Islamism into post-Islamism, as it pertains to art and recreation, is related to several developments.

The Iranian Revolution of 1979 has been one of the crucial factors in the present "Islamic Revival" in many Muslim countries. Throughout the 1980s and 1990s, conservative Islamists battled against playfulness and entertainment, which were considered a "counter value" because they distracted the believer from prayer and supplication toward film and art (Bayat 2007). Popular artists who were somehow associated with "nudity" and other "immoral" signifiers were demonized and started leaving the country. Although traditional and folk musics were promoted against the "Westernized, inauthentic" cultural industries, most popular musics were banned (Hemmasi, this volume). Morals police "cleansed" the public space and even invaded private parties. Unlike Islamic states such as Saudi Arabia and Afghanistan, the postrevolutionary state in Iran faced a population that had been largely accustomed to secular diversion for about fifty years. Throughout the 1980s, the country's war with Iraq strengthened the revolutionary fervor and surveillance. During the 1990s, the young began to challenge the state's political and moral authority through what Bayat calls "subversive accommodation" (2007, 441). They, for instance, used legitimate rituals such as Muharram—austere occasions of mourning the death of Imam Hussein—to invent "Hussein parties," which provided a legitimate space for fun and flirting. The government was not totally against pleasure, however, as long as it was rationalized and controlled, or a form of "pious pleasure" (Bayat 2007). Beginning in 1997, a period of liberalization started, in part to provide an ideologically correct alternative to the Iranian exile pop (Hemmasi, this volume).

Particularly Muhammad Khatami, the Iranian president between 1997 and 2005, has played a pioneering role in giving culture a more prominent role (Alagha, this volume). His "democratic Shi'ite discourse" and argument that "Islam is culture" were also transported to Lebanon's Hizbullah and paved the way for the transformation of the *hala Islamiyya* into a *saha Islamiyya*—that is, a movement from a political toward a cultural Islamic sphere. Hizbullah now has its own music bands that produce *nashid* (Islamic song, plural *anashid*) that are broadcasted from the mosques (Alagha, this volume). The Hizbullah cultural sphere mainly consists of controlled and ideologically motivated forms of art. Stellar (this volume) analyzes the reappearance of theatrical movement-based performance (*harikat-i mawzun*) in postrevolutionary Iran. Rhythmic movement, which enacted mystical and religious themes such as the Sufi ritual of Sama, were presented as "dance for the divine" rather than "worldly dances which serve no purpose but pleasure." Also, movement-based performances focusing on founding figures of Shi'a Islam, including Zaynab, Fatimah, Hussein, and 'Ali, were performed. Performances of the Holy Defense Theatre are regularly commissioned by governmental organizations for various occasions. A controlled form of art and entertainment has been created that embodies the state's ideology. The battle over art remains an important source of conflict between the reformist and the conservative wings of the government to the present day.

In Egypt, Islamist movements not only targeted popular artists and their publics but also the officially secular state that allowed and accommodated entertainment and art. As is the case for Turkey, Islamists were not hegemonic, but formed a counterpublic that tried to create alternatives to "immoral" art. In the 1980s, Islamist students dominated university campuses in Egypt. They not only disrupted performances of what they considered "immoral" art, but also developed alternative religious theater and reworked the imported genre of *anashid*, religious songs. As Boubekeur (2007) shows for France, important factors in the growing popularity of the genre were the vernacularization of the songs and the departure from strict religious or political activism toward the incorporation of social themes. No longer songs about holy struggle sung in classical Arabic or the Palestinian or Jordanian dialect, songs were sung in French or the Egyptian dialect, addressing topics that mattered to the everyday life experiences of the young. These songs developed into a genre that used authentic Islamic sources, as well as elements of global musical cultures. They thus became a way for religious outreach and political mobilization, as well as entertainment, for young Muslims.

Related to the emergence of a post-Islamist cultural sphere is a second trend: the development of a middle- and upper-middle-class "market Islam" (Haenni 2005). Besides "cool Islamic" artistic forms favored by youth, diverse forms of pious art are directed at middle- and upper-class audiences. From the campus environment in Egypt developed an alternative pious art scene that increasingly catered to the religious sensibilities of a wider circle of people, who accordingly invited the student-artists to their parties. An austere form of pious art would not please the audience, except for the most devout. Artists accordingly experimented with the addition of percussion instruments or lessened the explicit moral and religious imagery of their songs or plays in order to entertain a broader audience. The return from the Gulf of labor migrants who were accustomed to a wealthy and pious lifestyle created a demand for pious art and pious forms of recreation. There thus developed a large internal religious market (Van Nieuwkerk, this volume). Egypt had already, for the religiously conservative market in the Gulf, a considerable production of films and soaps that accommodated Wahhabi censorship (Shafik 2001). But now an internal demand for "prudish productions" developed: the so-called "clean cinema." These films are not strictly religious or moralizing, but women play "chaste roles," without embarrassing the moviegoer (Tartoussieh 2007). A general tendency is noticeable nowadays toward less preachy and more self-consciously pleasant forms of pious art. Yet, as the Muslim public is fragmented, so is the religious market: artists can cater to different religious publics by providing music with or without percussion, weddings with or without sketches, depending on audience demand.

With regard to the development of an internal pious market, Turkey makes an interesting comparison. With the coming into power of Turgut Özal in the mid-1980s, Muslim capitalists and small traders began to compete with secular businessmen in almost all sectors of the economy. Navaro-Yashin makes important observations about the processes of commodification behind any market, secular or religious (2002; see also Haenni 2005). Muslim businessmen advertised themselves as morally different from their competitors, but were after all implicated in the same capitalist consumption market. The rise of the Islamist movement in Turkey in the 1980s and 1990s also led to the creation of a specific market niche for Islamist consumer products such as headscarves, overcoats, and veils. Consumption habits differed between secularists and Islamists, but the production of Islamist commodities bore witness to similar processes of commodification. The Tekbir fashion company, named after the habit of calling "God is great" at public demonstrations, strove for worldwide prestige. Covered women began in time to discriminate veils according to brands and qualities rather than simply for the modesty they afforded. Yet despite the similar production processes implicated, the availability of Muslim capital and the growing religious sensibilities among the well-to-do stimulated a new market for leisure and entertainment: from Islamic tourist resorts offering segregated swimming along the Turkish coast to fashion and art.

In Turkey during the 1970s, an Islamic popular culture started to appear that consisted of rather ideologically determined artistic productions (Saktanber 2002). The first Islamic film company was established in 1968, featuring films in which the good, modest, and authentic person meets an individual who represents the corruptions of modernity. The good person inevitably falls in love with the bad one only to discover the true path, albeit too late for a happy ending. In the 1990s, cinema "sensitive to Islam" reflected the problems of youth more accurately. The dichotomizing approach that contrasts good and bad, moral and immoral, is also characteristic of the current popular Islamist fantasy serials that Ahu Yiğit (this volume) analyzes. These fantasy serials—deeply influenced by some Western productions—adopt magical plots such as time travel, angels disguised as ordinary people, and appearing or disappearing objects and people. Several serials are set in the afterlife, from which the main characters look back on their life on earth. These serials have become so popular that secular channels have copied the format, a development which suggests that a division along the lines "secular" versus "Islamist" is too simple. This Islamization of popular culture in Turkey also forms the context for the emergence of the Islamist rap discussed by Solomon (this volume). But not all such attempts to remake popular cultural forms in an Islamic image succeed, as evident, for example, in the Turkish state's effective censorship of Islamic rap around 2000 by excluding it from the market.

Third, moderate religious ideologies are gaining ground that support liberal religious views on art. 'Amr Khalid and Mo'ez Mas'ud are noticeable examples of preachers who encourage the production of pious art in Egypt (Van Nieuwkerk, this volume; Winegar 2008). Interesting in this respect is not only the increase of trendy messengers who support the "Islam lite" productions, but also the recent use of Sufi elements in pious art productions. Sufi mysticism, or *tasawwuf*, appeared in the Turkish Islamic cinema, the "Dream Cinema," that came into being in the 1990s. Jonathan H. Shannon (this volume) analyzes the "Suficization" of music in present-day Syria. He analyzes the present upsurge of Sufi music worldwide as a result of, amongst other factors, the so-called "War on Terror." In furthering the idea of Syria and Syrians as on the "right" side in the War on Terror, Suficized music helps to promote awareness of an Islamic heritage that is peaceful and "good." The Syrian state tries to portray itself as an ally in the War on Terror, and as a source of "good" Islam and "good" Muslims—Sufism and Sufis—versus the "bad" forms of Islam at its borders. In this highly politicized context, Sufi-related expressive cultural forms are used by the state to promote a message of tolerance to the world.

Equally important and interesting is another development related to the Suficization of music—that is, the crucial influence on the production of music of what Shannon calls the "World Stage" for World Music (Shannon 2003). When we see and hear Sufi music on the World Stage in the ever growing popular scene of World Music festivals, we are actually experiencing *Suficized* musics—those that are "created expressly for the stage and that bear sometimes only a passing relationship to their reputed referents" (Shannon, this volume). Whereas World Music and "World Beat" are generally associated with globalization and transnational cultural economies, "sacred music" is perceived as the domain of the spiritually "authentic" and the "local." The efforts of the Syrian ensembles to record and promote Sufi music reveals how spiritual traditions are in fact produced and authenticated within the practices of the World Music market. In the rush to perform on the World Stage, artists and managers participate in the Suficization of their performance repertoires. The Suficized music *is* in fact the World Stage music—that is, its production is intended for performance outside the original ritual context.

This brings us to a last development I would like to highlight with regard to the emergent post-Islamist cultural sphere: the influence of media, and the global transnational sphere and markets. Several studies indicate the influence of the global and transnational cultural sphere for the development of pious artistic genres. Boubekeur (2007) argues that politically engaged French Muslims desire to participate in the global public sphere. Their artistic products are not only bound to codes related to Islam but also to aesthetic norms of the West: it no longer suffices to sing in a religiously correct way, but the cover of the album should be of the latest design. Also a celebrity system is ascendant in the Muslim public sphere. "Celebrification," the importance of celebrity culture for everyday life, identity formation, and patterns of social interaction, has become a pervasive and global phenomenon (Gamson 1994; Rojek 2001). Also in the Muslim cultural sphere, fame has become as important as religious authority. Bart Barendregt shows the importance of the success of Western boy bands such as the Backstreet Boys in the 1990s for understanding the current form and celebrity status of *nasyid* (*nashid*) music. The transnationality of *nasyid* in Southeast Asia is reflected in the form and style of the music and in the song texts, as well as in the composition of the ensembles consisting of multinational members. Of some singers such as Waheeda, "the 2003 *nasyid* sensation," it was said that the sounds produced were merely World Music with a spiritual twist, that is, not authentic. The commercialism of some groups that seem to focus more on pop than religion is criticized as well.[2] Muslim performers, audiences, and ideologues take different positions as to what is the "right" balance between morals, mission, and the market (Van Nieuwkerk, this volume).

This challenge of balancing glamour and piety relates to manifold aspects of the performance, the most mundane of which is the extent of the remuneration that is acceptable. Monetary compensation can be a tricky issue for pious performers, because tensions can emerge as a result of their sincere pious intentions and their desire to be appropriately remunerated. Islam as (profitable) business was a sensitive issue during my research among female weddings bands in Egypt. Several female performers were slightly insulted when I talked about their performance as "work." It was done for spiritual *ajr*, recompense, not for material gain. This was an important element constituting the respectability, and influencing the religious imagery, of their "work." Also, the families of the women performing at the wedding processions as players of the *duff* (tambourine), were uncomfortable with their daughters "working" at weddings, whereas they did not mind their daughters being engaged in "Islamic calling." The bandleader, though, intending to increase the extent of professionalism in her band, deemed nothing wrong in earning a decent living from this work. She rhetorically asked why whenever something is "Islamic" it should be for free. "Is Islam against money?"[3] Her answer was clearly that morals and money go hand in hand. Yet, the pious performers can be easily attacked for "impious commercialism."

The challenge to translate Islamic ethics into Islamic aesthetics goes far beyond these mundane aspects and is related to sounds, images, movements, and bodily comportment. Pious performance is inscribed onto the body, and pious performances are made to embody certain missions. The relationship between religious mission and the sensorial, bodily form is the topic of the last section.

ISLAMIC ETHICS, AESTHETICS, AND THE BODY

For the study of Islam and performing arts it is crucial to examine discourses on the body. Within anthropology, the body already has a long career, and notions of the body, sensorial experiences, and embodiment are widely debated among scholars (Mauss 1979; Bourdieu 1977; Csordas 1999; Blackman 2008). As Blackman has argued, the body comes in manifold shapes: a disciplined body, a civilized body, a vitalist body, a feeling body, and a sensient body, to mention just a few. Yet the body-in-motion is still undertheorized. Desmond has tackled the dancing body, yet she mainly focuses on it as an arena of bodily discourse and argues for considering not only the body, but also its actions and movements, as a "text" (1993–1994, 34). I would like to consider the moving body in performance not only as a site of representation, but also as a source of experience and subjectivity (Csordas 1999). I will restrict myself to studies on the (moving) body in relation to Islam and piety. First, I will look at some of the theoretical insights on the body and embodiment in the field of Islam and Islamic piety that theorize the pious body at a religious-experiential level. This will give insights into the way religious sensibilities among large audiences have created a receptive climate for pious productions. Then I will come back to the moving body in performance as embodying Islamic ideologies and analyze the translation of these discourses into moving bodies.

Within the study of Islam and the Middle East, Bourdieu's elaboration of the concept of habitus has been taken up and criticized by Starrett (1995) and Mahmood (2005). Bourdieu's notion of bodily hexis is also considered a promising field for further study (Abu Lughod 1989; Starrett 1995). Bourdieu is interested in understanding how individuals contribute to the reproduction of social restrictions, a problem for which the concept of habitus offers an important tool. Habitus is defined as a system of durable, transposable dispositions—"structured structures"—that structure and generate human practice yet are not felt as enforcing and typically go unnoticed

(Bourdieu 1977, 72; Auslander 2008, 67–72). Bodily hexis refers to the way individuals' bodily movements come to feel natural to them; these move-ments are "*em-bodied*, turned into a permanent disposition, a durable man-ner of standing, speaking, and thereby of *feeling* and *thinking*" (Bourdieu 1977, 93–94). These notions, however, have been criticized for emphasiz-ing the unconscious character of the habitus and body hexis. Mahmood, for instance, in her study of the Egyptian piety movement (2005, 139), has highlighted the intentional and pedagogical training of the body as a site of moral virtue among the members.

Bourdieu is criticized not only for neglecting the pedagogical process of instilling disposition, but also for his lack of attention to the relationship between bodily hexis and the ideology or public discourse about hexis (Star-rett 1995). Instead of being an unconscious transmission of bodily habits, the embodiment of ideology in hexis is "a set of processes through which individuals and groups consciously ascribe meaning to—or learn to per-ceive meaning in—bodily disposition, and to establish, maintain, and con-test publicly its political valence" (Starrett 1995, 954). Starrett analyzed the relationship between body hexis and discourse as it pertains to prayer and showed the difference between the colonial discourse, in which the rocking body in prayer is perceived as irrational, and the discourse of Egyptian ed-ucators, who advocated a modern version of prayer as related to cleanliness and discipline. Embodying an ideology, in this case pertaining to prayer, is thus not an unconscious process but an explicit and discursive practice. This brings agency back into processes of embodiment and bodily habits, and underlines its learned, conscious, and contentious character.

The work of Foucault and Butler has been another source of inspira-tion for scholars working on Islam and piety, particularly Mahmood (2001, 2005). One of the central areas of analysis of both Foucault and Butler is the process of subjectivization, that is, the constitution of the subject. Subjec-tivity draws attention to the intricate processes through which subjects con-struct a liveable sense of self. Foucault explored how power—perceived both as oppressive and as resistant to oppression and emanating from discourses and material practices—operates to produce certain subjects. He explores the issue of the ethics of self and identified sexual, political, and religious "Technologies of the Self" (2003) that are constitutive of a sense of oneself (Foucault 2003, 146). The technologies are practices that discipline the body and mind. "Individuals can resist power and transform their own subjectiv-ity by applying techniques of the self. Techniques of the self are about dis-cipline, they are not simply about discipline as domination of the self; they also entail positive transformations of the self" (Auslander 2008, 101).

Mahmood (2005) has given an in-depth analysis of the piety movement in Egypt and the way the devotees train pious dispositions and work on the body to cultivate an ethical self. Participants in the mosque movement regard religious practices such as prayer, styles of comportment, dress, and the movement of the body as ineluctable means for training, cultivating, and realizing a virtuous self (2005, 27–31). Prayer is not simply the expression of piety, but also the means to develop piety. It is a positive way of discipline and ethical self-making. As Hirschkind (2001, 2006) has shown, one of the ethical practices of self-discipline can be to listen to tape-recorded sermons. By extension, listening to religious songs is not only an expression of the devoutness of listeners, but also a form of ethical self-improvement. Pious performances can thus help to inculcate pious dispositions and sensibilities into audiences.

Sensibility is a concept used by Strathern and Stewart to overcome mind-body dualism, as well as to point at the "moral and aesthetic dimension of choice in action" (2008, 70). Sensibility mediates between the mental and the sensory. It encompasses conscious thoughts and actions and also includes the senses, which are focal in the context of performances. It also incorporates the idea of culturally appropriate or habitual behavior (Stewart and Strathern 2002, 5–6). Pious productions do not simply cater to religious sensibilities, but also instill piety into the body and senses of the devout. This enables the realization of the virtuous self in an embodied way within the discursive field of the "appropriate." Pious art is thus for both producers and consumers a sensory means for ethical self-making in accordance with religious ideologies.

This brings us back to what counts as culturally or religiously appropriate. What ideologies or discourses are embodied in pious productions and how? How are bodies made to embody ideologies, particularly in performances? Working from Foucault's insight on forms of power and the processes of subjectivization, Judith Butler has investigated "body matters" with regard to gender and sexuality. Every social-symbolic order is consolidated by prohibitions and repeated performance of identities within that order. Identities are "performative" and constantly reiterated: "Gender is not being but doing; it is not who you are but what you do, that is, how you express your identity in word, action, dress, and manner" (1990, 25). As Butler explains in *Bodies That Matter* (1993), identity performance is not a voluntaristic free choice. Subjectivization—that is, the process by which a subject becomes a self-conscious agent—is not outside the working of power but is a product of these operations. Butler stresses the sustained enactment of norms, although there is a possibility for transformation in the performative reiteration of norms (Auslander 2008, 73–79; see also Mahmood 2005). Stellar (this volume), however, draws attention to the restrictions and controls on performance that hardly leave space for enactment of norms other than those reflecting the biopolitics of the postrevolutionary government in Iran.

We thus need to understand the performativity of normative performances. Which norms or scripts do pious productions in diverse cultural settings enact, embody, and perform? Several contributions highlight religious doctrines (Alagha, this volume; Yiğit, this volume), pedagogical projects (Van Nieuwkerk, this volume), or biopolitics (Stellar, this volume) of Islamist groups or states. Islamic discourse pertaining to the permissibility of art in general, the discussions about the lawfulness of certain instruments and of the female voice, and the conditions for the permissibility of listening to music all shape the artistic form of the performance. How are religious norms and ethics translated into aesthetics, and what does this mean for the sensorium and the body-in-motion?

There are various ways in which Islamic ethics are embodied in aesthetics, depending on the mission of the Islamist states or groups concerned. Yet the moving body appears to be a problem for many Islamists. As Bayat noted for Iran: "Sorrow, sadness, a somber mood, and dark, austere colors defined the Islamist public space, media, and religious rituals. In such a state of virtue, the shape and color of clothing, the movement of the body, the sound of one's voice, the level of laughter, and the intensity of looks all became matters of intense discipline and contestation" (Bayat 2007, 439). Saktanber noted for Turkey that Islamic youth are "over-cautious about any kind of bodily expression, other than presentational codes regarding veiling for girls and beards and hair for boys, and, in the same way that they carefully avoid dancing, . . . [they seem] not to be interested in sport, apart perhaps from martial arts like karate and judo" (2002, 269). Yet, the contrast between the ideal body-at-rest versus the negatively valued body-in-motion is not an assumption restricted to Islamists, but was also part of the colonial discourse (Starrett 1995). As Desmond has argued, in many cultures bodily expressiveness is often linked to nondominant groups, races, classes, and ethnicities, and to gender and sexuality. Several dances introduced into Europe and the USA, for instance, those coming from Latin America, became over time more codified and stylized, less sexually explicit, and more restrained in movement of the body in order to become "appropriate" (Desmond 1993–1994).

In Egypt, the Islamic Revival and religious sensibilities of performers and audiences have affected the domain of cinema to a large degree. The "clean cinema" is one of the expressions of the normative religio-ethical projects of the Islamic Revival (Tartoussieh 2007). An important facet of piety is bodily modesty, and any representation of explicit sexuality is avoided. Women's bodies have to be silenced and sanitized, their sexuality erased. Any "hot scene"—that is, sexually explicit scene—is removed, and new ways of suggesting love scenes are developed. Clean cinema actresses "inhabit a body that is at once chaste, ascetic, and overwhelmingly appealing, even prurient in its modesty and morality" (Tartoussieh 2007, 37). Actresses cultivate the image of the clean body also in order not to lose their fan base and disappoint their pious audience. Clean cinema is a light comical genre because, as Tartoussieh argues, the comic's sexual innocence and chasteness make slapstick an appropriate vehicle for modesty.

Other productions in accordance with the recent Islamist "art with a mission" project are less light and more missionizing (Van Nieuwkerk, this volume). They go beyond erasing hot scenes. Women are veiled, both in real life and on stage, and their bodies are fully covered. They embody religious values such as piety, chastity, and modesty, and gendered values such as motherhood, obedience, and patience. Islamic soaps featuring veiled artists show not only a chaste body but, foremost, a pious body. The use of religious imagery and props, as well as bodily comportment, way of dressing, and moving, enact piety. Whether doing the five-day prayers or supplicatory prayer, holding and reading the Qur'an, or consoling and advising women to be patient and obedient with gestures of submission and patience, the body avoids restlessness and agitation in order to embody the value of religious calmness, *sakina* (Van Nieuwkerk, this volume).

Early-twentieth-century Iranian Islamist discourse rejected "dance" (*raqs*) as the activity of the Western-driven "modernists" (*mutijadid*), deeming it a "religion-destroying and Islam-murdering performance." While in the genre of "national dance" (*raqs-i milli*), constructed under the rule and patronage of the Pahlavi dynasty, a new "authentic" dancing body was introduced, the performing body in the postrevolutionary rhythmic movements had to embody chastity, modesty, and spirituality. While rhythmic movements often showcases Iranian identity like its predecessor national dance, Islamic ideology is a common theme for these postrevolutionary performances. This genre was renamed from "dance" (*raqs*) into "rhythmic movements" in order to dissociate it from immorality. An inspection committee previews and examines the performances for their appropriateness. Female bodies-in-motion are particularly scrutinized, and the female dancers have to cover their bodies with a loose costume. They have to move for a defined purpose, such as carrying props, or move in a way that resembles prayer. The general trend is that they are to embody and perform the expressions of heaviness, modesty, chastity, and austerity, and in order that dancers embody these qualities, movements should have a purpose and are literally "slowed down" movements (Stellar, this volume).

Gender and the sexuality of performing bodies on stage remain a prime problem for Islamists, and for that reason the body must be neutralized or desexualized. This can be done in several ways, of which veiling and covering it are the most obvious ones. Removing certain agitated movements such as the shimmy with the hips and shoulders is another strategy. Rhythmic movement is fairly fixed around the vertical midline of the body and restrains the free flow of movements of the wrist and arms in the common Iranian solo improvised dance (Stellar, this volume). The director of the Egyptian National Folklore Troupe deemed all the folkloric dance acts "art with a purpose" and appropriate also as a pastime during the holy month Ramadan, except for the *milaya laff* dance, which contains many shimmy movements and resembles belly dance. This dance was skipped during Ramadan.[4] Even with these desexualized movements and covered bodies, female performances remain a sensitive issue because of the male gaze, which tends to sexualize female bodies-in-motion. Yet male singers must perform the "art of no seduction," too. Male bodies should refrain from moving too much while singing, and they should also avoid imitating "feminine" movements. Abundant swaying on stage can tip the balance from religion to pop.[5]

Excessiveness also marks poor moral quality in women in Turkish Islamist fantasy serials. Whether in the form of excessive makeup or loud laughter, it is always considered bad for women (Yiğit, this volume). So there is a complex set of contrasts between heaviness and lightness, slowness and rapidity, restlessness and calmness, excessiveness and austerity in moral-religious terms. Heaviness signifies moral solemnity and lightness connotes triviality in Persian (Bayat 2007, 438). In other parts of the Middle East as well, the relationship between movement and morality is noted. Algerian men are considered "heavy"—that is, in control of their movement—whereas women have to overcome their natural tendency to be light (Jansen 1987, 183). Lightness of movement stands for lightness in morals. This is connected to the contrast between slow and fast. Iranian rhythmic movement has slowed down the movements; Egyptian actresses embody solemnity by avoiding agitated movements.

Whereas the Islamist cultural sphere tends to "slow down," the post-Islamist cultural sphere shows a tendency to "speed up." Shannon discusses the different tempi in which Sufi music created for the World Stage is packaged and consumed (this volume). He argues that this Suficized music is akin to "fast food"—that is, highly embedded in capitalist social relations and marketing strategies characteristic of advanced industrial economies: "Suficized musics are those that are produced for global consumption with the same attention to form and presentation as fast food: Sufi music and dance may be slow and ecstatic (think of the whirling dervishes doing their slow turns), but the aesthetic regimes of value that create them are very much *fast*" [emphasis added]. The opening up of the Islamist movement toward the global market and the emergent post-Islamist cultural sphere thus also translate into other aesthetic forms. I have mentioned already the celebrity culture that has gained ground in the Muslim cultural sphere and the aesthetic regime of the global markets that affect pious productions. The Islamist fantasy serials are deeply influenced by the Western genres (Yiğit, this volume). This points at the global aesthetics' contentious character within the Muslim cultural sphere. It is deemed an enormous challenge to carefully strike a balance between "East" and "West" and between commercialism and spirituality. The balance between religion and pop, morals and market, and ethics and aesthetics remains a contested issue.

THE CONTRIBUTIONS IN THIS VOLUME thus try to bring together several crucial developments in the Muslim cultural sphere by providing in-depth case studies of performing arts. They will highlight the conditions that impede or facilitate the emergence of a post-Islamist cultural sphere in different areas, a development that is highly contested within and outside Islamist movements. Several chapters will examine the development of religious sensibilities of audiences, which increasingly include the well-to-do and educated young. The contributions thus point out the emergence of local and global religious markets. The changing discourses that provide more space for religious productions are examined as well.

Finally, the contributions indicate how ethics and aesthetics are related. Several examples of pious art productions are elaborated, showing how these productions embody different ideologies and affect the body-in-motion.

NOTES

1. Bart Barendregt, presentation during ESF workshop, Amsterdam, October 2008.
2. Ibid.
3. Interview with author, February 11, 2006.
4. Interview with author, February 10, 2008.
5. Barendregt presentation.

REFERENCES

Abu Lughod, L. 1989. "Zones of Theory in the Anthropology of the Arab World." *Annual Review of Anthropology* 8:267–306.

———. 2005. *Dramas of Nationhood: The Politics of Television in Egypt.* Cairo: American University in Cairo Press.

Auslander, Ph. 2008. *Theory for Performance Studies: A Student's Guide.* London and New York: Routledge.

Bayat, A. 2002. "Piety, Privilege and Egyptian Youth." *ISIM Review,* no. 10, 23.

———. 2005. "What Is Post-Islamism?" *ISIM Review,* no. 16, 5.

———. 2007. "Islamism and the Politics of Fun." *Public Culture* 19 (3): 433–460.

Blackman, L. 2008. *The Body: The Key Concepts.* Oxford and New York: Berg.

Boubekeur, A. 2007. "Post-Islamist Culture: A New Form of Mobilization?" *History of Religions* 47 (1): 75–95.

Bourdieu, P. 1977. *Outline of a Theory of Practice.* Cambridge: Cambridge University Press.

Butler, J. 1990. *Gender Trouble: Feminism and the Subversion of Identity.* New York: Routledge.

———. 1993. *Bodies That Matter: On the Discursive Limits of "Sex."* New York: Routledge.

Carlson, M. 2004. *Performance: A Critical Introduction.* New York and London: Routledge.

Csordas, Th. J. 1999. "The Body's Career in Anthropology." In *Anthropological Theory Today*, ed. H. L. Moore, pp. 172–234. Cambridge and New Malden: Polity Press.

Desmond, J. C. 1993–1994. "Embodying Difference: Issues in Dance and Cultural Studies." *Cultural Critique*, no. 26 (Winter): 33–63.

Fabian, J. 1990. *Power and Performance: Ethnographic Explorations through Proverbial Wisdom and Theater in Shaba, Zaire.* Madison: University of Wisconsin Press.

———. 1998. *Moments of Freedom: Anthropology and Popular Culture.* Charlottesville and London: University Press of Virginia.

Foucault, M. 2003. "Technologies of the Self." In *The Essential Foucault*, ed. P. Rabinow and N. Rose, pp. 144–170. New York: New Press.

Fraser, N. 1990. "Rethinking the Public Sphere: A Contribution to the Critique of Actually Existing Democracy." *Social Text*, no. 25/26, 56–80.

Gamson, J. 1994. *Claims to Fame.* Berkeley: University of California Press.

Gazzah, M. 2008. *Rhythms and Rhymes of Life: Music and Identification Processes of Dutch-Moroccan Youth.* Amsterdam: Amsterdam University Press.

Haenni, P. 2005. *L'islam de marché. L'autre révolution conservatrice.* Paris: Seuil.

Harb, M. 2006. "Pious Entertainment. Al-Saha Traditional Village." *ISIM Review*, no. 17, 10–12.

Hirschkind, Ch. 2001. "The Ethics of Listening: Cassette-Sermon Audition in Contemporary Cairo." *American Ethnologist* 28 (3): 623–649.

———. 2006. *The Ethical Soundscape: Cassette Sermons and Islamic Counterpublics.* New York: Columbia University Press.

Jansen, W. 1987. *Women without Men: Gender and Marginality in an Algerian Town.* Leiden: Brill.

Kepel, G. 2000. "Islamism Reconsidered: A Running Dialogue with Modernity." *Harvard International Review* 22 (2): 22.

Kirshenblatt-Gimblett, B. 2004. "Performance Studies." In *The Performance Studies Reader*, ed. H. Bial, pp. 43–56. London and New York: Routledge.

LeVine, M. 2008. "Heavy Metal Muslims: The Rise of a Post-Islamist Public Sphere." In "Creating an Islamic Cultural Sphere: Contested Notions of Art, Leisure and Entertainment," ed. Karin van Nieuwkerk, special issue, *Contemporary Islam* 2 (3): 229–251.

Mahmood, S. 2001. "Feminist Theory, Embodiment, and the Docile Agent: Some Reflections on the Egyptian Islamic Revival." *Cultural Anthropology* 16 (2): 202–236.

———. 2005. *Politics of Piety: The Islamic Revival and the Feminist Subject.* Princeton, NJ: Princeton University Press.

Mauss, M. 1979. "Body Techniques." In *Sociology and Psychology: Essays*, pp. 95–124. London, Boston and Henley: Routledge and Kegan Paul.

Navaro-Yashin, Y. 2002. "The Market for Identities: Secularism, Islamism, Commodities."

In *Fragments of Culture: The Everyday of Modern Turkey*, ed. D. Kandiyoti and A. Saktanber, pp. 221–254. London: I. B. Tauris.

Nooshin, L. 2005. "Subversion and Counter-Subversion: Power, Control and Meaning in the New Iranian Pop Music." In *Music, Power and Politics*, ed. A. J. Randall, pp. 231–272. New York: Routledge.

Otterbeck, J. 2008. "Battling over the Public Sphere: Islamic Reactions to the Music of Today." In "Creating an Islamic Cultural Sphere: Contested Notions of Art, Leisure and Entertainment," ed. Karin van Nieuwkerk, special issue, *Contemporary Islam* 2 (3): 211–229.

Rojek, Chr. 2001. *Celebrity*. London: Reaktion Books.

Roy, O. 2004. *Globalized Islam*. London: Hurst and Company.

Saktanber, A. 2002. "'We Pray Like You Have Fun': New Islamic Youth in Turkey between Intellectualism and Popular Culture." In *Fragments of Culture: The Everyday of Modern Turkey*, ed. D. Kandiyoti and A. Saktanber, pp. 254–277. New Brunswick, NJ: Rutgers University Press.

Schechner, R. 1987. "Victor Turner's Last Adventure," Foreword in *The Anthropology of Performance*, by Victor Turner. New York: PAJ Publications.

———. 2002. *Performance Studies: An Introduction*. London and New York: Routledge.

Shafik, V. 2001. "Prostitute for a Good Reason: Stars and Morality in Egypt." *Women's Studies International Forum* 24 (6): 711–725.

Shannon, J. H. 2003. "Sultans of Spin: Syrian Sacred Music on the World Stage." *American Anthropologist* 105 (2): 266–277.

Starrett, G. 1995. "The Hexis of Interpretation: Islam and the Body in the Egyptian Popular School." *American Ethnologist* 22 (4): 953–969.

Stewart, P. J., and A. Strathern. 2002. *Gender, Song and Sensibility*. Westport and London: Praeger.

Strathern, A., and P. J. Stewart. 2008. "Embodiment Theory in Performance and Performativity." *Journal of Ritual Studies* 22 (1): pp. 67–72.

Tammam, H., and P. Haenni. 2003. "Chat Shows, Nashid Groups and Lite Preaching: Egypt's Air-Conditioned Islam." *Le Monde diplomatique*, September.

Tartoussieh, K. 2007. "Pious Stardom: Cinema and the Islamic Revival in Egypt." *Arab Studies Journal* 17 (1): 30–44.

Van Nieuwkerk, K. 1995. *"A Trade like Any Other": Female Singers and Dancers in Egypt*. Austin: University of Texas Press.

———. 2008. "Creating an Islamic Cultural Sphere: Contested Notions of Art, Leisure and Entertainment. An Introduction." In "Creating an Islamic Cultural Sphere: Contested Notions of Art, Leisure and Entertainment," ed. Karin van Nieuwkerk, special issue, *Contemporary Islam* 2 (3): 169–176.

Winegar, J. 2008. "Purposeful Art: Between Television Preachers and the State." *ISIM Review*, no. 22, 28–30.

Wise, L. 2003. "'Words from the Heart': New Forms of Islamic Preaching in Egypt." Master's thesis, Oxford University. http://users.ox.ac.uk/~metheses/Wise.html (accessed November 28, 2006).

PART ONE

THE POWER OF PERFORMANCE

CHAPTER I

HARDCORE MUSLIMS:
ISLAMIC THEMES IN TURKISH RAP
BETWEEN DIASPORA AND HOMELAND

THOMAS SOLOMON

AT THE BEGINNING OF THE twenty-first century, Islam had, according to various estimates, between 900 million and 1.4 billion adherents in more than fifty countries, making it the second-largest religion in the world. Rap music and hip-hop youth culture have also, in their brief history, achieved global status, as the essays in Tony Mitchell's edited volume *Global Noise* (2001b) illustrate. It is perhaps not surprising that the long-standing world religion Islam[1] and the more recently global musical genre of rap have intersected in various ways.[2] Both the religion and the musical style have spread over the globe as people and ideas move around and people use the material and expressive resources at their disposal in practices of identity construction. It is not necessarily contradictory or paradoxical that some people may find it useful and compelling to imagine their identities using both Islam *and* rap music.

Recent research on globalization and popular culture provides a framework for exploring how people may create and explore Muslim identities through rap music. Researchers have explored local adaptations and uses of globally circulating culture, especially focusing on cases where these uses are by people in places perceived to be geographically or socially marginal or peripheral to an imagined white Euro-American cultural "center." Some key terms in this discourse—each with its own nuances or implications—include "cultural reterritorialization," "indigenization," "domestication," "glocalization," and "creolization" (Appadurai 1996; Bennett 2000; Hannerz 1992; Mitchell 2001a; Slobin 1993; Solomon 2005a). While such accounts have focused on how local actors have reinterpreted and locally emplaced the objects and genres of global popular culture—how Afro-American rap music and hip-hop youth culture are locally emplaced in Tokyo, Istanbul, and Sydney, for example—comparatively less attention has been paid to the other side of the glocalization coin—how locally significant issues and discourses are adapted to and embodied in these globally circulating cultural forms.

In this chapter I explore some of the ways Turkish rappers have imagined Islam. By "imagining Islam," I mean the ways in which people go beyond issues strictly pertaining to faith and doctrine to creatively imagine their own identities as Muslims.[3] I examine "Islamic" themes in Turkish rap lyrics, comparing rappers living in Turkey to those in the Turkish diaspora in Germany, and I discuss some of the differences between the uses of Islam in Turkish rap in songs from these two different settings. I use three Turkish rap groups, one from Frankfurt, Germany, and two from Istanbul, as case studies of the different subject positions self-consciously Muslim rap groups can create through their music. I explore these issues primarily through the discussion of rap song texts, but also draw on ethnographic fieldwork in Istanbul. I argue that there is no one genre of Turkish "Islamic rap," but rather that "Islam" is a sign that can be deployed in different ways to various cultural and political ends, and I suggest that the signs "Islam" and "Muslim" as deployed in these rap songs cannot be equated with a unitary "Turkish Muslim" identity or with any particular political or religious ideology.[4]

TURKISH RAP IN THE TURKISH DIASPORA

Turkish-language rap and hip-hop are a transnational movement. Accounts of the history of Turkish rap describe how it started not in Turkey, but in Germany, practiced by members of the Turkish "guestworker" (*Gastarbeiter*) community, especially in, but not limited to, the cities of Berlin and Frankfurt (Diessel 2001; Kaya 2001; Robins and Morley 1996).[5] Rappers who use the Turkish language are also active in Holland, France, Switzerland, England, and the United States.

In Europe, especially in Germany, Turkish hip-hop was created in a context of sociocultural marginality, reflecting very real experiences of racism and social exclusion (Çağlar 1995; Çınar 2001; Kaya 2001; Robins and Morley 1996). During the early 1990s Turks in Germany experienced a wave of physical and psychological attacks by neo-Nazis, skinheads, and other xenophobic, racist far-right groups. Besides the everyday racism and xenophobia directed at them, Turks in Germany have also been the target of violent racist attacks, infamously including a series of arson attacks on Turkish homes during the early 1990s, as in the events described in the following news report:

> On November 23, 1992, two Skinheads, aged 19 and 25, firebombed two houses in Mölln, Schleswig-Holstein, killing a Turkish woman, her 10–year-old granddaughter, and 14–year-old niece. Several others were severely injured. The perpetrators telephoned the police station and announced,

FIGURE 1.1. Inside of inlay card from Sert Müslümanlar's cassette *Ay Yıldız Yıkılmayacak*

"There's fire in the Ratzeburger Strasse. Heil Hitler!" They made an identical call to the fire brigade regarding the second address. Michael Peters and Lars Christiansen were tried and convicted in December 1993, and sentenced to life imprisonment, and 10 years, respectively. (ADL Report, n.d.)

Perceiving that the genre of Afro-American rap music, with what they perceived as its characteristic discourse of protest and social commentary, would be an appropriate vehicle for responding to these attacks, Turkish youth in Germany began making rap songs, first in English and German, and then in Turkish. The most prominent of these groups and solo artists, such as Karakan ("Blackblood"), Da Crime Posse, and Erci-E, created and deployed in their music a kind of playful cultural nationalism (Kaya 2001, 182–188) modeled in part on the hyperbole of Afro-Nationalist American rap groups like Public Enemy, rapping against racism and fascism.

While the majority of antiracist songs by German-Turkish rappers drawing on nationalist discourse can be characterized as invoking a cultural and political nationalism that privileges ethnic and national identity, a few groups have made a "Muslim" identity part of their discourse as well. One German-Turkish rap group that has in particular cultivated an explicitly Muslim identity is Frankfurt-based Sert Müslümanlar (Figure 1.1), whose name can be translated as "Tough Muslims," or, borrowing from a line in one of their verses rapped in English, "Hardcore Muslims." The group raps mostly in Turkish, but also with verses in German and English on some tracks.

An example of Sert Müslümanlar's invocation of a Muslim identity can be heard in their song "Solingen," about attacks on German Turks by neo-Nazis, specifically the firebombing of a house in Solingen in May 1993 in which five Turkish citizens were killed—three girls ages 4, 9, and 12, and two women ages 18 and 27. In this song the rappers suggest that the unity of a shared Muslim identity is a way to find strength. This Muslim identity is, however, in no way passive. The rapper adopts the aggressive rhetoric of US gangsta rap and says he will use his gun to defend himself and his fellow Muslims against those who attack them.

SERT MÜSLÜMANLAR—"SOLINGEN" (EXCERPT)

[depressed speaking voice:]

Ah gurbet ah	Oh, living away from the homeland, oh
Yaktın harcadın bizi	You've ruined us, you've done us in
Suçumuz neydi?	What was our fault?
Müslümanlığımız mı? Türklüğümüz mü?	Our being Muslim? Our being Turks?
Yoksa insanlığımız mı?	Or was it our being human?
Allah rahmet eylesin	May God have mercy
Ölenler kalbimizde yaşıyor	The dead go on living in our hearts

[agitated speaking voice, sounds of large fire and a crowd:]

Yavrularım yanıyor!	My children are burning!
Kurtaran yok mu?	Can no one save them?
Yardım eden yok mu?	Can no one help?
İnsanlık bu mu?	Is this humanity?
Yavrularım yanıyor! [sobs]	My children are burning! [sobs]

[rap, chorus:]

Bizler Müslüman kardeşiz, kardeşiz	We are Muslim brothers, we're brothers
Hep beraber olup gavurları yeneriz	Together we'll defeat the unbelievers

[rap, 1st verse]

Ne haber getirdin gene bana?	What news have you brought me again?

Ey Müslüman nöbette kim buralarda?	Hey Muslim, who's standing guard here?
Al eline tabancayı çık dışarı	Get your pistol and go outside
[onomatopoeia] tabancayı çek	[onomatopoeia] draw your gun
Çek çek çek çek	Draw it, draw it, draw it, draw it
Acıma hepsini vur tek tek	Don't feel sorry, shoot them one by one

In a way parallel to that in which the Iranian diasporic musicians in Los Angeles discussed by Farzaneh Hemmasi (this volume) engage with political and cultural issues in the homeland, another concern of many German Turkish rappers was the civil war in the predominantly Kurdish region of southeast Turkey, which reached its height in the 1990s. A number of German Turkish groups made songs calling for an end to the conflict, alluding to the concept of the *umma*, or the shared world community of Muslims, and pointing to the shared Muslim identity between Turks and Kurds. An example of this is Sert Müslümanlar's song "Allahu Ekber Bizlere Güç Ver" ("God Is Great, Give Us Strength"). The song begins with the sampled sound of the *ezan*, or Muslim call to prayer (more about which below), overlaid with the sound of machine gun fire, followed by raps urging an end to the conflict. The song goes on to develop even further the idea of Muslim brotherhood, evoking not just the Kurds as belonging to the wider Muslim community, but also the two main branches of Islam in Turkey, the Sunni and Alevi.

The Alevi are a heterodox Islamic sect and quasi-ethnic group in Turkey. Like Shi'a Muslims, they regard 'Ali as the first rightful successor to the prophet Muhammed. But their form of Islam incorporates numerous heterodox religious practices, with devotional rituals including music and dance, sometimes claimed to have their origins in old Central Asian Turkic pre-Islamic shamanistic practices (Bozkurt 1998, 86; Markoff 1986, 1993, 1995, 2002; Mélikoff 1998, 3; Seufert 1997, 173; Vorhoff 1998, 27, 33). For these and other reasons, Turkish Alevis are often regarded with suspicion by the majority Sunni (Mandel 1990; Markoff 1986; Seufert 1997), and their worship practices are often associated with, or confused with, Sufism. Estimates of the number of Alevis in Turkey vary widely, from 9–10 million, or 15–20 percent of the total population (Shankland 2003, 20), to 20–26 million (Clarke 1999, 2), including a sizeable number of Kurdish Alevis (Çelik 2003; Leezenberg 2003; Neyzi 2002, 2003; Seufert 1997; P. White 2003). Mandel (1990, 165; 2008, 251) suggests that Alevis are proportionally over-represented in the Turkish diaspora in Germany, though according to data analyzed in a recent study published by the German Federal Office for Migration and Refugees, the number of Alevis in Germany represents about 17 percent of Turkish-origin migrants in Germany (Haug, Müssig, and Stichs 2009, 99), comparable to estimates of the proportion of Alevis living in Turkey.[6] Mandel also suggests that an important motivation for Turkish Alevis to migrate to Germany is that in the diaspora they find "an environment conducive to expressing their Alevi identity free from what they perceive as the pressures of a Sunni-dominant, repressive, hegemonic order in Turkey" (Mandel 1990, 163). The Alevi are particularly known for their tolerance of difference, and for their affinity with left-wing politics and progressive causes such as gender equality.

SERT MÜSLÜMANLAR—"ALLAHU EKBER BIZLERE GÜÇ VER" (EXCERPT)

[Song begins with the sound of the call to prayer, overlaid with the sound of machine gun fire.]

[Chorus:]	
Allahu ekber bizlere güç ver	God is great, give us strength
Allahu ekber Müslümanlara güç ver	God is great, give Muslims strength
[1st verse:]	
Bundan sonra Müslümanlar için konuşuyor	This is spoken for Muslims
Pa pa pa Müslüman olmaya bak	Bang bang bang, look what it's like to be Muslim
Bırakalım savaşı yaşayalım insan gibi	Let's abandon the war, let's live like human beings
Bu senin sonuncu şansın kaçırayım deme sakın	This is your last chance, don't miss it
Bırakalım bu pis silahları elimizden	Let's leave these filthy weapons behind
Hepimize sesleniyorum ve lütfen	I'm talking to all of us and please
Kürt, Alevi, Sünni kardeşiz hepimiz çünkü	Because Kurd, Alevi, Sunni, we're all brothers
Kardeş kardeşi öldürmekten zevk mi alıyon?	Does a brother take pleasure in killing his brother?
Sen bu yaptıklarından hiç mi utanmıyon?	Aren't you embarrassed by what you've done?
Ne oldu bize girişiyoruz birbirimize?	What has happened to us, that we're fighting?

Biraz düşün taşın gebereceksin belki yarın	Think about it carefully, you could die tomorrow
Evlerde çoluk çocuğunuz bekliyor	Your wife and children are waiting at home
Babamız ne zaman geliyor diye ağlıyor	They're crying "When is father coming home?"
Çocuğu babasız mı bırakmak istiyon?	Do you want to leave your children fatherless?

The call to prayer heard at the beginning of the recording is sampled not from an actual muezzin's reading of the *ezan*, but from a well-known mid-1990s recording of the song "Aziz Istanbul" by the singer Bülent Ersoy in the Turkish art music genre (*Türk sanat müziği*). On the original recording by Ersoy that the sample comes from, the singer performs the call to prayer in the service of the song's nostalgic evocation of the landscape (or rather soundscape) of Istanbul. As Martin Stokes (1996a; 1997, 680–683; 2000, 235) discusses, this recording of "Aziz Istanbul" aroused the ire of Islamists in Turkey, not just because of its use of the sacred sound of the call to prayer in a recording of a secular entertainment song, but because the singer Bülent Ersoy is well known as a male-to-female transsexual, so her performance of the *ezan* on the recording was heard by many to be blasphemous.

Bülent Ersoy was also well known to Turks living in Germany, as she too lived in Germany in virtual exile because she had been banned for a time from performing in Turkey. That Sert Müslümanlar would sample the transsexual Ersoy's controversial performance of the call to prayer and incorporate it into their own song suggests that they did not, however, find her performance blasphemous or objectionable.

It is also significant that Sert Müslümanlar should make it a point in this song to stress that the Alevi and the Sunni are brothers. This song came shortly after an incident in July 1993 that became known as the Sivas Massacre (Sivas Katliamı). In the Anatolian town of Sivas, a large group of Alevi intellectuals had gathered for a conference and cultural festival. Among the invited participants at the conference was the Turkish poet Aziz Nesin (himself not Alevi), who had publicly declared his intent to translate into Turkish Salman Rushdie's controversial novel *The Satanic Verses* and have it published in Turkey. After Friday prayers, a crowd of Sunni protesters gathered at the hotel where the conference participants were staying and set it ablaze, killing thirty-seven people, including a number of Alevi intellectuals, writers, and artists, though Aziz Nesin himself escaped the blaze. The Sunni-dominated local police and emergency services stood by, without rendering aid to those trapped in the hotel. This violent incident, as well as others

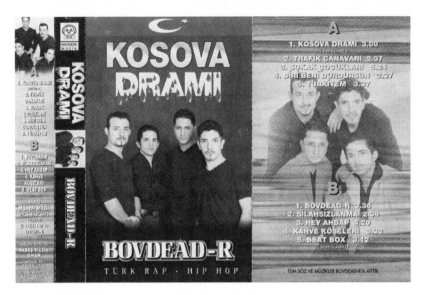

FIGURE 1.2. Inlay card from Bovdead-R's cassette *Kosova Dramı*

in the predominantly Alevi neighborhood of Gazi in the city of Istanbul in 1995, had the result of raising consciousness about the distinctiveness of Turkish Alevi identity both in Turkey and in the Turkish Alevi diaspora, especially in Germany (Greve 2000; Kaya 1998; Olsson, Özdalga, and Raudvere 1998; Rigoni 2003; Stokes 1996b). By specifically including the Alevi in their call for brotherhood among Muslims, Sert Müslümanlar thus argued against antagonism between Sunni Muslims and Alevis at a time when tension between the two communities was high.

Some rappers extend further the idea of a shared Muslim identity to show solidarity with Turkish and Muslim populations elsewhere in Europe, both diasporic and indigenous. During the Balkan wars of the 1990s, many German-Turkish rappers were especially concerned with the fate of the Muslim populations of Kosova and Bosnia. An example of a rap song addressing the situation in Kosova is the title song of the German-Turkish group Bovdead-R's cassette *Kosova Dramı* (*The Tragedy of Kosova*) (Figure 1.2).

Sert Müslümanlar's track "Bosna" ("Bosnia") similarly addresses the fate of the Muslim population there. In their discussion of Islam and globalization, Ahmed and Donnan discuss how

> Bosnia has become a rallying point for Muslims throughout the Muslim world. The case of Bosnia . . . has driven home the point that Muslims tend to see the world through Islamic spectacles and interpret the suffering of

the Bosnia Muslims as brought about by a West indifferent to the plight of ordinary Muslims: the feeling is that had they been Jews or Christians, the Western response would have been very different. (Ahmed and Donnan 1994a, 7)

Sert Müslümanlar draw on this discourse in their rap about Bosnia, arguing again, as in their songs discussed earlier, that Islam should be the basis of a shared identity across ethnic and national boundaries, and that Muslims everywhere should defend one another from attacks from outside the worldwide community of Muslims.

SERT MÜSLÜMANLAR—"BOSNA" (EXCERPT)

[Chorus:]

En büyük Allah için savaşanlar	Fighters for Allah, the all-great
[onomatopoeia] Sen ve ben, sert Müslümanlar	Bang! Bang! You and me, tough Muslims
En büyük Allah için savaşanlar	Fighters for Allah, the all-great
Sen ve ben, sert Müslümanlar	You and me, tough Muslims

[1st verse:]

Sert Müslüman deyince acaba aklına ne geliyor	When I say "tough Muslim" what do you think of?
Haydi bana söyle durma öyle	Come on and tell me, don't be so passive
Ben sana anlatayım can kulağıyla dinle	I'll tell you, listen up
En büyük Allah için savaşanlar	Fighters for Allah, the all-great
Örnek—Bosna'daki sert Müslümanlar	For example, the tough Muslims in Bosnia
Müslümanlığı yayan Hazreti Muhammed	The prophet Muhammed is the one who spread Islam
Sen de gel bize, Müslümanlığı kabul et	You too come with us, accept Islam
Allah için öleceğine bile yemin etmiş	He even swore he'd die for Allah,
Bosna'daki bir Müslüman askerimiz	One of our Muslim soldiers in Bosnia
Sonunda da bomba parçalayıp bitmiş	In the end a bomb exploded and finished him off
İşte buda Müslümanlık için vefat etti	This is how he died for Islam

Bu da sert Müslümanlardan biriydi	He was also one of the tough Muslims
Bir sert Müslüman kardeş daha	One more tough Muslim brother
Ölüyor Bosna'daki savaşta	Is dying in the war in Bosnia

Significantly, the rapper never uses in the song the word *İslam*, which is a perfectly good word in Turkish. The word he uses, *Müslümanlık*, also a common word in Turkish, and which I have translated as "Islam," actually literally means "being Muslim," or "Muslim-ness." The other songs by Sert Müslümanlar that I discussed earlier also do not used the word "Islam" itself, but refer instead to Muslims and Muslim-ness, again focusing not on religion per se, but on being Muslim as a kind of identity.

I suggest that the construction of Islam in these songs by Sert Müslümanlar, and in other similar songs by German Turkish rap groups, is at least in part an "ethnicized" Islam (Swedenburg 2001, 57, 77) or "cultural Muslim identity" (Kaya 2001, 159; Vertovec 1998, 101). In this way of making religion part of one's identity, people may claim what Alex Hargreaves describes as "affective identification with doctrinal detachment" (1995, 121, quoted in Vertovec and Rogers 1998, 2). As Vertovec and Rogers explain, people who self-identify as Muslims may engage in expressive practices that have the effect of "making their Muslim identity more a matter of culture than religion" (1998, 18). Writing about Algerian *rai* music in relation to "the secularization of Franco-Maghribi sociocultural life," Gross, McMurray, and Swedenburg similarly argue that for many "Muslim" North Africans living in France, "Religion has become another form of ethnic identification, like holidays, cuisine, language and music" (1992, 14; see also Gross, McMurray, and Swedenburg 2001, 133). While these analyses see the creation of "cultural Muslim identities" as the bottom-up result of expressive practices based on affect, Y. Soysal notes that an "ethnicized Islam" can also emerge as a consequence of top-down political pressures, in her argument that the strategic use by labor-migrant Muslims in Europe of "the categories of European states" to foster a collective identity has had the consequence of a "recasting of Islam as an ethnicized political entity" (1997, 509).

In their introduction to an edited book on Muslim youth in Europe, Vertovec and Rogers describe how "European Muslim youth identities are often forged in reaction to negative and essentialist representations of both Islam and migrants" (Vertovec and Rogers 1998, 15). Vertovec also argues, on the basis of empirical ethnographic research among Pakistani youth in West Yorkshire, that such a "strong 'Muslim' identity . . . often does not necessarily entail an enhanced knowledge of Islam nor an increased participation in religious activity" (Vertovec 1998, 101). Besides the more general appeal to a Muslim cultural identity, however, songs like the examples discussed above are specific to the experiences of Turks living in Germany, especially the second generation born and brought up there in the 1970s and 1980s. Making rap is for these young people a practice for the creation of diasporic identities, as they negotiate through rap both their understanding of their place in German society and their relationships with the homeland of Turkey (Çınar 2001; Kaya 1996, 2001, 2002). They are constantly reminded by the German society in which they live as a minority that they are Turks and Muslims, even if they are not actually practicing Muslims and do not have any particular attachment to the doctrines of the Islamic faith. The strategy of rappers like those in Sert Müslümanlar, who understand that their Muslim-ness is negatively valued by the majority society, is to revalorize this identity as something positive to be proud of, similar to the way Afro-Americans in the 1960s revalorized being Black from something negative to something beautiful.

FROM DIASPORA TO HOMELAND

Since the mid-1990s, Turkish rap made in Europe has spread back to Turkey itself, and a two-way flow of people, recordings, and information has continued between the homeland and the diaspora. Rappers from Europe come to Turkey to perform, and may do guest spots on recordings by rappers based in Turkey, and the latter likewise perform abroad, especially in Germany. Rappers in Turkey thus get ideas and practices not only directly from US rappers, but also as mediated through Turkish rappers in Europe, especially Germany.

While the Frankfurt-based Sert Müslümanlar are known to rappers in Turkey (several of their albums from Germany have also been released in Turkey), for the most part, Turkish rappers in Turkey avoid direct references to Islam or Muslims in their song texts. One group that did, for a time, cultivate Islamic themes in its songs is R.A.K. Sabotaj (R.A.K. stands for the English phrase "Rappers Against Kaos"). I met one of the members of R.A.K. Sabotaj, who calls himself Tuzak (meaning "Trap," Figure 1.3), at a hip-hop party in Istanbul in February 2001.

Tuzak explained to me that his group made what he called "Islamic rap," discussing the problems of Muslims under the secular regime in Turkey. He said he would like to see the return of the caliphate to the Muslim world. (The founder of the modern Turkish Republic, Mustafa Kemal Atatürk, abolished the caliphate in 1924 as part of his program of remaking the remains of the Ottoman Empire into a modern secular state.) Tuzak also expressed interest in the problems of Muslims in Chechnya, Palestine, and Su-

FIGURE 1.3. The rapper Tuzak from the group R.A.K. Sabotaj

dan. Unlike Sert Müslümanlar, however, he said he advocates solving the problems of Muslims without using violence or making war. He told me his group had recorded an album, but he could not get it released in Turkey because of censorship of any statements critical of the official secularism of the Turkish state. A number of the songs from this unreleased album were, however, made available on the Internet, and the group was eventually able to place one of its songs, "Keskin Sirke" ("Strong Vinegar"), on the compilation album *HipHop Menü*.

Tuzak was especially interested in having dialog with Islamic rappers elsewhere in the world. He told me he was in contact with the group Soldiers of Allah from the United States, who have a similar agenda of promoting Islam and what they understand to be Islamic ideals and values, including the return of the caliphate. While Tuzak regards Muslims in Turkey as oppressed by the secular state, his group's songs are generally not openly combative calls to violent action like the antiracist songs of some German Turkish groups like Sert Müslümanlar. Rather, R.A.K. Sabotaj's songs elaborate Islam as a moral code that one should submit to. There are in the songs, however, references to state censorship of antisecularist ideas, as in the ironically whispered intro to the song "Keskin Sirke," where Tuzak says, "Şşşşt! İslamik underground, ama kimse duymasın!" ("Ssshh! Islamic underground, but don't let anybody hear it!"), referring to the need to keep these sentiments below the radar of the state.

R.A.K. SABOTAJ—"KESKIN SIRKE" (EXCERPT)

[whispered:]
Şşşşt! İslamik underground   Shhh! Islamic underground
Sssss! ama kimse duymasın!   Shhh! But don't let anyone hear it!

[Verse 1, rap:]

Bak bunu da dinle	Pay attention and listen to this
Gel tepene de vur	Come, get your head straight
Gör kimmiş bu ülkeyi soyan	See who is robbing this country blind
Namuslulara namussuzca dil uzatan	Who is dishonorably defaming the honorable
Bağır sahtekâr bu bestekâr sana hesap soracak	Cry out, imposter! this composer will call you to account
Verilecek çok cevap arar	He looks for many answers
Ama görülecek hesap daha kabarık	But the reckoning to come is even greater
Kopmadı mı benden acaba hayırsızca?	Didn't I stop him in his tracks like a good-for-nothing?
Ecel gelip dikilecek senin kapına	When your appointed time comes it will wait at your door
Kaçış yok bundan, sen de göreceksin bunu	There's no escape from this, you too will see it
Tuzak şimdi gelip hemen ölçer boyunu	Tuzak is coming now to measure your worth

A number of songs by R.A.K. Sabotaj from their unreleased album draw on the language of Turkish political Islam. Some of these songs criticize, implicitly or explicitly, the official secularism of the Turkish state, suggesting that the Turkish legal system is untenable and should be replaced with an Islamic legal system (*şeriat*). The song "2000 Intro," which would have been the introductory track to the unreleased album, explains the group's agenda of using the idiom of rap to deliver their Islamic message, in spite of the Turkish state's secular legal system, which officially bans advocacy for *şeriat*; the song "Gerçek Ritm" ("Real Rhythm") suggests that no matter what opinions one may hold during life, in the end Islam is the unavoidable truth.

R.A.K. SABOTAJ—"2000 INTRO" (EXCERPT)

İslam işte gerçek hayat düsturu	Islam is the true path for life
Sana doğru gelecek olan R.A.K. clan	The R.A.K. clan is coming your way
Legal yöntem illegal sözler söylev doğuruyor	The legal system is the reason for our speech with illegal words

R.A.K. SABOTAJ—"GERÇEK RITM" (EXCERPT)

Koş hadi yanımızdaki gerçek kurtuluşa	Come on, run to the true salvation right next to us
Buluşmaya hazır ol âhir zamanda	Get ready to meet at time's end
Kuşatma altında insanoğlu dar ovada	Humanity is under siege on the narrow plain
Konuşamadan gideceksin karanlığa	You will go speechless into the darkness
Kıracağın asıl sonuç yine İslam	Your final destination will be Islam
Hızı kesmeden böyle sözlere devam	May these words continue without slowing down

Besides specifically mentioning Islam and advocating an Islamic legal system, the rappers in the group also inflect their raps with a Turkish-language Islamic vocabulary heavy with religious terms borrowed from Arabic, including words such as *âhir zaman* ("the end of the world"), *ahiret* ("the afterlife"), *nizam* ("order"), *nefis* ("desire"), *ecel* ("the time at which a person is fated to die"), and *ihlâs* ("purity," "refinement"; also the name of one the surahs of the Qur'an). The average Turkish speaker would readily understand these words, but would also recognize that the words evoke a specifically Islamic religious discourse, especially because so many of these terms are used in the texts of the songs, making the songs unusually dense in this religious vocabulary, compared to what one would typically hear in popular song texts. R.A.K. Sabotaj's peppering their raps with Arabic-language religious terminology is also consistent with Saktanber's observation that self-consciously Islamic youth in Turkey "like to show how fluently they can use terminology from both Ottoman and modern Turkish, as well as Arabic" (2002, 266).[7]

Another song in which R.A.K. Sabotaj develops Islamic themes is called "Sınav Hayatı," literally "Test Life." The central conceit of this song is that life on this earth is a kind of test, and our behavior during this life will determine our fate in the next life. A striking example of the use of religious language in this song is a pun that turns on the identical pronunciation of a religious term and an everyday Turkish phrase. The religious term *tekbir* comes from Arabic, and refers to a specific prayer acknowledging the greatness and absoluteness of God, beginning with the phrase *Allahu ekber* ("God is great"). The two syllables can also be understood, however, as the Turkish phrase *tek bir*, a common phrase meaning simply "the only one," without any specifically religious connotations. In the song's climax at the end of the second verse, the singer uses the phrase *tek bir* twice in its everyday, nonreligious meaning to modify words that do refer to religion, and then constructs the text so that the word can be understood both as *tek bir* in its nonreligious meaning and as the religious term *tekbir*, culminating in a line that describes the sound of the call to prayer reverberating over the land, thus reimagining officially secular Turkey as a distinctly Islamic landscape (and soundscape). Like the whispered intro to "Keskin Sirke" already mentioned, the song also makes a dig at those who would rather that Islamic hip-hop not have a place in the Turkish soundscape.

R.A.K. SABOTAJ—"SINAV HAYATI" (EXCERPT)

Hadi evlat mikrofonun başına göster gücünü
Come on, boy! show your strength at the microphone

Göster düşünceyi, göster asıl olan ivmeyi
Show your thoughts, show real action!

Görsünler, dinlesinler nasıl olurmuş
Let them see, let them hear how it really is

İslamik hip-hop kudurturmuş dimi?
Islamic hip-hop infuriates them, doesn't it?

Asi gençlerin birliği, el emeği göz nuru
The confederation of rebellious youth, the fruit of our labor

Bu iş alnımızın akı, ahiret pasaportu
This work is the thing that makes us proud, the passport to the afterlife

Sırtımızı dayadık *tek bir* kurala, *tek bir* nizama
We have faith in *only one* rule, in *only one* order

Tekbir allahu ekber sesleri yurdumun üzerinde inler
The sound of *the prayer/the one and only allahu ekber* echoes over our land

Songs like these of R.A.K. Sabotaj, in which the rappers bring the specifically religious dimension of Islam to the forefront, contrast significantly with the songs of Sert Müslümanlar that I discussed earlier, in which the rappers stress Muslim-ness as a kind of identity that people have, rather than Islam as a set of religious beliefs and practices. In a short presentation of his new group Ondaon[8] published in a Turkish music magazine in 2002, Tuzak himself wrote about the difference between being Muslim in Germany and being Muslim in Turkey:

> In Germany the situation is a little different; there Muslim Turks live in a Christian society; because of this they are trying to put [their being Muslim] in the forefront. When you listen to [their raps] . . . they are using their being Muslim to distinguish themselves from other groups. In Turkey the majority is Muslim; who would we distinguish ourselves from by doing this?

> [Almanya'da durum biraz farklı, orada hristiyan bir toplum içinde yaşayan müslüman Türkler var, bu nedenle bunu öne çıkartmaya çalışıyorlar. Dinlenildiği zaman . . . kendini diğer gruplardan ayırmak için kullanıyorlar müslüman olmayı. Türkiye'de zaten çoğunluk müslüman, biz bunu kullanarak kendimizi kimden ayırabiliriz ki?] (Tuzak 2002, 40)

In contrast to the songs of Sert Müslümanlar discussed above, then, the songs of R.A.K. Sabotaj construct not an ethnicized or "cultural" Islam, but Islam as a religion and a moral code for how to live one's life, especially in the context of an officially secular Turkey where open display of Islamic sentiment has historically been closely watched over by the government, and censored if it goes too far over the line and criticizes the officially secular basis of the Turkish state.

The Islamic raps by Tuzak and R.A.K. Sabotaj should also be understood, however, not simply as an affirmation of faith, but also in the context of the recently stepped-up revitalization of Islam in urban Turkey and the accompanying discourses of political Islam. The early architects of the new, officially secular Turkish Republic embarked on a project of erasing Islam from public life, arguing that religion properly belonged in the private sphere. During the period of one-party rule by the CHP (Republican People's Party) from the founding of the republic in 1923 until 1950, the state abolished or reorganized the institutional bases for religion in its efforts to banish Islam from the public sphere. With the beginning of multiparty democracy in 1950, various political parties with Islamist roots began to reverse this project, in efforts to reclaim space for Islam in Turkish urban life (Ayata

1996). The project of reclaiming space for Islam gained steam when the Islamist Welfare Party won significant advances in the local elections in 1994, including mayorships in Istanbul and Ankara, and most recently culminated in the victory of the AKP (Justice and Development Party), which has roots in the Welfare Party, in the national elections in 2002.

R.A.K. Sabotaj's Islamist raps were recorded circa 2000, after the Welfare Party took over the mayorship of Istanbul, but before the AKP's big national win in 2002, and thus represent a transitional period during which the Islamist movement had made significant local gains that had newly emboldened it, but before it had gained comparable power at the national level. Welfare Party propaganda during the 1990s criticized "the oppressive rule of the corrupt and unjust society that exploits and humiliates the poor Muslim" (Ayata 1996, 54). The rap texts quoted above draw on this discourse in their criticism of those who are "robbing this country blind" and are "dishonorably defaming the honorable."[9] The texts of the raps are also consistent with Nakshibendi Sufi teaching, echoed in the Welfare Party's position, that "Muslim renewal requires moral recovery" (Ayata 1996, 54). R.A.K. Sabotaj's Islamist raps should thus be seen as part of a ongoing project of using popular culture as a vehicle for moving Islam from the realm of the private back into public life in Turkey. In this way the raps are similar to other practices of the creation and performance of oppositional Islamic identities during the pre-2002 period through the engagement with and resignifying of popular culture and commodity forms circulating in Turkey (Navaro-Yashin 2002a, 2002b; Saktanber 1997, 2002; J. White 1999, 2002; see the papers by Pierre Hecker and Ahu Yiğit in this volume for more recent developments post-2002, especially Yiğit's discussion of "the reappearance of Islam in cultural consumption" and her analysis of Turkish TV fantasy serials that recast in an Islamist mold plots and themes from American TV series). Saktanber in particular discusses the recasting in Islamic form of commodity forms prevalent in youth culture in general, such as movies, cartoons, comic strips, graffiti, stickers, and posters, by injecting them with Islamic content (2002, 264). If Turkish popular culture, and popular music in particular, have been an important arena for the playing out of the historic antagonism between Islam and the officially secular Turkish state (Stokes 1992), R.A.K. Sabotaj's use of the rap idiom to communicate an Islamic message is emblematic of "the rather subtle and creative ways in which Turkish Islamists encounter and engage with modernity, rather than rejecting it out of hand" (Stokes 2002, 331). Creating Islamic rap is thus part of a larger process of the development of an Islamic popular youth culture in Turkey, which entails "the deployment of cultural symbols as the principal weapons in the battle between Islamic and secular forces in society" (Sak-

FIGURE 1.4. Illustration on CD by Eastila

tanber 2002, 267). It should also be noted, however, that the medium of rap has so far not been a successful way of getting an Islamist message out to lots of people. If Turkish-language rap as a whole had a marginal place on the Turkish cultural landscape throughout the 1990s and early 2000s (Solomon 2005b), then such underground tracks as the ones discussed here are doubly marginal. Because R.A.K. Sabotaj's music has never been commercially released (with the exception of one song on a low-circulation compilation cassette), few people have heard or will ever hear it beyond a small number of fans who know where to look for the tracks in cyberspace.

While Tuzak has since left the Turkish rap scene, another performer who similarly raps on religious themes has more recently emerged. The rapper Alfa performs as the one-man-group named Eastila, a pun on the English word *east* and the Turkish word (derived from Arabic) *istila* ("invasion"). Like Tuzak, Alfa also uses rap as a didactic tool for communicating the requirements of Islam and critiquing local and international events from an Islamist point of view. His self-representation as teacher is made explicit in the visual material accompanying the recorded sounds. In the illustration printed on the Eastila CD *Ahir Zamanda Uyanış* (*Awakening at the End of Days*, Figure 1.4), Alfa is portrayed sitting and gazing pensively off into the distance, his right hand grasping a *tespih* (string of prayer breads). Sitting next to him in a similar posture is a *hoca* (learned man, teacher) whose face is illuminated by the light emanating from the Qur'an he holds open in front of him. This tableau thus presents the rapper as another kind of *hoca* who is knowledgeable about Islam and who communicates that knowledge through his rapping.

Eastila also continues mostly in the textual vein that Tuzak and R.A.K. Sabotaj started, drawing on the language of political Islam, but the raps also include evocations of Turkish nationalist discourse. For example, the song "Ahalım Uyan" ("Wake Up, My People!") refers positively to Mustafa Kemal Atatürk, founder of the modern Turkish state, whereas R.A.K. Sabotaj vilified Atatürk as the person who abolished the caliphate. The song also brings Turkish Islamic rap into the post-9/11 era, referring to the controversy over the Muhammed cartoons first published in Denmark, the Israeli occupation of East Jerusalem, and the occupation of Baghdad by the American-led coalition force after the Second Gulf War.

EASTILA—"AHALIM UYAN" (EXCERPT)

Bazıları çok büyük yanılgı içinde	Some of them are greatly deluded
Sapkınlık emperyalizme vurdu heralde	Looks like the aberration has struck imperialism
Onlar hep saldırdı biz bölündükçe	They have always attacked us when we were divided
Kudüs, Bağdat esir batılın öfkesine	Jerusalem, Baghdad are captive to the rage of the false
Bu aralar şeytan iyi çalışmakta	The devil is working hard nowadays
Ahlak tükendi ve bozulma çoğalmakta	Morality has faded and corruption is on the rise
Peki ya umrumuzu gören var mıydı	So, is there anybody who understands our concern
Rasul'ın karükatür yarışmasında? . . .	During the contest of cartoons of the Messenger?[10] . . .
Onlarda silah, bizde nuru Mustafa olanın	Weapons are their glory, Mustafa is ours
Müminler doğrulun, İslam'a sarılın	Believers, straighten up! embrace Islam

This song also creates a specifically Muslim soundscape through its sonic invocation of *zikr*. *Zikr*, which literally means "remembrance," is the practice of chanting the names of God and/or other sacred phrases in accompaniment to rhythmic breathing, used by many Sufi orders in devotional ceremonies that may include the achievement of ecstatic states. The chorus of the song consists of the repeated, breathy chanting in the style of *zikr* of the Arabic-language phrase (in the pronunciation typically used in Turkey) *lâ ilâhe illallah* ("There is no God but Allah"), the first part of the *şehadet*, the Islamic profession of faith.

While R.A.K. Sabotaj had found it impossible to get their album released around the year 2000, the growing acceptance of Islamic expressions in the cultural sphere in Turkey following the AKP's victory at the national level in 2002 (see Yiğit's paper in this volume for more on this development) included an environment more conducive to the local production of Islamic popular music. Eastila's CD was released circa 2005–2006 by the media company Asir, which specializes in music with religious themes (including Turkish licensing of recordings by internationally known *nasheed* [composition in popular song form with religious text] artists such as the Malaysian singer Imad, Indonesian Haddad Alwi, and American Mustaqiim Sahir), as well as audio recordings of the Qur'an.

CONCLUSIONS

The case studies I have discussed here provide examples of how Turkish rappers may use the idiom of rap music to create and explore different kinds of subjectivities that can be called Muslim. While the two approaches to Islam and Muslim identity that I identify in these examples—an ethnicized "cultural Muslim identity" in the diaspora, and an identity based in the discourses of Turkish political Islam in the homeland—are very different, what they have in common is that they both draw on the performers' perceptions of the rap genre as especially appropriate for the expression of oppositional identities.

I don't want to give the impression that all Turkish rappers rap constantly on Islamic themes. Many rappers (perhaps even most) studiously avoid this topic entirely. But the case studies I have discussed of a group from Germany and two groups from Turkey show that in the case of groups that do rap about Muslims and Islam, the meaning of Islam and the way it is rhetorically deployed in specific songs can be quite different and specific to the localities and experiences of those making the songs. I also do not want to give the impression that the ideas expressed in Sert Müslümanlar's songs stand for all German Turkish rappers' subject positions (or for that matter all German Turks who identify as Muslims[11]). As Nederveen Pieterse points out, "not all migrants adhere or turn to Islam nor would it carry the same meaning for those who do" (1997, 179). The ways the rappers in Sert Müslümanlar construct and deploy Muslim identities in their songs do illustrate, however, how "In the matrix of migration, local and global processes interpenetrate. The global standing and aspirations of Islam are locally meaningful: they inspire a sense of identity and self-worth among the Muslim diaspora" (Nederveen Pieterse 1997, 184).

I also do not want to claim that the songs of R.A.K. Sabotaj or Eastila represent the subject positions of all rappers in Turkey. In fact, the Islamist subjectivity created in the songs by those two groups is a decidedly marginal one within the overall range of perspectives represented in Turkish rap music made in Turkey. The three case studies taken together do show, however, that there is not just a single "Islamic" position or discourse in Turkish rap. Rather, rappers may take many different approaches to Islam, both in the Turkish diaspora and in the homeland itself. I would further suggest that these different approaches are the result of the specificity of individual rappers' experiences and subjectivities, though this needs to be further explored not just through the discussion of songs as media texts as I have done here, but through an ethnographic approach engaging with these rappers as individuals through interviews and participant-observation in the scenes where this music is created and used.

NOTES

Special thanks to Tunca Arıcan for transcribing from the recordings the texts of the songs by R.A.K. Sabotaj, and for help in translating those texts and explaining some of the vocabulary and idioms in them. This article is a revised and expanded version of a paper originally published in *Yearbook for Traditional Music*, volume 38 (2006); thanks to the International Council for Traditional Music (ICTM) for permission to reprint the paper here.

1. For discussions of Islam as a global religion and a religion in constant movement, see Ahmed and Donnan (1994b), AlSayyad and Castells (2002), Eickelman and Piscatori (1990), Manger (1999), Mohammadi (2002), Nederveen Pieterse (1997), and Vertovec and Rogers (1998).

2. Ted Swedenburg has discussed the intersection of Islam and hip-hop from several directions, including the Afronationalist rap of rappers from the Nation of Islam and its offshoot the Five Percent Nation (1997), and uses of rap and hip-hop by progressive artists in England and France to combat Islamophobia (2001). Further discussion of rap and the Nation of Islam/Five Percent Nation can be found in Allen (1996), Decker (1994), Eure and Spady (1991), and Miyakawa (2005).

3. I am influenced here by Turkish sociologist Ayşe Öncü's evocation of "different ways of knowing Islam" (1994, 13). While Öncü is primarily concerned with different ways Islam is "packaged" for mainstream audiences of Turkish commercial television,

I try here to explore subjectivities created through engagement with Islam and being Muslim. For further discussion of the many ways that Muslims live Islam, see the edited volume *Muslim Diversity: Local Islam in Global Contexts* (Manger 1999).

4. This paper is part of a broader project on Turkish rap and transnationalism. See also Solomon (2005a, 2005b, 2008a, 2008b, 2009).

5. See also Greve (1997, 2003), Kaya (1998, 1999, 2000, 2001, 2002), Nohl (1999), and L. Soysal (1999, 2001) on diasporic cultural formation among German Turks, and Bennett (2000, 138–148), Çağlar (1998), Cheesman (1998), Çınar (1999, 2001), Diessel (2001), Elflein (1998), Greve (2003, 440–456), Greve and Kaya (2004), Kaya (1996, 2001, 2002), Klebe (2004), Robins and Morley (1996), and L. Soysal (1999, chapters 3–4) on rap by German Turks.

6. Thanks to Pierre Hecker for alerting me to this study.

7. On the complex relationships among everyday Turkish, Arabic, and Persian, see Mardin (2002).

8. After I talked with Tuzak in early 2001, his group R.A.K. Sabotaj joined together with another Istanbul rap group, Sözlü Taarruz (Verbal Assault), to make the group Ondaon (TenOutOfTen). This group has released two albums, but for these new recordings the group has stayed away from any explicit mention of Islam in their songs.

9. Saktanber discusses similar discourses in Islamic-themed Turkish movies, which have portrayed "the theme of the sufferings of Muslims under an unjust, non-Islamic system" (2002, 263).

10. The word *rasul* ("messenger") here refers to one of the titles of Muhammed—*Rasúlullâh*, "the Messenger of God."

11. For a discussion of the diversity of religious practices and beliefs among Turks in Germany, see Yalçın-Heckmann (1998).

REFERENCES

ADL Report. n.d. "ADL Report: 'Skinhead International': Germany, 1995." http://www .nizkor.org/hweb/orgs/american/adl/skinhead-international/skins-germany.html (accessed December 3, 2003).

Ahmed, A. S., and H. Donnan. 1994a. "Islam in the Age of Postmodernity." In *Islam, Globalization and Postmodernity*, ed. A. S. Ahmed and H. Donnan, pp. 1–20. London: Routledge.

———, eds. 1994b. *Islam, Globalization and Postmodernity*. London: Routledge.

Allen, E., Jr. 1996. "Making the Strong Survive: The Contours and Contradictions of Message Rap." In *Droppin' Science: Critical Essays on Rap Music and Hip Hop Culture*, ed. W. Perkins, pp. 159–191. Philadelphia: Temple University Press.

AlSayyad, N., and M. Castells, eds. 2002. *Muslim Europe or Euro-Islam: Politics, Culture and Citizenship in the Age of Globalization*. Oxford: Lexington Books.

Appadurai, A. 1996. *Modernity at Large: Cultural Dimensions of Globalization*. Minneapolis: University of Minnesota Press.

Ayata, S. 1996. "Patronage, Party, and State: The Politicization of Islam in Turkey." *Middle East Journal* 50 (1): 40–56.

Bennett, A. 2000. *Popular Music and Youth Culture: Music, Identity and Place*. New York: St. Martin's Press.

Bozkurt, F. 1998. "State-Community Relations in the Restructuring of Alevism." In *Alevi Identity: Cultural, Religious and Social Perspectives*, 2nd ed., ed. T. Olsson, E. Özdalga, and C. Raudvere, pp. 85–96. Istanbul: Swedish Research Institute in Istanbul.

Çağlar, A. Ş. 1995. "German Turks in Berlin: Social Exclusion and Strategies for Social Mobility." *New Community* 21 (3): 309–323.

———. 1998. "Popular Culture, Marginality and Institutional Incorporation: German-Turkish Rap and Turkish Pop in Berlin." *Cultural Dynamics* 10 (3): 243–261.

Çelik, A. B. 2003. "Alevis, Kurds and Hemşehris: Alevi Kurdish Revival in the Nineties." In *Turkey's Alevi Enigma: A Comprehensive Overview*, ed. P. J. White and J. Jongerden, pp. 141–157. Leiden: Brill.

Cheesman, T. 1998. "Polyglot Politics: Hip-hop in Germany." *Debatte* 6 (2): 191–214.

Çınar, A. 1999. "Cartel: Travels of German-Turkish Rap Music." *Middle East Report* 29:43–44.

———. 2001. "Cartel'in Rap'i, Melezlik ve Milliyetçiliğin Sarsılan Sınırları: Almanya'da Türk Olmak Türkiye'de Türk Olmaya Benzemez" [Cartel's Rap, Hybridity and the Shaken-up Limits of Nationalism: Being a Turk in Germany Is Not Like Being a Turk in Turkey]. *Doğu Batı* 15:141–151.

Clarke, G. L. 1999. *The World of the Alevis: Issues of Culture and Identity.* Istanbul: AVC Publications.

Decker, J. L. 1994. "The State of Rap: Time and Place in Hip Hop Nationalism." In *Microphone Fiends: Youth Music and Youth Culture*, ed. A. Ross and T. Rose, pp. 99–121. London: Routledge.

Diessel, C. 2001. "Bridging East and West on the 'Orient Express': Oriental Hip-hop in the Turkish Diaspora of Berlin." *Journal of Popular Music Studies* 13 (2): 165–187.

Eickelman, D. F., and J. Piscatori, eds. 1990. *Muslim Travellers: Pilgrimage, Migration, and the Religious Imagination.* London: Routledge.

Elflein, D. 1998. "From Krauts with Attitudes to Turks with Attitudes: Some Aspects of Hip-hop History in Germany." *Popular Music* 17 (3): 255–265.

Eure, J. D., and J. G. Spady, eds. 1991. *Nation Conscious Rap: The Hip Hop Vision.* New York: PC International Press.

Greve, M. 1997. *Alla Turca: Musik aus der Türkei in Berlin.* Berlin: Die Ausländerbeauftragte des Senats.

———. 2000. "Alevitische und musikalische Identitäten in Deutschland." *Zeitschrift für Türkeistudien* 13 (2): 213–238.

———. 2003. *Die Musik der imaginären Türkei: Musik und Musikleben im Kontext der Migration aus der Türkei in Deutschland.* Stuttgart: Verlag J. B. Metzler.

Greve, M., and A. Kaya. 2004. "Islamic Force, Takım 34 und andere Identitätsmixturen türkischer Rapper in Berlin und Istanbul." In *Rap: More Than Words*, ed. E. Kimminich, pp. 161–179. Frankfurt am Main: Peter Lang.

Gross, J., D. McMurray, and T. Swedenburg. 1992. "Rai, Rap, and Ramadan Nights: Franco-Maghribi Cultural Identities." *Middle East Report* 178:11–16, 24.

———. 2001. "Arab Noise and Ramadan Nights: *Rai*, Rap, and Franco-Maghrebi Identities." In *Displacement, Diaspora, and Geographies of Identity*, ed. S. Lavie and T. Swedenburg, pp. 119–155. Durham, NC: Duke University Press.

Hannerz, U. 1992. *Cultural Complexity: Studies in the Social Organization of Meaning.* New York: Columbia University Press.

Hargreaves, A. G. 1995. *Immigration, "Race," and Ethnicity in Contemporary France.* London: Routledge.

Haug, S., S. Müssig, and A. Stichs. 2009. *Muslimisches Leben in Deutschland.* Nürnberg: Bundesamt für Migration und Flüchtlinge. http://www.deutsche-islam-konferenz.de /cln_110/nn_1876234/SubSites/DIK/DE/InDeutschland/ZahlenDatenFakten /StudieMLD/studie-mld-node.html (accessed June 22, 2010).

Kaya, A. 1996. "Türk Diasporasında Hip-hop Milliyetciliği ve 'Rap' Sanatı" [Hip-hop Nationalism and the Art of "Rap" in the Turkish Diaspora]. *Toplumbilim* 4:141–148.

———. 1998. "Multicultural Clientelism and Alevi Resurgence in the Turkish Diaspora: Berlin Alevis." *New Perspectives on Turkey* 18:23–49.

———. 1999. "Türk Diyasporasında Etnik Stratejiler ve 'Çok-KÜLT-ürlülük' İdeolojisi: Berlin Türkleri" [Ethnic Strategies and "Multi-CULT-uralist" Ideology in the Turkish Diaspora: Berlin Turks]. *Toplum ve Bilim* 82:23–55.

———. 2000. "Ethnic Group Discourses and German-Turkish Youth." In *Redefining the Nation State and Citizen*, ed. G. G. Özdoğan and G. Tokay, pp. 233–251. Istanbul: Eren Yayıncılık.

———. 2001. *"Sicher in Kreuzberg": Constructing Diasporas: Turkish Hip-Hop Youth in Berlin*. Bielefeld: Transaction Publishers.

———. 2002. "Aesthetics of Diaspora: Contemporary Minstrels in Turkish Berlin." *Journal of Ethnic and Migration Studies* 28 (1): 43–62.

Klebe, D. 2004. "Kanak Attak in Germany: A Multiethnic Network of Youths Employing Musical Forms of Expression." In *Manifold Identities: Studies on Music and Minorities*, ed. U. Hemetek, G. Lechleitner, I. Naroditskaya, and A. Czekanowska, pp. 162–179. London: Cambridge Scholars Press.

Leezenberg, M. 2003. "Kurdish Alevis and the Kurdish Nationalist Movement in the 1990s." In *Turkey's Alevi Enigma: A Comprehensive Overview*, ed. P. J. White and J. Jongerden, pp. 197–212. Leiden: Brill.

Mandel, R. 1990. "Shifting Centers and Emergent Identities: Turkey and Germany in the Lives of Turkish *Gastarbeiter*." In *Muslim Travellers: Pilgrimage, Migration, and the Religious Imagination*, ed. D. F. Eickelman and J. Piscatori, pp. 153–171. London: Routledge.

———. 2008. *Cosmopolitan Anxieties: Turkish Challenges to Citizenship and Belonging in Germany*. Durham, NC: Duke University Press.

Manger, L., ed. 1999. *Muslim Diversity: Local Islam in Global Contexts*. Richmond, Surrey: Curzon.

Mardin, Ş. 2002. "Playing Games with Names." In *Fragments of Culture: The Everyday of Modern Turkey*, ed. D. Kandiyoti and A. Saktanber, pp. 115–127. London: I. B. Tauris.

Markoff, I. 1986. "The Role of Expressive Culture in the Demystification of a Secret Sect of Islam: The Case of the Alevis of Turkey." *The World of Music* 28 (3): 42–56.

———. 1993. "Music, Saints and Ritual: Sama' and the Alevis of Turkey." In *Manifestations of Sainthood in Islam*, ed. G. M. Smith and C. W. Ernst, pp. 95–110. Istanbul: Isis Press.

———. 1995. "Introduction to Sufi Music and Ritual in Turkey." *MESA Bulletin* 29 (2): 157–160.

———. 2002. "Alevi Identity and Expressive Culture." In *The Garland Encyclopedia of World Music, Volume 6: The Middle East*, ed. V. Danielson, S. Marcus, and D. Reynolds, pp. 793–800. New York: Routledge.

Mélikoff, I. 1998. "Bektashi / Kızılbaş: Historical Bipartition and Its Consequences." In *Alevi Identity: Cultural, Religious and Social Perspectives*, 2nd ed., ed. T. Olsson, E. Özdalga, and C. Raudvere, pp. 1–7. Istanbul: Swedish Research Institute in Istanbul.

Mitchell, T. 2001a. "Another Root—Hip-hop outside the USA." In *Global Noise: Rap and Hip-Hop outside the USA*, ed. T. Mitchell, pp. 1–38. Middletown, CT: Wesleyan University Press.

————, ed. 2001b. *Global Noise: Rap and Hip-Hop outside the USA*. Middletown, CT: Wesleyan University Press.

Miyakawa, F. M. 2005. *Five Percenter Rap: God Hop's Music, Message, and Black Muslim Mission*. Bloomington: Indiana University Press.

Mohammadi, A., ed. 2002. *Islam Encountering Globalization*. London: Routledge Curzon.

Navaro-Yashin, Y. 2002a. *Faces of the State: Secularism and Public Life in Turkey*. Princeton, NJ: Princeton University Press.

————. 2002b. "The Market for Identities: Secularism, Islamism, Commodities." In *Fragments of Culture: The Everyday of Modern Turkey*, ed. D. Kandiyoti and A. Saktanber, pp. 221–253. London: I. B. Tauris.

Nederveen Pieterse, J. 1997. "Travelling Islam: Mosques without Minarets." In *Space, Culture and Power: New Identities in Globalizing Cities*, ed. A. Öncü and P. Weyland, pp. 177–200. London: Zed Books.

Neyzi, L. 2002. "Embodied Elders: Space and Subjectivity in the Music of Metin-Kemal Kahraman." *Middle Eastern Studies* 38 (1): 89–109.

————. 2003. "*Zazaname*: The Alevi Renaissance, Media and Music in the Nineties." In *Turkey's Alevi Enigma: A Comprehensive Overview*, ed. P. J. White and J. Jongerden, pp. 111–124. Leiden: Brill.

Nohl, A. 1999. "Breakdans ve Medresse: Göçmen Gençlerin Çok Boyutlu Habitusu" [Breakdance and Medrese: The Multidimensional Habitus of Migrant Youth]. *Toplum ve Bilim* 82:91–112.

Olsson, T., E. Özdalga, and C. Raudvere, eds. 1998. *Alevi Identity: Cultural, Religious and Social Perspectives*. 2nd ed. Istanbul: Swedish Research Institute in Istanbul.

Öncü, A. 1994. "Packaging Islam: Cultural Politics on the Landscape of Turkish Commercial Television." *New Perspectives on Turkey* 10:13–36.

Rigoni, I. 2003. "Alevis in Europe: A Narrow Path towards Visibility." In *Turkey's Alevi Enigma: A Comprehensive Overview*, ed. P. J. White and J. Jongerden, pp. 159–173. Leiden: Brill.

Robins, K., and D. Morley. 1996. "Almancı, Yabancı." *Cultural Studies* 10 (2): 248–254.

Saktanber, A. 1997. "Formation of a Middle-class Ethos and Its Quotidian: Revitalizing Islam in Urban Turkey." In *Space, Culture and Power: New Identities in Globalizing Cities*, ed. A. Öncü and P. Weyland, pp. 140–156. London: Zed Books.

————. 2002. "'We Pray Like You Have Fun': New Islamic Youth in Turkey between Intellectualism and Popular Culture." In *Fragments of Culture: The Everyday of Modern Turkey*, ed. D. Kandiyoti and A. Saktanber, pp. 254–276. London: I. B. Tauris.

Seufert, G. 1997. "Between Religion and Ethnicity: A Kurdish-Alevi Tribe in Globalizing Istanbul." In *Space, Culture and Power: New Identities in Globalizing Cities*, ed. A. Öncü and P. Weyland, pp. 157–176. London: Zed Books.

Shankland, D. 2003. *The Alevis in Turkey: The Emergence of a Secular Islamic Tradition*. London: Routledge Curzon.

Slobin, M. 1993. *Subcultural Sounds: Micromusics of the West*. Hanover, NH: Wesleyan University Press.

Solomon, T. 2005a. "'Listening to Istanbul': Imagining Place in Turkish Rap Music." *Studia Musicologica Norvegica* 31:46–67.

————. 2005b. "'Living Underground Is Tough': Authenticity and Locality in the Hip-hop Community in Istanbul, Turkey." *Popular Music* 24 (1): 1–20.

————. 2008a. "'Bu Vatan Bizim' [This Land Is Ours]: Nationalist Discourse in Turkish

Rap Music." In *Freedom and Prejudice: Approaches to Media and Culture* ed. S. Kırca Schroeder and L. Hanson, pp. 204–222. Istanbul: Bahçeşehir University Press.

———. 2008b. "Diverse Diasporas: Multiple Identities in 'Turkish Rap' in Germany." In *Music from Turkey in the Diaspora*, ed. U. Hemetek and H. Sağlam, pp. 77–88. Vienna: Institut für Volksmusikforschung und Ethnomusikologie.

———. 2009. "Berlin-Frankfurt-Istanbul: Turkish Hip-Hop in Motion." *European Journal of Cultural Studies* 12 (3): 305–327.

Soysal, L. 1999. "Projects of Culture: An Ethnographic Episode in the Life of Migrant Youth in Berlin." PhD diss., Harvard University. UMI number 9949808.

———. 2001. "Diversity of Experience, Experience of Diversity: Turkish Migrant Youth Culture in Berlin." *Cultural Dynamics* 13 (1): 5–28.

Soysal, Y. N. 1997. "Changing Parameters of Citizenship and Claims-making: Organized Islam in European Public Spheres." *Theory and Society* 26 (4): 509–527.

Stokes, M. 1992. "Islam, the Turkish State, and Arabesk." *Popular Music* 11 (2): 213–227.

———. 1996a. "History, Memory and Nostalgia in Contemporary Turkish Musicology." *Music & Anthropology*, no. 1. http://www.levi.provincia.venezia.it/ma/index/number1/stokes1/st1.htm (accessed June 8, 2009).

———. 1996b. "Ritual, Identity and the State: An Alevi (Shi'a) Cem Ceremony." In *Nationalism, Minorities and Diasporas: Identities and Rights in the Middle East*, ed. K. E. Schultze, M. Stokes, and C. Campbell, pp. 188–202. London: Tauris Academic Publishers.

———. 1997. "Voices and Places: History, Repetition and the Musical Imagination." *Journal of the Royal Anthropological Institute* 3 (4): 673–691.

———. 2000. "'Beloved Istanbul': Realism and the Transnational Imaginary in Turkish Popular Culture." In *Mass Mediations: New Approaches to Popular Culture in the Middle East and Beyond*, ed. W. Armbrust, pp. 224–242. Berkeley: University of California Press.

———. 2002. "Afterword: Recognising the Everyday." In *Fragments of Culture: The Everyday of Modern Turkey*, ed. D. Kandiyoti and A. Saktanber, pp. 322–338. London: I. B. Tauris.

Swedenburg, T. 1997. "Islam in the Mix: Lessons of the Five Percent." Paper presented at the Anthropology Colloquium, University of Arkansas, February 19.

———. 2001. "Islamic Hip-hop versus Islamophobia: Aki Nawaz, Natacha Atlas, Akhenaton." In *Global Noise: Rap and Hip-Hop outside the USA*, ed. T. Mitchell, pp. 57–85. Middletown, CT: Wesleyan University Press.

Tuzak. 2002. "Tuzak: Onda On." *Gezgin Yabancı* (Istanbul) 2:40.

Vertovec, S. 1998. "Young Muslims in Keighley, West Yorkshire: Cultural Identity, Context, and 'Community.'" In *Muslim European Youth: Reproducing Ethnicity, Religion, Culture*, ed. S. Vertovec and A. Rogers, pp. 87–101. Aldershot: Ashgate.

Vertovec, S., and A. Rogers. 1998. "Introduction." In *Muslim European Youth: Reproducing Ethnicity, Religion, Culture*, ed. S. Vertovec and A. Rogers, pp. 1–24. Aldershot: Ashgate.

Vorhoff, K. 1998. "Academic and Journalistic Publications on the Alevi and Bektashi of Turkey." In *Alevi Identity: Cultural, Religious and Social Perspectives*, 2nd ed., ed. T. Olsson, E. Özdalga, and C. Raudvere, pp. 23–50. Istanbul: Swedish Research Institute in Istanbul.

White, J. B. 1999. "Islamic Chic." In *Istanbul between the Global and the Local*, ed. Ç. Keyder, pp. 77–91. Lanham, MD: Rowan & Littlefield Publishers.

————. 2002. "The Islamist Paradox." In *Fragments of Culture: The Everyday of Modern Turkey*, ed. D. Kandiyoti and A. Saktanber, pp. 191–217. London: I. B. Tauris.

White, P. J. 2003. "The Debate on the Identity of 'Alevi Kurds.'" In *Turkey's Alevi Enigma: A Comprehensive Overview*, ed. P. J. White and J. Jongerden, pp. 17–29. Leiden: Brill.

Yalçın-Heckmann, L. 1998. "Growing Up as a Muslim in Germany: Religious Socialization among Turkish Migrant Families." In *Muslim European Youth: Reproducing Ethnicity, Religion, Culture*, ed. S. Vertovec and A. Rogers, pp. 167–191. Aldershot: Ashgate.

DISCOGRAPHY

All titles are Turkish pressings, unless otherwise noted.

Bovdead-R. 1999. "Kosova Dramı." *Kosova Dramı*. Modem Müzik [cassette].

Eastila. n.d., ca. 2005–2006. *Ahir Zamanda Uyanış*. Asır [CD].

Orhanca. 1998. *Sert Müslümanlar*. Umut Plak ve Kasetçilik [CD and cassette].

R.A.K. Sabotaj. 2001. "Keskin Sirke." *HipHop Menü* [compilation album]. Zihni Müzik [cassette].

————. n.d. "Gerçek Ritm," "Sınav Hayatı," "2000 Intro." [Underground songs distributed on the Internet beginning ca. 2001.]

Sert Müslümanlar. 2000a. "Bosna," "Solingen," "Allahu Ekber Bizlere Güç Ver." *Ay Yıldız Yıkılmayacak*. At-Ek Müzik Yapım [cassette].

————. 2000b. *Dönelim Vatana*. At-Ek Müzik Yapım [cassette].

————. 2004. *Best of Sert Müslümanlar 2004*. Özdiyar Music [CD, Nürnberg].

CHAPTER 2

CONTESTING ISLAMIC CONCEPTS OF MORALITY: HEAVY METAL IN ISTANBUL

PIERRE HECKER

"I GOT NO PROBLEM with religion or religious people. My problem is they got a problem with me," my counterpart with the long, blond dyed hair so aptly sums up. With his tattooed arms and the "pilot shades" on his head, he could easily be considered as the Turkish incarnation of American glam rock star Bret Michaels, who had just dropped by to have a couple of beers before hitting on the beautiful young women in the bar where we were doing the interview. Lighting another cigarette, he disdainfully adds: "You know, when they saw me on TV or out in the streets, they shit on me."[1] Saying this, he refers to how he is being perceived in the eyes of the Turkish public. And indeed, the appearance and behavior of Turkish rockers and metalheads—with their long hair, black clothes, tattoos, earrings and piercings, and their love for Turkish *rakı* and beer—are still often labeled as deviant and contradictory to prevalent concepts of morality and religion.

If we look at Turkish heavy metal from a perspective of resistance and power (Karin van Nieuwkerk, introduction to this volume), we need to address contemporary discourses on secularism and Islamism in Turkish society. Islamic actors, who, for a long time, have found themselves in a marginalized position resisting the laicist doctrines of the Kemalist state, are blaming Turkish rockers and metalheads for their supposedly loose morals and disrespect to Islamic traditions. Today, however, political Islam no longer represents an oppositional counterpublic, but with the electoral victory of the Muslim conservative Justice and Development Party (AKP), has taken the dominant power position in state and society.

While adherents of the Turkish hip-hop scene in the 1990s countered what they perceived as the domination of secularist Kemalism (Thomas Solomon, this volume), Turkish metalheads today, by the same token, see themselves in a marginalized position in which they resist the dominance of Islamic revivalism. The present government's Islamization policies are usually seen as evidence for its intentions to subvert the secularist principles of

FIGURE 2.1. Levent, alias "Nikki," in a bar in Istanbul

the Turkish state. Consequently, many Turkish metalheads openly speak of their fears of Turkey "becoming Iran" (see Farzaneh Hemmasi, this volume) and losing their individual freedoms to the orthodox interpretations of political Islam.

This chapter aims to explore how particular cultural practices associated with heavy metal are contesting Islamic concepts of morality in Turkish society. After briefly introducing the history of Turkish heavy metal and providing an insight into the Islamization policies of the present government, it examines the public discourse on heavy metal, shedding light on the different forms of moral subversiveness ascribed to it by the Turkish media. Finally, it investigates how heavy metal culture is contesting Islamic morality in everyday life. In this respect, the text refers to aspects of gender, religion, and anti-Christian blasphemy in a Muslim context.

THE ART OF TRANSGRESSION

It was not so long ago that conducting research on heavy metal in Turkey earned me the disbelieving and amused looks of many colleagues and friends. The very idea of Muslim metalheads appeared absurd to them, for it did not fit into anything they had associated with Turkey and the Muslim world at the time. Could there really be young Muslim men and women shaking their heads to the extreme sounds of metal music and performing the same deviant practices as their counterparts in the West? Furthermore, hardly anyone could imagine how studying metal could be of academic interest at all.

Happily enough, academic interest in heavy metal has risen significantly over recent years,[2] and meanwhile, even studies on heavy metal in various Muslim contexts have been published—whether it be Egypt (Swedenburg 2000), Indonesia (Wallach 2003, 2008), Bali (Baulch 2003, 2007), Turkey (Hecker 2005, 2010), Morocco, Pakistan, or Iran (LeVine 2008, 2010). All of these studies, one way or another, stress the subversive and countercultural potential of heavy metal within predominantly Muslim societies. Personal interviews with metalheads from Syria, Lebanon, Jordan, the UAE, and Turkey, as well as a limited analysis of newspaper articles on the "satanic panic" in Morocco in 2003, suggest that heavy metal, above all, is publicly perceived to subvert Islamic concepts of morality. This, actually, perfectly corresponds with early perceptions of heavy metal in predominantly Christian contexts.

Throughout the 1980s and 1990s, North America and Western Europe have seen widespread allegations, lawsuits, and charges against heavy metal artists, blaming them for seducing youngsters into Satanism, suicide, violence, and drug abuse (Walser 1993, 137–171; Weinstein 2000 [1991], 245–263; Christe 2004, 290–303; Kahn-Harris 2007, 27–29; Klypchak 2007, 12–15, 101ff). Heavy metal has even been said to convey subliminal messages and to possess supernatural powers over its listeners. While the irrational, false, and often politically motivated allegations were usually ridiculed by fans and bands, they were frequently taken seriously by a wider public. Consequently, heavy metal, for a long time, has been publicly perceived as contradictory to Christian concepts of morality as well.

Considering the subversive potential of heavy metal, I agree with British sociologist Keith Kahn-Harris, who describes "extreme metal" as a culture of "transgressive practices" (Kahn-Harris 2007, 25–49).[3] Yet I would argue that the production of transgression is not limited only to those subgenres of heavy metal described by him as "extreme" (e.g., thrash metal, death metal, black metal, grindcore), but rather is found in metal music and culture as a whole. Though the modes of transgression have been constantly changing, heavy metal has been transgressive throughout its history. While, for instance, on the eve of the hippie movement, long hair on men was something odd to see even in the United Kingdom or the United States, it is, today, no longer regarded as something deviant. In other words, what is considered transgressive today may no longer be considered transgressive tomorrow.

Metal has always been following a creative urge to test and break musical and nonmusical boundaries. While extreme sounds push for sonic transgression—as, for instance, through screamed or growled vocals, heavily distorted and downtuned guitars, complex rhythms, or extremely fast tempos—verbal and visual means aim to subvert various nonmusical boundaries. Lyrical themes of gore and horror, sex and excess, despair and paranoia, or death and rebellion commonly merge with symbolic representations of horror, death, sex, and blasphemy. Blasphemy usually relates to anti-Christian sentiments. Symbolic representations depicting the devil, the inverted cross—which refers to the Roman Empire's execution of St. Peter by having him crucified with his head down as an act of mocking his religious belief—or 666, the number of the beast—which derives from St. John's Book of Revelation and symbolizes the approaching Apocalypse—were all appropriated from a Christian tradition. To such symbols are added elements of pre-Christian pagan traditions, as the pentagram or Thor's hammer. Also common are explicit sexual illustrations, human and animal skulls, and the color black. All these icons are displayed in various forms on album covers, T-shirts, patches, band logos, tattoos, and basically all kind of metal fashion.

TURKISH METAL HISTORY

The rise of rock music in Anatolia dates back to the second half of the 1960s, when a number of young Turkish musicians pioneered a sound that is nowadays known as Anatolian Rock (Anadolu Rock). Merging traditional Anatolian melodies with the sounds of electric guitars, bass, and rock beats, artists such as Erkin Koray (b. 1941), Cem Karaca (1945–2004), Barış Manço (1943–1999), and the band Moğollar (f. 1967) laid the foundations for an indigenous Turkish rock tradition (see Solmaz 1996; Tireli 2005), paving the way for the emergence of Turkish heavy metal in the 1980s and 1990s.

In the early and mid-1980s, local metal scenes initially formed in Istanbul, Ankara, and a few other major Turkish cities. Although heavy metal music, on a global scale, witnessed a tremendous boost in popularity and commercial success throughout the 1980s,[4] the emergence of a Turkish metal scene could not be taken for granted. On September 12, 1980, Turkey experienced a military coup d'état followed by political repression and economic hardship. The military intervention, which, in the first place, was directed against Turkey's powerful socialist movement, forced numerous leftist-oriented rock musicians into exile. Due to the openly socialist attitudes of artists like Cem Karaca or the band Moğollar, rock music was considered politically subversive. As a consequence, musical performances remained restricted for years, requiring official permission by the authorities.

Beyond political hardship, the situation was further aggravated by a series of economic factors. Import taxes, the devaluation of the Turkish lira (TL), and a general decrease of purchasing power made European and American music imports almost unaffordable to Turkish customers. Albums, magazines, instruments, amplifiers, stereo equipment, and any kind of metal-related accessories, including patches and T-shirts, were virtually unavailable in the Turkish market. It was not until the mid-1980s that a small number of internationally popular heavy metal albums were licensed to Turkish record companies and sold at more moderate prices.

In addition to that, the national media were still monopolized and controlled by the state. Consequently, rock, let alone metal, programs were extremely rare on Turkish radio and TV. This did not change until the early 1990s, when the national broadcasting monopoly was finally lifted and countless private radio and TV stations began to emerge (see Çaplı 1998; Barış 2006). Parallel to this development, Turkey's economy entered an era of recovery and liberalization, providing easier access to cultural resources from abroad. Until then, however, Turkish metalheads had to rely on informal networks to get hold of albums, merchandise, and information on bands and trends.

A common way of getting connected with the global metal underground was tape trading. The term describes an informal practice of exchanging and distributing recordings at a mostly nonmonetary level. Before the advent of the Internet, the global metal scene had been relying on postal mail for sending and exchanging demo tapes, flyers, fanzines, and personal information around the globe. In so doing, the scene finally generated a widely ramified network consisting of thousands of individuals, bands, distributors, and independent record labels. Turkish metalheads began to participate in the global tape trading network in the late 1980s and early 1990s and managed to establish contact with such faraway places as Norway, South Africa, and Malaysia. On several occasions, tape trading contacts were even used to attract to Turkey foreign metal bands, whose concerts further boosted the emergence of the Turkish scene.

Although the dissemination of new media and communication technologies have made metal music and culture more easily accessible since then, metal still remains a predominantly urban culture—at least as far as the cultural infrastructure of bands, rock bars, concert venues, fanzines, and scene-specific music shops is concerned. While the big cities have always granted greater individual freedoms, providing space for almost all kinds of subcultures and scenes, social and cultural constraints in rural areas usually remain high, and the metal scene's deviant codes and styles (e.g., earrings on men, tattoos on women) are met with open, sometimes violent, disapproval.

FIGURE 2.2. Demo tape of Turkish thrash metal band Metalium, ca. 1990

Since the early days of Turkish metal, countless media reports depicted the scene as a threat to Turkey's national and religious identity. Although most of these reports—including accounts of Satanism, suicide pacts, and perverted sexual practices—were highly imaginative, metalheads are indeed violating traditional concepts of morality. Having extramarital relationships, celebrating the drinking of alcohol as an integral part of the metal lifestyle, and distancing themselves from religious practices in everyday life (ritual prayers, religious services, fasting, wearing of the Islamic headscarf) are indicators expressing dissent from dominant codes in Turkish society. But can these practices be seen as acts of resistance toward Islam?

Turkish metalheads mostly regard themselves as a product of Turkish secularism, which, in the wake of Islamic revivalism, needs to be defended. Imagining metal without secularism appears impossible to them. The idea of Turkey "becoming Iran" and, one day, individual freedoms losing out to state-implemented religious doctrines are, for many metalheads, real and imminent threats.[5] With regard to the present political situation, the Turkish metal scene shows strong antipathy against the Muslim conservative government and its two leading figures, Prime Minister Recep Tayyip Erdoğan and the president of the state, Abdullah Gül. Their opposition is particularly directed against the government's Islamization policies.

ISLAMIZATION OF THE PUBLIC SPHERE

It has been almost a decade since the Muslim conservative Justice and Development Party first took office after securing a landslide victory in the Turkish national elections of November 2002. Since then, its representatives have been promoting a policy that appears to result in a gradual Islamization of the public sphere. A bundle of provisions enacted in recent years underline the government's ambitions of subverting the laicist character of the Turkish state. Under the cover of social and educational reform—and always careful to take a cosmopolitan and modern line of argument—it supports Islamic cultural practices while, at the same time, it aims to restrict what is regarded as un-Islamic.

The government's most popular and, at the same time, most controversial move of Islamizing the public sphere was its struggle to ease the ban on Islamic headscarves at Turkish universities. Promoting the visibility of Islamic symbols and practices in formerly well-guarded secular spaces such as universities was an effective means of demonstrating power and contesting the secularist legacy of the state. Yet the government presented its political move as a campaign for women's rights rather than an attempt at Islamization. Stressing the fact that young Muslim women were denied university education on the basis of refusing to remove their headscarves, government representatives persisted in saying that they were only implementing international antidiscrimination policies, as, for instance, demanded by the European Union. By turning the headscarf issue into an antidiscrimination matter, the government, moreover, aimed at avoiding confrontation with Turkey's powerful Constitutional Court and military, which both regard themselves as guardians of the secularist legacy of the state.

In early February 2008, the government effectively eased the ban on headscarves on the basis of two constitutional amendments. While the first amendment provided for the right to equal treatment from state institutions for everyone, the second amendment guaranteed that no one can be deprived of his or her right to higher education. Accordingly, Islamic headscarves were repermitted at Turkish universities. Yet the new provision compromised with the secular system by only allowing traditional, loosely tied headscarves that could hardly be interpreted as a symbol of political Islam. Women lecturers and civil servants continued to be banned from covering their heads. Despite concessions to the secular system, the Turkish Constitutional Court, on June 5, 2008, annulled the government's constitutional reforms on the grounds of violating the secular founding principles of the Turkish state. As a consequence, the ban on Islamic headscarves was reimposed. Nevertheless, the move proved to be a huge political success for the prime minister, for the reform attempt publicly underlined his commitment to strengthen the role of Islam in the Turkish state and society.

Further moves to promote conservative Islamic ethics within the educational system have been revealed in increased financial support for the so-called Imam Hatip High Schools, which had been originally established to educate government-employed imams. Meanwhile, however, they appear to primarily function as secondary education institutions for boys and girls from families that place high value on religious and moral education. In addition to that, Turkey has been witnessing sporadic censorship of teaching materials on moral grounds. In 2006, for instance, the National Education Ministry removed Eugene Delacroix's famous painting *Liberty Leading the People* from a seventh-grade schoolbook for depicting a bare-bosomed woman leading French revolutionaries into battle. Beyond that, the national broadcasting authority banned several pay-TV channels specializing in erotic movies for offending public moral values.

Apart from issues of veiling, nudity, and sexuality, the issue of Islam and alcohol has been high on the government's agenda. Since coming to power in late 2002, AKP officials imposed a variety of new taxes, laws, and licensing restrictions in order to legally restrict the consumption of alcohol in the public sphere. Though the production and sale of alcoholic beverages have always been limited under licensing laws, public drinking has been a common practice in Turkish society for a long time. Even Mustafa Kemal, the highly venerated founding father of the Turkish republic, enjoyed drinking and smoking in public.

The first in a series of steps taken to restrict and partially ban the consumption of alcohol from the public sphere was to impose a private consumption tax on alcoholic beverages. As a result, consumer prices for alcohol have been skyrocketing. The average price for a half-liter bottle of Turkish-produced beer more than doubled—climbing from 1.08 TL in early 2003 to 2.23 TL in Summer 2009. The average price for a bottle of *rakı*, Turkey's anise-flavored "national drink," temporarily almost tripled during the same period.[6]

Furthermore, AKP-controlled municipalities frequently refuse to issue new sales licenses for alcohol or to extend existing permits. Consequently, the number of businesses selling alcohol in Turkey has decreased significantly under Muslim conservative rule. Besides, the government issued regulations that restrict the sale of alcohol in public places: In November 2005, it imposed a ban on serving alcohol in state-run cafés and restaurants on the grounds of protecting family values. In Spring 2008, a new law banned the sale of alcoholic beverages outside their original packaging. Speaking in practical terms, this means that bars and restaurants that want to sell drinks by the glass need to acquire particular licenses.

The government's latest move, as of July 2009, is a series of new provisions on alcohol advertisement. From now on, alcohol companies are prohibited from presenting items in their advertisement campaigns that could be associated with Turkey's geographic, cultural, historic, and artistic values. It is, for instance, no longer allowed to display Turkish *rakı* together with its most popular accompaniments, white cheese and fish.

The new regulations are officially rationalized as precautionary measures for the benefit and protection of children and youth. Possible religious intentions go completely unmentioned. Current discussions on future regulations even include propositions to ban alcohol from city centers and establish prescribed "drinking zones" as the only areas where alcohol can be legally sold and consumed in public. Turkish critics, in response to the previously described measures, have been pointing a heavily accusing finger at government officials for subverting the laicist principles of the Turkish state. In Summer 2009, several metalheads temporarily found themselves at the forefront of public resistance against the government's Islamization policies.

ACTS OF RESISTANCE

On July 18, 2009, the second day of a major heavy metal festival in Istanbul, a group of young metalheads had gathered on the green in front of the venue. The so-called Uni-Rock Open Air Festival hosted a huge variety of national and international bands, attracting thousands of Turkish fans who were joined by metalheads from neighboring countries like Greece, Iran, and Syria. According to Turkish media reports, the just-mentioned group of youngsters were just enjoying themselves—hanging out, banging their heads to the music, and drinking beer—when, coincidentally, the motorcade of Prime Minister Recep Tayyip Erdoğan drove by. Some of them, then, apparently vented their dislike and anger by raising their hands and pointing the sign of the horns in the direction of the passing limousine. This, however, prompted the prime minister's bodyguards to arrest them on the grounds of showing "disrespect to a statesman."[7] According to the media, four young men and one woman were thereupon taken to a nearby police station, where they were held and interrogated for twenty-one hours.

The particular gesture, which apparently prompted the arrest, is done by stretching the index and the little finger of one's hand while holding the middle and the ring finger down with the thumb. In the 1960s, the sign of the horns had been popularized as a satanic salute and is therefore also known as "devil's horns," or simply "devil sign." Within the realms of global metal, it has become a significant indicator of shared identity that should be understood as a symbol of rebellion and individual emancipation from social constraints rather than a cultural representation of Satanism. Whatever meaning had been ascribed to it by the prime minister's bodyguards and the Turkish police, the incident triggered some political repercussions.

When the event received publicity, many Turkish artists, intellectuals, and politicians were quick to declare their solidarity with the detained metalheads. At the time, the youngsters were threatened with being officially charged for insulting the head of government. While the prime minister himself was quoted with the words "The state of [our] youth is distressing. That sort of unlimited moral erosion makes us sad,"[8] Gürsel Tekin, the Istanbul chairman of the main opposition party, the Republican People's Party (CHP), emphasized his willingness to support the metalheads' cause. The CHP subsequently mocked the prime minister's disproportionate and apparently undemocratic reactions. Several major newspapers published a photo showing Gürsel Tekin together with two of the "perpetrators," all of them making the sign of the horns in front of a large CHP banner. Furthermore, a Republican MP even requested to hold a public hearing on the case in parliament.[9] In the eyes of the opposition, the five metalheads were a symbol of laicism and resistance against political Islam. This, however, only reflected the latest stage in the public discourse on heavy metal in Turkey, whose roots date back to the late 1980s.

PUBLIC DISCOURSE ON HEAVY METAL

In the late 1980s and early 1990s, the growing visibility of metal in urban public spaces began to increasingly attract the interest of the Turkish media. Newspaper journalists and television commentators overwhelmingly depicted metal as a phenomenon of deviant behavior and consequently as a threat to the established way of life. The situation was exacerbated when a series of teenage suicides and the murder of a young girl in an Istanbul cemetery triggered a series of panics over metal and Satanism. The Turkish media, emphasizing the commonalities of the events, constructed a coherent scenario of interrelated incidents, though they had nothing to do with each other.[10]

The most serious accusations against metal were raised in connection with the so-called "Ortaköy murder." In the late summer of 1999, Turkish police recovered the naked, half-buried body of a young woman from a cemetery in the Istanbul neighborhood of Ortaköy. The girl's head reportedly had been smashed with a stone, and her body showed signs of rape. By the time the newspapers published the story, the police had already arrested two young men and a young woman, who all confessed to murdering twenty-one-year-old Şehriban Çoşkunfirat on the night of September 13th. When pictures showing the long-haired perpetrators dressed in black and holding the remains of a dismembered cat surfaced, rumors of necrophilia and satanic rituals dominated the news. In the following days and weeks, the media coverage snowballed into a major moral panic with rock and heavy metal music at the forefront of public concern: parents warned their children to stay away from long-haired men in the streets, and the police conducted crackdowns on rock bars, record labels, fanzines, record stores, and individuals who had long hair or wore black clothes.

The invention of Satanism in the Turkish media resembles similar events in the United States and Europe apparently providing a blueprint for the writings of many Turkish journalists. In the Turkish case, the prototype for allegations of Satanism, sexual perversion, and different kinds of immorality was written by well-known newspaper journalist Engin Ardıç. His outright antimetal polemic in an article for *Sabah* on October 14, 1990, made him a staunch enemy of the Turkish metal scene:

As if there were not enough "species" in the country [already], yet another one has emerged: metalheads. Calling themselves "children of Satan," their main features are tattered clothes and iron pieces and shackles [attached] to their backs and heads. Some of them are wearing swastikas and some are cutting themselves with razor blades here and there, ripping themselves left and right and making themselves bleed. . . .

Last Monday, you saw a photo report of our [colleague] Tayyar Işıksaçan on our back page: As many as 2,000 "metalheads" had gathered in the [Harbiye] Open Air Theatre, enjoying themselves [and drinking alcohol].[11] On their foreheads crosses—yes, young ladies with makeup and the official "sign of the infidels." . . .

They have symbols. You stretch the index and the little finger of the right hand into the air and yell, bursting out "metaaaaal" from deep inside your throat!

. . . I would like to address another and bigger aspect of degeneration to you, a squalor that is [even] more inconceivable: Satan worshippers have been springing up! Yes, in Turkey!

. . . Every Saturday the 15th, they gather in order to celebrate a mass with wads of smoke, black cowls, crosses, sharp knives, and a mystic number of magic murmurs. Stark-naked chicks. The abbot mixes the blood of the person attending the ritual with his own blood and signs a contract with Satan. After that they copulate like dogs in front of the group!

In any case, there has to be sexual intercourse between man and woman [during the rituals]. They are the servants of Satan—everything is permitted; homosexual relationships are fostered. Among them, there are even villains who are molesting small children.

. . . A bloke named A.K. explains their principles in the following way: be antisocial, live only for yourself . . . be egoistic, live up to your desires . . . be strong, evolution proceeds through the perishing of the weak . . . obliterate all moral values . . . destroy what is not created by yourself, strike back against everything done to you . . . spread chaos . . . do not limit your sexuality to only one gender . . . live without responsibility . . . You see, we are unaware of how "westernized" the country is, for heaven's sake.[12]

Putting Ardıç's assertions in a nutshell, heavy metal is subverting public morality. The text is replete with evocative images of deviance that seek to strengthen this argument. With regard to the variety of images used in the text, it appears necessary to define some sort of classificatory system that helps to transform the empirical material into manageable categories. Accordingly, I decided to use four "categories of immorality" to which the different images will be allotted. The lines between these categories are, however, fluid. Some images could be assigned to more than just one of them.

RELIGIOUS SUBVERSIVENESS

A central argument in Ardıç's polemic against metal is the putative renunciation of Islam. According to what he says, metalheads ascribe to themselves apostasy and Satanism. He depicts them as "children of Satan," "Satan worshippers," and "servants of Satan." The text culminates in a portrayal of a black mass that ends in signing "a contract with Satan" before finally engaging in a ritual act of sexual intercourse.

In order to present more "evidence" for the apostate nature of metal music, he refers to photographs by his colleague Tayyar Işıksaçan, reportedly showing young women with crosses painted onto their foreheads. Though I did not have access to these photographs, I suppose that the girls had painted inverted crosses onto their skin. This, however, points to the ambivalence of anti-Christian symbols in a Muslim context: in the eyes of a Muslim society that is not familiar with metal iconography, a cross, inverted or not, is perceived as an expression of Christian creed. Consequently, the "sign of the infidels" upon the skin of young Turkish girls must have come as a shock to newspaper readers, as it implies the girls' conversion to Christianity. This poses a threat not only to Islam, however, but also to the country's national identity, for Sunni Islam is an important element of Turkish nationalism—despite the Kemalist doctrine of laicism.

SEXUAL SUBVERSIVENESS

The text clearly mentions several forms of sexual subversiveness, namely, promiscuity ("they copulate like dogs," "there has to be sexual intercourse between man and woman"), homosexuality ("homosexual relationships are fostered"), and child molestation ("molesting small children"). The concept of morality addressed through these images is mainly religious. Concerning sexuality, Islamic sources do condemn two particular practices: anal intercourse and extramarital intercourse. Both practices are sinful and shameful and, at least according to religious sources taken from the *hadith/ahadith*, to be punished by law (Schmitt 2002). This refers equally to heterosexual and homosexual relationships. Neither men nor women are allowed to engage in anal and/or extramarital sex. Accordingly, religious scholars generally deduce a prohibition of homosexuality, since (male) homosexuality supposedly involves both aforementioned practices. From a religious perspective, any violation of these prohibitions represents a disregard for the divine revelation and is therefore considered subversive.

A second, traditional concept of morality addressed here is that of honor and shame. Very briefly speaking, the idea of honor and shame is based upon the principle of separating the masculine from the feminine in order to ensure the sexual integrity of the female body. Any harm to that is equivalent to a complete loss of social prestige for the whole family. Consequently, metal, described by Ardıç as propagating promiscuity, must be seen as a threat to traditional social order.

POLITICAL SUBVERSIVENESS

From a political perspective, Ardıç blames metalheads of adhering to subversive ideologies such as National Socialism ("some are wearing swastikas") and—as mentioned in a second article by Ardıç published only a couple of days later—Communism.[13] With regard to Turkish national history, it was open conflict between the Communist Left and the Fascist Right that led the country into political instability culminating in the coup d'état of 1980.

As outlined above, Ardıç assumes metal to be apostate, thus posing a threat to the country's religious identity. Religious identity, in that case, is equivalent to national identity. Another verbal attack along the same line is his final résumé that the emergence of metal and Satanism is a result of westernization ("You see, we are unaware of how 'westernized' the country is, for heaven's sake!"). The Turkish Republic was born from a war of independence, after European imperialist powers had already agreed on a territorial partitioning of Ottoman Anatolia by the end of World War I. Therefore, Turkish nationalism is highly sensitive to any kind of foreign interference in the country's internal affairs. From this perspective, Westernization—seen as a matter of cultural alienation—could breed discord among the population, finally contributing to a weakening and disintegration of the country. Metal, in this sense, is undermining Turkish national identity.

SOCIAL SUBVERSIVENESS

The text dwells on multiple images that can be categorized as socially subversive. It starts with some brief remarks on the metalheads' clothing. What Ardıç describes ("tattered clothes") flouts the prevailing dress codes of Turkish society. The question of what is seen as adequate in terms of clothing is based on principles such as decency, tidiness, and cleanliness.

On another occasion, he denounces Turkish metalheads as "our homemade rich bastards" who are wearing expensive sports shoes. In doing so, he alludes to the enormous social, cultural, and economic disparities in Turkish society. When he wrote his antimetal polemic, Westernization in terms of having access to cultural resources from Western Europe and North America was widely limited to a relatively well-off Turkish middle class. Accordingly, Ardıç implies that metal is an exclusively upper-middle-class phenomenon, which, at least today, it is not. In other words, he draws a line between an allegedly morally corrupted, Westernized elite and a socially deprived, but morally superior, lower class. As a result, the originally social rift attains the connotation of a moral rift, with metal functioning as an indicator for that scenario.

Beyond that, Ardıç claims that metalheads indulge in acts of self-mutilation ("some are cutting themselves with razor blades") and are committed to the principles of egoism and hedonism. Accordingly, they disregard the well-being of others ("be antisocial," "evolution proceeds through the perishing of the weak"), seek to maximize their own pleasure ("live up to your desires"), and act solely to serve their own interests ("live only for yourself," "live without responsibilities"). Finally, he imputes to them a nihilist attitude ("spread chaos," "obliterate all moral values"), thereby completing the picture of social subversiveness.

Since Ardıç wrote his polemic twenty years ago, the moral impact of heavy metal on the younger generation has been widely discussed by the Turkish public. Yet, as far as Ardıç's general line of argument is concerned, he appears to have provided the blueprint for critical debate on heavy metal in Turkey. In 2003, a group of Islamic writers took up the issue of Satanism. In an edited volume entitled *Satanizm Girdabı ve Sahte Metafizik Akımlar* (*The Satanic Vortex and False Metaphysical Movements*), the above-mentioned stereotypes reappear with a religiously motivated intention. The volume includes articles by prominent Islamic intellectuals such as Fethullah Gülen, the leader of the Islamic reform movement named after him, Ahmet Güç, a professor of theology at Uludağ University, and Mehmet Şeker, a writer for the religious-conservative newspaper *Yeni Şafak*. The following two excerpts, from psychiatrist Nevzat Tarhan's contribution, "Satanism: Its Nature, Reasons for Its Dissemination, and Ways of Its Prevention," and Ahmet Güç's article, "Our Youth's Search for Identity and Satanism,"[14] illustrate how heavy metal, in a religious discourse, is being blamed for disseminating allegedly satanic ideas:

Rituals and crazy music

Slaying cats and dogs, making fun of religious services, humiliating sacred things, torturing and raping those who had been chosen for sacrifice, having group sex, taking drugs, practicing black magic and magic rites are the Satanists' main features. Essential for them is black, dark, and hard music—music such as black metal and heavy metal. . . . Their rituals resemble an orgasm. Actually, hard music is an outcry of the Satanists' inner distress. (Tarhan 2003)[15]

How does Satanism spread in Turkey?
Among [the means of] disseminating Satanism are computers and the Internet, some books, magazines, brochures, cassettes, CDs, etc. Apart from the technical means, other factors are being used—mainly women, alcohol, drugs, concerts, friends, parties, and to a considerable degree money. . . . satanic thoughts are being imposed through music. Inasmuch as this effect is well known, today Satanist thoughts and ideas are being conveyed to their young minds particularly through metal and rock music. . . . In Satanism there is an understanding of "free sex." Young girls are in the [bad] situation to accept that. . . . Satanists do not only sacrifice cats, but also animals like roosters and rabbits. (Güç 2003)[16]

Both authors repeat the same narrative as countless newspaper reports, comments, and articles before. In so doing, they are connecting the issue of Satanism with heavy metal music and culture. They depict the same images of immorality as Engin Ardıç, thereby pointing toward multiple acts of sexual and religious subversiveness.

CONTESTING ISLAMIC CONCEPTS OF MORALITY

As the previous paragraphs have shown, the public discourse on heavy metal has been widely dominated by allegations of subverting public morality. What should have become clear from the above is that these allegations were often highly imaginative and designed to produce moral panics among the Turkish public. Media polemics such as that by newspaper journalist Engin Ardıç may illustrate how metal is publicly perceived in Turkey—thereby revealing the different layers of moral subversiveness ascribed to it—yet they provide no information about "real life." In order to investigate how heavy metal is contesting Islamic concepts of morality in everyday life, it is necessary to let the metalheads speak for themselves and retrieve some qualitative data from the field. The subsequent paragraphs aim to do this by addressing aspects of gender, Muslim-ness, and blasphemy.

METAL AND GENDER

Gender relations in Turkish society have been changing—not only since the emergence of rock and metal culture. Today, the question of how men and women are expected to behave cannot be answered easily and, by no means, in a universally valid way. In contemporary political discourse, the female body, or more precisely, particular modes of female behavior, have become an important matter of marking, claiming, and contesting secular and religious spaces in everyday life. The following paragraphs will illustrate how metal culture helps to define secular spaces in an urban context, and how it is contesting prevalent gender identities.

The Kemalist model of modernity put women's emancipation at the fore-front of its reform efforts from the very beginning (Göle 2000, 51; Kadıoğlu 2002, 73; Arat 2005, 16–19). In the 1920s and 1930s, new laws strengthened women's position in society. Women were given the right to vote, provided with access to education, and increasingly given the opportunity to enter the public sphere and the workplace. Within this process, the unveiled, en-lightened woman became a symbol for national progress and modernity. Although Kemalist reform efforts proceeded against prevalent traditions, female behavior was still expected to be characterized by modesty, chas-tity, and a general acceptance of male dominance (Kadıoğlu 2002, 76; Arat 2005, 18).

During the early 1990s, debates over how women should act (and dress) in public became an important factor of Islamic revivalism (cf. Göle 1995; Kadıoğlu 2002; Navaro-Yashin 2002; Arat 2005). Islamic actors pushed their way into the public realm by promoting particular visual codes and practices that marked them as Islamic. Particularly young women placed emphasis on their Islamic identity by wearing the *türban*, a modern, though conserva-tive, version of the Islamic headscarf. The visibility of the Islamic veil in the public sphere represented a demonstration of power and often functioned to demarcate religious from secular urban spaces. For many Turkish women, wearing the *türban* became an important means to underline their Islamic, and accordingly modest and chaste, behavior. Today, gender issues in Turk-ish society are still highly politicized, thereby usually bearing religious con-notations. In order to illustrate the meaning of metal with regard to gender issues, I will proceed with a situational description from the field.

In March 2008, I had the chance to join a conference at Kayseri Erciyes University. In Turkey, the central Anatolian city of Kayseri is famous for be-ing a stronghold of the governing conservative Justice and Development Party, the AKP. The conservative atmosphere of the place could be easily felt during the conference sessions. In response to the conference program, which was meant to discuss the EU Turkey Agenda for the 21st Century, students placed remarkable emphasis on questions of cultural alienation and religion. Even more striking was the fact that for the first time in a Turkish university, I witnessed female students wearing the Islamic headscarf. Un-til recently, Islamic-style headscarves had been banned from state schools and universities, though the AKP, since its coming to power in 2002, had been pushing hard to ease the ban by amending the country's constitution. The final move of easing the ban has been bitterly opposed by hard-line Kemalists and intellectuals who fear damage to secularity. For conservative

Muslims, however, the headscarf has become an important visual symbol to demonstrate their religious aspirations in public.

In addition to wearing headscarves, the young women participating in the conference sat in small groups separate from their fellow male students, an apparent expression of modesty. Female students, though they were actively involved in the conference discussions, noticeably effaced themselves in the breaks between conference sessions, while their male counterparts besieged the predominantly male speakers with questions. Speaking in more abstract terms, the young women's behavior revealed a set of gender-specific practices that, in the particular conservative context, were regarded as morally adequate.

The day after the conference, I got on a plane to Istanbul in order to meet old friends and gather new material to complement previous research on Turkish metal. The same night, I went to DoRock, a popular rock bar in the center of Istanbul, to watch a concert by the metal bands Murder King and Postmortem. The bar was packed with people, and when I entered, Postmortem were already live on stage. Pushing my way to the front, I finally encountered a crushingly brutal sound with growled vocals that was produced by three ferociously headbanging young women and a heavily tattooed male drummer. None of the women was covering her hair—neither on stage nor in the audience. Instead, they were wearing skin-tight, sleeveless shirts and were socially interacting with the mixed male and female audience. All in all, their confident and extroverted performance appeared to represent the antipode to the behavior of the modest, chastely dressed women I had met in Kayseri the day before.

Turkish traditional society places strong emphasis on maintaining a clear line between the sexes. Though separating the masculine from the feminine does not necessarily relate to forms of spatial segregation, as it has, commonly, in Turkish rural societies, it is strongly related to gender-specific forms of behavior. In other words, particular social practices are either coded male or female. Any behavior that departs from these norms is considered deviant and therefore frequently sanctioned by society.

If we regard gender, in accordance with an exploration by the sociologist Mary Holmes, as the "practiced differences between masculinity and femininity" (Holmes 2009, 13), Turkish metalheads are violently contesting the imaginative line that runs between gender identities. While a respectable woman, from a traditional point of view, would be expected to be passive and act in a chaste and modest way, the young female metalheads described above are displaying a decisively masculine form of behavior. They are active, extroverted, and aggressive, thereby standing at the center of public attention.

FIGURE 2.3. Postmortem live in Istanbul, 2008

Beyond the example of the band Postmortem, female metalheads are violating gender-specific concepts of morality by, for instance, smoking cigarettes, drinking beer, or hanging out in rock bars until late at night. In other words, they are appropriating particular social practices that had been reserved to men. Male metalheads, by the same token, are violating gender-specific forms of behavior by, for instance, having long hair or wearing ear-rings. They appropriate an allegedly nonmasculine aesthetics and therefore represent an antithesis to what is considered socially appropriate male be-havior. As far as female metalheads and their admirers are concerned, it ap-pears obvious that metal provides a means of female emancipation.

METAL AND MUSLIM-NESS

As already mentioned, public discourse usually depicts metal as contradic-tory to Islam. Even today, accusations of Satanism, atheism, and immoral, anti-Islamic practices are a common feature of many media reports. Turk-ish metal does, indeed, emerge as a secular culture that opposes an Islamiza-tion of the public sphere as proposed by the Muslim conservative govern-ment. Turkish metalheads, in interviews and conversations for the present study, usually displayed a vehement antipathy toward the policies of the AKP. This, however, does not mean that Turkish metalheads are necessar-ily anti-Islamic, and, to paraphrase the quotation from the very beginning of this chapter, Turkish metalheads generally do not have a problem with re-ligion or religious people. Their problem is that religious people appear to have a problem with them. This, however, raises questions of religious iden-tity that can only be answered by looking at the individual level. What be-came apparent during my research is that Turkish metalheads all showed in-dividualized notions of religiosity and Muslim-ness. This became evident, for instance, in an interview with an Ankara death metal band conducted in December 2003. Questioned about their personal religious beliefs, the mu-sicians replied:

Oral: It's a necessity. I believe in God. I'm a Muslim. It makes me better. I believe in religion.

Pierre: Can you elaborate a bit on what it means to believe in God and be a Muslim?

Oral: I'm not a hard believer, but I think you need to be a good person. I believe in all religions, whether it is Christianity or Islam or Judaism. It's not important. If it makes people well-charactered and well-behaving per-sons, if it makes them good people, religion is necessary, I think. For exam-ple, I don't support the sacrificing [of animals] on the religious days of Is-lam.[17] I don't support this. . . . The important thing is to be a good person.

Başar: I don't believe in God. . . . And I don't think there's need to be-lieve in something or someone—except in myself.

Taylan: I just believe in a creator. So, religion doesn't matter. I just be-lieve in God or something like that. You know, it's deism. So, it's just like this, and it doesn't matter. I don't make a difference between people who are atheist or who believe in God.[18]

The text reveals three distinct individual positions of religious belief that typically surface in discussions on religion within the Turkish metal scene. First, we can speak of a secular Muslim position. That is to say, interviewees, though they emphasize their Muslim identity, do not attach much relevance to daily religious routines. In fact, many of them behave rather indifferently toward religious practices and provisions in everyday life—e.g., they do not conduct ritual prayers and/or abstain from alcohol. Generally speaking, the commitment to adhere to a strictly Islamic code of living is low. However, they may, for example, fast during the holy month Ramadan, pray and go to mosque from time to time, reject having tattoos, or keep to Islamic dietary rules. Yet religious practices are subject to individual variation. In summary, the group of secular Muslim metalheads can be described as following an individualized interpretation of Islam, as being tolerant toward other religions, and as supportive of the idea of a secular state and society. The following interview excerpt further illustrates this position:

> Engin: I believe in God. I have a belief. You know, I am Muslim. I believe in religion. I mean, not in the way I've been raised. It's a way that I choose. I mean, I believe in God, and I believe that religion is the path, but it's also just one way. And it's a personal thing I believe. I mean, nothing more. I believe and it's just an interest. For example, nobody thinks that I'm a believer. Especially with long hair, it's very odd for Turkish people. Most people think that you are an atheist. At least, you are an atheist, because you have long hair and you are living this heavy metal lifestyle let's say. What else? I mean religion doesn't take a huge part of my life. . . . What I'm trying to do is being a good person. . . . This is one of the main things of religion I mean.[19]

In addition to secular notions of Muslim-ness, deist notions of religiosity are being expressed. The deist position can be described as the belief in a universal creator or God that is often combined with a clear rejection of religious ideology. Religion is mostly perceived as suppressive, irrational, dogmatic, and divisive in terms of separating human beings from each other by drawing sectarian and confessional lines. Turkish metalheads expressed the idea in the following ways:

> Taurnas: We believe in a creator, but we don't believe in religions.[20]

> Erdem: It's a lie [i.e., religion]! As I said before, it's a swearing at God. I believe in God, but not in religion. Maybe it was important in the old ages, but now it's worthless. It's not worth anything. Because most of the things written in the holy books are lies.[21]

Both interviewees draw a clear line between God and religion. In the second quotation, religion is connoted negatively and described as a lie and an insult against God ("swearing at God"). In addition to containing very personal statements, the next example provides at least some information on the role of religion within the family. It is extracted from an interview with one of the few metalheads in the Turkish scene from a Christian background:

> Maksim: Before high school, before college, I was a really religious guy. I believed in Christ, and I was a very strong Christian. I was pushing my father and mother to go to church each Sunday. But it's so strange: my mother and my father, they are real Communists! My father is a real Communist. He says: "Why are we going to church? To hold His balls?" [laughs] He's a crazy guy. He's a funny guy. But they never pushed me to be like that. . . . But in high school I learned too many problematic things about religion. I mean . . . The problem is that they are using religion for political purposes, and they . . . Anyway, . . . I started to realize: OK. Christ is a big philosopher. He's a good man. He wanted all people to be as good as possible. . . . I started to think like that. Then, in university, I was an atheist. I started not to believe in God as well. But some years passed and right now, I'm a deist. . . . I believe in a power, but I can't name it God. I believe in a power . . . Maybe it's a god . . . Let's say I believe in God, but I don't believe in religions.[22]

An atheist family background and a father with a tendency toward blasphemous remarks may be something of a rarity, but at least it is possible to say that many metalheads grew up in a secular context. Yet this does not finally support the conclusion that a secular family background necessarily spawns secular or atheist attitudes among children, as the above-quoted interviewee, who speaks of a strong religious belief during his teenage years, demonstrates. Moreover, a considerable number of interviewees described their families as religious or even strongly religious and claimed to be raised in a religious context. Apart from information on the family background, the interview excerpt contains a reference that relates religion to politics ("they are using religion for political purposes"). This connection was often mentioned as a reason to reject religion in itself.

Finally, we find an atheist position that, in brief, can be reduced to the renunciation of God and religion. The following interviewees distance themselves from both:

> Zehra: It's bullshit! I mean I renounce it. I didn't strongly believe, anyway. You know it's not like I didn't believe at all. I was a Muslim, but I neither

believed in God nor in the ritual worship, nor in anything else. . . . You
know religion is bullshit. And God is also bullshit I think. There is neither
religion nor God.[23]

Güray: Religion means nothing [laughs]! I'm an atheist. Well, I don't care.
I think it's a lie. I don't like it. Too many crazy people in both religions.
You know a lot of religious people are hypocrites. And there is a lot of
bullshit, there is a lot of sexism in it. There is a lot of fascism in it. Lots of
stuff. I don't wanna be part of it![24]

Taylan: I read the Koran. I read the discussions [i.e., Koran exegesis, *tafsir*].
I read the Bible. I read the Torah. There was a short period of Satanism
[laughs out loud]. And I came to be an atheist. That was the logical thing.
But I had to find it myself. . . . I tried to find my own truth.[25]

The reasons for drawing a line between religion and their personal lives
are diverse. Atheism is either described as the logical consequence of self-
reflection and human reason or explained by the assertion that religion is responsible for hypocrisy, sexism, fascism, and other maladies that are not further specified.

All three positions—secular, deist, and atheist—are subversive to the
point that the individual claims authority over his or her religious beliefs.
Islamic authorities are either being rejected, ridiculed, or simply not taken
into account as far as individual religiosity is concerned. The importance
of individual autonomy is underlined by the fact that individual notions of
Muslim-ness frequently contradict the teachings of religious authorities, or,
as a young metalhead puts it: "I am Muslim and I drink beer, but it's an individual thing between me and God."[26]

BLACK METAL BLASPHEMY

As mentioned earlier, global metal culture draws on symbolic representations of evil that originally derive from a Christian or, more precisely, anti-
Christian context. Visual depictions of the devil, the inverted cross, the
number 666, as well as the Latin phrase *non serviam* ("I will not serve"),
which refers to Satan's biblical refusal to submit to the will of God and vow
to accept no masters (Jeremiah 2:20), can be found within local metal scenes
all around the globe—with Turkish metalheads being no exception. However, the use of these symbols has been mostly popular within black metal.

Black metal is a subgenre within global metal that distinguishes itself by
what can be best described as the ultimate cultivation of negativity, hope-
lessness, and evil. Concerning its musical aesthetics, black metal stands out

FIGURE 2.4. Swedish black metal band Marduk live in Istanbul during Ramadan, 2005

for its high, shrieking vocals, the use of chromatic scales, highly distorted guitars, and up-tempo blast beats. Additionally, it developed its own visual aesthetics, characterized by a misanthropic, pagan, and evil imagery. In accordance with this, many black metal musicians dye their hair black and put on facial corpse paint, spike-studded leather gauntlets, and in some cases, medieval weaponry while performing live on stage. As far as the verbal representations of black metal are concerned, band names and lyrics usually incorporate pagan, satanic, morbid, and misanthropic themes.

More than any other metal subgenre, black metal is famous for displaying antireligious and pagan symbols. It is difficult to specify exactly when black metal appeared in Turkey for the first time, although the influence of international black metal bands such as Venom, Bathory, and Celtic Frost dates back to the second half of the 1980s. Among the first Turkish black metal bands, which formed in the early 1990s, were Witchtrap and Sadistic Spell from Ankara, as well as an all-female band from Istanbul called Ebonsight. All of them used to incorporate corpse paint and inverted crosses in their performances. As far as the inverted cross is concerned, it appears in a variety of forms, even beyond the realms of black metal. It is either directly incorporated into band logos—usually replacing the letter "t"—or worn as bracelets.

Given that cultural representations assume different meanings in different contexts, it is obvious that anti-Christian symbols transferred from a Christian to a Muslim context assume different meanings as well. As the cross is commonly known as a Christian symbol used by Christian believers to demonstrate their faith, the person wearing it is consequently identified as a Christian. Therefore, it does not matter whether the cross is inverted or not. That is, the practice of wearing an inverted cross is frequently not recognized as an expression of anti-Christian or antireligious sentiments and therefore decoded "wrongly" as a symbol of Christian creed and apostasy from Islam. This begs the question as to why Turkish metalheads use anti-Christian symbols in a Muslim context. As there is no simple answer to the question, I will briefly outline a series of explanations that have been put forward by Turkish metalheads: To begin with, the aforementioned symbols are part of a cultural code of identification and therefore do not have any particular meaning except for marking someone as "being metal." Further, the symbols have been used by musicians in order to underline their bands' brutal image—along the lines of "brutal music needs a brutal image." Moreover, some black metal musicians claimed a general lack of anti-Islamic symbols ("We worked hard on finding an anti-Muslim symbol . . . we tried something with the crescent, but it didn't look good"),[27] thereby justifying their use of anti-Christian symbols. Apparently, many musicians were afraid of displaying anti-Islamic symbols in public, for blasphemous activities would trigger violent reaction against them. Finally, it has to be said that many Turkish metalheads ridicule the use of anti-Christian symbols, for they "have no meaning in a Muslim context."

A black metal band that stands out for its attempt to incorporate a combination of anti-Christian and anti-Islamic symbols is the Istanbul black metal band Satanized, which formed in 2005. The band's logo shows two topless angels forcibly holding an inverted crescent that embraces an equally inverted pentagram. The two angels are nailed to the lower arc of the crescent, while blood is dripping from their eyes and wounded arms and torsos. The image is an adaptation of the Turkish national symbols—crescent and star. While the crescent has been rotated clockwise by ninety degrees so that it appears to be inverted, the star has been turned into a pentagram. A second version of the logo, which can be found on the band's MySpace site,[28] presents a decapitated Jesus nailed to the inverted pentagram. Blood is seeping from the crescent and the five-pointed star.

In its promotional photos and live performances, the band is celebrating the typical black metal image: black clothes and black hair, corpse paint, spike-studded wristbands, medieval weaponry, and lots of blood and gore. At the present stage, it is not possible to say whether or not Satanized represent a new generation of Turkish black metal bands that finally dares to publicly challenge Islamic symbols. For this, further developments need to unfold.

CONCLUSION

Metal iconography, as the preceding discussion has shown, poses a provocative challenge to religious sensibilities in Turkish society. Herein, however, also lies the metal scene's power to symbolically resist Islamic revivalism. The two rival public spheres of Islamists and secularists in Turkey have been reacting differently toward metal aesthetics, though occasionally, even Kemalist writers accused Turkish metalheads of subverting the principles of Islam, stressing the importance of Muslim identity for the Turkish nation. Turkish metalheads usually view themselves as advocates of secularism who remain suspicious of political Islam, for they fear it will bring an oppressive end to their ways of life.

Particularly with regard to the Turkish government's present policies, heavy metal provides various modes of symbolic resistance to an Islamization of the public sphere. Symbolic resistance is expressed through bodily practices such as drinking alcohol in public, rejecting the Islamic headscarf, or displaying antireligious symbols. As the case studies on gender, Muslimness, and blasphemy have shown, Turkish metalheads are contesting Islamic morality to the extent that they are subverting traditional Islamic concepts of femininity and masculinity, challenging the authority of religious institutions by promoting individual notions of Muslim-ness, and (in some cases) questioning the legacy of religion in itself. Yet this does not make Turkish metal anti-Islamic in the sense that it rejects Islam completely. Many Turkish metalheads do indeed attach importance to their belief in God and Islam, as the above-mentioned examples have shown. At the present stage, however, it is possible to conclude that Turkish metalheads overwhelmingly stand against any form of political Islam.

On a final note, it must be added that the public discourse on heavy metal only recently began to change. Not only did the Kemalist opposition in parliament, the CHP, use the aforementioned incident during Istanbul's Uni-Rock Festival in order to criticize the prime minister, but even religious authorities appear to have been discovering heavy metal for themselves. In preparation for the 2009 Ramadan celebrations, Turkey's highest religious body, the Directorate of Religious Affairs, released a poster series that was meant to promote that year's Ramadan motto, "Paylaşmak güzeldir" ("It's good to share"). One of these posters depicted a young, long-haired bearded man wearing a black T-shirt of British heavy metal band Iron Maiden cordially smiling at and putting an arm around the shoulders of an old, white-haired bearded man with a prayer cap on his head who is likewise smiling at the young man. Photos of the president of the Directorate of Religious Affairs, Ali Bardakoğlu, standing in front of the described poster have been circulated by numerous Turkish newspapers and TV channels, triggering debate on the apparent change of attitude toward the former "Satanists." Whether or not metal music and culture are really going to lose their transgressive character in terms of no longer being perceived as anti-Islamic by the Turkish public needs to be examined in the future.

NOTES

1. Personal interview, conducted in English, Istanbul, June 18, 2003.

2. Recent international workshops and conferences on heavy metal mark the birth of an academic field that nowadays is often referred to as "metal studies." The first global conference on heavy metal, Heavy Fundamentalisms: Music, Metal and Politics, was held in Salzburg from November 3 to 5, 2008. Only one year later, an international congress called Heavy Metal and Gender was organized in Cologne in October, succeeded by a follow-up conference on global metal in Salzburg from November 10 to 12, 2009.

3. Under the term "extreme metal" Kahn-Harris (2007, 2–5) summarizes a variety of subgenres of heavy metal—thrash metal, black metal, doom metal, death metal, grindcore—that are outstanding for their transgressive character. Kahn-Harris differentiates three types of transgression: sonic transgression, discursive transgression, and bodily transgression.

4. According to Robert Walser (1993, 3), heavy metal's commercial success peaked in 1989, when it accounted for 40 percent of the record sales in the United States.

5. These assertions are based on dozens of conversations and interviews that I conducted with Turkish metalheads between 2002 and 2009.

6. According to the Turkish Statistical Institute's Consumer Price Index 2009.

7. Quoted from "Metalci selamı'na gözaltı," CNN Turk, July 25, 2009 (http://www.cnnturk.com/2009/turkiye/07/25/metalci.selamina.gozalti/536446.0/index.html); translated by the author from Turkish into English.

8. Quoted from "Başbakan'a hoşgörüsü çağrısı," Milliyet, July 23, 2009 (source: http://www.milliyet.com.tr); translated by the author from Turkish into English.

9. According to a report by Zaman, see "CHP, 'metalci' gençleri Meclis'e taşıdı," July 28, 2009, Zaman Online, http://www.zaman.com.tr/haber.do?haberno=874139.

10. For a detailed analysis on how Turkish newspaper reports triggered moral panics over heavy metal and Satanism, see Hecker 2009, 119–177.

11. Ardıç does not explicitly speak about alcohol here, but using the Turkish verb dağıtmak implies wild partying and heavy drinking.

12. Quoted from E. Ardıç's article "Metaaal!," Sabah, October 14, 1990; translated by the author from Turkish into English.

13. See E. Ardıç, "Metalciler bozulmuşlar," Sabah, October 21, 1990.

14. For the sake of simplicity, both titles have been translated by the author from Turkish into English; for details see the bibliographical section.

15. Quoted from the Internet edition of "Satanizm: Mahiyeti, Yayılma Sebepleri ve Önleme Yolları" (http://kitap.yeniumit.com.tr/satanizm/index.php [accessed January 11, 2005]); translated by the author from Turkish into English.

16. Quoted from the Internet edition of "Kimliğini Arayan Gençliğimiz ve Satanizm" (http://kitap.yeniumit.com.tr/satanizm/index.php [accessed January 11, 2005]); translated by the author from Turkish into English.

17. The interviewee refers to the Festival of Sacrifice, during which Muslim believers are supposed to bring an animal sacrifice—preferably a sheep or lamb. The celebrations mark the end of the annual pilgrimage to Mecca.

18. Personal interview, originally conducted in a mixture of Turkish and English (Turkish parts translated by the author from Turkish into English), Ankara, December 14, 2003.

19. Personal interview, conducted in English, Istanbul, December 1, 2003.

20. Personal interview, originally conducted in Turkish, translated by the author into English, Istanbul, July 13, 2004.

21. Personal interview, conducted in English, Istanbul, July 10, 2003.

22. Personal interview, conducted in English, Antalya, July 18, 2004.

23. Personal interview, originally conducted in Turkish, translated by the author into English, June 4, 2004.

24. Personal interview, conducted in English, Istanbul, August 6, 2004.

25. Personal interview, conducted in English, Istanbul, May 31, 2004.

26. Personal interview, conducted in English, Istanbul, September 12, 2009.

27. Personal interview, conducted in English, Istanbul, December 4, 2003.

28. See http://www.myspace.com/truesatanized.

REFERENCES

Arat, Y. 2005. *Rethinking Islam and Liberal Democracy: Islamist Women in Turkish Politics.* New York: State University of New York Press.

Ardıç, E. 1990. "Metaaal!" *Sabah*, October 14, 1990.

Barış, R. 2006. *Media Landscape Turkey*. Maastricht: European Journalism Centre.

Baulch, E. 2003. "Gesturing Elsewhere: The Identity Politics of the Balinese Death/ Thrash Metal Scene." *Popular Music* 22 (2): 195–215. Cambridge: Cambridge University Press.

———. 2007. *Making Scenes: Reggae, Punk, and Death Metal in 1990s Bali*. Durham, NC: Duke University Press.

Bennett, A. 2001. *Cultures of Popular Music*. Buckingham: Open University Press.

Çaplı, B. 1998. "The Media in Turkey." Paper presented at the British Council, Ankara, March 3.

Christe, I. 2004. *Sound of the Beast: The Complete Headbanging History of Heavy Metal.* New York: Harper Entertainment.

Göle, N. 1995. *Republik und Schleier: Die muslimische Frau in der modernen Türkei.* Denklingen: Babel Verlag.

———. 2000. "Global Expectations, Local Experiences: Non-Western Modernities." In *Through a Glass, Darkly: Blurred Images of Cultural Tradition and Modernity over Distance and Time*, International Studies in Sociology and Social Anthropology, ed. W. Arts, pp. 40–55. Leiden: Brill.

Güç, A. 2003. "Kimliğini Arayan Gençliğimiz ve Satanizm." In *Satanizm Girdabı ve Sahte Metafizik Akımlar*, ed. A. Güç. Istanbul: Işık Yayınları.

Hecker, P. 2005. "Heavy Metal in a Muslim Context." In "Youth: Music, Movements, Politics, Practices, Cultures, Consumption," ed. D. Douwes and L. Herrera, special issue, *ISIM Review* (Leiden), no. 16, 8–9.

————. 2009. "Heavy Metal in a Muslim Context: New Social Spaces in Istanbul." PhD diss., University of Leipzig.

————. 2010. "Heavy Metal in the Middle East: New Urban Spaces in a Translocal Underground." In *Being Young and Muslim: New Cultural Politics in the Global South and North*, ed. A. Bayat and L. Herrera, pp. 415–434. Oxford and New York: Oxford University Press.

Holmes, M. 2009. *Gender and Everyday Life*. London and New York: Routledge.

Kadıoğlu, A. 2002. "Women's Subordination in Turkey: Is Islam Really the Villain?" In *Islam: Critical Concepts in Sociology*, vol. 3, *Islam, Gender and the Family*, ed. B. S. Turner, pp. 70–86. London and New York: Routledge.

Kahn-Harris, K. 2007. *Extreme Metal: Music and Culture on the Edge*. Oxford and New York: Berg.

Klypchak, B. C. 2007. "Performed Identities. Heavy Metal Musicians between 1984 and 1991." PhD diss., Graduate College of Bowling Green State University.

LeVine, M. 2008. *Heavy Metal Islam: Rock, Resistance, and the Struggle for the Soul of Islam*. New York: Three Rivers Press.

————. 2010. "Rockmusik als Gegengift: Jugendliche im Iran äußern im Heavy Metal ihren Protest." *Welt-Sichten: Magazin für globale Entwicklung und ökumenische Zusammenarbeit* 6-2010:26–29.

Mudrian, A. 2004. *Choosing Death: The Improbable History of Death Metal and Grindcore*. Los Angeles: Feral House.

Navaro-Yashin, Y. 2002. *Faces of the State: Secularism and Public Life in Turkey*. Princeton, NJ: Princeton University Press.

Saymaz, I. 2009. "Başbakan'a metalci işareti yapmak suç değil!" *Radikal*, August 1, p. 10.

Schmitt, A. 2002. "Liwat im Fiqh: Männliche Homosexualität?" *Journal of Arabic and Islamic Studies* (Edinburgh) 4:49–110.

Solmaz, M. 1996. *Türkiye'de Pop Müzik: Dünü ve bugünü ile bir infilak masalı*. Istanbul: Pan Yayıncılık.

Swedenburg, T. 2000. "Satanic Heavy Metal in Egypt." Paper presented at the American Anthropological Association Annual Meeting, San Francisco.

Tarhan, N. 2003. "Satanizm: Mahiyeti, Yayılma Sebepleri ve Önleme Yolları." In *Satanizm Girdabı ve Sahte Metafizik Akımlar*, ed. A. Güç. Istanbul: Işık Yayınları.

Tireli, M. 2005. *Bir Metamorfoz Hikayesi. Türkiye'de Grup Müziği: 1957–1980*. Istanbul: Arkaplan.

Türkiye Istatistik Kurumu. 2009. "Temel Yıllı Tüketici Fiyatları Endeksleri," Ankara. Available online: http://www.turkstat.gov.tr.

Wallach, J. 2003. "'Goodbye My Blind Majesty': Music, Language, and Politics in the Indonesian Underground." In *Global Pop, Local Language*, ed. H. M. Berger and M. T. Carroll, pp. 53–86. Jackson: University Press of Mississippi.

————. 2008. *Modern Noise, Fluid Genres: Popular Music in Indonesia, 1997–2001*. Madison: University of Wisconsin Press.

Walser, R. 1993. *Running with the Devil: Power, Gender, and Madness in Heavy Metal Music*. Middletown, CT: Wesleyan University Press.

Weinstein, D. 2000 [1991]. *Heavy Metal: The Music and Its Culture*. Rev. ed. New York: Da Capo Press.

Yıldırım, B. 2009. "Başbakan'a hoşgörüsü çağrısı." *Milliyet*, July 23, 2009.

CHAPTER 3

IRANIAN POPULAR MUSIC IN LOS ANGELES: A TRANSNATIONAL PUBLIC BEYOND THE ISLAMIC STATE

FARZANEH HEMMASI

Oh devout ones, devout ones . . .
If you're on the road to Heaven and I'm on the path to Hell,
It's none of your business . . .
If I am drunk, it's none of your business
If I am sober, it's none of your business!
"BE TO CHE" ("NONE OF YOUR BUSINESS")
BY HASSAN SHAMAIZADEH, 2004[1]

Above are the words to a song by Hassan Shamaizadeh, a well-known Iranian vocalist, instrumentalist, and composer who has lived in Southern California since the Iranian Revolution, which took place some three decades ago. These lyrics are set to a rollicking, driving rhythmic instrumental accompaniment that recalls urban musical styles linked to dance and Tehran's cabarets of the mid-twentieth century. After the establishment of the Islamic Republic of Iran (IRI) in 1978–1979, such cabarets and nightclubs were closed, mixed-sex social dance was banned, and popular musics were restricted as the country's religious leaders sought to bring state, culture, and society into line with Islamic and revolutionary principles. In "Be To Che," Shamaizadeh speaks back to the "devout ones" (*zāhed-hā*)[2] who wish to regulate his personal life, while he employs sonic references, and their contextual connotations, that flout the Islamic state's cultural regulations.

Produced in Los Angeles—far from its implied clerical addressees—Shamaizadeh's musical statement is representative of much more than a single exile's grumbling taunts to a country in which he is no longer welcome. Rather, the singer is one of hundreds of musicians and media producers active in the Iranian culture industries that coalesced in Southern California after the Islamic Republic heavily restricted popular culture and media. Fed by the mass exodus, beginning in the early 1980s, of many of the country's most famous musical stars and most skilled media producers, these exile culture industries have produced music and media to serve the area's local Iranian community, the largest in the world outside of Iran. Much exile-produced popular music takes the Iranian homeland as its main focus, a typical orientation for first-generation migrants that helps situate diasporic subjects by simultaneously referring to place and aiding in emplacement.[3] But this exilic preoccupation with Iran serves another function as well: it provides different forms and avenues for Iranian identification than are available either in Western or official Iranian media.

Whether inside or outside the country, music plays a special role in debates about Iranian identity, engaging Iran's relationship with Islam and the West, and raising questions regarding rights to expression, sexuality, youth, and gender, making it an ideally situated cultural form to examine in order to understand the conflicts facing the Iranian nation. Today, LA-produced music and media, and the national concerns expressed therein, are not only diasporic but transnational, reaching dispersed Iranian communities around the world, as well as audiences in Iran, where they are illegal but widely consumed. As I show in this chapter, Iranian exile popular music's homeland orientation is driven by its creators' financial and emotional motives, but also by a desire to extend Iranian culture, identity, and political expression beyond the ideological and territorial bounds of the Islamic Republic. From their positions abroad, Iranian exile popular musicians contribute to what I argue is a transnational public containing views and representations of Iranian-ness that deviate from dominant state-approved discourses. What versions of Iranian identity are explored in this music, and how might these contrast with those identities and practices promoted in the Iranian Revolution or by the Islamic state? Further, how effective is exile popular music in reaching widespread Iranian audiences both inside and outside of the country, and how can we evaluate its influence?

The chapter begins with a brief overview of the salient postrevolutionary Iranian state policies regarding expression and culture that provide the context for both the initial establishment of the LA-based Iranian exile culture industries and the particular forms Iranian popular music and media have taken in Los Angeles. Drawing on ethnographic fieldwork conducted in Southern California in 2007, I outline the LA cultural industries and focus on popular music's transnational circulation to Iranians abroad and in their homeland, a topic that has not been covered in the few previous accounts of Iranian popular music in Southern California (Naficy 1993; Shay 2000). Sketching out some of the main functions and themes of both pre-revolutionary pop preserved and reproduced in Los Angeles and the newly created Iranian popular music known locally as *musiqi-ye pop-e los ānjeles* (henceforth MPLA),[4] I show some of the ways these musics present alter-

native versions of Iranian culture and identity, especially through their representations of women and female sexuality, notions of cultural authenticity, and uses of Iranian history in song and video. The chapter concludes by
evaluating the impact of MPLA in Iran as contributing to an alternative,
transnational public in a context where the national public sphere is already
contested.

MEDIA, POLITICS, AND CULTURE IN
THE ISLAMIC REPUBLIC OF IRAN

Recent literature has emphasized the growing significance of Muslim publics
and counterpublics in Muslim-majority states where secular governments are
in power (Hirschkind 2006; Salvatore and Eickelman 2004; Eickelman and
Anderson 2003; Van Nieuwkerk 2008). Iran presents a very different case
than Egypt, Lebanon, and other countries represented in these studies, as it
possesses an Islamic state that controls the majority of media outlets. While
state media dominance and censorship also characterized Iran's prerevolutionary monarchical government (Baraheni 1977; Sreberny-Mohammadi
and Mohammadi 1994), since the revolution civil society and the public
sphere have been circumscribed by a combination of religious and instrumental political state power that presents significant obstacles for alternative
viewpoints in media (Khiabany 2007, 2008).[5] In addition, after 1979, public
space, education, and economic and foreign policy were all transformed to
align with the particular combination of Shi'ite Islam and populist and anti-
imperialist philosophies embodied in the revolution.[6]

If political expression has been curtailed in postrevolutionary Iran, so
has artistic expression. Since the establishment of the Islamic Republic, performing arts have been carefully monitored by the state through a number
of permit-issuing organizations—chief among them the Ministry of Culture
and Islamic Guidance[7]—that regulate performance, recording, broadcasting, and dissemination. Music and dance have been the most challenging
art forms to reconcile to the pious, revolutionary vision of Iranian culture,
both because they have long histories of being considered morally suspect
in Iran and because of their prominence in prerevolutionary Iranian popular culture.

While the Pahlavi monarchy that had ruled Iran prior to the revolution
had promoted Iranian popular music as part of its national modernization
and Westernization projects (Nooshin 2005a), popular music was rejected
entirely in the early years of the revolution. In 1979, Ayatollah Ruhollah
Khomeini unambiguously stated his disapproval of music in general in the
Islamic Republic:

Music [*musiqi*] is like a drug; whoever acquires the habit can no longer devote himself to important activities. It changes people to the point of yielding to vice or to preoccupations pertaining to the world of music alone. We must eliminate music because it means betraying our country and our youth. We must completely eliminate it. (Quoted in Youssefzadeh 2000, 138; originally in the newspaper article "Radio and Television Must Strengthen the Young," *Keyhān*, 1 mordād 1358/1979)

Following this pronouncement musical activity was dramatically curtailed and heavily restricted on state radio and television. Vigilante groups and revolutionary guards sometimes took matters into their own hands, harassing instrument makers, burning cassette tapes in the streets, stopping cars playing pop music, and breaking up parties with music and dancing (Youssefzadeh 2000; Nooshin 2005a).

Despite the unequivocal tone of Khomeini's statement, these restrictions did not apply to all kinds of sound art, but to *musiqi*, an Arabic term of Greek derivation that refers to nonreligious sonic forms of questionable morality.[8] Among those forms and styles initially considered irreligious, profane, or otherwise incompatible with the ideals of the fledgling Islamic Republic were Iranian art and folk music, as well as urban entertainment musics played by *motreb*, or professional entertainers, music associated with cafés and cabarets, sometimes called *kāfe-i* ("of the cafés"—see Fatemi 2005), and Westernized, mass-mediated popular music (*musiqi-ye pop*) from both inside and outside of the country. In keeping with conservative interpretations of Muslim law regarding interaction between the sexes, women were forbidden from singing before men and from making solo vocal recordings. Also prohibited were songs containing debauched or sensual themes.

But music policies were not only inspired by Muslim law, the Koran, or *hadith*; in some cases, these were also resonant with long-standing and widely held negative attitudes toward performers of entertainment musics. For instance, prior to the revolution, the *motreb* profession was disproportionately the province of Iranian Jews, because many Muslims did not want to be associated with such unethical employment. While Iranian Jews did not share the same religion-based prejudices toward *musiqi* as Muslims, Jewish *motreb* nonetheless occupied a low status in their own communities as well, ranking only above beggars, butchers, and corpse washers (Loeb 1972, 8–9). In other cases, the objections to certain musics and musicians were the result of revolutionary aims of political and cultural transformation. For instance, singers and instrumentalists whose reputation was "judged incompatible" with postrevolutionary moral and political values were barred from professional musical activities (During 1992). Likewise, cultural "inauthenticity" in popular music, much of which bore heavy Western influences characterized during this period as "Westoxification,"[9] was also important to its restriction during this period of ideological consolidation.

Those genres initially allowed for public performance by men included unaccompanied Shi'ite vocal genres such as *nowheh* (responsorial sung verses) and *rowzeh* (sung narratives about the martyred imams); these were a major part of television and radio broadcasts, especially during the 1980s. Another form promoted in this period was the *sorud-e enghelābi,* or "revolutionary march-hymn," a marchlike choral piece often using Western harmonies and accompanied by Western and Iranian instruments that celebrated the revolution.[10] The fact that the term *sorud* was sometimes used as a euphemism for other types of *musiqi* gives an idea of the sensitive atmosphere surrounding music during the early years of the Islamic Republic (Chehabi 1999; Youssefzadeh 2000).

Dance likewise became a very problematic category of cultural practice for the state after the revolution. The National Ballet Company was shuttered after 1979, and the country's dance schools were ordered closed (Meftahi 2005). Social dance in mixed-sex private settings like parties and weddings was not permitted, and private gatherings were regularly interrupted by morality police who heard dance music from outside and who could arrest (or seek bribes from) partygoers on grounds of immorality. Dance was later permitted on stage after the first decade of the revolution as a subcategory of theater, but only by the euphemism of *harikat-i mawzun,* a phrase that is usually translated in English as "rhythmic movement" (see Zeinab Stellar, this volume). *Harikat-i mawzun* in fact constituted a new, generally slow-tempo concert performance form that was devoid of the many sensual shoulder and hip movements (called *qir*) commonplace in Iranian urban social dance, staged cabaret dance, and films. In keeping with the restrictions on dance, musics with danceable rhythms—especially those recalling urban entertainment genres like *motrebi* musics associated with morally ambiguous performance—were also restricted.

The limitations on music loosened somewhat at the end of the first decade following the revolution. Just months before he died in 1989, Khomeini issued a religious ruling, or fatwa, that explicitly allowed the sale of instruments and the performance of music so long as they were for "ethical" purposes (Movahed 2003–2004). This opened the way for an explosion of traditional art and folk music activity in the country, which, once sanitized of any offending sensual or romantic elements, was rationalized as both "ethical" and "learned" and was seen to support the ideals of cultural authenticity promoted in the revolution (Youssefzadeh 2000; Movahed 2003–2004; Nooshin 2005a). However, even after the fatwa many restrictions were still in place. In addition to limitations on sexual and romantic topics and criticisms of the state and Islam, which were also in effect in film and publishing, those musics or works considered *mobtazal* (trite or banal) remained officially unacceptable (Adelkhah 1991). Encompassing moral, political, and aesthetic values, the term *mobtazal* implies banality, cliché, lack of creativity and worth, and cheapness, but also suggests a cultural form that disorients a listener and can promote disengagement with the world through harmful distraction. In a period when state culture—including military marches—was developed with the express purpose of inculcating revolutionary Islamic ideology, those cultural forms that took the listener out of a revolutionized or pious state of mind were inappropriate.

Then in 1997, during another period of liberalization, popular music was also approved for local production and broadcast. As Nooshin (2005a) has suggested, pop's reappearance at this moment was engineered to appeal to the country's growing youth population and to provide a politically correct alternative to the torrents of illegal Iranian exile pop from LA widely consumed inside Iran. At present, a wide variety of government-approved popular music bearing a strong resemblance to contemporary Western styles, prerevolutionary *musiqi-ye pop*, and Los Angeles Iranian pop is sung by male vocalists and is also broadcast heavily on state television and radio. This music is subject to oversight by several permit-issuing boards that monitor lyrics, style, and other elements and have frequently prevented musicians from performing, recording, or disseminating their music. The combination of bureaucratic obstacles and the use of popular music as a "political football" by battling factions within the Iranian government has made producing music within official channels challenging (Nooshin 2005b). This situation has led many musicians to make their music "underground" (*zirzamin*), performing in private spaces and circulating their music hand-to-hand or online, which allows them to circumvent governmental hurdles, but also means they cannot be broadcast on state-controlled radio or television and are therefore limited in the audiences they can reach (Nooshin 2005b, 2008).

While many younger musicians and a few lesser-known prerevolutionary performers could work within the parameters of postrevolutionary Iran, the *musiqi-ye pop* celebrities of the 1960s and 1970s—many of whom were widely considered emblematic of the Pahlavi state's now dismantled programs of Westernization and secularization—were in a much more difficult situation, since their risqué roles and performances and often scandalous personal lives were well known. As a result of fear of persecution and the practical impossibility of continuing to work in Iran, great numbers of the country's celebrities and skilled industry personnel fled during the 1980s, eventually landing in Los Angeles, where they began their musical activities in exile. This generation of established musicians, composers, lyricists, and producers was joined by others who entered the entertainment field after immigrating, and eventually, by younger 1.5 and second-generation Iranians. It is to their activities in exile that we now turn.

LOCAL AND GLOBAL IRANIAN POPULAR MUSIC IN LA: TRANSNATIONAL RECORDINGS, TOURS, AND TELEVISION

Los Angeles County is home to the most Iranians anywhere in the world outside of Iran. While Iranians lived in Southern California in large numbers prior to 1978, it was the revolution and the ensuing war with Iraq (1980– 1988) that drove hundreds of thousands to flee the country. Many of the nation's wealthy elite—including large numbers of those who were involved with the overturned Pahlavi government—landed in Los Angeles. Today, Iranians live in large numbers from San Diego to Ventura County, with especially visible populations in the western Los Angeles neighborhoods of Westwood, Beverly Hills, and Santa Monica, and throughout the towns lining LA County's San Fernando Valley. Shi'ite and Sunni Muslims, Jews, Christians, Baha'is, and Zoroastrians are all represented here, as are Iranians of Persian, Azeri Turkish, Armenian, Assyrian, Kurdish, and Arab ethnicity (Kelley, Friedlander, and Colby 1993; Bozorgmehr 1997).

While this diversity extends to political viewpoints as well, Iranians in Southern California, and in Los Angeles in particular, have a reputation for opposition to the current Iranian state and for keeping the flame of the Pahlavi era alive. Here, the flag of the Islamic Republic never flies: at local events, in Iranian establishments, and in the media produced in Los Angeles, it is nearly always the prerevolutionary flag bearing the lion, sword, and sun that is present, an enduring symbol for the refusal of many in this population to accept the Iranian government as their own. This continuity with the past is also manifest in the large number of businesses and organizations bearing the names of well-known and now-defunct establishments from Tehran in the 1970s (Adelkhah 2001).

Arts and entertainment are central to producing an Iranian identity distinct from that promoted in the Islamic Republic. Much of this cultural production reflects the secular values and Westernized aesthetics linked to the Pahlavi past. Cabaret Tehran, a posh supper club in the San Fernando Valley, is a popular spot where prerevolutionary star vocalists come to perform their classic songs for an almost exclusively Iranian audience. Working-class and upscale cabarets were important venues for public life in Tehran from the 1920s to 1979 (Fatemi 2005), but Cabaret Tehran would not fit in today's Iran, with its bans on alcohol consumption, mixed-sex social dance, and

solo female vocalists and proscriptions on many prerevolutionary performers. Instead, Cabaret Tehran is a remnant of the past that seems to highlight its difference with Iran. The Music Box, a small shop in Westwood well
stocked with albums and films from the 1950s to the 1970s, along with newer
products of the LA music industry, is one of several stores that give local
audiences access to prerevolutionary popular culture. A number of dance
schools in the LA area teach urban and folk dance styles to classes of Iranian
women and girls, who perform at parties and in cultural festivals. Taken with
the ever-present sound of dance music at Iranian social events and the prevalence of Iranian "club nights" (one-night parties), in which social dance,
mixed-sex interaction, and alcohol consumption are the primary activities,
the version of Iranian culture and sociality one can experience in Los Angeles is very different from what is permitted and promoted in Iran.

But the Los Angeles version of Iranian culture is not limited to Southern California, or even the United States in its geographical reach. Instead,
it travels to the rest of the Iranian world through a variety of transnational
mediated means, of which music, television, and the Internet are the most
important. The San Fernando Valley is the seat of a thriving music and media industry, with many magazine offices, music stores, record labels, and recording and television studios situated within a few miles of each other in
strip malls and office parks along Ventura Boulevard, the Valley's main thor-
oughfare. Music is central to LA's Iranian culture industry, and Los Angeles has been likened to a "Persian Motown" (Naficy 1993, 54), with between
five and ten record labels putting out dozens of albums and music videos every year since the early 1980s. These albums are sold in Iranian music and
book shops and in Arab and Iranian groceries in cities around the world,
and they are also widely available via bootlegging and smuggling within Iran
(Adelkhah 1991). These recordings are readily accessible online through legitimate electronic music stores such as iTunes and on a plethora of illegal
download sites that have a similar global reach.

Live performances are another important means for making LA popular
musics available to transnational audiences. In Los Angeles, well-known performers play shows at the Shrine Auditorium and the Greek Theater, as well
as in smaller venues like Cabaret Tehran, but successful LA stars also regularly embark on international tours. These tours take well-known performers to cities across North America and Northern Europe with large Iranian
populations, including Houston, Chicago, New York, Vancouver, Toronto,
Amsterdam, Gothenburg, London, Cologne, and Goa. During the Christ-
mas season, a large number of LA-based pop singers give annual concerts
in hotel nightclubs in Las Vegas, when Iranian vacationers from across the
United States take over the city. Concerts by exiled musicians are, of course,

impossible within Iran, but annual music festivals in nearby Dubai featuring LA-based performers reportedly regularly attract audiences of thousands who fly to the Emirates for the occasion.

Persian-language television provides many possibilities to access LA-produced pop music. The LA Iranian music industry was highly integrated with television throughout the 1980s (see Naficy 1993). Though their numbers fluctuate, as of 2009 there are between ten and fifteen Iranian television stations that regularly program Los Angeles popular music, many of which are owned by Iranian exiles and are headquartered in Southern California. On some channels, such as the Persian Music Channel (PMC, located in Dubai) or PEN (Persian Entertainment Network, located in Woodland Hills, California), the programming is almost entirely music videos and commercials. Even on television stations that air other sorts of programs (health advice programs, news, or political discussions are all popular formats), music videos and music-related advertising and programming make up a large percentage of air time, and can include variety shows with musical performances, interviews with singers, commercials for new albums and concert tours, and call-in shows hosted by singers themselves.[11] Record labels and stations are often located in close physical proximity to one another; for instance, during my fieldwork the television station Jam-e Jam and the record label Avang were on the same floor of a Ventura Boulevard office building, while the record label Taraneh and the television station Omid-e Iran were located in the same industrial park.

As with the Iranian music industry, these television stations initially served the local LA Iranian community, but since the early 2000s many stations broadcast internationally via free-to-air satellite[12] and online. Satellite dishes are illegal in Iran, where they have frequently been blamed for ushering in the "cultural invasion by the West" that governmental officials have referred to since the end of the war with Iraq (Kian 1995; Alikhah 2008).[13] They are, however, widely available on the black market and prevalent in Iran, as well as in the diaspora. Likewise, many foreign and exile websites are blocked by state-implemented Web filters, but filter-breakers are also available within the country. Advertising on these satellite stations promotes products and services from urban diasporic hubs around the world, from Persian carpet stores in Houston, to legal services for emigration to Canada, to real estate in Dubai. Advice programs, music video request shows, and political discussion programs that use the call-in format also reveal this transnationality, as viewers identify themselves as dialing in from Shiraz, Muscat, Berlin, and San Francisco.

For generating audiences within Iran, satellite television station owners' main business strategy is to give viewers access to what they cannot have on local state-run television stations. According to Kourosh Bibiyan, who with his father runs the Jam-e Jam satellite and cable television stations in the Los Angeles area, popular music was the primary product he believed his station and others in LA could provide Iranians inside the country. He explained this through a point-by-point comparison with what Iranian state television had on offer:

> At the end of the day, music is the key because [the Iranian government] cannot compete [with those of] us [in LA]. They have a big budget for serials. They have all the access to sports. We are stealing the feed from them most of the time [and replaying it on our channel], but they have better access [to sports], and more money. For movies, okay, all the movies made in Persian are in Iran . . . The only thing we've got is music. (Interview with K. Bibiyan, May 2007)

Bibiyan acknowledged he enjoyed much of the post-1997 pop music and said that his station broadcast this government-approved music in addition to exile videos. But his perception was that LA pop's appeal was not (only) at the level of sound, as he made clear elsewhere in our conversation: "We are not better than them [the IRI] except in music because they cannot have [Iranian exile pop singer] Andy with ten half-naked girls singing and dancing!" Audiovisual titillation is a marked attribute of many pop music videos produced in the Iranian (and American) culture industries and is likely a draw for audiences inside and outside of the country, but it is not the only aspect that separates LA pop from its counterparts in Iran. Equally important is MPLA's focus on the prerevolutionary past, which further consolidates forms of Iranian identity not sanctioned by the state.

PRESERVATION AND CANONIZATION OF ALTERNATIVE HISTORIES IN LOS ANGELES

Preservation and canonization of prerevolutionary music and media are a central function of the Los Angeles culture industries in which recordings and performance play central roles. Many music and media producers in Los Angeles believe that they are responsible for preserving for posterity Iranian music and culture that the revolution would have destroyed. This threat of destruction was quite literal in the case of recording-session masters and films that some smuggled out of the country during the early days of the revolution, when vigilante groups reportedly looted homes for cassette tapes. In the handful of Iranian music and video reproduction companies that sprang up in Los Angeles, these recordings were carefully preserved and transferred to cassettes, and then were remastered for release on compact disc in the 1990s. While prerevolutionary popular musics were mostly illegal in postrevolutionary Iran, among exiles in Los Angeles and in Iranian migrant communities elsewhere, they were treasured remnants of their past and, as I learned from my interviews with music industry personnel, remain some of the most profitable aspects of the Iranian music business. For Iranian migrants to Southern California, who are physically separated from their homelands and largely ideologically opposed to their home state's postrevolutionary government, these musics allow sensory and emotional access to a homeland that, because of irrevocable transformation, is gone, but also frozen and repeatable via recorded media.

Many of these prerevolutionary sound recordings are released in "Best of . . ." collections. While these rereleases provide exile audiences contact with their past, they also provide a new script through which to comprehend these preserved fragments by explicitly designating the collections as valuable. The grounds for this value can be mass popularity, as implied in the title of the collection *52 Melodies from the Most Popular* Kucheh Bāzār *Songs*, or a suggestion of enduring significance, as in *The Golden Hits of Homeyra*.[14] As in any case of canonization, the collections claim to constitute those parts of Iranian culture worthy of preservation. While the rerelease format and accompanying laudatory language are commonplace in US music markets as a way of boosting sales from old catalogs, in the Iranian market these take on additional valences tied to the revolutionary condemnation of popular music, its creators, and the sentiments and activities to which its stars, styles, and imaginaries were thought to give rise. The collections do not only manifest the preservationist instinct and search for continuity seen among exile and diasporic cultures; they also represent a counterdiscourse to the revolutionary revision of history that would exclude these singers and musicians from the Iranian past.

Covering prerevolutionary songs and song forms in updated arrangements is an extremely common practice on Iranian pop albums recorded in Los Angeles that contributes to their canonization. To name just a few examples recorded in the 2000s, the singer Leila Foruhar covered the beloved prerevolutionary *tasnif* (light classical song) "Shab-e Mahtāb-e" ("Night of the Moonlight" by the composer Sheida) in a house music style, while another singer named Mansour has transformed the famous slow-tempo romantic song "Marā Bebus" ("Kiss Me" by Gol-Naraghi) from a sad piece about separation (and including what many believed were political undertones) into an optimistic song about the beginning of a new relationship. The prerevolutionary patriotic *sorud* "Ey Iran" ("Oh Iran" by Khaleqi), often described as the unofficial Iranian national anthem, has probably been covered more in the diaspora than any other single piece. "Ey Iran" was first a choral piece with orchestral accompaniment, but it has been recorded in a variety of styles from soft instrumentals on acoustic guitar (Babak Amini) to ballad (Andy) to techno (Kiki). These new arrangements often change the original spirit of the songs considerably through faster tempos, intensified percussion, and other additions to make them palatable to younger generations who seem to relate more to the dance pop format. This stylistic translation may contribute new memories for younger generations, while also educating them (perhaps without their awareness) in Iranian popular music history. This is another way in which Iranian *musiqi-ye pop*—one of the key symbols of cultural degradation and depravity in revolutionary discourse— is claimed and elevated by Iranians in Los Angeles as a way of marking off their version of Iranian culture and history from that of the Islamic Republic they left behind.

NEW POPULAR MUSIC IN LOS ANGELES: EPITOMIZING QUALITIES REJECTED IN THE REVOLUTION

Not all of the music produced in Los Angeles is from the prerevolutionary era; there are also hundreds of new songs recorded and released through the exile culture industries every year. The majority of the new music produced in LA is known as *musiqi-ye pop*, or *musiqi-ye pop-e los ānjeles* (MPLA). However, there are many similarities between prerevolutionary popular music and those new albums produced in Los Angeles. This sense of continuity is communicated most clearly through the large number of prerevolutionary singers, composers, and lyricists—many of whom are now in their sixties and seventies—who are still actively producing music in Los Angeles. As in its prerevolutionary iteration, the popular music produced in Los Angeles is oriented primarily toward songs rather than instrumental music, and solo singers with anonymous studio or live musicians rather than groups or ensembles. While much MPLA is devoted to nostalgic reflections on the lost homeland (see Naficy 1993), most MPLA is dance music with uncomplicated lyrics that shows strong Western musical influences, leading its disparagers inside and outside of Iran to consider it both "Westoxified" (*gharbzadeh*) and *mobtazal*. In MPLA music videos, male and female singers wear the latest American and European fashions while groups of women are frequently on display, both conventions that comport with both contemporary Western music videos and Iranian pop visuals from the 1960s and 1970s. This section considers those qualities in Los Angeles productions that depart from postrevolutionary Iranian music and media guidelines.

MPLA continues the predilection for cultural borrowing and Western emulation that characterized *musiqi-ye pop* in the prerevolutionary era. In LA, the gentle cha-chas and disco influences of the Shah's era have been replaced over the years by a swirling mixture of contemporary global dance musics, including salsa, Hi-NRG, house, and trance combined with identifiably Iranian musical instruments and samples and Persian lyrics. This hybridity is perhaps enhanced by increased contact with the world of musical styles available in Southern California. Throughout the 1980s and for most of the 1990s—before the Iranian state permitted the renewed production of popular music—the LA industry's embrace of stylistic diversity and Western trends represented a vision of Iranian culture sharply contrasting with that officially permitted in the Islamic Republic. It was, after all, these Western elements of Iranian *musiqi-ye pop* and the political and historical context in which it emerged that made it simultaneously attractive to the Pahlavi state and—initially, at least—a pariah for the revolutionary government.

Much of the popular music produced in LA is fast-paced, upbeat dance music with light, simple lyrics on romantic themes. Many of these songs employ a mixture of the diverse non-Iranian contemporary musical styles mentioned above, Persian texts, and a narrow range of rhythmic patterns, mostly in a 6/8 meter derived from established Iranian musical styles such as *motrebi* (urban entertainment music), *bandari* (Persian Gulf music), and the *reng*, or dance-inspired instrumental pieces, that typically close performances of a *dastgāh* (a set of pieces similar to a suite) in Iranian art music. While dance rhythms became one of the most predominant features of MPLA, they were largely absent from music produced within Iran until the late 1990s because they were considered "sensually arousing" (Youssefzadeh 2000, 39). When combined with frankly amorous lyrics that often focus on the physical attributes of female objects of desire, MPLA dance songs produce a sonic experience focused on sensuality that runs counter to the pious dispositions encouraged by Iranian state policy.

But LA pop songs do not only work at the level of sound; their treatment in music videos amplifies their communicative power.[15] A look at Armenian-Iranian MPLA singer Andranik Madadian's song and video "Āreh Āreh" ("Yeah Yeah") reveals these tendencies. Known simply as Andy, the singer is now in his fifties and has been active in the Los Angeles music industry since the early 1980s. His music retains a youthful edge by incorporating contemporary Western, Arabic, and Indian musical trends along with the aforementioned Iranian dance rhythms, and by sticking to uncomplicated romantic lyrics. Following this pattern, "Āreh Āreh" has extremely simple lyrics (the chorus: "Yeah, yeah / He loves you / Every day and every night / He thinks of his beloved"[16]) accompanied by synthesizers and a continuous thumping beat. The video underscores the cultural hybridity

and youthful sound by taking place in a quintessentially 1950s American setting of a diner, which is filled with attractive, fashionably attired, plausibly
Iranian dark-haired young women.[17] Andy appears in the restaurant and flips
a coin into the air that lands precisely in a jukebox that begins playing his
song. This brings on a stampede of even more young women who suddenly
appear outside the diner, screaming and beating on the windows in a manner that recalls the hysterical crowds of teenage girls who swooned over El-
vis during his early years. The women rush into the restaurant and dance to
the song as they lip-sync the song's chorus. Throughout the video, the camera cuts between shots of Andy in wraparound mirrored sunglasses, white
T-shirt, and varsity letterman's jacket as he dances among the women, and
close-ups of the smiling women's faces and their scantily clad, shimmying
hips and posteriors. These shots are interspersed with scenes of the diner's
parking lot, where an all-female dance corps of young women and girls ex-
pertly performs a coordinated choreography blending American video dance
and Iranian dance styles.[18]

How should one evaluate this example in light of MPLA musicians' often oppositional stance toward the IRI? On the one hand, Andy's video
for "Āreh Āreh" epitomizes the combination of cultural hybridity and un-
checked sensuality that was targeted in the revolutionary revision of Iranian culture. Further, the video relentlessly focuses on uncovered, sexualized female bodies and seems designed to put as many women on display
as possible—every corner of the diner and parking lot is absolutely packed
with them, while Andy is the only male present throughout the video. Given
the fact that some government officials and clerics have espoused the notion that women's veiling can act as a counter to "cultural invasion by the
West" (cf. Ayatollah Azari-Qomi in Mir-Hosseini [1999]) and long-standing
Iranian clerical attacks on dance and dancers (Stellar, this volume), Andy's
video could be taken as suggesting the inverse position: it revels in the delight of unbridled female sexuality inspired by a Westernized soundtrack in
an American diner.

At the same time, the combination of male musicians and a silent, desir-
ing female dance corps is a tried and true formula in American music videos, where women are frequently used as "props" to emphasize the sexual
desirability of the male vocalist (Andsager 2006). The formula's ubiquity
in American videos from rock to hip-hop is evidence of its financial success, and Andy has also employed female dance corps repeatedly in his other
videos.[19] Attempting to decipher whether Andy adopts this convention out
of a desire to emulate American fashions, for monetary gain, or to undermine the IRI's strictures on women and culture (or all three) points to the
ambiguity of statements made through such aesthetic choices: they cannot

be simply read as "resistant," but neither are they purely innocent. However, no matter the intentions, two facts remain important: first, as in America, viewers in Iran seem to be attracted to videos in this format (or at least LA cultural producers believe this to be the case—recall Kourosh Bibiyan's statement on Andy, above); and second, Iranian policy-makers have considered such videos an affront to the country's territorial sovereignty and have dealt harshly with perpetrators. We will turn to the consequences of exile cultural production shortly, but first, we must consider a far less ambiguous category of exile communication: songs that deal directly with topics sensitive to the Iranian state.

FINDING A VOICE THROUGH MPLA: FEMALE SINGERS, WOMEN'S ISSUES, AND OPPOSITION TO THE STATE

In MPLA, women do not only appear as sexual objects; they are also political subjects who sometimes take positions in song that can be difficult to assume publicly within Iran. Prior to migration, Iranian poets, composers, and professional entertainers working in both high and low cultural forms had also crafted songs and performance pieces that addressed political events and cultural issues (Chehabi 2000; Fatemi 2005), but such topics appeared only occasionally in the mass-mediated, state-supported popular music of the 1960s and 1970s. While romantic love is the primary focus of MPLA song texts, a number of Los Angeles–based artists have treated song and video as public forums in which they make critical statements about the Iranian state at a safe distance from any physical consequences. Given the global scope of MPLA, and particularly its penetration into Iran, these songs are also a means for sharing these views with compatriots, and, in their mediated transnational forms, they have the potential to overcome government attempts to monitor expression within the country.

One of many areas in which MPLA musicians have explicitly countered the state is regarding female singers and women's rights. Men outnumber women in every segment of the LA Iranian music industry, but women are successful and well known in MPLA especially as vocalists and lyricists. The most famous Iranian pop vocalist in both the prerevolutionary era and today is Googoosh, the diva of Iranian pop who remained in the country until 2000, when she moved to Toronto and then to Los Angeles and restarted her career in exile to worldwide acclaim. With twenty-odd other female singers in Los Angeles recording albums and videos, performing for mixed-sex audiences, and almost never wearing veils, Googoosh's and other LA-based female vocalists' activities are highly visible (and audible) examples of noncompliance with postrevolutionary law. Thus, women in MPLA singing otherwise innocuous love songs are something like Andy's female dance corps: they appear to be making a statement about Iranian laws without uttering a (critical) word. But some male and female vocalists and lyricists have made their sentiments obvious through songs that deal with gender issues, often in tandem with criticisms of other cultural restrictions in postrevolutionary Iran.

One such issue is the Iranian state policy of compulsory veiling, which has been addressed a number of times in MPLA songs in both direct and indirect fashion. In Iranian Islamic revolutionary thought, female veiling was conceptualized not only as a means of complying with Islamic practices, but of releasing women from the tyranny of Western cultural imperialism and empowering them to enter public spaces unencumbered by the male sexual gaze.[20] However, among many non-Muslim and secular Iranians, of whom there are many in Los Angeles and especially within the culture industries, compulsory veiling is often viewed as Islam's or the Iranian state's sanction of women's oppression or as a traditional cultural vestige to be cast aside by "modern" (read Westernized) women. When veiling is addressed in MPLA, it is usually to criticize it.

One song, called "Lady Sun" ("Khorshid Khānum"), sung by the female vocal trio Silhouettt is an example that exploits the common Iranian characterization of the sun as female.[21] Using poetic metaphor in an upbeat pop song, the young vocalists sing the following opening line in three-part harmony, "Lady Sun, come out again, let fall your veil (*hejāb*) of clouds and come into the middle of the sky," repeating it throughout the piece. Some lines later, the notion of women as captive emerges as one of the vocalists asks Lady Sun to "come out of [her] cage."[22] Another song, by the male vocalist Ebi, also called "Khorshid Khānum," makes use of the same sun-as-woman poetic formula, but in a more direct manner: "Lady Sun doesn't want a black scarf."

A more direct approach to women's issues is exemplified in Googoosh's song "Oh People, I'm Dying" ("Āy Mardom Mordam"), with lyrics by male lyricist Shahyar Ghanbari.[23] This song is crystal clear in its condemnation of women's suffering at the hands of men, as the song's chorus makes plain:

Oh people, I'm dying
I'm disappointed again
I'm dying because of these cowardly men
Not only me, but all women, have suffered

The lyrics paint a grim picture of Iranian women's lives; in one line, veiled women are portrayed as being wrapped "in twisted felt, rotting without air," a far cry indeed from the emancipatory depiction of veiling in revolutionary rhetoric and by many pious Muslim women. Elsewhere in the song, the lyrics compare women's bodies to "white *sofreh*" (a cloth laid on the ground upon which meals are served) that "burns where the belt buckle hit," linking two objects associated with the domestic sphere to depictions of female subservience and physical abuse.

This outspokenness stretches back to Googoosh's first songs after she emerged from Iran in the early 2000s. This is most evident in "Zartosht" ("Zoroaster"), named for the founder of Zoroastrianism, the dominant religion in Iran prior to the introduction of Islam, and also the name of her first album since the revolution. At the song's opening, Googoosh sings, "If I sing it is a crime, if I don't sing it is a crime," succinctly communicating her disagreement with Iranian policy on musical expression and its personal challenges for her, a professional vocalist who is compelled to sing by her own desire and perhaps by a sense of responsibility. The following lines further elaborate Googoosh's dispute by calling on an ancient past imagined to be hospitable to music:

> *In the body of this good, green kingdom*
> *Which is older than history*
> *When could singing have become a sin*
> *When Zoroaster planted this earth with hymns?*[24]

Here the lyrics' assertion of the importance of hymnody in the Zoroastrian religion presents a contrast to the comparatively negative treatment of musicians and music in the Iranian state's version of Islam. This declaration of the ongoing legitimacy of Iran's Zoroastrian lineage and the attitudes toward music supposedly contained therein becomes a means of undermining the authority of the Islamic texts, practices, and interpreters setting policy in Iran. The fact that Zoroastrians presently make up only a tiny fraction of Iran's population does not diminish the significance of this association, which is not in any case related to actual Zoroastrians but to the idea of a deeply rooted Iranian identity and culture that stretches back thousands of years and, in its lastingness, also transcends the present. This is not a new strategy by any means; the symbolic invocation of Iran's pre-Islamic past was a long-standing tactic for disassociating Iran from Islam (and particularly clerical political influence) throughout the Pahlavi period, which extends throughout Iranian modernity (Tavakoli-Targhi 2001) and back even further, to the poet Ferdowsi's celebrated and highly influential Iranian epic the "Shāhnāmeh" ("Book of Kings," AD 1010), which chronicles ancient Iran's heroes, kings, and cultures prior to Islam.[25] This symbolic identification resembles Thomas Solomon's (this volume) description of contemporary Turkish youth's selective appropriation of Muslim signifiers in their attempts to carve out a nonsecular identity in their Berlin- and Istanbul-based hip-hop productions, but instead grows out of Iranian exile musicians' desires to counter the Islamicization of Iranian national identity. In exile, the long-standing trope of pre-Islamic Iranian authenticity and national culture is employed to counter the Islamic state on yet another level.

As we see, MPLA singers have at times adopted stances on Iranian women and cultural and religious identity that compete with those projected in Iranian state media and policy. This activity has been ongoing since the inception of the LA culture industries and extends to new political issues as they arise. Most recently, musicians in Los Angeles have continued this role by releasing a number of songs addressing the violence following the contested reelection of President Mahmood Ahmadinejad on June 12, 2009, with contributions coming from Googoosh, Andy, and many others.[26] Measuring the reception and impact of these songs within the United States is difficult, but one can point to their frequent airings on satellite television and numerous page views on websites like YouTube, where these videos are also available, for some idea of their reach. But far more challenging—and far more charged—is the task of determining the effects of these MPLA in Iran, where so many musicians and media producers in Los Angeles insist they are influential and revered. It is to this question that we now turn.

EVALUATING THE LA CULTURAL INDUSTRIES' TRANSNATIONAL REACH

Despite its best efforts, the Iranian state has never had a complete monopoly over its citizens' media consumption. Access to nonapproved media has been especially documented among upper- and middle-class secular, urban youth (cf. Rouhani 2001; Basmenji 2005; Alikhah 2008; Mahdavi 2009), and consuming these media is frequently portrayed as an act of dissent against the state. Shahram Khosravi, whose research also focused primarily on these privileged populations, has asserted the importance of unofficial media for Iranian youth in this way:

> How young Tehranis imagine themselves and their nation is influenced by their access to the media. While ignoring entirely Iranian state media products, they are avid consumers of alternative media—satellite TV channels and radio programs, the Internet, and video—in which they can find alternative representations of what it means to be Iranian. (2008, 173–174)

Some of these media, such as blogs, websites, and underground music, are produced inside the country outside of official channels and suggest the presence of a vibrant, varied public sphere with both local and transnational components.[27] But Khosravi goes on to suggest that "the popular culture industry in the diaspora" is paramount in providing those "alternative representations" of Iranian-ness.

My own experiences in Iran in 1997, 2000, and 2004 among similar urban populations revealed myriad instances of Los Angeles cultural industries' penetration into the country, especially through popular music. I witnessed MPLA recordings, along with other Western and Arabic pop music brought in from abroad, being played in taxicabs, in private cars, and at parties in homes. Home television sets were often tuned to Persian Entertainment Network and Persian Music Channel, both satellite stations that play mostly music videos from LA. These were often left on all day like a radio, receiving the latest emanations from exiles abroad. In one home without a satellite dish, I observed residents playing a purchased bootlegged VCD of a satellite television feed that featured exile and Western music videos. Over the course of my visits, MPLA was an unremarkable part of daily life, an entertainment option that happened to be slightly more difficult to obtain than some others, but which was enjoyed along with government-approved pop, traditional musics, and "underground" MP3s without any apparent moral or political controversy. However, as Khosrokhavar (2007) has demonstrated, listening to MPLA or other forms of music (approved or not) is not so simple for pious residents of the religious city of Qom, who sometimes struggle to justify their enjoyment. All the same, Khosrokhavar shows that those observant Muslims he interviewed often reject the notion that "Los Angeles music is banned by religion," as some conservative clerics assert (2007, 461), and develop their own interpretations of appropriate behavior. As he suggests, this personal decision-making around music—an area of culture that many conservative clerics have forbidden even despite governmental support—may contribute to the gradual secularization of Iranian society (ibid.).

Besides accounts of individual reception in Iran, perhaps the greatest evidence for MPLA's impact is state responses to MPLA and the figures associated with it. The most notable of these reactions was the legalization of popular music after 1997, which was intended to counter the flow of exile and Western music into the country by providing a local, government-approved alternative. These approved singers have not infrequently competed with LA exiles by borrowing melodies from prerevolutionary or MPLA songs and changing their lyrics to meet oversight board approval and to further distance them from the original versions. Some singers even possess voices that strongly resemble those of popular exiled singers who now work through LA-based music companies. For instance, the Iran-based singer Khashyar Etemadi sounds remarkably like the prerevolutionary exiled icon Dariush,

Nader Meschi's voice resembles that of the LA-based singer Mansour, and Mohsen Chavoshi is incredibly similar to prerevolutionary vocalist Siavash Gomeishi. Such moves have the effect of denying the legitimacy of MPLA while tacitly acknowledging—and attempting to capitalize on—its popularity. The government's adoption of pop music also undermines its subversive potential and is an attempt to remove its secularist associations (Nooshin 2005a).

MPLA musicians I spoke with were aware of their influence in Iran and sometimes pointed to their impact on officially approved pop as an example of, rather than a challenge to, their popularity there. Again and again I was told by well-known vocalists—many of whom had begun their careers before the revolution—that they regularly received e-mails and even telephone calls from fans within Iran who emphasized how important exiled musicians were to Iranians inside the country. In their efforts to maintain and grow these connections, many MPLA singers reach out to audiences in Iran by affirming in interviews in transnational Iranian media that they "never forget those in Iran," by using lyrics written by Iranians within the country in their songs in order to "give them a voice," and by producing songs that refer to Iranian current events. As suggested in this chapter's introduction, songs focusing on the homeland also serve an important function for diasporic audiences, who often seek out connections to Iran and to different representations of Iranian culture than those they find projected in either official Iranian or Western media. These music and media may thus do double service, first by appealing to diasporic audiences who can purchase recordings and concert tickets and thereby support the LA industry, and second by attracting Iran-based audiences, from whom LA musicians receive more intangible—but still significant—rewards.[28]

Ironically, whether or not MPLA musicians intend their productions to reach Iran or wish to take a stand on Iranian issues, their participation in exile cultural industries opens them up to potentially serious consequences that underscore the lingering subversive potential of MPLA. This is evidenced in the state's sharp response toward those LA-based musicians and figures that have returned to Iran for a visit. The majority of Iranian musicians and media personnel working in the Southern California Iranian culture industries do not travel back to Iran, because they fear repercussions, especially if they are well known. These fears are not unfounded, as Babak Amini, a young guitarist and composer who led Googoosh's band on her first tour and composed songs for her first album, learned when he returned after their tour. On his first and only visit back to Iran, he was questioned for several days about his relationship to Googoosh and his activities outside of the country. Ultimately, Amini was fined, held in Iran for six months, and forced to sign a statement promising never to work with Googoosh again. A similar incident was the arrest and imprisonment of Iranian-American aerobics instructor and dancer Mohammad Khordadian, who was charged with propagating corruption via his dance and exercise videos that had been circulating back into Iran from Los Angeles (Papan-Matin 2009). Khordadian has protested that he was unaware of the restrictions on dance in Iran and that, as with Babak Amini, his arrest came as a complete surprise to him. These consequences were not surprising, apparently, to the passengers on Amini's flight, who, he said, warned him that he should expect problems entering the country. These performers' claims to naïveté complicate the notion that exile cultural producers necessarily intend to undermine IRI media, but at the same time, since the Iranian government has sometimes considered those involved in LA media hostile to its sovereignty, they are nonetheless implicated in this alleged transgression.

But MPLA and its performers are not always taken so seriously in Iran, even in media approved by government oversight boards. A 2005 Iranian comedic feature film called *MAXX* parodied exiled pop musicians through the story of a fictional cabaret singer named Maxx who has been living in Los Angeles since the revolution.[29] In the film, Maxx, a ponytailed New Ager given to outlandish outfits, mistakenly receives a letter of invitation for a classical musician and returns to Iran in the artist's place to receive a warm welcome by government officials. Maxx's subterfuge slowly becomes apparent through his performances of prerevolutionary songs and LA-style dance pop and his use of American-slang-inflected Persian that, together, communicate his complete unawareness of cultural shifts in postrevolutionary Iran. In this way, the film pokes fun at exile musicians (and diasporic Iranians more generally) who are nostalgically focused on Iran but are not at all familiar with life in the Islamic Republic.

At one level, *MAXX* appears to be an acknowledgment of exile musicians' illegal penetration into Iran, which can be recognized in the state's approval of a film in which exiles are ridiculed. On another level, however, the film also levels implicit criticism at the government's sensitivity to exile music and musicians by portraying Maxx as utterly harmless. While some characters find Maxx's performances offensive and the story ends with the singer being ejected from the country by an intelligence officer, those characters closest to Maxx find his personality, many foibles, and sincere love for Iran amusing and even admirable. Perhaps even more provocatively, throughout the film Maxx's audiences are shown knowingly demonstrating their enjoyment of his music, smiling and shyly sketching the outlines of Iranian dance movements with their bodies to the beats of his undeniably *mobtazal* musical numbers. The film seems to ask, what is so threatening about this hapless lounge singer and his pop songs? And what is so wrong with our enjoying them?

CONCLUSION

Evaluating the importance of alternative media for youth in Iran, Khosravi asserts that "[f]or many Iranians the 'authentic' Iran comes, ironically, from Los Angeles" (2008, 174). This may be true for some audience members, but as the examples above show, responses to exile popular music within Iran are diverse and often contradictory. Rather than attributing authenticity to exile cultural producers, the Iranian state, or any other group, I have tried to show here that producers of MPLA are expressing multiple identities, viewpoints, and practices that extend beyond those represented in state-supported culture and media. These include assertions of the enduring relevance of both ancient and prerevolutionary periods of Iranian history, in which Islam is imagined to have played a diminished or nonexistent role in Iran and in which music is presented as having been a valued part of Iranian culture. The pleasures of dance, sexuality, and cultural appropriation are also on display in MPLA music and video in ways that depart from the moral dispositions and cultural attitudes that have been promoted by the Islamic state. Taken together, the ways MPLA engages gender, sexuality, involvement with the West, and Iranians' complicated relationship to their own history and culture do not make it more authentic, but rather allow it to serve as an alternative to state visions of Iran.

MPLA's focus on the homeland has the possibility of serving both diasporic Iranians and Iranians within the country in search of expanding their aesthetic and expressive horizons beyond what is available to them in either official Iranian or Western media. While undeniably constrained by economic pressures and exiles' own internal politics and predilections, MPLA also contributes to a transnational, multimedia alternative public in which criticisms of the Iranian state and of Iranian culture more generally can be aired within a readily accessible, yet politically and morally disputed, popular musical form. Whether LA cultural producers' foremost intentions are to counter the IRI through these statements and aesthetic choices or whether these themes emerge as a result of primarily commercial or artistic impulses is less the issue than the fact that by virtue of their participation in this public, MPLA and its producers ultimately become implicated in struggles over Iranian cultural and national sovereignty. That this music has produced a contest of legitimacy and power between exiles and state actors speaks to the importance of the issues Iranian popular music engages and to its influence, which, while ambiguous, is also undeniable. As our understandings of the forms and activities constituting emergent publics extend to include cultural production and transnational media (cf. Warner 2002; Hirschkind 2006; Fraser 2007; Wedeen 2008), popular music should also occupy our attention.[30] And as Iranians on both sides of the border debate the shape and contents of their national identities and the arc of their future, MPLA will likely continue to play an important role.

NOTES

Research for this chapter was supported by grants from Columbia University and PEO Sisterhood International. I would like to extend my thanks to Karin van Nieuwkerk and the two reviewers for the University of Texas Press for their helpful suggestions. Several colleagues and friends also generously provided me with feedback on this paper, especially Ana María Ochoa Gautier, Aaron Fox, Chris Washburne, Sandhya Shukla, Tyler Bickford, Morgan Luker, Ida Meftahi, Anna Stirr, and Lauren Ninoshvilli. Special thanks to Mohammad Hemmasi. My transliteration approximates spoken Persian.

1. Lyrics and music by Hassan Shamaizadeh. Discographic information appears in the discography.

2. *Zāhed* is also sometimes translated as pious or ascetic.

3. For more on the relationship of music, place, and emplacement, see Feld and Basso (1996); Leyshon, Matless, and Revill (1998); and Diehl (2002).

4. *Los ānjelesi* and *musiqi-ye los ānjelesi* are terms also sometimes used to refer to this music in Iran, but are not generally employed by LA-based musicians themselves. Sometimes the borrowed *muzik* is used in place of the Persian *musiqi*. MPLA is an abbreviation I derived for convenience. It is not a term used by Iranians in everyday speech.

5. Khiabany calls the state Iran's "dominant media capitalist" (2007, 487) and asserts that "[b]y any standard and any definition it is hard to suggest that the press in Iran is distinctly located outside the realm of the state" (2008, 31).

6. See Abrahamian (2008, Chapter 6) for a succinct overview of these changes.

7. *Vezārat-e farhang va ershād-e eslāmi*, often referred to simply as *Ershād*.

8. Lois Ibsen al-Faruqi (1985) has described a number of sources and rationales supporting the general permissibility of certain aural forms among Muslims, such as unaccompanied religious chants, which are not *musiqi*, versus the impermissibility of instrumental music or sung poetry, which are generally considered *musiqi*. However, the question of whether a "musical" form is or is not *musiqi* does not solve the issue of its ultimate legitimacy; in practice as well as in jurisprudence, delineation of *halāl* (permissible) from *makruh* (disfavored, disapproved) sonic arts varies widely between time periods, locations, and interpretive communities.

9. Iranian intellectual Jalal Al Ahmad popularized the term *gharbzadegi*, which is translated variously as "Westoxification," "Occidentosis," and "Plagued by the West," in an influential essay written in the 1960s (Al Ahmad 1982). This eventually became a key term in Iranian revolutionary discourse.

10. The *sorud*, or "march-hymn," is not itself a postrevolutionary genre, however; it was developed in the mid-twentieth century and often featured texts celebrating the secular Persian-centric nationalism espoused by the Pahlavi monarchs. See Chehabi (1999) for a detailed history of the prerevolutionary national *sorud*, or *sorud-e melli*.

11. The Los Angeles–based Iranian pop stars Dariush and Shahbal Shabpareh both

had television shows on the Reseda-based television station Omid-e Iran ("Hope of Iran") in 2007.

12. Free to air means that no subscription service is needed to access the channels—a dish pointed toward the correct coordinates will open viewers up to an array of Iranian-owned and -oriented channels, as well as to others from Europe and the Middle East. Alikhah (2008) counted thirty-seven such stations available in Iran.

13. "Cultural invasion by the West" (*tahājom-e farhangi-e gharb*) is a slogan that refers to Western plots to overtake Iran by cultural means.

14. *52 Tarāneh az Mardomitarin Āhang-hā Kucheh Bāzār* and *Āhang-hā Talāi Homeirā*, both on the Southern California–based label Taraneh Records. Homeyra was a beloved female vocalist who specialized in pop and light classical songs.

15. For more on LA Iranian music videos, see Naficy 2002.

16. Lyrics by Paksima Zakipour and music by Mohammad Moghaddam. On *Platinum*, 2004. As Persian pronouns are genderless, these lyrics could also be interpreted in the feminine.

17. Many women who appear in Iranian music videos are not in fact Iranian. For an interesting reading, see Naficy 1993, 180–181.

18. For a description of Iranian "solo improvised dance" as performed in Iranian Southern California, see Shay (1999).

19. See also Andy's videos for the songs "Che Khoshgel Shodi Emshab" ("How Pretty You Are Tonight") and "Khoshgelā Bāyad Beraqseh" ("The Pretty Ones Must Dance").

20. See Moghissi 1994 on Ayatollah Motahari and the intellectual Ali Shari'ati, whom she credits with delineating *hejāb* as central to revolutionary ideology.

21. Silhouettt is spelled with three T's to represent the three vocalists.

22. Lyrics by Homa Mir Afshar and music by Farzin Farhadi.

23. Music by Mehrdad.

24. Lyrics by Nosrat Farzaneh and music by Babak Amini.

25. See Chehabi 1999 for texts of patriotic art songs and anthems from the early and mid-twentieth century that also glorify pre-Islamic Iran.

26. For instance, see Googoosh's song "Man Hamun Iran-am" ("I Am That Very Iran," http://www.youtube.com/watch?v=SuBSrYEwN44, and Andy's 2009 performance of the 1961 hit American song "Stand By Me" with Jon Bon Jovi, http://www.youtube.com/watch?v=RASKaZFZtS8.

27. Some of these alternative media are radio (e.g., Voice of America, BBC Persian, and Radio Zamaneh), websites, and satellite television stations produced and funded by Western governments and staffed by Iranian journalists and media producers, many of whom were well known in Iran prior to emigration. Music also plays an important role in these media outlets. This is a very interesting area of Iranian cultural production that should be investigated further.

28. Several record label owners in Los Angeles told me that they had accepted that they couldn't receive any profits from sales in Iran, though "that is where our biggest audience is," as one put it. On the other hand, several LA musicians I spoke with suspected that industry personnel were profiting from sales in Iran and being dishonest about it. More research is necessary to confirm either suggestion.

29. *MAXX*, directed by Saman Moghaddam, 2005.

30. See Gautier (2006) for another take on the aural public sphere as constituted by Latin American popular musics.

REFERENCES

Abrahamian, Ervand. 2008. *A History of Modern Iran.* Cambridge, UK, and New York: Cambridge University Press.

Adelkhah, Fariba. 1991. "Michael Jackson Ne Peut Absolument Rien Faire: Les Pratiques Musicales En République Islamique d'Iran." *Cahiers d'études sur la Méditerranée orientale et le monde turco-iranien,* no. 11.

———. 2001. "Les Iranienes De Californie: Si La République Islamique N'existait Pas . . ." *Les Etudes de CERI* 75.

Al Ahmad, Jalal. 1982. *Plagued by the West (Gharbzadegi).* Modern Persian Literature Series. Delmar, NY: Center for Iranian Studies, Columbia University.

Alikhah, Fardin. 2008. "The Politics of Satellite Television in Iran." In *Media, Culture and Society in Iran: Living with Globalization and the Islamic State,* ed. Mehdi Semati, pp. 94–110. London and New York: Routledge.

Andsager, Julie L. 2006. "Seduction, Shock, and Sales: Research and Functions of Sex in Music Video." In *Sex in Consumer Culture: The Erotic Content of Media and Marketing,* ed. Tom Reichert and Jacqueline Lambiase, pp. 31–50. Mahwah, NJ: L. Erlbaum Publishers.

Baraheni, Reza. 1977. *The Crowned Cannibals: Writings on Repression in Iran.* New York: Vintage Books.

Basmenji, Kaveh. 2005. *How Iranian Youth Rebelled against Iran's Founding Fathers.* London: Saqi.

Bozorgmehr, Mehdi. 1997. "Internal Ethnicity: Iranians in Los Angeles." *Sociological Perspectives* 40 (3): 387–408.

Chehabi, H. E. 1999. "From Revolutionary *Tasnif* to Patriotic *Surud*: Music and Nation-Building in Pre–World War II Iran." *IRAN* 37:143–154.

———. 2000. "Voices Unveiled: Women Singers in Iran." In *Iran and Beyond: Essays in Middle Eastern History in Honor of Nikki R. Keddie,* ed. Rudi Mathee and Beth Baron, pp. 151–166. Costa Mesa, CA: Mazda Publishers.

Diehl, Keila. 2002. *Echoes from Dharamsala: Music in the Life of a Tibetan Refugee Community.* Berkeley: University of California Press.

During, Jean. 1992. "L'oreille Islamique: Dix Années Capitales De La Vie Musicale En Iran: 1980–1990." *Asian Music* 23 (2): 135–164.

Eickelman, Dale F., and Jon W. Anderson. 2003. *New Media in the Muslim World: The Emerging Public Sphere.* Bloomington: Indiana University Press.

al-Faruqi, Lois Ibsen. 1985. "Music, Musicians and Muslim Law." *Asian Music* 17 (1): 3–36.

Fatemi, Sasan. 2005. "La Musique Légère Urbaine Dans La Culture Iranienne: Réflexions Sur Les Notions De Classique Et Populaire." PhD diss., Universite Paris X-Nanterre.

Feld, Steven, and Keith H. Basso. 1996. *Senses of Place.* School of American Research Advanced Seminar Series. Santa Fe, NM: School of American Research Press.

Fraser, Nancy. 2007. "Transnationalizing the Public Sphere: On the Legitimacy and Efficacy of Public Opinion in a Post-Westphalian World." *Theory, Culture & Society* 24:7–30.

Gautier, Ana Maria Ochoa. 2006. "Sonic Transculturation, Epistemologies of Purification and the Aural Public Sphere in Latin America." *Social Identities* 12 (6): 803–825.

Hirschkind, Charles. 2006. *The Ethical Soundscape: Cassette Sermons and Islamic Counterpublics.* New York: Columbia University Press.

Kelley, Ron, Jonathan Friedlander, and Anita Colby, eds. 1993. *Irangeles: Iranians in Los Angeles.* Berkeley: University of California Press.

Khiabany, Gholam. 2007. "Iranian Media: The Paradox of Modernity." *Social Semiotics* 17 (4): 479–501.

———. 2008. "The Iranian Press, State and Civil Society." In *Media, Culture and Society in Iran: Living with Globalization and the Islamic State,* ed. Mehdi Semati, pp. 17–36. London and New York: Routledge.

Khosravi, Shahram. 2008. *Young and Defiant in Iran.* Philadelphia: University of Pennsylvania Press.

Khosrokhavar, Farhad. 2007. "The New Religiosity in Iran." *Social Compass* 54 (3): 453–463.

Kian, Azadeh. 1995. "L'invasion Culturelle: Myth Ou Realité?" *Cahiers d'études sur la Méditerranée orientale et le monde turco-iranien,* no. 20 (juillet–décembre).

Leyshon, Andrew, David Matless, and George Revill, eds. 1998. *The Place of Music.* New York: Guilford Press.

Loeb, Laurence D. 1972. "The Jewish Musician and the Music of Fars." *Asian Music* 4 (1): 3–14.

Mahdavi, Pardis. 2009. *Passionate Uprisings: Iran's Sexual Revolution.* Stanford, CA: Stanford University Press.

Meftahi, Ida. 2005. "Learning to Dance in Iran in the 1990s." Conference paper presented at the Dance and Human Rights Conference, Congress on Research in Dance, Montreal, Quebec.

Mir-Hosseini, Ziba. 1999. *Islam and Gender: The Religious Debate in Contemporary Iran.* Princeton Studies in Muslim Politics. Princeton, NJ: Princeton University Press.

Moghissi, Haideh. 1994. *Populism and Feminism in Iran: Women's Struggle in a Male-Defined Revolutionary Movement.* New York: St. Martin's Press.

Movahed, Azin. 2003–2004. "Religious Supremacy, Anti-Imperialist Nationhood and Persian Musicology after the 1979 Revolution." *Asian Music* 35 (1): 85–113.

Naficy, Hamid. 1993. *The Making of Exile Cultures: Iranian Television in Los Angeles.* Minneapolis: University of Minnesota Press.

———. 2002. "Identity Politics and Iranian Exile Music Videos." In *Music, Popular Culture, Identities,* ed. R. Young, pp. 229–247. Amsterdam and New York: Editions Rodopi.

Nooshin, Laudan. 2005a. "Subversion and Counter-Subversion: Power, Control and Meaning in the New Iranian Pop Music." In *Music, Power and Politics,* ed. Annie Janeiro Randall, pp. 231–272. New York: Routledge.

———. 2005b. "Underground, Overground: Rock Music and Youth Discourses in Iran." *Iranian Studies* 38 (3): 463–494.

———. 2008. "The Language of Rock: Iranian Youth, Popular Music, and National Identity." In *Media, Culture and Society in Iran: Living with Globalization and the Islamic State,* ed. Mehdi Semati, pp. 69–93. London and New York: Routledge.

Papan-Matin, Firoozeh. 2009. "The Case of Mohammad Khordadian, an Iranian Male Dancer." *Iranian Studies* 42 (1): 127–138.

Rouhani, Farhang. 2001. "The Home as a Site of State Formation: The Politics of Transnational Media Consumption in Tehran." PhD diss., University of Arizona, Tucson.

Salvatore, Armando, and Dale F. Eickelman. 2004. *Public Islam and the Common Good.* Leiden and Boston: Brill.

Shay, Anthony. 1999. *Choreophobia: Solo Improvised Dance in the Iranian World.* Costa Mesa, CA: Mazda.

————. 2000. "The 6/8 Beat Goes On: Persian Popular Music from Bazm-E Qajariyyeh to Beverly Hills Garden Parties." In *Mass Mediations: New Approaches to Popular Culture in the Middle East and Beyond*, ed. Walter Armbrust, pp. 61–87. Berkeley, Los Angeles, and London: University of California Press.

Sreberny-Mohammadi, Annabelle, and Ali Mohammadi. 1994. *Small Media, Big Revolution: Communication, Culture and the Iranian Revolution*. Minneapolis: University of Minnesota Press.

Tavakoli-Targhi, Mohamad. 2001. *Refashioning Iran: Orientalism, Occidentalism, and Historiography*. New York: Palgrave.

Van Nieuwkerk, Karin. 2008. "Creating an Islamic Cultural Sphere: Contested Notions of ⟵ Art, Leisure and Entertainment. An Introduction." In "Creating an Islamic Cultural Sphere: Contested Notions of Art, Leisure and Entertainment," ed. Karin van Nieuwkerk, special issue, *Contemporary Islam* 2 (3): 169–176.

Warner, Michael. 2002. *Publics and Counterpublics*. New York and Cambridge, MA: Zone Books; distributed by MIT Press.

Wedeen, Lisa. 2008. *Peripheral Visions: Publics, Power, and Performance in Yemen*. Chicago: University of Chicago Press.

Youssefzadeh, Ameneh. 2000. "The Situation of Music in Iran since the Revolution: The Role of Official Organizations." *British Journal of Ethnomusicology* 9 (2): 35–61.

DISCOGRAPHY

All titles are US pressings unless otherwise noted.

Ebi. 2000. "Khorshid Khānum" ("Lady Sun"). *Khorshid Khānum*. Avang Records [CD].

52 Tarāneh Mardomitarin Āhang-hā Kucheh o Bāzār (*52 of the Most Popular Songs of the Street and Bazaar*). 2001. Taraneh Records [CD].

40 Golden Hits of Homeyra. 2000. Taraneh Records [CD].

Foruhar, Leila. 2000. "Shab-e Mahtāb-e" ("Night of Moonlight"). *Tasvir* (*Image*). Caltex Records [CD].

Googoosh. 2001. *Zartosht* (*Zoroaster*). Label unknown, produced in Canada [CD].

————. 2005. "Āy Mardom Mordam" ("Oh Men, I'm Dying"). *Manifest*. MZM Records [CD].

Kiki. 2002. "Ey Iran" ("Oh Iran"). *Persiatronica*. Pars Video [CD].

Madadian, Andy (Andranik). 1998. "Ey Iran." *Jādeh-ye Abrisham* (*Silk Road*). Taraneh Enterprises [CD].

————. 2004. "Āreh, Āreh" ("Yeah, Yeah"). *Platinum*. Caltex Records [CD].

Mansour. 2005. "Marā Bebus" ("Kiss Me"). *Farāri* (*Escapee*). Taraneh Enterprises [CD].

Shamaizadeh, Hassan. 2002. "Be To Che" ("None of Your Business"). *Miss*. Caltex Records [CD].

Silhouettt. 1995. "Khorshid Khānum" ("Lady Sun"). *Āb, Ātash va Khāk* (*Water, Fire, and Earth*). Caltex Records [CD].

PART TWO

MOTIVATIONS

CHAPTER 4

RITUAL AS STRATEGIC ACTION:
THE SOCIAL LOGIC OF MUSICAL
SILENCE IN CANADIAN ISLAM

MICHAEL FRISHKOPF

LIVING IN EGYPT FOR MANY YEARS, I became accustomed to Islamic ritual as sonically rich, hence socially and spiritually compelling. From Qur'anic recitation (*tilawa*), to the Sufi liturgy (*hadra*), from the saint's day festival (*mawlid*) to ordinary congregational prayer (*salah*), Egyptian sounds of Islam are variegated, often moving, and frequently virtuosic. In short, they are often (though certainly not always) "music," if this word is understood in its broad English sense of "aesthetic sound," rather than as a cognate of the Arabic *musiqa* (implying instrumental music, a word not typically applied to Islamic practices). After moving from Cairo to Canada in 1998, and visiting numerous Canadian mosques, I was struck both by the social dynamism of Canadian Muslim communities (most of them established only recently) and by the relative *musical silence* of Islamic ritual there (sometimes actively applied, for instance in the lukewarm reception given by second-generation Muslims to a traditional Qur'anic reciter whom I brought from Egypt to Edmonton, due to expressed fears that his spiritual-musical practices may "transgress the boundaries of the Quraan and Sunnah").[1]

Why is Islamic ritual practice in Canada comparatively bereft of musical sound? More generally, why is Canadian Islamic practice *relatively* lacking in those aesthetic media—especially architecture, calligraphy, poetry, and the vocal arts—whose practical procedural knowledge has been (for the most part) transmitted orally, and that have, for centuries, accompanied Islamic ritual, offering powerful means for gathering worshippers, and for developing, expressing, communicating, and instilling spiritual feeling, transmitting and catalyzing an immediate experience of the numinous, in its transcendent and immanent dimensions, the *mysterium tremendum et fascinans* (Otto and Harvey 1925; Nasr 1987)?[2]

In this chapter, I explore the relatively limited practice and acceptance of music—and more broadly, of aesthetic spirituality—in Islamic ritual in Canada as a consequence of (1) a distinctively modernist Islamic reformism, one that developed in a dialectical relation with the West from the mid-nineteenth century onwards, and that persists today as one set of Islamic discourses (among many others); and (2) Canada's being a place of emigration that is particularly hospitable to these discourses, and particularly inhospitable to others.

Here, I'm not alluding to broader antimusic Muslim *discourses* for which music *qua* aesthetic entertainment is anathema (nowadays widespread via reformist propaganda—if relatively inconsequential—among segments of the Canadian Muslim population, as elsewhere in the world). Nor am I claiming that the Canadian Muslim population (more than others) actually avoids making or listening to music in *practice* (a statement that I believe would prove untrue). Rather, my discussion centers on music in Islamic ritual: I wish to interpret the absence of aesthetically compelling sound and, correspondingly, sonically generated affect in Canadian Muslim spiritual practice, as compared to Muslim practices in historically Islamic regions.

RITUAL TRANSMISSION: HUMAN MEDIATION
VERSUS ORIGINARY MODELS

Islamic ritual almost invariably centers on the socially marked recitation (individual or collective) of sacred texts, what I have called *language performance* (Frishkopf 1999). Textual recitation entails pitched vocal sound, the paralinguistic carrier for vowels and voiced consonants. The resulting sonic contours offer potential parasemantic power—via tonal, timbral, temporal, and social organization—as moving aesthetic sound, transcending the assertional content of the text itself. This affective-aesthetic power, extolling the text through sonic adornment, serves both text and ritual, by drawing and focusing attention, clarifying meaning, facilitating retention, forging social solidarity among participants, and developing emotion confirming the felt certainty of the textual message and the efficacy of the spiritual practice in which its recitation is embedded (see Frishkopf 2002).

In Islamic ritual the full power of aesthetic sound appears in the intricate tonal arabesques of the call to prayer (*adhan*), in Qur'anic recitation (*tilawa*) performed in the *mujawwad* style, and in the elaborate echoings of the *muballigh*, responding to the imam of congregational prayer with "*Allahu akbar*" or "*assalamu ʿalaykum wa rahmatullah*" in melodic style. It includes the ascending tonal arches of the public *duʿaʾ* (supplication) as performed by the prayer leader, and the otherworldly *ibtihalat*, ornamented predawn vocal solos performed by specialists (*mubtahilin*) in the mosques. It encompasses the wide range of musicality displayed in liturgies of the Sufi orders (*al-turuq al-sufiyya*), whether in the chanted textual formulae of *dhikr*, *awrad*, and *hizb*; in accompanying religious hymns, *inshad dini*; or in spiritual-musical audition, *sama'*. And it includes popular devotional songs—most commonly praise (*madih*) and petition (*istighatha*) directed to the Prophet (and sometimes to saints); and glorification (*tasbih*), supplication (*ibtihalat*), and *salawat* (requests to bless the Prophet) to God—ranging from simple call-and-response singing, to elaborate musical ensembles featuring song, as well as instruments (especially frame drums and flutes). Thus Islamic ritual, while invariably centering on text, is nearly everywhere embellished by paralinguistic sound.

In the Arab world, these forms exploit a range of familiar (if indescribable) vocal timbres and ornamental styles, along with the system of Arab musical modes, the heptatonic *maqamat*. Elsewhere in the Muslim world, tonal and timbral practices may be quite different. Thus Muslim Hausa speakers of West Africa deploy contrasting instruments, timbres, and tonalities (e.g., pentatonic scales) in their religious genres. In Turkey vocal characteristics may resemble the distinctive sound of the Mevlevi order, in Iran vocal ornaments used in religious recitations sound Iranian, and in Pakistan the musical style of Sufi performance is adapted from Hindustani traditions (Qureshi 1987). In many cases, the texts are the same, however; even when appearing in local languages, poetic themes (praise, supplication, exhortation, spiritual love) recur widely. The same Islamic messages, then, are projected in a multitude of sonic forms, which serve powerfully to channel the religious feeling of the performer, and to evoke religious feeling in the listener, by means of musical idioms that are available, local, familiar, and potent.

Because the aesthetics of these sonic forms—unwritten and passed through (usually informal) oral transmission—resist discursive specification, and because they defer to the referential texts they support, they tend to go unremarked among Muslims (as that which "goes without saying because it comes without saying," as Bourdieu quipped [1977, 167]), as, for instance, in Sufi texts (including mystical manuals) or in guides for Qur'anic cantillation, where the melodic details of recitation are virtually always omitted. Furthermore, as they typically carry no particular referential meaning themselves, such forms cannot easily be contested via critical discourse, which (outside the hands of a few specialists) serves as a kind of blunt instrument capable only of accepting or rejecting them en masse (as attested by antimusical polemics). And yet these forms carry tremendous emotional force for those in whom they are inculcated—for those (to continue with Bourdieu) in whom they are inscribed, almost bodily, in the aesthetic habitus through repeated ritual practice, accumulating (via both individual memory and collective oral transmission) indexical meanings (by juxtaposition to use-contexts), while providing "presentational" (Langer 1960) and expressive ones, the combination generating the "effervescence" elaborated by Durkheim as crucial to the solidarity of social groups (Durkheim 1976).

As in other religious ritual, sonic forms are powerful forces in naturalizing embodied, affective social identities (at the phenomenological level), and thus (at the sociological level) in actually unifying or dividing socioreligious solidarities, despite their nondiscursivity—indeed all the more powerful for lying outside the discursive realm (Frishkopf 2009c). Aesthetic forms that cannot be expressed in language may nevertheless express one another very well.

All of these aesthetic-sonic practices of Islam, along with many intellectual ones, have been transmitted and developed across the centuries by chains (*silsilas, isnads*) of *human mediation.* By this I mean that the transmission path links a series of people, engaged in extended intersubjective relationships, sharing a lifeworld—and, consequently, soundworld (Frishkopf 2009b)—each receiving from a teacher (formally or not) through intensive social-sonic interactions and transmitting (in the same manner) to a relatively small number of students, rather than receiving a mass broadcast emanating directly from a privileged point of fixed cultural reference, an "originary model."

Indeed it cannot be otherwise. In contrast to texts, such models have never existed for Islamic ritual sound, and as a result cannot exist, for the music of Islam (unlike, say, Protestant hymnals) has developed tremendous performative flexibility and adaptability, as a result of its freedom from fixed models, which can therefore no longer be easily recaptured in any model at all. If Islamic reformism has tended to postulate the early Muslim community, Qur'an, and Sunna as primary discursive reference points, the fact is that these have virtually nothing to say regarding so many matters of aesthetic content. The result of human mediation over many generations is thus a highly ramified transmissive genealogy, and a highly localized Islam, in which neighboring villages may boast of distinctive sonic styles, even while performing exactly the same texts.[3] The process of human mediation not only produces continual sonic variation, in dynamic adaptive relation to local sociocultural circumstances (including acoustic ecologies), but also entails an accretion of meaning and practice, the continual "sedimentation of tradition" (Husserl 1970) across an entire history of such changes, which may be preserved beyond its immediate adaptive value through hysteresis, that is, a temporal lag reflecting respect for the practices of past venerable masters, i.e., a deference to the transmissive system itself.

Human mediation centers on the stability of an inner (*batin*) meaning, allowing outer (*zahir*) forms to vary adaptively throughout time and space (not least via translation), in part as a means of ensuring mediative continuity, relevance, and affective power across multiple social settings. In this way, the process of human mediation (primarily via oral tradition, though often supplemented by technologies of writing) itself offers a metaphysical metacommentary, underscoring that that which is essential is not the variable surface, but the eternal core; not the symbolic form, but the interior substance—a proposition common to mystical interpretations of Islam, and perhaps to mysticism generally. Sufism, Islamic mysticism (*tasawwuf*), supplies the quintessential instance of such mediation in the *silsilas* (initiatory chains) of its social orders (*turuq*), transmitting gnosis (*ma'rifa*) and blessing (*baraka*), though Islamic tradition is full of other examples from other fields, including music itself.

This concept of human mediation—aesthetic or intellectual—has always been counterposed by a completely different—indeed, converse—mode of transmission, through mass dissemination of *originary models*. Such models fix the form of a message, without ensuring uniformity of its interpreted meaning, thus precluding the ramifying genealogies of *human mediation*, ensuring an outward unity, without any guarantee of a corresponding inward one. In the past, these models (when they existed) necessarily assumed the linguistic form of a sequence of *discrete signs*, since it was only the sequence of sign pairs (signifier-signified) that could assure perfect reproduction, without change (much as digital media have enabled perfect reproduction today). Continuous aesthetic media (such as music) could not be reduced to such sequences, and, therefore, could not be fixed, without reductive quantization supplemented by additional technologies, either a rich symbolic notation approximating continuities (which the Islamic world, by and large, did not develop for music[4]), or—only recently—digital representations.

The outstanding example of an originary model is the Qur'an itself, required to appear always in Arabic, and to be recited in highly prescribed ways, as fixed by the so-called *ahkam al-tajwid* (Nelson 2001). The fact is that for many Muslims (the vast majority of whom are not fluent in Arabic), the text's mystery is founded, in part, on the simple fact that they cannot comprehend its language, though they may be able to recite it; they master the sonic phenomenon without mastering the text itself. The experience—perhaps often quite moving—of pronouncing incomprehensible sequences of sounds, almost a kind of incantation, can have little in common, however, with its largely lucid meaning for an Arabic speaker.

In fact, early on, Qur'anic transmission was humanly mediated. Following an initial period of genealogical branching in both written and oral forms, the tree was quite suddenly and drastically pruned, resulting in a single *mushaf* (written text), qualified by multiple *qira'at* (readings), as human mediation threatened to split the nascent community (Frishkopf 2009c).

The Prophet Muhammad began to receive revelations around 610 CE, as a quasi-aural communication from the Angel Jibril (aka Gabriel, who received them, likewise quasi-aurally, from God), not as a written text. Muslims affirm this aurality as critical to the proof of the Qur'an's status as revelation (*wahy*). The Prophet Muhammad was completely illiterate, a fact understood by Muslims to substantiate the Qur'an's divine origins[5] and the miracle (*mu'jiza*) validating his message (every genuine prophet being associated with one or more *mu'jizat*).

However, the Prophet's spiritual companions (*sahaba*) did write down his recitation of Qur'anic verses, using the simple Arabic script at their disposal (at this stage, Arabic letters not only omitted vowels, but also the dots that would later distinguish completely different consonants, such as /b/, /y/, /n/, /t/, /th/). Copies were made, and copies of copies, and soon variants were in circulation. The third caliph, 'Uthman, put a stop to this incipient diversity as a means of ensuring the unity of the Umma. As a *hadith* records:

> Narrated Anas bin Malik: Hudhaifa bin Al-Yaman came to 'Uthman at the time when the people of Sham and the people of Iraq were waging war to conquer Arminya and Adharbijan. Hudhaifa was afraid of their (the people of Sham and Iraq) differences in the recitation of the Qur'an, so he said to 'Uthman, "O chief of the Believers! Save this nation before they differ about the Book (Quran) as Jews and the Christians did before." So 'Uthman sent a message to Hafsa saying, "Send us the manuscripts of the Qur'an so that we may compile the Qur'anic materials in perfect copies and return the manuscripts to you." Hafsa sent it to 'Uthman. 'Uthman then ordered Zaid bin Thabit, 'Abdullah bin AzZubair, Said bin Al-As and 'AbdurRahman bin Harith bin Hisham to rewrite the manuscripts in perfect copies. 'Uthman said to the three Quraishi men, "In case you disagree with Zaid bin Thabit on any point in the Qur'an, then write it in the dialect of Quraish, the Qur'an was revealed in their tongue." They did so, and when they had written many copies, 'Uthman returned the original manuscripts to Hafsa. 'Uthman sent to every Muslim province one copy of what they had copied, and ordered that all the other Qur'anic materials, whether written in fragmentary manuscripts or whole copies, be burnt. Said [Zaid] bin Thabit added, "A Verse from Surat Ahzab was missed by me when we copied the Qur'an and I used to hear Allah's Apostle reciting it. So we searched for it and found it with Khuzaima bin Thabit Al-Ansari. (That Verse was): 'Among the Believers are men who have been true in their covenant with Allah.'" (33.23) (Sahih Bukhari, Volume 6, Book 61, Number 510)

Thereafter, through 'Uthman's extraordinarily bold move, there emerged a single, authoritative, written text, an originary model known as the Uthmanic *mushaf* (Sa'id 1975).

Additional problems, however, developed with the recitation (*tilawa*) of this unitary written version, since the absence of dots and vowel markings could lead to multiple linguistic vocalizations within the oral tradition of Qur'anic recitation (*tilawa*). In this case, diversity could not be eliminated entirely, but the number of variant "readings" (*qira'at*), each with a number of subreadings (*riwayat*), was fixed, as attributed to established reciters in a genealogy (Sa'id 1975). Differences could also be legitimized by the theory of so-called *ahruf*, which held that the Qur'an was revealed in seven different dialects as a means of enhancing comprehension among the various Arab tribes (*qaba'il*) of Arabia.

> Narrated 'Abdullah bin 'Abbas: Allah's Apostle said, "Gabriel recited the Qur'an to me in one way. Then I requested him (to read it in another way), and continued asking him to recite it in other ways, and he recited it in several ways till he ultimately recited it in seven different ways." (Sahih Bukhari Volume 6, Book 61, Number 513)

With the addition of diacritical markings on the 'Uthmanic base, the *mushaf* could be notated so as to indicate acceptable readings, while all other readings were rejected. Finally, human mediation had been removed from these notated readings, corresponding to those discrete aspects of *tilawa* (mainly, phonemic) that could be notated: the *qira'at* henceforth comprised a set of originary models, with which no reciter could ever tamper. But other paralinguistic sonic aspects of recitation—continuous parameters such as melodic shape, timbre, and timing—remained as "free variables" (Frishkopf 2009c) and continued to be transmitted via human mediation, enabling stylistic localizations to occur.

Much the same process led to the codification of four schools of law (*madhahib*) among the Sunnis and the codification of Hadith. In this way, the inherent diversity of human mediation, if not eliminable, could at least be managed—with respect to the linguistic phenomenon of texts.

SONIC PRACTICES AND REFORM

If the unity of the core Islamic text—the Qur'an itself—and legal schools could be assured in this way, the same was certainly not true of paralinguistic sonic practices (most classed as "music"), continuous and unbound by reference, which could not be systematically codified, and which therefore depended entirely on human mediation. Even the sound of the recited Qur'an, whose tonal characteristics were never regulated (or regulable) by *ahkam al-tajwid*, was not immune to sonic diversity; the improvisatory character of *tilawa* was required by some scholars, on theological grounds, to avoid melodic associations with the Qur'an, considered nearly a kind of *shirk* (associationism; see Nelson 2001). Sonic flexibility in timbral, tonal, and temporal domains, allowed even for the Qur'an, was enacted, a fortiori, for sonic practices more remote from the sacred core, including *adhan*, *ibtihalat*, and *madih*, which developed completely different sounds in Egypt, Turkey, Iran, and West Africa, for instance. But these differences, not easily represented in verbal discourse, tended not to cause problems for theories of Muslim unity during the period of Muslim ascendancy, perhaps in part because the territorialized differences were rarely juxtaposed in practice.

Least regulable were the "popular" ritual-sonic practices that ramified worldwide through human mediation, primarily in oral form. Such localization of "popular Islam" occurred primarily in two species of context: birthday celebrations for the Prophet and saints (*mawalid*) (Schacht 1965; Hiskett 1973; Boyd 1981; Monts and Monts 2001; al-Hilawi 1984; Boyd 2001; Faruqi 1986; Giles 1989; *Égypte: ordre chazili* 1992; Karrar 1992; Kaptein 1993; *Comores* 2004; Shadhiliyah and Helbawy 1999; Corke et al. 2003; Foulani 2000; Orwin 2001; Topp Fargion 2000; Waugh 2005) and rituals of the Sufi orders (Gilsenan 1973; Qureshi 1987; Diagne 1996; Karrar 1992; Frishkopf 1999, 2001; Ben Mahmoud 2000; Aichi 2001; Duvelle 2003; Waugh 2005; Trimingham 1998), since these occasions, themselves the result of human mediation, fell outside the scope of canonical Islam of the *madhahib*. Thus musical and ritual developments tended to accumulate, through human mediation, together. But they occurred more generally—because logically—in performance culture, especially music, that could not be fixed by written expressions.

Modern Islamic reform can be traced to nineteenth- and early-to-mid twentieth-century thinkers such as Sayyid Ahmad Khan (1817–1898), Jamal al-Din al-Afghani (1838–1897), Muhammad Abdu (1849–1905), Rashid Rida (1865–1935), Muhammad Iqbal (1876–1938), Sayyid Abu al-Ala Mawdudi (1903–1979), and Sayyid Qutb (1906–1966). Only since the mid-twentieth century have Islamic reform movements based on their ideas developed a mass appeal beyond a relatively narrow stratum of intellectuals. The real diversity of these movements—including what have been labeled Islamic reform (*islah*), revival (*tajdid*), Salafism, and Wahhabism—also masks a fundamental similarity, by comparison to earlier currents of reform and revival. These earlier waves of reform, having a primary objective of correcting spirituality, occurred while Islam was still globally ascendant to some degree, from the seventh-century al-Hasan al-Basri (Knysh 2000), to Ibn Taymiyya, to eighteenth-century reformists such as Muhammad ibn Abd al-Wahhab (Haj 2009) and Ahmad al-Tijani (Abun-Nasr 1965).

By contrast, modern Islamic reform has developed as a strategy for a subaltern Islam, designed to homogenize ritual practice, unify the global Umma, and thereby re-empower Islam against the West, following a precipitous decline resulting from the onslaughts of European colonialism (and later from the spread of Western-originated secular-nationalist ideologies, capitalism, and globalization).

Where modern reform differed from earlier thinkers and movements was in its response to this decline (and the forces behind it), and in its ironic tendency to adopt paradigms and content—albeit selectively—from the very Western civilization it ostensibly opposed, stressing, in particular, reason over emotion, rationality over mysticism, unity over diversity, and derivations from first principles (in the Qur'an and Sunna). In search of exoteric social unity, modern reformers from the nineteenth century onwards emphasized replicable discursive messages—originary models—to the detriment or even exclusion of the spiritual-aesthetic riches carried by human mediation, since the latter, for all of their localized spiritual-social value, also underscored the outward cultural divisions of the Umma. If the way of spiritual feeling could demonstrate the inner, essential unity of Islamic spirituality as a single message clothed in multiple outward forms for the mystic, the same multiplicity—each form representing the localization effected by a long chain of human mediation—simultaneously contradicted that unity for the nonmystic more concerned with political empowerment than spiritual essences. Mystical ecstasy was henceforth to be perceived not only as antithetical to Islamic dynamism, unity, and empowerment, but to Western values of reason and modernity as well.

The new reformers, seeking unity (beyond culture) and reason (toward social action), became increasingly intolerant of Islam's cultural differences and impatient with mystical emotion (at best producing torpor and lassitude, at worst representing *shirk* of the most noxious kind, culminating in mystical identity with God). The diversity of ritual localizations was not only criticized as politically ineffective, but also charged as instantiating *bid'a*, "innovation." From early on, the Arabic concept of *bid'a* was developed in religious terms as denoting a practice (usually a ritual practice) not grounded in Sunna. Originally carrying a pejorative meaning, the term became nuanced through legal usage, with the differentiation of positive (*bid'a hasana*) and negative (*bid'a sayyi'a*) types (Fierro 1992; Rispler 1991). During this period, the *bid'a* label did not necessarily constitute a condemnation. Judgments about *bid'a* occurred throughout Islamic history as a corrective to spiritual practice.

However, in the modern period *bid'a* tends to be used increasingly in its negative sense, and in a strategic manner: not as a means of fostering proper Islamic spirituality, but as a social tool for censure, seeking the elimination of ritual diversity and the unification of the Umma, as a strategy toward re-empowerment. In reformist circles one constantly hears a *hadith*, offered as a means of reducing ritual variety, emphasizing *bid'a* as unequivocally neg-ative: "the worst of all things are novelties (*muhdathat*); every novelty is in-novation (*bid'a*), every innovation is error (*dalala*) and every error leads to hell" (attributed to Imam Ahmad al-Nasa'i). While not all reformists uni-formly reject *bid'a*, there is a general tendency to reject diversity of ritual practice through accusations of *bid'a*, while the most uncompromising re-formists reject all *bid'a* absolutely.

Thus one contemporary reformist website asks, "WHY ARE WE SO DI-VIDED?," answering, "Because of Shirk, innovations and leaving the Sun-nah . . . Allah has informed us in the Qur'an that He has completed this reli-gion of Islam. . . . Since the religion is complete how can it be that we need to add new things and ways of worship to Islam? . . . So how can we come together upon something as dangerous as innovations, such as the innova-tions of mystics, who practice all kinds of weird and innovated invocations?" (Hoor al-Ayn). The same website unequivocally denounces the *mawlid* as equally *bid'a*.

This tendency toward intolerance of religious differences, even those in-ternal to Islam, could be supported through reference to another *hadith*, cited by al-Tirmidhi:

> 'Abdullah ibn 'Amr reported that Allah's Messenger (peace and blessings be upon him) said, "My Umma will face that which the Banu Isra'il faced. . . . the Banu Isra'il divided into seventy-two sects and my Umma will divide into seventy-three sects, all of whom will enter the Fire except one." (The Prophet's companions) asked (him), "Which one, O Messenger of Allah?" He said, "That of myself and my companions." (Sunan al-Tirmidhi, Book of Faith, 2641; translation by author)

Modern reformism became a mass political movement in the mid-twentieth century with the founding of the Muslim Brothers (*al-ikhwan al-muslimun*) by Hasan al-Banna in Egypt, cross-fertilizing with the older Wahhabi move-ment in Saudi Arabia and inspiring like movements elsewhere. Egypt's losses in the 1967 war with Israel, and the consequent discrediting of Nasserism, provided a boost to Islamism as a viable alternative.

However, the rise of global Islamic reformism only occurred after 1973, when Arab oil producers cut production and Saudi Arabia suspended petro-leum shipments to the United States. The price of oil tripled overnight, and producers—especially Saudi Arabia—enjoyed a dramatic increase in revenues and global influence (Vassiliev 2000, 401). King Faisal (r. 1964–1975) exploited post-1973 windfalls to develop his country, a policy continued by King Khaled (r. 1975–1982). Many Muslims interpreted this new wealth and power as a divine vindication of Saudi-style piety. Saudi Arabia's newfound wealth and global power modernized Wahhabism, which subsequently drew closer to Egypt's more progressive, and burgeoning, reformist trends. Through the early twentieth century, many Wahhabis had rejected even technological "innovations" such as electricity. From the mid-twentieth century, however, mainstream Wahhabi views were tempered—and empowered—by oil wealth (and concomitant close relations to Western powers), as well as by interactions with Egyptian reformism. Such "neo-Wahhabism" embraces modern technology, capitalism, and consumerism and, buoyed by oil, has become extremely powerful worldwide (Peskes and Ende 2006).

CANADA AS A MODERN REFORMIST LANDSCAPE

In traditionally Muslim regions of the world, modern reformism, with its emphasis on originary models, overlaid older Islamic cultural patterns, as evolved via human mediation, without ever erasing them entirely. In competition, each discourse laid its claims: one to the literate authority of the intelligentsia (typically educated in global centers such as Cairo or Saudi Arabia, and oriented toward an understanding of the West), the other to the localized heritage of "popular Islam" (Gaffney 1992). Frequently, discursive conflict would pit local Islamic culture against the reformist worldview, e.g., in Egypt, where dozens of Sufi orders thrive, and tens of thousands of *mawalid* are celebrated, if open to criticism (Johansen 1996; Frishkopf 1999), or in Ghana, where a well-established Sufi order, the Tijaniyya, regularly clashes with a Wahhabi-inspired reformist group, the Ahl al-Sunna wa al-Jamaʿa, over ritual differences, especially in regards to celebration of the Prophet's *mawlid*, veneration of *shaykhs*, use of musical instruments, and mixed-gender dance (Ryan 1996; Frishkopf 2009a). But Canada provides a receptive environment for a particular brand of reformist thought, one that is necessarily tolerant of non-Muslims, but not at all tolerant of Muslim difference, and which consequently provides little space for ritual diversity and its aesthetic elaborations, including musical ritual.

This fact is not merely a feature of Muslim communities in the West, for Canada evinces a stronger presence of reformism even when compared to other Western sites of Muslim immigration, especially in Europe, whose Muslim practices are more diverse. Why should this be the case? And why is musical ritual so scarce? Before exploring the social dynamics of Islam in

Canada, it is helpful to consider the historical and demographic dimensions of Muslim immigration there.

DEMOGRAPHIC BACKGROUND

Muslims began to emigrate to Canada during the late nineteenth century, though in 1931 there were still reportedly only 645 Muslim residents in Canada, mostly Arabs; Canada's first mosque (al-Rashid) was founded in Edmonton in 1938, by twenty Lebanese Muslim families (Abu Laban 1983, 80–81). Drawing heavily on the Middle East and South Asia, Muslim populations across Canada expanded rapidly after 1990 (see Figure 4.1 for the distribution of Muslims over the different provinces). In 2009, Canada's Muslim population was estimated at 657,000, or roughly 2 percent of the population, considerably higher than other immigrant societies of the developed world, such as those in the USA (0.8 percent, or 2,454,000 Muslims), Australia (1.7 percent, or 365,000), or New Zealand (0.9 percent, or 37,000), though not as high as those in the Netherlands (5.7 percent, or 946,000), Germany (5 percent, or 4,026,000), France (6 percent, or 3,554,000), or Britain (2.7 percent, or 1,647,000) (Mapping the Global Muslim Population 2009). As is shown in Figure 4.2, the ethnic background of the Muslim population of Canada is highly diverse.

Another important characteristic of the Canadian Muslim population is its high educational level. The Muslim full-time school attendance rate is more than double that of the general population, indicating a relatively well-educated population (see figure 4.3). Rates for master's and PhD degrees within the Muslim population are more than double those of the general population; bachelor's rates are 1.7 times the general rate (see figure 4.4).

By contrast, Muslims are far less likely to receive working-class credentials, such as a trades certificate (0.56 times the general rate; see figure 4.5) (StatsCan 2001e). The Muslim rate of employment in science and technology (mostly requiring postsecondary education) exceeds that of the general population by a ratio of nearly 2:1, while Muslims are proportionally underrepresented in the trades, and primary industry jobs (StatsCan 2001c), most of them working-class. Muslim participation rates in social science and arts/culture are significantly below the national average, implying relative lack of participation in civil society, though Canadian Islamic organizations such as the Canadian Islamic Congress are actively addressing this issue.

Despite well-established roots, the bulk of the Muslim community is first-generation. As figures 4.6 and 4.7 indicate, immigrants among the Muslim population greatly exceeded (over 70 percent) those in the total population (less than 20 percent) in 2001, when measured as a percentage of the total number in each group.

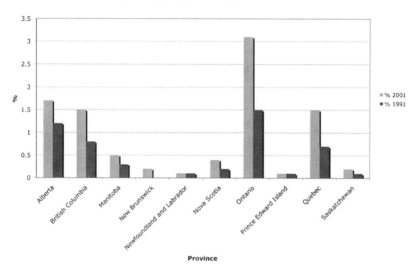

Muslims as percentage of provincial populations: 1991 and 2001

FIGURE 4.1. Muslims in Canada, as a percentage of provincial populations (1991, 2001) (StatsCan 2001b).

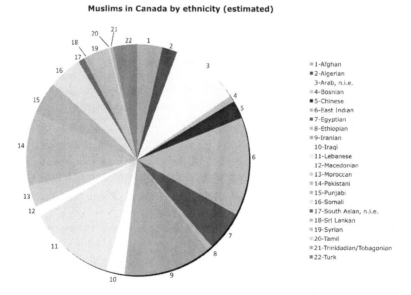

Muslims in Canada by ethnicity (estimated)

* 1-Afghan
* 2-Algerian
  3-Arab, n.i.e.
* 4-Bosnian
* 5-Chinese
* 6-East Indian
* 7-Egyptian
* 8-Ethiopian
* 9-Iranian
  10-Iraqi
  11-Lebanese
  12-Macedonian
* 13-Moroccan
* 14-Pakistani
* 15-Punjabi
  16-Somali
* 17-South Asian, n.i.e.
* 18-Sri Lankan
* 19-Syrian
  20-Tamil
* 21-Trinidadian/Tobagonian
* 22-Turk

FIGURE 4.2. Muslims in Canada are ethnically diverse. Estimate derived from Pew Report (Mapping the Global Muslim Population 2009), combined with Statistics Canada 2001 census data on ethnicity (StatsCan 2001f). (n.i.e. = not included elsewhere)

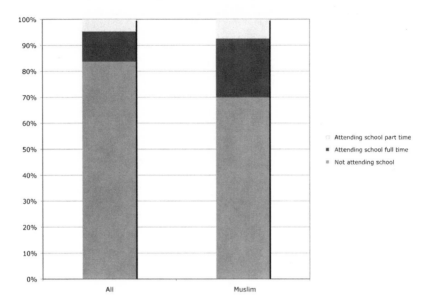

FIGURE 4.3. School attendance rates in Canada, Muslim vs. All (2001 census data) (StatsCan 2001e).

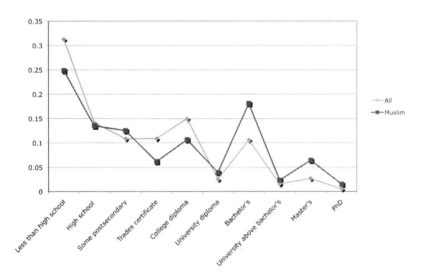

FIGURE 4.4. Educational level rates in Canada, Muslim vs. All (2001 census data), demonstrating Muslim professionalism in Canada (StatsCan 2001e).

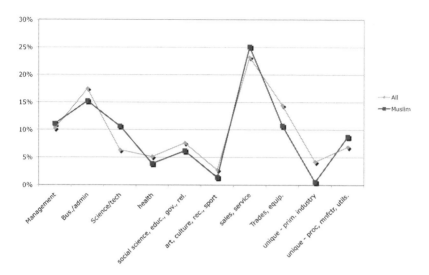

FIGURE 4.5. Census data indicate a high Muslim rate of employment in science and technology (StatsCan 2001c).

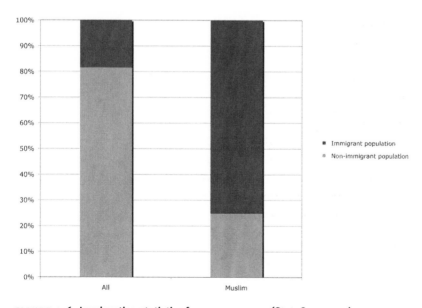

FIGURE 4.6. Immigration statistics from 2001 census (StatsCan 2001a).

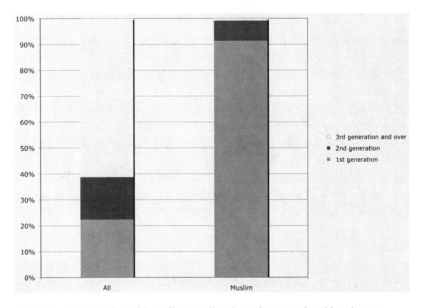

FIGURE 4.7. Proportion of Canadian Muslims in each generational bracket, as compared to the general population (2001 census data) (StatsCan 2001d).

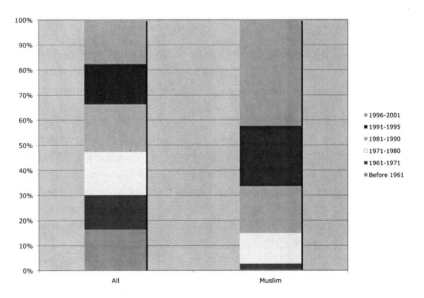

FIGURE 4.8. Proportion of Canadian Muslim immigrants by immigration period, as compared to the general immigrant population (StatsCan 2001a).

Muslim immigration in Canada is also comparatively recent: in 2001, nearly 70 percent of Muslim immigration had taken place in the previous ten years, as compared to only 32 percent for the general immigrant population (see figure 4.8).

In summary, Islam in Canada presents some sui generis demographic attributes: Canadian Muslim immigration is relatively recent, ethnically diverse, geographically far-flung, and significantly weighted toward higher educational levels and elite professions.

THE LOGIC OF MUSICAL SILENCE

In speculating about my opening "why" questions, I will rely on system theoretic concepts, applied to the particular context of the Muslim diaspora in Canada: as a religious minority (itself doctrinally heterogeneous), and as a diverse collection of linguistic-ethnic minorities, embedded within a multicultural, pluralistic, open civil society. This Canadian society is theoretically tolerant of difference, but rife with prejudice in practice, always rent not just by the contradiction between subcultural practices and the Canadian Charter of Rights and Freedoms (Canada's bill of rights), but also, at a logical level, by the paradox of "the tolerance of intolerance."

Here I'll introduce two key system theoretic ideas, one psychocultural and the other sociological.

On the psychocultural side is a kind of functionalism I derive primarily from anthropologist Mary Douglas, holding that the essential problem confronting human beings is to make sense of a chaotic environment, thus mitigating the existential strain of living. Social groups establish classificatory coherence by creating and maintaining sharply defined symbolic boundaries (establishing "pure" categories), and forbidding that which challenges their clarity: the danger of symbolic impurity (Douglas 2005). Ritual is a domain whose clear boundaries must be maintained by safeguarding the separation between ritual space-time and ordinary life. Music, while frequently crucial to the symbolic and affective power of ritual performance, also challenges ritual boundaries by crossing back and forth into entertainment, and many of the critiques hurled against ritual musical practices throughout Islamic history can be understood as a reaction to what may be perceived as a dangerous blurring of boundaries between ritual space-time and music's profane environment. This psychocultural observation provides insights in many social contexts, but, I will argue, with special significance in the Canadian diaspora.

On the sociocultural side, I will invoke Gregory Bateson's concept of schismogenesis, the progressive polarization of relations between social groups as a result of communicative feedback between them (Bateson 1972).

In this case, I'm interested in what he termed "complementary schismogenesis" between unequal groups, here between the Muslim diasporic community and the broader non-Muslim society. Indeed, the same cybernetic concept can help explain the progressive separation and crystallization of symbolic categories (such as what is ritually proper, and what is not) resulting from the dangers of symbolic impurity highlighted by Douglas.

ANTIMUSIC POLEMICS IN ISLAM . . .
AND ISLAM IN CANADA

Certainly there is a long history of antimusic polemic in Islamic cultures (Shiloah 1997; Nelson 2001), and the contemporary Canadian case has to be interpreted in this context, which is, however, insufficient to explain it completely. In other words, the lack of musical ritual in Canada cannot be understood as yet another case of Muslim antimusic sentiment.

Within Islamic jurisprudence (*fiqh*) and Sufism, the question was often raised, throughout Islamic history, as to whether music is *halal* (acceptable). And the usual answer was "no," music is *haram* (forbidden), or (for the Sufis) "yes" but only under particular conditions.

The case against music was really twofold: (1) musical entertainment is a distraction from God, and guilty by long-standing association with other *haram* practices, particularly alcohol and illicit sex; (2) musical practice *qua* ritual worship (*samaʿ*) is a heretical innovation (*bidʿa*), linked to the evils of music generally, and more specifically to fears, among *ʿulama*, of deviation from Islam's straight path via aesthetic-mystical experiences. Even voices relatively favorable to *samaʿ*, such as that of al-Ghazzali, carefully circumscribed the proper conditions for its spiritual performance (al-Ghazzali and Macdonald 1901).

However, despite this long-standing and often fierce polemic, a few facts should be borne in mind: First, until contemporary times, neither Islam nor Islamic civilization could ever be characterized as predominantly antimusic, even if certain legists railed against particular practices.[6] Second, throughout some 1,300 years of successful Islamic expansion, globalization occurred via localization, including absorption of local musical practices into Islamic ones. Rather than producing sectarianism and weakness, outward diversity became essential both in adapting to a wide array of pre-Islamic cultures and in demonstrating Islam's inner spiritual unity, and ironically supported the cohesion of the Umma through affective potency deriving from local rootedness. Third, musicality in Islamic ritual is carried by long-standing oral traditions; legal critiques from a small minority coexisted with acceptance, for centuries, from the vast majority.[7] Besides, the intellectual sources of a widespread popular movement generally opposing accretion of diverse Islamic oral traditions (including musical rituals) as irrational, divisive, enfeebling, backwards, and heretical innovations (*bid'a*) and advocating a global return to origins (Qur'an and Sunna) only began to flourish in the late nineteenth century with modern reformists, such as Shaykh Muhammad Abdu. Moreover, these reformist trends only developed a mass popular following with the advent of the Muslim Brothers in Egypt, in the late 1920s. This movement focused on fostering an active, "rational," dynamic Islam and outwardly unified Umma, as opposed to what was perceived as a passive, mystical, emotional Islam of inaction, apparently divided by the highly ramified, localized oral traditions that had developed, over the course of many centuries, via human mediation.

As a consequence, global Islam shifted its preferred mode of transmission from the ramified and locally adapted "human mediation" mode of the past to a centralized, mass-disseminated originary model, to be imitated throughout the Umma for all time. That which could not be clearly established by reference to the Qur'an and Sunna, a vastly variegated spiritual heritage that had developed gradually over time through humanly mediated transmission, whose value and originary legitimacy could not be rationally demonstrated, was frequently eviscerated as *bid'a*. This originary model not only critiqued musical rituals, but was also intrinsically incapable of representing them. For instance, *tajwid* manuals, supposedly rooted in prophetic practice, never elaborate the melodic principles of recitation, despite the widely acknowledged importance of melody and melodic modes (*maqamat*) in *tajwid* (Nelson 2001).

Even then, the social scope of antimusic Islamic discourse remained relatively limited until the 1970s explosion of political Islam and the oil-fueled empowerment of conservative Wahhabi propaganda. Since then, a new global Islam has emerged, extending beyond political concerns, claiming for itself the label of a universal Islam, and seeking to erase its own historicity, as well as competing models.

Despite all this, one finds highly musical rituals throughout the Muslim-majority world, still carried via humanly mediated transmission, now operating in parallel with the newer originary, reformist models . . . and not only in narrowly defined Sufi contexts. Indeed, it would even be entirely wrong to stereotype Wahhabism as antimusic in the general terms I've outlined— by non-Muslim standards, at least, the call to prayer in Mecca is a musical masterpiece, performed by dedicated and widely appreciated specialists, who have developed their talents through humanly mediated oral traditions.

Thus the lack of musicality, the aesthetic deficiency, of Canada's Muslim community cannot be understood simply as a local manifestation of a global phenomenon. The particular dynamics of Islam in Canadian society require further scrutiny, with reference to the nature of Canadian society, and via theoretical recourse to concepts of purity, danger, and schismogenesis.

SYSTEM THEORY AND MUSICAL RITUAL IN CANADA

If modern reformism were strongly shaped by the challenges and values posed by the West, then logically reformism should thrive among Muslims based in the West, in a proximate environment placing primary value on reason, unity, and principles, rather than humanly mediated oral traditions. But Canada is also different than Europe.

Canada boasts an open immigrant society, multicultural, pluralistic, and theoretically tolerant. Ironically, however, the cultural politics of Canadian multiculturalism pushes minority groups toward closure, stifling internal diversity as a means of translating "minority capital" into political capital. Subgroups strive for internal unity in order to empower themselves within the broader multicultural social environment.

The Canadian Muslim community is unprecedented in its cultural diversity. But for many Canadian Muslims of reformist disposition, the intra-community juxtaposition of cultural contrasts highlights the need to unify Islam by excising humanly mediated localizations imported from immigrants' home countries, i.e., by differentiating "Islamic religion" (defined via originary models) from "Muslim cultures," in order to emphasize a "purely Islamic" basis for unity. This process, I would argue, is structurally compatible with the strategies of the Muslim reformers, who have for the past century likewise sought to erase internal difference: to homogenize via appeal to originary models as a means of unifying the Umma in practice. But the necessity for such an operation is accentuated when cultural differences are juxtaposed in a single community, a phenomenon that hardly arises in historically Muslim regions of the world, where localized practices are territorialized.

Since the prevailing globalized Islamic discourse is reformist, and because the intersubjective lifeworld processes of human mediation tend to be broken by Canadian immigration, which admits primarily well-educated professionals (this phenomenon is further discussed later on), reformist discourse, disseminated via circulation of an originary model independent of human mediation, has achieved a powerful sway in Canada.

Official Canadian tolerance also masks a logical paradox, the problem of the "tolerance of intolerance," an issue repeatedly raised with respect to Muslim communities regarded by many Canadians as hopelessly backwards in various practices, particularly regarding the status of women. Muslim communities are not pressured to assimilate, but neither are they generally accepted. Muslim communities, in turn, are rightly on the defensive, particularly in the wake of 9/11, due to the prevalence of stereotypes, Islamophobia, and resulting discrimination.

At the same time, the Muslim immigrant lacks the social connections to the broader society enjoyed by, say, a Christian Ghanaian, who may find a more ready social acceptance through church groups, or by Jews, most of whom are not visible minorities and who have been widely accepted (along with their interests) by the North American political-economic establishment for several decades. De facto anti-Muslim intolerance in the broader society is matched by Muslim intolerance, expressed in discourse about living in the *dar al-harb* ("land of war," i.e., outside Muslim rule) and *hadith* warning against mixing with non-Muslims.

As a result, a schismogenetic cycle emerges, pushing Muslim and non-Muslim communities apart. For their part, reformist Muslims may seize on any feature of the wider society by which to differentiate themselves, and one of these is the prominent role of music in both secular and Christian religious contexts. Proclaiming "music is forbidden in Islam" (among other reformist slogans) thus becomes one means of expressing Muslim identity within Canadian society, at once a statement of reformist identity and a force for unification by denying intrareligious cultural difference. It's also a way of prioritizing issues: as did Muslim modernists of the nineteenth century, members of Muslim organizations in Canada often feel more keenly the need to address social concerns—discrimination and stereotyping, and the dangers of assimilation—than to pursue pure spirituality, a fortiori the aesthetic kind. Thus schismogenetic differentiation is accompanied by a countervailing pursuit of power in Canadian society at large.

Nevertheless, I hold that ritual (even when drained of its sonic-aesthetic force) remains critical to the constitution of Muslim community in Canada. Whereas in Egypt or Syria one's Muslim identity can be taken for granted regardless of practice, the same is not so for Canada. Social theorists have recently emphasized performativity in the construction and maintenance of identity. I suggest that perhaps performativity plays a more critical identity-maintenance role for minority groups living within a multicultural secular society that constantly threatens to absorb them. If this is so, then ritual purity is likewise more critical than it would otherwise be. And reformist ritual is oriented toward developing social unity, and consequent social power, at a moment when Muslims in the West are threatened from multiple quarters.

Under such conditions, the prevailing response to any ritual change not supported by the widely disseminated originary models—injecting a musical component, for instance—is not primarily condemnation, but fear. Overtly, this fear is expressed in the religious discourse of *bid'a*—the danger of spiritual innovations—but sociologically it can be understood rather differently as the fear of identity loss, perhaps via the conflation of multifarious "cultures" threatening the desired unity of "religion," and resulting in disunity and disempowerment. Among first-generation immigrants, reasoned rejection and fear of musical ritual may be accompanied by a pleasantly nostalgic emotional response deriving from memories of familiar practices of the homeland; however, the second generation, lacking such nostalgia, is more likely to respond with rejection, intellectual and emotional (Frishkopf 2009b).

For the most part, Canadian Muslims have marked themselves off from the broader society as those who fast in Ramadan, eat no pork, drink no alcohol, pray, and perhaps (especially for females) dress in a particular way. These practices are strategies for defining differences as a means of identity maintenance; in Canada it is difficult for anyone to claim to be an authentic Muslim (especially vis-à-vis other Muslims) without performing them in public, at least in the mosque (and in certain situations they are actually enforced[8]). By contrast, Muslim identity in traditionally Muslim regions of the world tends to be far less dependent on its performance; indeed, the status of being Muslim exists as a quasi-embodied property (akin to gender), nearly independent of the degree to which it is performed. But for the sake of emphasizing one's Muslim identity in Canada, "ritual music" is most usefully invoked not to be performed, but to be denied, thus generating a productive marker of difference.

Furthermore, immigration tends to break whatever chains of oral tradition remain active in global Islam. An immigrant Muslim community, particularly in its second generation, relies to a greater extent on the written word for religious guidance, and is thus ever more susceptible to the effects of global Islamism, advocated and carried by originary models. Particularly when languages of the homeland are lost (in the second generation), and connections to sacred places (e.g., saints' shrines) associated with affecting ritual performance are broken, the immigrant community tends to fall back upon Islamic texts translated and globally distributed by reformists. Such discourses become powerful tools for inducing collective amnesia, erasing centuries of oral tradition as if it had never existed.[9] As a corollary, it is clear that the value of the arts and aesthetic experience, along with mystical experience, is lost in the process, because the production of the spiritual arts depends crucially on human mediation, and because the experience of the spiritual arts resists linguistic capture.

Thus far much the same might be surmised for European Muslim communities. But particularities of the Canadian immigration processes play a critical role in shaping the particularities of Islam in Canada. There, immigration only began opening up to non-Europeans in the late 1960s, according to a rationalized "point system" rewarding higher education, particularly in practical fields the government deemed critical to the Canadian economy. As a consequence of this "high-pass filter" system, an overwhelming majority of recent Muslim immigrants arrive in Canada with training in applied science, especially engineering. The same filter tends to preclude immigration of artists and intellectuals. As in Egypt, where the Muslim Brothers draw the bulk of their membership from professions centered on closed and bounded systems, including medicine (the body), law (legal code), or engineering (the project at hand), a system approach tends to transfer to religious practice as reformism.

In the reformist model, Islam is itself such a closed system: a practice derivable—like mathematics—from axiomatic texts (Qur'an and Sunna) necessary and sufficient for regulating human life on earth. According to these very texts, the system is closed, bounded, and complete, regulating order within a formless and chaotic environment.[10] To admit any other truth or interpretation is impurity, danger—*kufr* (unbelief). One does not blur the line between system and environment (lest one jeopardize this certainty), much less critique the system itself. Everything is built with apparently unassailable rationality and logic—as attested by a prevalent apologetic reformist discourse regarding the compatibility between Islamic faith and modern science.

Here, then, lies the primary difference between Islam in Europe and in Canada. European Muslim immigrants, many of whom arrived as unskilled laborers, are more uniformly spread across social classes and professions than in Canada, whose Muslims are more highly educated than the general population. As a result, Muslim communities in Britain, Germany, France, and elsewhere in Europe, typically dominated by the cultures of former colonies (e.g., South Asia in Britain, North Africa in France), are better able to reconstitute (in microcosm) the Muslim communities of their home countries, including musical-ritual experts capable of reproducing musical-ritual practices. Muslim migration to Canada, by contrast, drawing primarily on the upper and professional classes across a wide array of Muslim countries, tends to produce new kinds of Muslim community in Canada, of a sort not found in the countries of origin. These communities typically lack musical-ritual experts carrying oral traditions of localized Islam. Indeed, in these communities, contrasting practices, carried by immigrants from multiple sites of Islamic localization, are highlighted for removal as merely "cultural," and hence extraneous to "true Islam."

Rather, when Muslim immigrants choose to practice Islam in Canada,[11] these relatively elite, well-educated Muslims center their attention on "proper" ritual performance according to originary sacred texts (mainly Hadith and originary reformist texts) circulated globally (ever more rapidly via cyberspace). For Canadian reformist Muslims, the inner spiritual wealth produced by adaptive chains of humanly mediated culture is construed as a threat to Islamic unity, particularly in urban, ethnically heterogeneous Muslim communities where such culture can be expected to be diverse.

Whereas earlier reformists sought a modernist unity as a means to reestablish the *khilafa* and ultimately to challenge the West on its own terms, Canadian reformists (and many others who succumb to peer pressure), professionally successful and inhabiting a relatively tolerant society, tend to harbor more modest goals: to establish unified Muslim communities enjoying freedom of religious expression, without persecution or discrimination, and to ensure the reproduction of that community via the Muslim upbringing and marriage of their children. At first these communities remained aloof from the broader society, focusing on building a modern Islamic practice in conformity to reformist ideology, in an inward-looking strategy of social unity and Islamic reform, a result of the schismogenetic cybernetic loop traced earlier.

These goals have proved difficult to achieve, however, especially in the post-9/11 world, in which the non-Muslim majority increasingly associates Islam with militancy and terrorism, and Islamophobia is rampant. Therefore Islamic reform in North America has had to counteract the systemic tendency toward schismogenetic differentiation in certain respects, reorienting itself for broader social engagement on a nonspiritual level, to combat discrimination, stereotyping, and journalistic bias. Muslim leaders began to realize that Muslims, occupying comfortable niches in professions such as medicine, engineering, and small business, needed to involve themselves also in social leadership and public policy and encouraged Muslim youth to pursue careers in law, politics, journalism, and broadcasting (see Shaikh 2006 below). This is now beginning to happen, particularly in the second and higher generations. Nevertheless, ritual (and, more broadly, performative) conformity remains a key strategy for unifying Muslim communities as they begin to engage the broader society, as a means for achieving social influence.

This new outward-looking reformism is visible in the public discourse of two prominent Canadian Muslim organizations. Neither discourse prioritizes spiritual development, much less the aesthetic means traditionally developed for its facilitation.

NATIONAL AND LOCAL STRATEGIES

Perhaps the most prominent national Muslim organization in Canada is the Canadian Islamic Congress (CIC), which provides a good example of strategic reformism directed toward social goals (internal and external) in a recent article posted on its website:

On Monday July 3, 2006 nearly 70 Canadian Muslims from Toronto, Vancouver, Winnipeg, London, Ottawa, Montreal and Waterloo gathered at
the Islamic Centre of York Region to generate a common strategy for the
Muslim community in Canada.

The six-hour meeting, which took a 90–minute break for lunch and
Zuhr prayer, was jointly organized by the Canadian Islamic Congress, Toronto Muslim Unity Group, and the Muslim Council of Montreal. Their
aim was to create a forum through which the Muslim community's challenges could be identified, as well as to generate both short- and long-term
solutions to these challenges. (Shaikh 2006)

The Congress identified the following challenges facing Canadian Muslims:

1. Negative stereotyping of Muslims by the media.
2. Islamophobia.
3. The need for more integration; including removal of discrimination bar-
   riers against Muslims and by encouraging more Muslim participation in
   Canada's political process.
4. The effects of Canada's move toward the political right.
5. Internal divisions in the national Muslim community along lines of gender, generation, culture, wealth, ethnicity, language, religious practices,
   etc.
6. Improving the quality and quantity of Canadian Muslims who can successfully manage their economic, social and political environment.
7. A Canadian foreign policy that appears to be increasingly against the
   Muslim world.
8. The lack of consensus and community building mechanisms among Canadian Muslims.
9. The need for more Muslims in significant professions, such as law, journalism, etc. (Shaikh 2006)

Reformist ideology is clearly in evidence here in the importance assigned
both to unity and identity, as well as integration and assumption of more
influential social positions. The Congress focuses exclusively on sociopolitical problems of ordinary Canadian social reality. Challenges posed by metaphysical reality are not in evidence. Nor are the aesthetic catalysts traditionally deployed to accelerate spiritual advancement.

An example at the local level is provided by the al-Rashid mosque of Edmonton. The original al-Rashid mosque, built in the 1930s, has been moved
to a historical park (Fort Edmonton), while a new facility, known as the Canadian Islamic Centre, includes a mosque and additional services. Discourse
from the Centre's website clearly exhibits strategic emphasis upon social in-

fluence, education, and unity, framed in the typical business-speak of management consultants ("mission," "vision," "goals").

> *CIC Mission Statement:*
> The CIC strives to foster better citizens and effective leaders for the future of the community; by providing a proper, financially stable and most conducive environment for the Muslims of Edmonton through quality religious, cultural, educational and social services & programs. An environment supported by a solid and sustainable organizational capacity.
> *Vision Statement:*
> Muslims of Edmonton are a strong community; well educated and knowledgeable; financially stable and independent; positive and influential leaders. Contributing constructively to society's betterment and advancement.
> *Goals:*
> 1. Produce 100 community leaders
> 2. Establish a progressive and dynamic youth organization
> 3. Establish financial stability throughout the organization
> 4. Establish quality programs and services (profitable and social)
> 5. Increase community and volunteer engagement involvement
> 6. Improve communications
> 7. Build a strong and organized internal foundation (CIC Mission and Vision 2009)

Neither the Canadian Islamic Congress nor al-Rashid mosque centers its discourses on Islam's central metaphysical aim (to worship God through submission, *islam*, in preparation for the hereafter) or Sufism's more mystical interpretation (to experience the Divine Reality in this life), much less on the sacred aesthetic media traditionally deployed for achieving it. Rather, these organizations emphasize strategies for solving this-worldly social problems characterizing a minority religious community in a theoretically tolerant immigrant society promising social influence for subgroups who can unify themselves by rallying round common concerns.

RITUAL AS STRATEGIC ACTION AND
THE ERASURE OF AESTHETIC PRACTICE

Modern Islamic reformism has tended to delete localized aesthetic Muslim ritual (as it had adaptively developed after centuries in Muslim regions from West Africa to Indonesia, the end product of long chains of human mediation) brought to Canada by immigrants, in favor of a deaestheticized ritual uniformity. For modern reformists, sacred, localized aesthetic culture is *bidʿa*, not grounded in originary canonical texts (indeed often not representable in language and thus not susceptible to originary formulation), and both symptom and cause of a premodern devotional diversity that has induced disunity and torpor in the Umma, and thus its disempowerment in the modern world.

A number of factors have accentuated modern Islamic reformism in Canada. Canada is primarily an immigrant society. Most Canadian Muslim immigration is recent, drawing heavily on post-1970 currents of global reformism, and it is culturally diverse. Generally speaking, immigration tends to disconnect Muslims from those sacred places, times, and rituals—scattered throughout their lands of origin—marking the multiple Islamic localizations that are anathema for reformers. Canadian immigration's "high-pass" social filtering also breaks the chains of oral traditions carrying localizations. In Canada, these factors further combine with a felt need for social unity among a religious minority subjected to schismogenetically amplified unifying forces, both exogenous (e.g., theoretical multicultural tolerance combined with Islamophobia in practice) and endogenous (e.g., the juxtaposition of Muslim cultural differences, thereby highlighted for elimination as extra-Islamic). The practical need for Muslims to solve pressing social problems (discrimination, the dangers of assimilation, and the lack of Muslim education) and the system mentality of Canadian Muslim professionalism have also favored dominance of the reformist approach.

But why doesn't Canadian Islam develop its own—if limited—aesthetic forms, as even such a strongly reformist country as Saudi Arabia (where particular forms of chant, architecture, and incense are deemed "*halal*") has done? Certainly the immigration filters have tended to limit the influx of specialists in the manipulation of aesthetic media (including musicians). But this isn't the whole story. If Canadian Muslim communities comprised a unified, fully communicating group or set of groups, such aesthetic forms might develop naturally.

Part of the problem is the fact that the locus of Islamic authority does not lie within Canada; Canadian Muslims tend to accept external authorities as representing "true Islam," rather than shaping a Canadian Islam for themselves. There are, for instance, no Islamic theological seminaries in Canada capable of training Canadian imams who understand Canadian society from within. On the contrary, Canadian mosques (of whatever doctrinal orientation) typically import their imams from traditional centers of Muslim learning, such as al-Azhar University in Cairo, as if these places could bestow authenticity on Canadian Islam by providing "the real thing." Many of these imams, while perhaps well trained, cannot even speak English or French, and have few prospects of communicating directly to their congregations, much less fostering a spiritual community and developing sonic forms adapted to the Canadian environment.

However, in the final analysis, the erasure of the aesthetic in Canadian Islam can be interpreted most deeply, it seems to me, as an instance of modernity's shift from communicative action toward strategic action, an example of the ongoing colonization of the lifeworld, to invoke social philosopher Jürgen Habermas's theoretical concepts, while simultaneously broadening them (Habermas 1984). In his theory of communicative action, Habermas is concerned primarily with the role of rational discourse in renewing a lifeworld replete with understanding and consensus. But just as the lifeworld can never be wholly rationalized, so rationality is never sufficient for full human communication, even in the (post?)-modern world, in which "traditional" mythical-emotional structures, supposed to have passed away, have nevertheless maintained their vitality to a surprising degree (as demonstrated by the continued prominence of organized religion). Rather, moral convictions and durable social relationships, whatever their rational dimensions, remain always crucially supported by affective expressive communication, carried, often enough, through aesthetic media.

Of all such media, live musical performance, with its intensive face-to-face social dimension and proximity to linguistic expression, is undoubtedly the most powerful. Musical performance supports powerful social relationships capable of transmitting meaning and shared understanding, the same kinds of social relationships privileged in human mediation. This is nowhere truer than in religious ritual, whose affective-aesthetic dimensions undergird the felt truth of the worldview it affirms, as well as social relationships forged among participants, providing channels for powerful nonverbal expressive communications. Drained of aesthetic media, constrained to fixed formal structures, religious ritual becomes coercive rather than communicative, a form of strategic action aiming proximately at coordinating internal unity, and ultimately at power in the society at large.

Reformist Islamic ritual is a case in point. Traditional humanly mediated Muslim ritual centers upon a localized linguistic expression fused with paralinguistic sound, enabling *expressive communicative action* to occur, comprising an enveloping soundworld through which intersubjective meanings are developed and transmitted, and rich social relationships are sustained, and thus supporting the process of human mediation itself. Live musical expression and experience constitute a complex form of musical-communicative action, nourishing the overlapping lifeworlds by which participants are connected through multiple feedback loops in the course of performance. But under circumstances of political threat (such as those in which Islam has found itself for the past two hundred years or so), such localized subjective nourishment has been construed as undermining objective strength.

Reformism's originary models include ritual models, uniformly applied and enforced as a form of *strategic action*, displacing aesthetic performance rendered meaningful by its adaptation to local social contexts and acoustic ecologies. Modernist Islam's insistence on a global ritual uniformity (enforced by accusations of *bidʿa*) centered on immutable texts, and the attendant evisceration of localized musical practices, is a manifestation of the social system, colonizing the individual Muslim's lifeworld as a means of unifying and strengthening the Umma in its exoteric aspects. The muting of the ritual soundworld instantiates reformist Islam's broader aim, to foster internal social unity and external social power through ritual conformity. In seeking this unity and power via collective action, the social system treats cultural differences (including aesthetic media and experience) as obstacles to be swept aside rather than as rich resources for interpersonal understanding and spiritual development. Reformist strategic action opposes the cultivation of aesthetic-spiritual practices (socially ramified and ramifying), centered on social relationships, place-specific traditions, human mediation, and expressive-communicative action, and contributing to an intensification of individual spiritual meaning. Such action centers instead upon coercive originary models for homogenizing thought and practice, developing social unity in order to serve a social agenda.

Whereas in the historic Muslim world this reformist ritual trend exists alongside older strands of human mediation, in Canada it expands to fill nearly the entire Islamic social space. Reminiscent of Husserl's critique of science (Husserl 1970), Canadian Islam seems, on the whole (and myriad exceptions notwithstanding), to have lost its connection to the human world, a world that is localized, affective, and rooted in human relationships, having been reoriented instead to address social problems inherent in a putatively multicultural society.

This situation is entirely understandable given the circumstances. Yet one hopes that the second or third generation of Canadian Muslims may succeed in localizing their religion through expressive-communicative ritual action, reclaiming a local authority, resisting colonization by the social system in favor of a richly spiritual lifeworld, and filling musical silences with sound.

NOTES

1. The present chapter builds on an earlier essay explicating this reception (see Frishkopf 2009b). The author is indebted to the editor for her constructive comments, as well as to the two anonymous readers.

2. While it is no doubt possible to find numerous counterexamples of Islamic music in Canada, including practices of particular Muslim communities (such as the Ismailis, or Sufi orders such as the Naqshabandiya of Montreal, whose highly musical *hadra* I attended in 2005), particular singers (such as Dawud Wharnsby Ali), and the occasional

musical muezzin, this chapter takes an empirical approach toward understanding the statistically dominant sonic profile of Islam in Canada, in which musical sound in Islamic ritual is the exception rather than the rule. In the social sciences, at least, the former does not disprove the latter.

3. For instance, the small Egyptian Delta town of Tanah is locally acclaimed for its distinctive tradition of Qur'anic recitation, despite proximity to the much larger urban centers of Mansura (23 km) and Cairo (147 km), hosting far more influential traditions.

4. Perhaps the reason may be that in the Muslim world, musical sound (as opposed to poetry itself, which was frequently written) has always centered on text, and (until recently) on transmission via human mediation, rather than being driven by system-level institutions (religious, political, or capitalist) carrying symbolic technologies for control and standardization via originary models. Until the advent of recording, even the melodic contours of Qur'anic recitation have never been regulated by originary models (see the following sections), whereas cantillation of the Bible has frequently relied upon ekphonetic notations.

5. Some thinkers have viewed Muhammad's illiteracy as structurally equivalent to Mary's virginity, providing a pure matrix for the deposit of the sacred Word (Schuon 1963).

6. From seventh-century Medina onwards, music flourished in Muslim courts, and the sonorous voice was highly esteemed in religious worship, starting with the Prophet's expressed preference (preserved in *hadith*) for the beautifully recited Qur'an.

7. For instance, for his public opposition to widely accepted beliefs and practices (including what he perceived as the innovations of saint veneration, including its musical ritual aspects in *sama'*), Ibn Taymiyya (1263–1328) was jailed several times and ultimately died in prison (Laoust 2010; Shehadi 1995, 95ff).

8. For instance, girls enrolling in Edmonton's Islamic Academy (a private Islamic school) are required to veil starting from elementary school (Edmonton Islamic Academy 2009, 36); no such formal requirement pertains to Egyptian schoolgirls, who generally do not wear the veil until they reach grades three or four.

9. How often have Canadian-born second-generation Muslim students told me: "There's no music in Islam" or "Sufism has nothing to do with true Islam!" despite the centuries-long prevalence of Sufism and music in traditional Muslim societies. Such statements may be heard in Muslim countries as well, but only in blatant juxtaposition to ethnographic evidence contradicting them, and hence with considerably different import.

10. E.g., the oft-cited Qur'an 5:3, "This day have I perfected your religion for you" (Yusuf Ali translation).

11. And many Muslim immigrants do, even among those who were formerly Westernized and secular, as a means of assuming a ready identity and joining a community, especially in the face of discrimination, and as an emotional compensation for social dislocation.

REFERENCES

Abu Laban, Baha. 1983. "The Canadian Muslim Community: The Need for a New Survival Strategy." In *The Muslim Community in North America*, ed. Earle H. Waugh, Baha Abu-Laban, and Regula Qureshi, pp. 75–92. Edmonton, AB: University of Alberta Press.

Abun-Nasr, Jamil M. 1965. *The Tijaniyya, a Sufi Order in the Modern World.* London and New York: Oxford University Press.

Aichi, Houria. 2001. *Khalwa: Chants sacres d'algerie.* Virgin Classics.

Bateson, Gregory. 1972. *Steps to an Ecology of Mind: Collected Essays in Anthropology, Psychiatry, Evolution, and Epistemology.* San Francisco: Chandler.

Ben Mahmoud, Abdelaziz. 2000. *Soulamia de Tunisie chants des confréries Soufies.* Paris: Arion.

Bourdieu, Pierre. 1977. *Outline of a Theory of Practice.* Cambridge and New York: Cambridge University Press.

Boyd, Alan. 1981. "Music in Islam: Lamu, Kenya, a Case Study." In *Discourse in Ethnomusicology II: A Tribute to Alan P. Merriam,* ed. Caroline Card et al., pp. 83–98. Bloomington: Ethnomusicology Publications Group, Indiana University.

———. 2001. *Music of the Waswahili of Lamu, Kenya. Maulidi. Volume one.* Custom compact disc series. Washington, DC: Smithsonian Folkways Records.

CIC Mission and Vision. 2009. http://www.alrashidmosque.ca/site/mission__vision.

Comores: Musiques traditionnelles de l'île d'Anjouan. 2004. Paris: Maison des cultures du monde.

Corke, Penny, Dennis Marks, John Miller Chernoff, Abhaji Ibrahim Abdulai, and Louis Mahoney. 2003. *The Drums of Dagbon. Repercussions: A Celebration of African-Influenced Music.* Princeton, NJ: Films for the Humanities & Sciences.

Diagne, Boubacar. 1996. *Tabala Wolof: Sufi Drumming of Senegal. African Percussion.* Seattle: Village Pulse.

Douglas, Mary. 2005. *Purity and Danger: An Analysis of Concepts of Pollution and Taboo.* London and New York: Routledge.

Durkheim, Emile. 1976. *The Elementary Forms of the Religious Life.* New York: Free Press.

Duvelle, Charles. 2003. *Soufis d'Algérie Mostaganem.* [Antony]: [Universal Division Mercury].

Edmonton Islamic Academy. 2009. Parent-Student Policy Handbook 2009–2010. http://www.islamicacademy.ca/sitewyze/files/Parent-Student_Handbook_2009-2010.pdf.

Égypte: ordre chazili "al-tariqa al-Hamidiyya al-chaziliyya." 1992. Musique soufi, v. 4. [France]: Arion.

Faruqi, L. L. A. 1986. "The Mawlid and Music in Muslim Ceremony." *World of Music* 28:79–89.

Fierro, M. 1992. "The Treatises against Innovations (kutub-al-bida')." *Der Islam-Zeitschrift für Geschichte und Kultur des Islamischen Orients* 69 (2): 204–246.

Foulani, Barka. 2000. *Chants sacrés du Sahara Algérie = Sacred Songs from the Sahara: Algeria.* Collection musicale. Paris: Institut du Monde Arabe.

Frishkopf, Michael. 1999. "Sufism, Ritual, and Modernity in Egypt: Language Performance as an Adaptive Strategy." PhD diss., University of California at Los Angeles.

———. 2001. "Tarab in the Mystic Sufi Chant of Egypt." In *Colors of Enchantment: Visual and Performing Arts of the Middle East,* ed. Sherifa Zuhur, pp. 233–269. Cairo: American University in Cairo Press.

———. 2002. "Islamic Hymnody in Egypt." In *The Garland Encyclopedia of World Music,* vol. 6, *The Middle East,* ed. Virginia Danielson, Scott Marcus, and Dwight Reynolds, pp. 165–175. New York: Routledge.

———. 2009a. Fieldnotes from Tamale, Ghana.

———. 2009b. "Globalizing the Soundworld: Islam and Sufi Music in the West." In *Sufis in Western Society: Global Networking and Locality,* ed. Ron Geaves, Markus Dressler, and Gritt Maria Klinkhammer, pp. 46–76. London and New York: Routledge.

————. 2009c. "Mediated Qur'anic Recitation and the Contestation of Islam in Contemporary Egypt." In *Music and the Play of Power in the Middle East, North Africa and Central Asia*, ed. Laudan Nooshin, pp. 75–114. Burlington, VT: Ashgate.

Gaffney, Patrick D. 1992. "Popular Islam." *Annals of the American Academy of Political and Social Science* 524 (1): 38–51.

al-Ghazzali, Abu Hamid Mohamed, and Duncan H. Macdonald. 1901. *Emotional religion in Islam as affected by music and singing. Being a Translation of a Book of the* Ihya 'Ulum ad-Din *of al-Ghazzali with Analysis, Annotation, and Appendices.* London: Royal Asiatic Society.

Giles, Linda L. 1989. "Spirit Possession on the Swahili Coast: Peripheral Cults or Primary Text?" PhD diss., University of Texas, Austin.

Gilsenan, Michael. 1973. *Saint and Sufi in Modern Egypt: An Essay in the Sociology of Religion.* Oxford: Clarendon Press.

Habermas, Jürgen. 1984. *The Theory of Communicative Action.* Boston: Beacon Press.

Haj, Samira. 2009. *Reconfiguring Islamic Tradition: Reform, Rationality, and Modernity.* Stanford, CA: Stanford University Press.

al-Hilawi, Muhammad 'Abd al-'Aziz, ed. 1984. *Kayfa tujawwid al-qur'an wa turattalu tartilan.* Cairo: Maktabat al-Qur'an.

Hiskett, Mervyn. 1973. "The Origin, Sources, and Form of Hausa Islamic Verse." In *Essays on African Literature*, ed. W. L. Ballard, pp. 127–153. Atlanta: School of Arts and Sciences, Georgia State University.

Hoor al-Ayn. http://www.hoor-al-ayn.com/docs/unity/.

Husserl, Edmund. 1970. *The Crisis of European Sciences and Transcendental Phenomenology: An Introduction to Phenomenological Philosophy.* Evanston, IL: Northwestern University Press.

Johansen, Julian, ed. 1996. *Sufism and Islamic Reform in Egypt: The Battle for Islamic Tradition.* Oxford: Clarendon Press.

Kaptein, N. J. G. 1993. *Muhammad's Birthday Festival: Early History in the Central Muslim Lands and Development in the Muslim West until the 10th/16th Century.* Leiden and New York: E. J. Brill.

Karrar, 'Ali Salih. 1992. *The Sufi Brotherhoods in the Sudan.* Evanston, IL: Northwestern University Press.

Knysh, Alexander D. 2000. *Islamic Mysticism: A Short History.* Leiden, the Netherlands, and Boston: Brill.

Langer, Susanne Katherina Knauth. 1960. *Philosophy in a New Key: A Study in the Symbolism of Reason, Rite, and Art.* 3d ed. Cambridge, MA: Harvard University Press.

Laoust, Henri. 2010. Ibn Taymiyya. *Encyclopaedia of Islam, Second Edition*, ed. P. Bearman, Th. Bianquis, C. E. Bosworth, E. van Donzel, and W. P. Heinrichs. Brill, 2010. Brill Online.

Mapping the Global Muslim Population: A Report on the Size and Distribution of the World's Muslim Population [electronic version]. 2009. http://www.pewforum.org/uploadedfiles/Topics/Demographics/Muslimpopulation.pdf.

Monts, Jeanne, and Lester Parker Monts. 2001. *Music of the Vai of Liberia.* [Washington, DC]: Smithsonian Folkways Recordings.

Nasr, Seyyed Hossein. 1987. *Islamic Art and Spirituality.* Albany: State University of New York Press.

Nelson, Kristina. 2001. *The Art of Reciting the Qur'an.* 2nd ed. Cairo: American University in Cairo Press.

Orwin, Martin. 2001. "Language Use in Three Somali Religious Poems." *Journal of African Cultural Studies* 14 (1): 69–87.

Otto, Rudolf, and John W. Harvey. 1925. *The Idea of the Holy: An Inquiry into the Nonrational Factor in the Idea of the Divine and Its Relation to the Rational.* London: Oxford University Press.

Peskes, Esther, and W. Ende. 2006. Wahhabiyya. In *Encyclopaedia of Islam* (Web edition), ed. P. Bearman, C. E. Bosworth, Th. Bianquis, E. van Donzel, and W. P. Heinrichs. Leiden: Brill Online.

Qureshi, R. B. 1987. "Qawwali: Making the Music Happen in the Sufi Assembly." *Asian Music* 18 (2): 118–157.

Rispler, Vardit. 1991. "Toward a New Understanding of the Term 'bid'a.'" *Islam* 68: 320–328.

Ryan, Patrick J. 1996. "Ariadne auf Naxos: Islam and Politics in a Religiously Pluralistic African Society." *Journal of Religion in Africa* 26 (3): 308–329.

al-Sa'id, Labib, ed. 1975. *The Recited Koran: A History of the First Recorded Version.* Princeton, NJ: Darwin Press.

Schacht, Joseph. 1965. "Notes on Islam in East Africa." *Studia Islamica* 23:91–136.

Schuon, Frithjof. 1963. *Understanding Islam.* London: Allen & Unwin.

Shadhiliyah, and Mohammed El Helbawy. 1999. *Chants soufis du Caire, Egypte. Sufi Chants from Cairo, Egypt.* France: Institut du Monde Arabe.

Shaikh, Sumaira. 2006. "Canadian Muslims Hold Productive Toronto Strategy Meeting." July 15. http://www.canadianislamiccongress.com/democracy/strategy.php.

Shehadi, Fadlou. 1995. *Philosophies of Music in Medieval Islam.* Brill's Studies in Intellectual History, vol. 67. Leiden: E. J. Brill.

Shiloah, Amnon. 1997. "Music and Religion in Islam." *Acta Musicologica* 69 (2): 143–155.

StatsCan. 2001a. Statistics Canada: Religion (95) and Immigrant Status and Period of Immigration (11) for Population, for Canada, Provinces, Territories, Census Metropolitan Areas and Census Agglomerations, 2001 Census—20% Sample Data. http://www12.statcan.ca/english/census01/products/standard/themes/RetrieveProductTable.cfm?Temporal=2001&PID=55824&APATH=3&GID=431515&METH=1&PTYPE=55440&THEME=56&FOCUS=0&AID=0&PLACENAME=0&PROVINCE=0&SEARCH=0&GC=0&GK=0&VID=0&VNAMEE=&VNAMEF=&FL=0&RL=0&FREE=0 (accessed January 5, 2011).

———. 2001b. Statistics Canada: Religions in Canada: Provincial and Territorial Highlights. http://www12.statcan.ca/english/census01/Products/Analytic/companion/rel/provs.cfm (accessed March 3, 2009).

———. 2001c. Statistics Canada: Selected Cultural and Labour Force Characteristics (58), Selected Religions (35A), Age Groups (5A) and Sex (3) for Population 15 Years and Over, for Canada, Provinces, Territories and Census Metropolitan Areas 1, 2001 Census—20% Sample Data. http://www12.statcan.ca/english/census01/products/standard/themes/RetrieveProductTable.cfm?Temporal=2001&PID=67773&APATH=3&GID=517770&METH=1&PTYPE=55496&THEME=56&FOCUS=0&AID=0&PLACENAME=0&PROVINCE=0&SEARCH=0&GC=0&GK=0&VID=0&VNAMEE=&VNAMEF=&FL=0&RL=0&FREE=0 (accessed January 5, 2011).

———. 2001d. Statistics Canada: Selected Demographic and Cultural Characteristics (104), Selected Religions (35A), Age Groups (6) and Sex (3) for Population, for Canada, Provinces, Territories and Census Metropolitan Areas, 2001 Census—20% Sample Data. http://www12.statcan.ca/english/census01/products/standard/themes/Retrieve

ProductTable.cfm?Temporal=2001&PID=67771&APATH=3&METH=1&PTYPE
=55496&THEME=56&FOCUS=0&AID=0&PLACENAME=0&PROVINCE
=0&SEARCH=0&GC=0&GK=0&VID=0&VNAMEE=&VNAMEF=&FL=0&RL=0
&FREE=0&GID=517770 (accessed January 5, 2011).

―――. 2001e. Statistics Canada: Selected Educational Characteristics (29), Selected Reli-
gions (35A), Age Groups (5A) and Sex (3) for Population 15 Years and Over, for Canada,
Provinces, Territories and Census Metropolitan Areas, 2001 Census—20% Sample Data.
http://www12.statcan.ca/english/census01/products/standard/themes/Retrieve
ProductTable.cfm?Temporal=2001&PID=67772&APATH=3&GID=517770&METH
=1&PTYPE=55496&THEME=56&FOCUS=0&AID=0&PLACENAME=0
&PROVINCE=0&SEARCH=0&GC=0&GK=0&VID=0&VNAMEE=&VNAMEF
=&FL=0&RL=0&FREE=0 (accessed January 5, 2011).

―――. 2001f. Statistics Canada: Selected Ethnic Origins, for Canada, Provinces and Territories—20% Sample Data. http://www12.statcan.ca/english/census01/products
/highlight/ETO/Table1.cfm?Lang=E&T=501&GV=1&GID=0 (accessed January 5,
2011).

Topp Fargion, Janet. 2000. *Zanzibar: Music of Celebration*. Topic World Series. London:
Topic Records.

Trimingham, J. Spencer, ed. 1998. *The Sufi Orders in Islam*. New York: Oxford University Press.

Vassiliev, Alexei, ed. 2000. *The History of Saudi Arabia*. New York: New York University
Press.

Waugh, Earle H., ed. 2005. *Memory, Music, and Religion: Morocco's Mystical Chanters*. Columbia: University of South Carolina Press.

CHAPTER 5

PIOUS ENTERTAINMENT:
HIZBULLAH'S ISLAMIC CULTURAL SPHERE

JOSEPH ALAGHA

HIZBULLAH'S SPOKESMAN SAYYID IBRAHIM AL-MUSAWI regards art as the most sublime achievement of humanity, since it brings man closer to the creator, to God, who asks man to be in a continuous struggle to ascend toward perfection.[1] Islamic art is a "cause, a passion, and a life." When a passionate activity is not related to revolution, then it is void of any worth and beauty. Revolutionary activity is part of Islamic art because it is purposeful; its purpose is to transform society and reform it. Herein lies its aesthetic dimension. Islamic art is the art of resistance (*al-fann al-muqawim*); it resists tyranny, oppression, and purposeless art: "art for the sake of art." Islamic art stresses creativity in relation to context and content, a transparent content that is the basis of influence and movement. By this it creates a realistic revolutionary art that aims at changing and reforming society. Thus, the message of the purposeful and committed Islamic art of resistance with a mission (*al-fann al-muqawim al-multazim al-hadif*)[2] is a different message; it is the message of ideologically motivated art (Murtada 2002, 55–94). Why is art accorded such an important mobilizational role? It has already been noted in the introduction of this volume that in other contexts and countries this *infitah* ("opening-up")—both generally and in art in particular— among Islamic movements is described by the concept of post-Islamism. Is a similar trend discernible in the case of the Lebanese Hizbullah?

Hizbullah, better known as the Islamic Resistance in Lebanon, which is infamous for its allegedly "terrorist" and militant face, is an interesting case study. In this chapter, I am going to convey another face of Hizbullah: its *al-saha al-Islamiyya* (Islamic cultural sphere). Available material on a Lebanese[3] Shiʻite view on the performing arts has not been adequately addressed in the literature, let alone Hizbullah's opinion on the topic, which remains sketchy and fragmented. Here I am going to shed light on Hizbullah's notion of pious entertainment and performing art, as well as limitations on them in the Islamic cultural sphere in relation to *al-fann al-muqawim*, as the organization labels it. In addition to primary Arabic Internet sources and secondary sources in English, I conducted two fieldwork visits, in the summer of 2009, to Lebanon, where I was able to obtain a host of primary Arabic sources, and in August 2009 I conducted interviews in Hizbullah's bastion in southern Beirut (*al-Dahiya*) with Shiʿite religious authorities and Hizbullah's rank and file on the issue of *al-fann al-muqawim*. Some notable figures I interviewed are the following: the late Ayatullah Sayyid Muhammad Husayn Fadlallah, the highest-ranking Shiʿite religious authority in Lebanon; Hajj Muhammad Raʿd, the head of Hizbullah's parliamentary bloc; Sayyid Abd Al-Halim Fadlallah, the head of the party's think tank the Consultative Center of Studies and Documentation (CCSD); Hajj Ghalib Abu Zaynab, party officer for Muslim-Christian dialogue; Shaykh Shafiq Jaradi, the rector of Al-Maʿarif Al-Hikmiyya College; and Hizbullah's spokesman Sayyid Ibrahim al-Musawi.

What are the contours of Hizbullah's *al-saha al-Islamiyya*? How is *al-fann al-muqawim*, resistance art with a purpose/mission, which means good Islamic art, bracketed from *al-fann al-habit*, lowbrow art (Khaminaʾi 2009, 102)?[4] I will highlight specific debates informed by scholarly tradition and will follow recent debates about the lawfulness of the performing arts— in particular singing, music, theater, and comedy—and their categorization scaling from the permitted, to the neutral, to the forbidden. What are the religious sensibilities of the Hizbullah constituency? Why does music play such a central role in this pious entertainment? What kinds of limitations are imposed on it, and which test cases stretch these limits?

Through analyzing discourses and interviews, on the one hand, and activities and artistic expressions, on the other, I discuss the constituents of *al-saha al-Islamiyya*. In other words, the chapter is divided into three main sections. The first deals with the discourses on work and leisure, music, and theater. The second offers extended examples of *al-saha al-Islamiyya*'s activities and artistic expressions. The third section deals with the question of how far Hizbullah goes in defending *al-fann al-muqawim*. It tests the limits of *al-saha al-Islamiyya* by addressing the contestations and tangible challenges to it.

FROM *AL-HALA AL-ISLAMIYYA* TO *AL-SAHA AL-ISLAMIYYA*

In this section I discuss the shift from Islamism to post-Islamism and how it comports with the transition from *al-hala al-Islamiyya* (Islamic religio-political sphere) to *al-saha al-Islamiyya* (Islamic cultural sphere), an eventuality noted by all my interviewees. In an interview with the late Ayatullah Fadlallah, he told me that a noticeable transformation has occurred from *al-*

hala al-Islamiyya to *al-saha al-Islamiyya*, arguing that he is a strong advocate of the latter. He noted that the former was a transitory stage that has served its purpose. He explained that *al-hala al-Islamiyya* was mainly concerned with establishing an Islamic state where minorities, such as Christians and Jews, were treated as *ahl al-dhimma*, i.e., residents holding limited rights and required to pay a tax in lieu of alms giving (*zakat*). Ayatullah Fadlallah clarified that in *al-saha al-Islamiyya* notions such as the Islamic state and *ahl al-dhimma* are bygone ideological constructs that do not exist anymore. According to him, *al-saha al-Islamiyya* is a pluralistic Islamic cultural sphere where the concept of citizenship (*muwatana*) reigns; where all people have equal rights and duties and where coexistence and mutual respect are the main norm and asset among Lebanon's eighteen ethno-confessional communities.[5] My other interviewees from Hizbullah's rank and file concur to the letter with Ayatullah Fadlallah's views.[6]

In the 1970s and 1980s, *al-hala al-Islamiyya*, which was fundamentally concerned with doctrinal-ideological Islamization, unified various sectors of the Shi'a community under the banner of an overarching Islamic ideology.[7] Members of *al-hala al-Islamiyya* converged and established Hizbullah in the wake of the victory of the Islamic Revolution. Since its inception, the party has been keen to control the Lebanese political system, initially through a top-down revolutionary process aimed at obtaining power and Islamizing society by military force. *Al-hala al-Islamiyya* was grounded primarily in Hizbullah's belief in pan-Islamism and the necessity of founding an Islamic order where the "oppressed" reign over the "oppressors." This radicalism proved futile in the 1980s. Sayyid Muhammad Husayn Fadlallah wielded power and influence over *al-hala al-Islamiyya*, being its godfather since the late 1960s. Many considered him Hizbullah's spiritual leader, an accusation both persistently and rightfully denied (Alagha 2006, 33–36).

Hizbullah changed as circumstances changed. *Al-saha al-Islamiyya* started to emerge in the early 1990s when Hizbullah altered its political strategy and endeavored to control the political system through a bottom-up process of a gradual participation in the democratic system, starting with the parliament, the municipal councils, and the Council of Ministers, the main executive body of the country. Thus, the party shifted to acceptance of, and engagement in, the democratic process under a sectarian-confessional political and administrative system in the wake of the emergence of a pluralist public sphere and mixed confessional space that compelled it to increase its openness toward other communities, political parties, and interest groups in the Lebanese myriad.[8] This led to the gradual waning of *al-hala al-Islamiyya* and contributed to the gradual growth of *al-saha al-Islamiyya*. In *al-saha al-Islamiyya* Hizbullah has repeatedly stated that its electoral campaigns represent a concerted effort between its resistance identity, on the one hand, and its socioeconomic, intellectual, and cultural work, on the other (Alagha 2006, 168).

Is the transition from *al-hala al-Islamiyya* to *al-saha al-Islamiyya* comparable to the transition from Islamism to post-Islamism in other contexts? Academic circles have identified them as almost the same trend. Arguing along the lines of Asef Bayat (2007b, 10–13; 1996), Olivier Roy (2004, 58–99; 1999, 85–86), Farhad Khosrokhavar (2002), Gille Kepel (2002, 368; 2008), Peter Mandaville (2007, 343–348), Amel Boubekeur (2007), and others, I would like to point to a general tendency of a gradual transition from Islamism to post-Islamism, from the "old" to the "new" (Mandaville 2007, 348), from *al-hala al-Islamiyya* (Islamic religio-political sphere) to *al-saha al-Islamiyya* (Islamic cultural sphere). These authors traced this development through the particular case studies of Egypt, Iran, France, and the UK, focusing on political openness. I will analyze similar trends and tendencies in Lebanon in Hizbullah's Islamic cultural sphere when it comes to culture and art production.

By post-Islamism Bayat means (1) a political and social *condition* in which Islamists became aware of their system's inadequacies and were thus compelled to reinvent it, and (2) a *project* or "a conscious attempt . . . to turn the underlying principles of Islamism on its head by emphasizing rights instead of duties, plurality in place of singular authoritative voice, historicity rather than fixed scriptures, and the future instead of the past" (Bayat 2007b, 10–11). Within this post-Islamist model, Amel Boubekeur highlighted the important role art plays for politically engaged Muslims. She writes, "Today art is a profession possessed of a genuine force of mobilization; its politically engaged dimension has become an intrinsic part of the ethic of peace and justice in Islam" (Boubekeur 2007, 90).[9]

Al-saha al-Islamiyya is primarily concerned with Islam as culture and social practice. Iranian reformist president Muhammad Khatami (1997–2005) has had a pioneering contribution in this regard, since he gave prominence to culture. Khatami argued, "If freedom of thought were to be suppressed then it would continue to be nurtured in the minds and hearts of the people. Therefore, the best system of government would be the one which would allow thought to be expressed without any limitation" (Alagha 2001, 40). Khatami articulates his cultural theory through the development of a "democratic Shi'ite discourse" on political freedom, pluralism, tolerance, and human rights. Khatami's cultural reforms included the following enhancements to the Iranian public sphere: making civil society the subject of common discourse; easing of censorship on books and films; a vigorous press and the releasing of dozens of new magazines and newspapers; and the formation of cultural and political associations. Khatami's domestic policy was directed toward civility and the rule of law as the most salient pillars of democracy. When Sayyid Hasan Nasrallah, Hizbullah's secretary general, visited Iran around the middle of October 1997, Khatami called on the party to pursue a policy of cultural openness toward the other sectarian-confessional communities in Lebanon and to graduate intellectuals in addition to freedom fighters. Khatami's discourse is paralleled by Nasrallah, who argues that upholding "public freedoms"[10] is a priority that goes hand in hand with the party's ideology and Islamic doctrine and serves the Lebanese society at large. According to Nasrallah, the establishment of civil society in Lebanon does not contradict Hizbullah's project; rather, it is concomitant with it, because one of the basic tenets of Islam urges the enactment of civil society (ibid., 40–42).

The crux of Khatami's argument is that Islam is not a normative, essentialist, elusive concept; rather, Islam is culture. From this perspective, it is interesting to note that Khatami's discourse was devoid of the use of the word "Islam"; in all his speeches and writings he employed culture (*farhang*), civilization (*tamaddun*), and religion (*din*). Thus, Khatami was recasting Islam in cultural terms (ibid., 41). To a lesser extent, the current leader of the Islamic Republic of Iran and Hizbullah's "spiritual leader," Imam Khamina'i, asserted that cultural work is always a precursor to political and military work, and added that the Islamic Revolution needs to have a strong, enriching cultural background (Khamina'i 2009, 66, 85). In turn, Khamina'i stressed that any message, or call, or revolution, or civilization, or culture, cannot be successfully disseminated if it is not expressed in artistic form (ibid., 10, 83), which represents another level of discourse. Khatami identifies Islam as culture, whereas Khamina'i believes that culture is one of the means to achieve the aims of the Islamic Revolution—in other words, an instrumentalist concept of culture which is rather different from post-Islamism. Imam Khumayni, the founder of the Islamic Republic, repeatedly stated that the purpose of "genuine" art (art with a purpose) is realized when it draws upon the core of the authentic Islamic culture, the culture of justice and purity. He added that from an Islamic cultural perspective, art is the clear presentation of justice and dignity.[11]

Hizbullah's *al-saha al-Islamiyya* is trying to emulate the above concepts and put them into practice through ideologically motivated art, or art with a mission (see van Nieuwkerk, Chapter 6). Hizbullah argues that the *shari'a* (Islamic law), as a socially constructed phenomenon, does not fall short of guiding a modern life, does have the flexibility and pragmatism to deal with man's progress, and addresses both the generalities and particularities that have to do with man's needs (Alagha 2006, 163, 203–205). From this perspective, one could argue that Hizbullah, as a post-Islamist movement, has been engaging in pragmatic attempts to construct an "alternative modernity" that incorporates modern democratic and religious principles (Bayat 2007b, 13; 1996).

Thus, the old motif of *al-hala al-Islamiyya* gradually gave way to the new theme of *al-saha al-Islamiyya*. In Boubekeur's words *al-saha al-Islamiyya* offers "consumable beauty, leisure, and well-being. Importantly, a population of militants is transformed into one of consumers and clients. From now on it is necessary to seduce one's public, to propose one's services through leisure . . . and mobilization around politically engaged art . . . [in order] to promote the emergence of new generations through the ethic of a 'conscious Islam'" (2007, 91). Based on all the aforementioned, I beg to differ with Mona Harb, who regards "*al-saha al-Islamiyya*" as a specific cultural manifestation of "*al-hala al-Islamiyya*," or what she calls the "Islamic sphere," where the masses consume piety. She gives an inconclusive opinion pending further research: "More fieldwork on the practices of consumption and the processes of commodification [is] necessary" (2006). I view *al-saha al-Islamiyya* and *al-hala al-Islamiyya* as discourses, or ways of thinking and acting belonging to different time periods, like Islamism, which has transformed into post-Islamism. Thus, rather than analyzing *al-saha al-Islamiyya* as a manifestation of *al-hala al-Islamiyya*, I would argue that *al-saha al-Islamiyya* entails a substantial transformation. In the remainder of the chapter, I will analyze the manifestations of *al-saha al-Islamiyya* through both discourses and artistic expressions.

DISCOURSES

In this section I will first go into the discourse with regard to work and leisure to demonstrate the general importance attached to purposefulness. Next I will deal with Shi'ite discourse with regard to music. Finally, I examine Imam Khumayni's and Ayatullah Fadlallah's rulings regarding television and theater.

WORK AND LEISURE

In response to the contention that Islam does not afford the individual with any leisure time, which is allegedly based upon the Qur'anic verses 94:7–8, Ayatullah Fadlallah asserted that "leisure time is meant to be the time in which one has no longer any social, religious and business duties. Even this free time is supposed to be refined from any deviation or any prohibited immoral deeds." Fadlallah added, "In Islam extravagance is rejected for God asks man to be moderate in his needs."[12] Thus, one ought to positively and constructively engage in purposeful, mobilizational art in order to fend off debaucheries (*fawahish*)[13] and inculcate Islamic values and norms (Bdir 2008).

According to Hizbullah, the Qur'an, *hadith*, and popular culture enjoin people to engage in purposeful activities and avoid emptiness and purposelessness.[14] Adnan Hammud, a regular contributor to Hizbullah's weekly *al-Intiqad*'s cultural section, adds that purposelessness and emptiness are diametrically opposed to work and praxis. Hammud asserts that emptiness that exceeds bodily and mental rest becomes more tiring than work, primarily because of the psychological pressure that torments the one enduring it. This emptiness leads to boredom, which most likely causes delinquency and deviance. The person who does not fill his time with purposeful activities or work will find himself an easy prey to excessive emptiness, which leads to frivolous pastimes, killing time by any means, even by committing immoral deeds. Thus, engaging in positive activities such as work is conducive to man's felicity (A. Hammud 2008). This is in line with the rulings of Khumayni and Khamina'i on laziness, boredom, and wasting time, and their admonishment to seek knowledge and purposeful activities in leisure time (Ma'had Al-Imam Al-Mahdi 2006, 31–33, 49).

Concerning youth and emptiness, Hammud stresses that destructive emptiness, especially among the youth who do not find ways to release their energy in a positive way, will negatively reflect upon them, destroying their life materially and morally, and will cause behavioral problems. The same applies to children (A. Hammud 2008). Rayya stresses the importance of planning purposeful activities that provide children with all kinds of pious entertainment. She argues that time is important and should not be wasted aimlessly; the decision should not be left to children to do as they please, so that they do not end up engaging in frivolous play; and there should be a cultural program, specially oriented toward the villages, aiming at promoting purposeful activities, *al-fann al-hadif*, and pious entertainment (Rayya 2008).

According to Hammud, the righteous prophets and Imams were all engaged in work, even manual labor and making handicrafts/artifacts (*hiraf*, i.e., works of art). He condemns laziness, arguing that the word lazy (*kasala*) is cited twice in the Qur'an in verses 4:142 and 9:54. Hammud adds that the seventh Imam, Musa al-Kazim, admonished against laziness and boredom, as did Prophet Muhammad. Hammud concludes that time is a blessing from God. Squandering it is a corruption (*mafsada*, the opposite of *maslaha*), both on earth and in heaven, a corruption that denies its perpetrator felicity, in this life and the life to come (A. Hammud 2008).

Shaykh Shafiq Jaradi, the rector of Al-Ma'arif Al-Hikmiyya College, conveyed to me that the essence of *al-fann al-muqawim al-multazim al-hadif* is the Qur'an. He stressed that the verses 38:27, 65:3, 75:36, 3:136, 3:57, 56:73, 84:25, among others, point to this direction—namely, that everything in life, including art, must have a telos: a purpose and a mission. Dr. Ahmad Majid, a colleague of Shaykh Jaradi, told me that in a world that is witnessing a struggle of cultures, it is of vital importance to present to the masses the culture of the resistance in a good way. The culture of the resistance is a humanistic culture that cooperates and thinks with others in order to make this world a better one by presenting an Islamic insight into dealing with things, where the human being always has precedence over anything else.

Dr. Majid affirmed that from this perspective, any work, any job you want to perform in society, has to be purposeful and committed in order to have a positive role and effect. Purposeful art is an embodiment and reflection of the pressing issues in society. It has a positive role of disciplining the self in such a way as to reveal the glory of God in the human being. For instance, revolutionary music glorifies the martyrs, the suffering of the handicapped and wounded, the pain of those who lost loved ones, etc. The purpose is to convey the message of human suffering. By serving society we realize the human project, whose ultimate telos is serving God. Man has a privileged status in this humanistic civilization, where everything points to God. Tariq 'Asayli told me that this view of "oneness of God" (*tawhid*) constitutes the essence of Islamic theosophy (*'irfan*),[15] a thinking in line with religious and human values that promote activism and mobilization whose main purpose is to safeguard individual and societal rights,[16] as Khumayni and Khamina'i repeatedly stated (Khamina'i 2009, 106–107).

Although art is an independent world in its own right, Ayatullah Fadlallah told me that there is no purposeful art without a purposeful artist. The human being, the artist, makes art purposeful or not. The committed artist lives the spiritual values and disseminates these to the public. The artist directs his art to the service of humanity, to a noble telos.[17] As we have seen above, purposeful art has a religious-jurisprudential dimension, on the one hand, and a cultural, artistic-innovative aspect, on the other, all directed to the aim of the intellectual love of God, the creator, and the provocation of religious and spiritual sensibilities in the service of mobilization and resistance, under the guidance of God (109:36): "Verily Allah is well aware of all that they do."

THE PURPOSE AND *MASLAHA* OF MUSIC

The transformation from *al-hala al-Islamiyya* to *al-saha al-Islamiyya* in the case of music is quite evident. As a case in point I refer to Khamina'i's discursive shifts. Khamina'i, Hizbullah's current religious authority, was skeptical about singing in the era of *al-hala al-Islamiyya*. According to him, what has been prohibited in Islam was singing, not music. He defined melody (*musiqa*) as every sound and rhythm emanating from the throat through the vocal cords according to a certain style or manner. Thus, he stressed that the only type of music that was prohibited at the time was the type related to singing (Khamina'i 2009, 56–57). Khamina'i called upon the religious scholars in Qumm to thoroughly research the issue of singing and music in order to come up with a ruling that would remove the confusion that engulfed common people (ibid., 59). In the *al-saha al-Islamiyya*, Khamina'i displays progressive views in this regard, since he sanctioned chanting religious or revolutionary *anashid* with musical instruments at the mosque in between two prayers or after the evening prayers, especially if they were used for mobilizational purposes, as long as this activity did not conflict with the duty of prayer (ibid., 171–172).

In *al-saha al-Islamiyya*, Khamina'i's view underwent a serious revision. "Singing is prohibited when it leads to *tarab* [enchantment],[18] and in the *marathi* [wailing rituals] there is no tarab" (M. Hammud 2005, 175); and by extension in *al-fann al-hadif* there is no *tarab*, since the rational faculty is in control of the spiritual faculty. This is the view of leading Shi'ite religious authorities such as Fadlallah,[19] al-Khu'i (1990, 702), Sistani,[20] Khumayni (in al-Hamidi 1994, 114), and Khamina'i (2009, 166). The following are examples that testify to this trend. The shaykh of al-Azhar, the most important religious establishment in Egypt, removed his turban as a gesture of respect in recognition of Umm Kulthum's purposeful singing. Signifying the strong message of purposeful art, Khamina'i mentioned that many artistic expressions move his heart, deeply affect him, and make him emotional to the extent of crying (Khamina'i 2009, 120). Ayatullah Fadlallah has progressive views concerning women's voice. He told me that love poetry (*ghazal*) is sanctioned, even if it is sung by a woman, as long as she abides by Islam's ethical values and norms, singing in a purposeful manner as Umm Kulthum used to do, for instance.[21]

Thus, according to Ayatullah Fadlallah's rulings, "Music that elevates the spirit and sublimates it such as the music of Chopin and Mozart is not prohibited. In general, we say that the classical music is not prohibited, as well as the music that soothes the nerves and elevates the soul and contains cultural elements that nourish the soul. . . . we have some musical groups whose songs are broadcasted at [Hizbullah's] 'Al-Manar' television. These songs are not prohibited from a religious point of view. Moreover, the Iranian media broadcasts high-class songs and beautiful music. Hence, art, whether singing, acting, drawing or poetry[,] aims at serving man [art with a purpose: *al-fann al-hadif*]. When art causes man spiritual or emotional behavioral damage, it will be dangerous." Fadlallah lays down the general jurisprudential rule according to which choices are being made concerning prohibition or sanctioning: "Everything that has negative effects and whose disadvantages [*mafasid*] [are] more than its advantages [*masalih*] is considered prohibited."[22]

Ayatullah Fadlallah is referring to an important secondary source in Islamic Law (*shariʿa*), which Muslim religious scholars (*ʿulama*) employ to determine if a certain practice—such as the performing arts—is permitted, neutral, or forbidden. In particular, Ayatullah Fadlallah is making reference to one of the maxims of Islamic jurisprudence (*qawaʿid al-fiqh*): "the warding off of vices is preferable to obtaining interests," or "the avoidance of vice is always preferable to any benefit that might accrue from the act" (*darʾ al-mafasid muqaddam ʿala jalb al-masalih*). This calls for an explanation. Ayatullah Fadlallah clarifies that when a person is confronted with two injunctions that require the exercise of his reason, reason (the mind) tells him that God has imposed on human beings injunctions for the sake of the *masalih* (advantages/virtues) and *mafasid* (disadvantages/vices, evils). In this case, what takes precedence is either the warding off of the grave disadvantage or the following of the most salient advantage. Thus, the injunction is carried out on the basis of waiving the less important injunction in favor of the more salient one. Ayatullah Fadlallah goes on to affirm that a religious (*sharʿi*) injunction could be frozen under pressuring circumstances that relegate this injunction to a category of lower importance, so that it can be overridden by an injunction that has higher priority or importance, i.e., takes precedence over it. Thus, the injunction remains in effect and binding, but it can be annulled under some circumstances, if necessity (*maslaha*) deems it to be so (Fadlallah 2009, 82–83).[23]

In conclusion, Ayatullah Fadlallah affirmed, "From the Islamic point of view, singing is not forbidden, simply because anything around us such as the sound of waterfalls, the singing of birds, and any other piece of art can provide delight in us, however, once this song pours in the channels of corruption and injustice and once it leads to the excitation of desires then it is prohibited. On the other hand, the songs that praise prophets, sing justice, curse savagery, and draw the awareness towards any political corruption are legitimate."[24]

Hizbullah's music is oriented toward these goals. Imam Khamina'i's recurrent statement that art is the most eloquent and effective means of Islamic propagation (2009, 6, 9, 27, 50, 83)[25] forms the crux of the party's justification of *al-fann al-hadif*. Indeed, Hizbullah is a strong supporter of *al-fann al-hadif* and is promoting it through its weekly newspaper *al-*

Intiqad and media institutions such as al-Manar satellite TV and al-Nour satellite radio.

TELEVISION AND THEATER

In a 1962 fatwa, in response to a question on theatrical plays, films played on TV, broadcasted music, and athletic programs such as boxing, judo, and swimming, Imam Khumayni affirmed that broadcasting and watching purposeful movies and plays are religiously sanctioned because of their pedagogical nature. The same applies to most athletic programs and music as long as they abide by the following prohibitions:

(1) Western popular music is prohibited;
(2) Women should be wearing the Islamic dress and should be accompanied by a *mahram*;[26]
(3) People should not look or listen in a lustful way; the intention (*niyya*) is important. (Al-Hamidi 1994, 113)[27]

In response to a question of when the media (TV, radio, cinema, theater, etc.) are considered legitimate (*halal*) and when illegitimate (*haram*), Ayatullah Fadlallah affirms, "The employment of media varies accordingly; if it serves Islam and its objectives, if it elevates humanity, widens man's knowledge, improves his morals then, doubtlessly, it is not only considered legitimate but is also regarded a must. However, once it includes any kind of wanton and dissolute activities and programs, which contaminate man's spirit, lower his humanity, serve the purposes of the tyrants and oppressors and support the international arrogance[,] . . . then it is automatically prohibited. Indeed, just as there is no absolute rejection to such kinds of media in Islam, there is also no absolute acceptance; the employment of such means determines its functionality and application in Islam."[28]

Again employing the contextual argument, in response to a question on the permissibility for a pious person to work in a domain of art that is known for its wantonness in a way that does not affect his/her morals and religious values, Ayatullah Fadlallah clarified, "These are two points in this domain. The first one depends upon the person himself and his abilities to withstand temptations. Indeed this person has to know himself; if this job is going to affect negatively his values and consequently lead him to the path of dissoluteness and licentiousness, then it is prohibited. The other point is related to his role which he plays either in a film or in a play. Once this role is advantageous [*maslaha*] to the Islamic situation, then there is no problem. However, once it supports the immoral habits and desires in a way that does not suit physically, spiritually, and realistically the Islamic situation then it is prohibited."[29]

To conclude this section, I have argued that the main characteristics of the aforementioned discourses are based upon these fundamental assumptions: an artistic practice or expression is sanctioned *if and only if*[30] it is: (1) purposeful and (2) the advantage (*maslaha*) behind it should outweigh the disadvantage (*mafsada*). This is Hizbullah's and Fadlallah's general rule of thumb, which is in turn based upon a progressive interpretation of Shi'ite jurisprudence (*fiqh*). In outlining the contours of this development, I questioned what kind of art is functioning in *al-saha al-Islamiyya* and which discourse is employed to legitimize it. Now we move from theory to practice, from discourses to actual, practical examples.

AL-SAHA AL-ISLAMIYYA: EXTENDED EXAMPLES

In this section I will give extended examples of the emergent *al-saha al-Islamiyya*. I will first go into popular and cultural activities that are in line with the discourse of purposefulness; next I will discuss examples of music and theatrical play.

PURPOSEFUL ACTIVITIES

Rayya argues that parents and the society at large have a grave responsibility toward the betterment of children by providing purposeful activities such as entertainment venues, summer camps, and cultural activities suitable to them. These activities promote pious entertainment and purposeful play, leaving no room for fruitless, foolish, and futile behavior and play. The aim is to give children a balanced, purposeful culture without burdening them with very high expectations and too much to do, leaving lots of room for happiness and joy. Engaging in beneficial activities accomplishes all of these. It must allow children to artistically express themselves by fully engaging in plastic and performing arts, most importantly by creative performances. Hizbullah's main pedagogical objective is to train children to behave in an effective, purposeful way (Rayya 2008).

Putting theory into practice, in conjunction with its summer camps, Hizbullah's Imam Al-Mahdi Scouts Association[31] in August 2008 inaugurated The Art's Unique Workshop (al-Muhtaraf al-Fanni Al-Namudhaji), dedicated to expressive activities and creative performances aimed at reducing psychological stress on children after all the traumas and calamities that they had passed through in war-torn Lebanon. The project helps gifted children and youth express their noteworthy capacities, talents, endowments, and thoughts, through all kinds of plastic arts, such as drawing; painting; graf-

fiti; making artifacts from wax, wood, and clay. Concerning the performing arts, the project encourages children and youth to engage in theatrical
works and puppet shows. It also provides for them to learn music and how
to play musical instruments under the supervision of professional teachers
and musicians. Among other things, the Workshop also offers entertainment
and amusement activities such as children's parks, computer games, chess
and Scrabble (spelling) tournaments, and a children's books library with a
special section dedicated to the Mahdi Magazine.[32]

MUSIC

Hizbullah's music bands Firqat al-Wilaya and Orchestra Shams al-Hurriyya
testify to this trend of *al-fann al-hadif.* The party's official music group
Firqat al-Wilaya[33] was established in 1985. It composed the party anthem[34]
and is mainly concerned with producing Islamic *anashid* (songs, hymns, and
anthems) that mobilize the Hizbullah constituency to perform *jihad* against
any aggressor. Women's Firqat al-Wilaya (Firqat al-Wilaya al-Nisa'iyya) followed suit, and a subsidiary group, Firqat Fajr al-Isra' al-Inshadiyya, also
branched from it.[35] Hizbullah is the only Islamic party that has an orchestra
in the full sense of the term. Orchestra Shams al-Hurriyya ("Freedom's Sun
Orchestra") has been producing symphonies since its founding in 2003. It is
a new endeavor to elevate purposeful music and *anashid* to the level of professionalism, as its reason d'être statement stipulates.[36] The mission of the
party's music bands is summarized as follows:

> Hizbullah's Islamic artistic bands professionally specialize in different kinds
> of musical arts and believe in art as a means to realize noble aims (*al-fann
> al-hadif*). They abide by the tenets of Islam and operate in complete har-
> mony with the Resistance's project of jihad with music as a nationalist, hu-
> mane option that rejects tyranny and calls for freedom of the human being
> and the liberation of the land in harmony with Islam's moral virtues and re-
> ligious sensibilities. The music bands have been producing art with a mis-
> sion, committed art (*al-fann al-multazim*), which satisfies the pious aspira-
> tions of the human taste in art.[37]

Hajj Ghalib Abu Zaynab, Hizbullah's officer for Muslim-Christian dialogue, told me that many religious symphonies produced by the Orchestra are influenced by Christian hymns.[38] It is remarkable to note that the
revolutionary *anashid* of Firqat al-Wilaya were broadcasted via loudspeak-
ers from the minarets of mosques in celebration of every military victory
Hizbullah accomplished against its enemies. With this practice, Hizbullah is
broadening the mandate of Imam Khumayni, who sanctioned broadcasting

anashid on TV and radio: "The *anashid* that have benefit (*maslaha*) such as mobilizing youth to revolution and war like the ones chanted in eulogizing martyr Mutahari [with musical instruments] are sanctioned" (Hamidi 1994, 112). Khumayni added that a *nashid* could become an obligatory duty in some battles.[39]

THEATER/MUSICAL PLAYS

Hizbullah also resonates the theme of art with a purpose, *al-fann al-hadif*, in theater and musical plays. Scenes from Hizbullah's 2008 musical play[40] *When Do We See You? (Mata Narak: 'Amal Inshadi Ida'i?*)[41] featured men, women, and children performing on stage (cf. van Nieuwkerk, Chapter 6).[42] As Ayatullah Fadlallah affirmed, "I do not consider the profession of dancing and singing, which preserves moral obligations, to be prohibited."[43]

In organizing the musical play *When Do We See You?* at the Risalat Theatre in the cultural center of Ghubayri district in Hizbullah's stronghold of Dahiya south of Beirut, the party catered to the religious sensibilities of its constituency, thus immunizing itself against potential criticism based on those religious prohibitions (*al-mahazir al-shar'iyya*) that usually keep Islamic movements from engaging in such cultural activities. Yes, true, there was a scene portraying Hizbullah fighters chanting, dancing, and performing with weapons on stage, but the scene was short and symbolic, emphasizing the centrality of the party's struggle against occupation. However, revolutionary orchestral music, coupled with special sound and lighting effects, contributed to an atmosphere of awe in a colorful, pious Muslim performance dedicated to Imam al-Mahdi, the twelfth Imam. This ambience, and in particular the colors, were conducive to a breathtaking atmosphere that divided day and night, symbolizing light versus evil and darkness.

Ayatullah Fadlallah sanctioned portraying the roles of the Prophet and Imams in the theater or the movies, especially if these roles are to the *maslaha* (benefit) of Islam and help disseminate its universal message: "There is no absolute rejection to this subject for there is no evidence, either in the Qur'an or in the hadith, that prohibits the representation of prophets or Imams by an actor in a play or in a movie. Yet here emerges a secondary level of consideration related to the role the actor is playing. The actor has to make sure that his role is not going either to weaken the personalities and the greatness of the holy religious people or undermine them. Indeed, if there is any slight disdain to their holiness, then it is prohibited. Briefly, the action, in itself, is not prohibited." Rather, the prohibition depends on whether the image of the Prophet or Imam is distorted or not.[44]

A common misconception about Islamic movements is that their fundamentalist nature does not leave room for women to express themselves in the public sphere. To the contrary, the majority of the working force in Hizbullah's NGOs and civil institutions, in particular the media institutions, are women, a trend reflected on stage, not in quantity, but in quality (since this is a public performance). In addition to women's classical roles as mothers, sisters, educators, etc., women were portrayed as professional, committed (*multazim*) actresses on stage, mixing with men and children in some scenes.

In this regard, Ayatullah Fadlallah legitimizes women's participation in the field of theaters and movies on the following grounds: "We do not see any illegitimacy so long as this job does not contradict with our Islamic path. Furthermore, I do not only encourage such activities, but I see them as a must since they help in enlightening our people on all levels politically, socially and morally as well. Therefore, I encourage the Muslim women to take part in this important field due to its greatest advantages to the Islamic cultural sphere (*al-saha al-Islamiyya*) and at the same time due to the greatest role the Muslim women could be performing."[45] Ayatullah Fadlallah told me that the issue is not putting a veil on her head, even if it is a religious obligation; rather, the actress should place a veil on her heart, instincts, and temptations. He reiterated that the main issue is to be a human being first and foremost, irrespective of gender. When a woman engages the public space, she goes out as a human being, not as a female body alone, which would demean her status. She goes out as reason, will, movement, and beautiful voice conducive to the promotion of *al-fann al-multazim*.[46]

Another distinguishing feature of the play was the presence of the children in an organized, expressive way in spite of all the lights, colors, sounds, movement, and special effects, which might have seemed scary and distractive to children of a young age. But they, like the youth, were acting with an attitude of reverence and anticipation. The context and purpose of the musical play overrode all other considerations. The context was the celebration of the birth of Imam al-Mahdi, and the purpose was to strengthen the believer's relationship with him until he appears again at the end of time. Due to their commitment (*iltizam*[47]), eighty people organized the whole work in the span of three weeks, dividing the chores according to their specializations in singing and acting, where Hizbullah's Women's Organization, Firqat al-Fajr al-Inshadiyya, and Firqat al-Wilaya al-Nisa'iyya took leading roles. Behind the scenes a large team of technicians, sound and light engineers, computer graphics artists, décor personnel, and fashion designers burned the candle at both ends contributing to the success and outreach of the work. The overall message behind the production was the common wisdom that purposeful-righteous work, sacrifice, and noble intention (*niyya*) will herald the reappearance of the Mahdi, as popular culture and Shi'ite traditions dictate.

In a similar vein, the artistic work *Dawn* (*Tulu' al-Subh*), to commemorate the birth of al-Mahdi in August 2009, targeted the same end; however, it was more creative and daring. With amazement, I watched the separate scenes of flame blowers performing on stage and acrobats walking on four-meter-high sticks. I wondered about the significance of these scenes, since we were not in a circus, but rather commemorating an austere, solemn religious event. It was the purposefulness of the scenes: the dialogue between the flame blowers and the audience centered upon the concepts of heaven and hell, while the dialogue between the audience and the towering acrobats promoted the values of humility and respect through the simple question of "Why are you so high?," an admonition to the acrobats to stop showing off and descend from their ivory towers to engage the common citizen as equals.[48] This leads us to a question: Is every artistic expression sanctioned in *al-saha al-Islamiyya* as long as it falls within the domain of art with a mission?

TESTING THE BOUNDARIES: LIMITATIONS OF THE ISLAMIC CULTURAL SPHERE

Actually, the answer is no; not every artistic expression could be legitimized in the Islamic cultural sphere, especially if it is deemed as insulting to the religious sensibilities of the pious audience and consumers of this kind of entertainment. The following three examples illustrate the relative vulnerability of artists within *al-saha al-Islamiyya*. I begin with the case of Marcel Khalife, then I discuss Sayyid Nasrallah's case, and finally I shed some light on Jad al-Maleh's case.

MARCEL KHALIFE: HURTING AND INSULTING RELIGIOUS SENSIBILITIES AND TESTING THE LIMITS OF FREEDOM OF EXPRESSION

Shi'ite jurisprudence defends *al-fann al-hadif* to a large extent. Marcel Khalife is a case in point. In 1995, from his CD entitled *Arabic Coffeepot*, the Christian Lebanese singer played on his *'ud* (lute) a song entitled "Ana Yusuf, Ya Abi," based on a two-line verse from Surat Yusuf of the Qur'an: "Behold! Joseph said to his father: 'O my father! I did see eleven stars and the sun and the moon: I saw them prostrate themselves to me!'" (12:4).[49] The song was written by the late Palestinian poet Mahmud Darwish. Its purpose was to portray the suffering of the Palestinian people (Freemuse 2006, 29–30).[50] Marcel Khalife earned the condemnation of the Sunni religious establishment headed by the Mufti of the Republic, while Ayatullah

Fadlallah came to his rescue and defended him to the very end until he was exonerated in court on December 14, 1999.

Since the release of his song till 1999, Khalife was summoned three times to court on the accusation of blasphemy against Islam, in conformity with the Sunni view that regards the use of Qur'anic text in itself as blasphemous, as the Mufti of the Republic repeatedly affirmed. In 1996 the late prime minister Rafiq Hariri put a lid on the case, but he was unable, ultimately, to stop the proceedings indefinitely. The case came emphatically to the fore again when on November 3, 1999, Khalife was summoned to court on the charge of insulting religious values, beliefs, and sensibilities—i.e., the charge of blasphemy surfaced again. Khalife was not alone; he had the backing of the civil society's constituents, including its elite, the intelligentsia, and most notably the Lebanese Bar Association. The case dragged on more than a month, and Khalife had the chance to address the "inquisition court," as he dubbed it, more than once. In his statements Khalife stressed that the main purpose behind his singing is to promote *jihad* with music: "I addressed people's sense of dignity and resistance, and was strengthened by their faith and their rightful claim to their land." Khalife added that as a "creative artist" he protested in a civilized way against indecencies and debaucheries, in particular "the banality and stagnation in which the Arab individual blissfully lives day and night exposed to the 'artistic' creations transmitted and aired by the Arab terrestrial stations and satellite networks" that offend people's religious sensibilities and sense of dignity (Korpe 2004, 135–137).[51]

He affirmed that his trial amounts to a "profound cultural shame," a disgrace to Lebanon's "moral heritage" and "rich tradition of artistic and cultural expression." He leveled harsh words in strongly condemning the Sunni religious establishment: "I believed that the spirit of religion was more broad and tolerant than the interpretations by those who appoint themselves as guardians of our faith and morality," questioning if they are "losing their authenticity" when Islam enriched Lebanon with a "rich tradition that has provided its people with a depth of intellectual and cultural dimension" (Korpe 2004, 136–137).

Khalife stressed the main aim behind his song was to elevate Arabic music to an empowering "cultural status" against a backdrop of indecencies and debaucheries. He forcefully stated that his song catered to Muslim religious sensibilities and was intended for a good purpose: "I shall not believe that quoting or incorporating a fragment of a Koranic verse in a poem, and reciting it with truth, reverence, and spiritual sensitivity, justifies this lawsuit. . . . I have formulated the song . . . with a densely symbolic texture in which Joseph [Yusuf] represents innocence, beauty, truth and sacrifice." The court proceedings concluded in declaring Khalife's innocence. In his final address Khalife expressed his delight with the Lebanese judicial system, which proved to be a supporter of the "human rights of freedom, culture, and art," against unfounded, demeaning accusations (Korpe 2004, 137–140). On which grounds did Hizbullah and Ayatullah Fadlallah applaud the decision?

In principle, Ayatullah Fadlallah argues, "All kinds of Qur'anic recitation, even the ones accompanied by music [*talhin*], are allowed, simply because we allow the kind of musical songs which include words of justice and right, so how about the Qur'anic verses which contain the words of God? Indeed, what is not legitimate in this sense is the kind of music, which might not suit the holiness of the Qur'an. My viewpoint in this respect is that music increases the effects on the soul and the spirit. For this reason, we prohibited the musical songs, which support injustice in order that such words might not penetrate into the people's minds, while we deemed lawful the songs whose words call for justice and fight oppression and tyranny. Most importantly, we encourage the Qur'anic reciting competitions, which take place everywhere, provided that they do not violate the Qur'anic atmosphere of piety."[52]

In this particular case, on April 10, 1999, Ayatullah Fadlallah issued his opinion in a statement entitled, "A response to the accusations that were leveled against Marcel Khalife for desecrating sanctities." After affirming the necessity to respect sanctities and to avoid any kind of sedition, Fadlallah stressed that this *talhin*—the poem (song) that contains a Qur'anic verse—expresses a humanistic content that does not encroach upon the sanctity of the Qur'an, since this *talhin* is in conformity with the Qur'anic atmosphere of piety and adheres to Muslim religious sensibilities. In an indirect reference to the Sunni Mufti of the Republic, Fadlallah cautioned those who deal with the general public to carefully evaluate the nature of the sensitivities that are aroused in such cases, weighing the positive and negative consequences (*masalih* and *mafasid*) before making any decision, especially if that decision might have dire consequences on Islamic causes.[53]

This incident did not tarnish Khalife's credentials in Hizbullah's eyes. Since the party employs Islamism as a guise for a certain notion of Islamo-nationalism, Hizbullah continued utilizing Khalife's nationalistic songs that preach *jihad* with music as a means of mobilization, precisely to arouse the motivation of the Hizbullah fighters, while keeping it under the control of the rational faculty, as the doctrine of greater *jihad* prescribes.

HURTING HIZBULLAH'S RELIGIOUS SENSIBILITIES: NASRALLAH MOCKED ON A LEBANESE TV COMEDY SHOW

On the evening of June 1, 2006, LBCI aired its weekly political satire show entitled *Basmat Watan*, the name a pun that could imply either "The Death of a Nation" or "The Laughs of a Nation." One of the actors, dressed like Hizbullah's leader in his black turban and religious attire, mocked Nasrallah as a political leader, and not as a religious leader, thus trying to avoid offending the religious sensibilities of the Hizbullahis. In spite of that, Hizbullah's constituency took to the streets chanting Imam Husayn's call in Karbala', "Death to humiliation" (*hayhat minna al-dhilla*), intending to go all the way to the Christian heartland to "burn" LBCI. On their way they committed mayhem in Sunni and Christian areas, almost physically engaging the people, who adhere to a diametrically opposed ideology, especially the youth residing in these areas. After Hizbullah's members of parliament and middle-rank cadres failed to contain their crowds, Nasrallah, personally, in an unprecedented call by way of Hizbullah's media, called on the demonstrators to return to their homes. Although they immediately obeyed, the riots tainted Hizbullah's image as an advocate of free speech and expression and upholder of public freedoms.

This event ought to be read in light of the following instance, in which Hizbullah's reaction matched that of the Vatican.[54] In line with the Vatican's stance and the condemnations of the Catholic and Orthodox bishops in Lebanon and elsewhere, on February 19, 2009, Hizbullah released a declaration vehemently censuring the Israeli comedian Yair Shlein, who, on Channel 10, ridiculed Jesus and Mary in a TV comedy series: "We are deeply saddened by the terrible insult to prophet Jesus and his immaculate, holy mother, Mary . . . We call upon human rights organizations and the international community to condemn the public desecration of religious beliefs and doctrines and to stop the derision of religious personalities." In turn, the Vatican blasted the show as an "offensive act of intolerance," a position that prompted the Israeli government to intervene to interrupt the transmission and make Shlein and Channel 10 offer a public apology.

So, which redlines were breached in the Nasrallah case? Which religious sensibilities were trampled upon? According to Hizbullah, the answer is straightforward: merely wearing the attire and turban of a Sayyid, a direct descendant of the Prophet, by a comedian is an unacceptable act (*batil*) that is very demeaning to Shi'ite traditions.

THE BAN ON A SOLO COMEDIAN:
THE CASE OF JAD AL-MALEH

Jad al-Maleh—a French comedian of Moroccan-Jewish descent who is famous for his one-man theatrical comic acts—was forced to cancel his shows in Lebanon in July 2009[55] after Hizbullah accused him of having served in the Israeli armed forces.[56] But there is more to this. What seemed on the surface to be a strictly ideological matter turned out to confirm more and

more Hizbullah's sensitivity and reservations toward comedy shows and comedians, as the previous case might suggest. It seems that Hizbullah did not
want to risk the chance of being indirectly mocked by al-Maleh as the LBCI
had done, or was interpreted to have done.

What is telling is that all twelve thousand tickets for the three-day show
were sold, suggesting that the Lebanese public did not buy Hizbullah's allegations. On June 27, 2009, the entertainer's manager held a press conference in order to fend off the charges. He argued that the picture of al-
Maleh in Israeli military uniform that Hizbullah's al-Manar TV aired was a
fake, as were the Internet pictures posted on Hizbullah's websites and affiliated sites. Fearing for his safety, al-Maleh canceled his shows and reim-
bursed all those who bought tickets. A wave of condemnations by civil society organizations ensued, as well as by Lebanese cabinet ministers who
argued that the politically motivated allegations amounted to racial profil-
ing and were an onslaught on arts and culture, damaging, at the peak of the
tourism season, Lebanon's image abroad as a civilized society. The minister of culture termed the campaign an insult against cultural diversity, stressing the need to differentiate between an artistic work and the religion of the
artist, between culture and politics. He rejected exercising hegemony in any
form, especially the imposition of cultural and artistic choices. The ministers of information, interior, and tourism added that Hizbullah's allegations
amounted to prior censorship on cultural activities and public freedoms,[57]
the very things the party prided itself on upholding. They warned that Hizbullah's censorship in the cultural sphere was a dangerous precedent pointing to a bid by the party to impose its own Islamic cultural sphere on Lebanon as a whole.

A FINAL WORD ON COMEDY

Does Hizbullah have a problem with comedy shows and comedians per se?
Could not these fall within the domain of pious fun and entertainment? Are
these too much for *al-saha al-Islamiyya* to bear when other artistic practices that promote fun and entertainment are sanctioned? Asef Bayat explains and conceptualizes this censorship in relation to fun. Bayat has argued
that Islamists have problems with amusement, entertainment, and fun, even
in what they label as "controlled fun" or "pious fun," because:

> Fun disturbs exclusivist doctrinal authority because, as a source of in-
> stantaneous fulfillment, it represents a powerful rival archetype, one that
> stands against discipline, rigid structures, single discourse, and monop-
> oly of truth. It subsists on spontaneity and breaths in the air of flexibil-

ity, openness, and critique—the very ethics that clash with the rigid one-dimensional discourse of doctrinal authority. (2007a, 457)

The preceding examples suggest that this is not Hizbullah's main bone of contention, since the party is not uptight when it comes to fun and does not mind political satire, and even encourages it as a purposeful art.[58] More importantly, Hizbullah, in line with the Shiʿa traditions, enjoins the pursuit of "purposeful fun" within the domain of certain religious safeguards, to the extent of arguing that Islam sanctions fun and urges disseminating happiness in the hearts of the believers, providing for those who do so a great remuneration in heaven, as Moses, the Prophet, the fifth Imam Muhammad al-Baqir, and the sixth Imam Jaʿfar al-Sadiq had admonished (Cultural Islamic Al-Maʿarif Association 2007, 6–7). In other words, Bayat's reasoning seems not to account for the banning of some comedy shows.

In response to my question "Is there a prohibition on comedy as such in Shiʿite discourse?," Ayatullah Fadlallah, Abd Al-Halim Fadlallah, the head of Hizbullah's think tank, and Shaykh Shafiq Jaradi assured me that "there are no jurisprudential reservations to comedy as such." Abd Al-Halim Fadlallah and Shafiq Jaradi attributed the dearth of comedy productions in Hizbullah's *al-saha al-Islamiyya* to the restrictive public space that stifles creativity and artistic innovation. Ayatullah Fadlallah stressed that in terms of the religious safeguards (*al-dawabit al-sharʿiyya*), comedy, like any other performing art, should be in the service of humanity and human values. Purposeful comedies that highlight the social, political, and economic ills that plague society in an artistic way are welcomed even if they employ a sharp sense of critical satire. If the comedies do not cater to the human values of internal worth and dignity, do not elevate man's status, and do not serve justice and the good, then they should be shunned. Ayatullah Fadlallah reiterated the need to judge and act according to the jurisprudential principle of *maslaha*, which stipulates weighing the advantages and disadvantages of every artistic work.[59] Hajj Muhammad Raʿd, the current head of Hizbullah's parliamentary bloc, clarified that Islamic movements, in general, and Hizbullah, in particular, can promote art and creativity as long as they do not conflict with their jurisprudential stipulations and religious safeguards.[60] Building on the foregoing, it seems that the sensitivity toward comedy might be toward the likelihood of insulting the sensibilities of Hizbullah's senior religious figures and, by extension, the Shiʿite tradition they represent. Conceptualizing this, it seems that the party is adamant in upholding its symbolic capital (honor and dignity), come what may. Symbolic capital corresponds to someone's reputation, honor, distinction, and prestige. Bourdieu defined

symbolic capital as the "degree of accumulated prestige, celebrity, conse-
cration or honour [possessed by someone and] founded on the dialectic of
knowledge and recognition" (1990, 111ff.). Since for Hizbullah "dignity is
the opposite of humiliation, and death to humiliation," then if prefers to die
a million times, rather than to let a comedian trample on its religious doctrines and beliefs.

CONCLUSION

Hizbullah is notorious for its austere face of alleged "terrorism" and militancy, a debate beyond the scope of this chapter. I intended to portray a
new face of Hizbullah—the cultural face it promotes through ideologically motivated art, or an "art of resistance"—by examining its discourses,
activities, and artistic expressions in relation to work, leisure, music, theater, and comedy. The party's post-Islamist trend resulted in a new dynamic
where the old motif of *al-hala al-Islamiyya* gave way to the new theme of
al-saha al-Islamiyya. Hizbullah argued that the *shari'a*, as a socially constructed phenomenon, is flexible and pragmatic to the extent of account-
ing for all the complexities of modern life in *al-saha al-Islamiyya*, including
performing art. The party does not believe in the theory of "art for the sake
of art," or purposeless art;[61] rather, Hizbullah promotes art with a purpose,
art with a noble mission, especially stressing the mobilizational role of art.
The party does exploit certain forms of performing art, especially music and
zealous theatrical plays, as effective means of mobilization in the service of
noble ends such as fighting aggression and occupation in order to promote
peace and justice (cf. Boubekeur 2007). In *al-saha al-Islamiyya*, art with a
purpose legitimizes using the mosque as a forum to disseminate revolutionary songs, hymns, and anthems. Hizbullah's religious authority Khamina'i
even sanctioned chanting religious or revolutionary *anashid*, with musical
instruments, at the mosque, as long as they do not interfere with the duty of
prayer. However, *al-saha al-Islamiyya* has its limitations. Although Nasrallah's and al-Maleh's cases might imply that, with regard to comedy, Hizbullah wants to exercise artistic censorship and curb the very public freedoms
Nasrallah promised to uphold, and even though there is no prohibition on
comedy itself in Shi'ite discourse, the dearth of comedy production is attributed to the limited public space allocated to it in the Islamic cultural
sphere. Marcel Khalife's case of playing a Qur'anic verse on his 'ud is different because he did not insult the religious sensibilities, according to Ayatullah Fadlallah and Hizbullah, since his song is regarded as being in line with
"*jihad* with music" and is employed in mobilization. However, the party
censored comedy shows that might encroach upon the Shi'ite doctrine or

hurt the religious sensibilities of the Hizbullah constituency. So it seems that the problems of satirists started when they included Hizbullah personalities in their satires.

Unlike with music and theatrical plays, it is most likely that religious prohibitions (*al-mahazir al-shar'iyya*) rule out certain comedies as artistic expressions, since, in Hizbullah's eyes, they seem to promote purposelessness, or since their disadvantages outweigh their advantages. Thus, they may threaten the very foundations upon which *al-saha al-Islamiyya* is erected: namely, that art should be in the service of noble human goals,[62] the mainspring for the well-being of the humanistic community, as Khamina'i clarified (2009, 73).

NOTES

1. Personal interview, August 11, 2009. Al-Musawi worked at al-Manar TV as political programs editor and was the editor-in-chief of Hizbullah's weekly mouthpiece *al-Intiqad*. He holds a PhD in Islamic Studies from Birmingham University. Unless otherwise specified, translations from Arabic are mine.

2. From now on this heavily value-laden terminology will be abridged to *al-fann al-muqawim*, unless the sources or my interviewees use another specific term to connote it.

3. I only brought Iran into the discussion heuristically, since Hizbullah's religious authority (*marja'*) is Sayyid 'Ali Khamina'i, the jurisprudent (*al-waliyy al-faqih*) of the Islamic Republic of Iran. Thus, I confine my discussion to the cultural, artistic productions of the Lebanese Hizbullah. For cultural productions in Iran, see, in this volume, Farzaneh Hemmasi, Chapter 3, and Zeinab Stellar, Chapter 8.

4. For comparative purposes, especially in order to highlight the similarities and differences with the Lebanese context, refer to van Nieuwkerk, Chapter 6.

5. Personal interview, August 4, 2009.

6. For an elaboration on these concepts see my article "Ahl Al-Dhimma in Hizbullah's Islamic State" (2008).

7. My interviewees defined Islamists as fervent Muslim believers or pious (religious) youth.

8. The Lebanese myriad, or mosaic, refers to the ethnic composition of the Lebanese communities that comprise Lebanon, including the officially recognized eighteen sects.

9. Based on fieldwork, interviews, and discourses, I can fairly claim that Hizbullah embraces this dimension of art, as all my interviewees repeatedly stressed.

10. Cf. the last section in this article, "Testing the Limits" (Alagha 2001).

11. http://www.orchestra-hlb.com/materials/works.htm; http://www.orchestra-hlb.com/materials/calender_all.htm (accessed July 17, 2009).

12. Jurisprudence of amusing games, http://english.bayynat.org.lb/se_002/jurisprudence/amusingames.htm (accessed July 17, 2009).

13. Verse 7:33: "The things that my Lord has indeed forbidden are: shameful deeds/debaucheries, whether open or secret."

14. Cf. Samuel Beckett, *Waiting for Godot* (New York: Grove Press, 1994).

15. In very simple terms, this corresponds to Sufism in the Sunni tradition.

16. It is worth mentioning that from a Shi'ite theological perspective, it is a religious

obligation to render each individual her/his own rights (Maʿhad Al-Imam Al-Mahdi 2006, 30).

17. Personal interview, August 4, 2009.

18. "Refers to emotions related to extreme joy or extreme sorrow and also employs sensual pleasure," and "Sensual pleasure caused by listening to music" (Baig 2008, 6 and 335, respectively).

19. Personal interview, August 4, 2009.

20. "Music, singing & dancing: General Rules," http://www.sistani.org/local.php ?modules=nav&nid=2&bid=53&pid=2808&hl=music (accessed July 17, 2009).

21. Personal interview, August 4, 2009.

22. "Ruling on Songs by M. H. Fadlallah part (2)," http://english.bayynat.org.lb /islamicinsights/elaph_p2.htm (accessed July 17, 2009).

23. See the section entitled "Imposing injunctions between *masalih* and *mafasid*" (*fard al-ahkam bayna al-masalih was al-mafasid*). In Shiʿite jurisprudence, *maslaha*, which is a secondary source of law, can take precedence over primary sources of law, even the five pillars, as Imam Khumayni's 1988 fatwa conveyed. Khumayni stipulated that the *maslaha* of the Islamic order, or its agencies, gains priority over any other principle in social and political affairs, including prayer, pilgrimage, and fasting (Alagha 2006, 88– 92, 164–165).

24. "The Jurisprudence of Art," http://english.bayynat.org.lb/jurisprudence/art .htm (accessed July 17, 2009).

25. Reiterated in personal interviews with Shaykh ʿAli Daher and Muhammad Kaw-tharini, the head and CEO, respectively, of Hizbullah's Cultural Unit, August 7, 2009.

26. A woman's husband or close unmarriageable relatives like father, brother, and son. Ayatullah Fadlallah is a bit more relaxed than Khumayni in this respect. Fadlal-lah argues that a woman cannot perform sanctioned singing (*al-ghinaʾ al-muhallal*) in front of a man who is not her *mahram*. Further, a man should not listen to a women's voice if it cases discord (*fitna*) and seduction that might lead to spiritual and ethical de-generation, as the Qurʾan stipulates: "O Consorts of the Prophet! Ye are not like any of the (other) women: if ye do fear (Allah), be not too complacent of speech, lest one in whose heart is a disease should be moved with desire: but speak ye a speech (that is) just" (73:32). See "Prohibited and sanctioned jobs," http://arabic.bayynat.org.lb/mbayynat /books/fatawa/j2m1b3f1m1.htm (accessed July 17, 2009).

27. Quoted from *Ettelaat* daily newspaper, October 1, 1962.

28. "The Jurisprudence of Art," http://english.bayynat.org.lb/jurisprudence/art .htm (accessed July 17, 2009).

29. Ibid.

30. "If and only if" is a mathematical formulation, which implies that it is a must that both conditions should be satisfied.

31. "Music," http://www.almahdiscouts.net/essaydetails.php?eid=500&cid=5 (ac-cessed July 17, 2009).

32. "The Opening of the Expressive Arts Project," *Al-Intiqadnet*, http://www .alintiqad.com/essaydetails.php?eid=902&cid=46 (accessed August 1, 2008).

33. http://www.welaya-hlb.com (accessed July 17, 2009).

34. http://www.youtube.com/watch?v=idLyEv2oETM&feature=related (accessed July 17, 2009).

35. http://www.welaya-hlb.com/sub.php?op=new# (accessed July 17, 2009).

36. See DVD entitled *Whisper*, produced by the Lebanese Association of Arts, and http://www.orchestra-hlb.com/materials/works.htm (accessed July 17, 2009).

37. Personal interview with band members Mahmud Yunis and Bashar Laqis, August 3, 2009.

38. Personal interview, August 10, 2009.

39. Personal interview with Muhammad Kawtharani, August 7, 2009.

40. Plays are not alien to Shi'ite culture and religious traditions; they are part and parcel of Shi'ite rituals, most notably the Ta'ziya of 'Ashura, commemorating the death of Imam Husayn, the grandson of the Prophet.

41. DVD produced by Risalat (Lebanese Association of Arts), a subsidiary non-profit organization of Hizbullah's Cultural Unit founded to promote *al-fann al-hadif al-multazim* as an expression of "culture of resistance," mainly in its audiovisual works, as its reason d'être statement stipulates. In 2005 it was licensed by the Lebanese government and it was registered in the Ministry of Interior under number 295/AD, as published in the Official Gazette. As Kawtharani told me, Risalat is actively engaged in implementing its three-year strategic plan (2009–2012) in order to keep on promoting "committed Islamic culture" (interview of August 7, 2009).

42. Van Nieuwkerk demonstrates in Chapter 6 that at the *halal* Egyptian weddings the segregation of the sexes is the norm, which contrasts with Hizbullah's artistic expressions/cultural productions, where the mixing of the sexes is the norm.

43. "The Jurisprudence of Art," http://english.bayynat.org.lb/jurisprudence/art .htm (accessed July 17, 2009). (Cf. Chapter 8, where Stellar's discussion of dance in Iran points to the very different ways that Hizbullah conceives of both culture and the role of religion in public life compared with its Iranian counterparts).

44. Ibid.

45. Ibid.

46. Personal interview, August 4, 2009.

47. Always has a religious connotation that is in line with Islamic religious sensibilities.

48. The show took place in the afternoon of August 7, 2009.

49. http://www.youtube.com/watch?v=V9fpiTY2pNI&feature=related; http://www.marcelkhalife.com/httpdocs/audio/yusif.mp3 (accessed July 17, 2009).

50. See also http://www.marcelkhalife.com (accessed July 17, 2009).

51. See article 15 entitled, "Defending Freedom: Blasphemy Trials and Censorship in Lebanon" (Korpe 2004, 135–140; and http://www.marcelkhalife.com [accessed July 17, 2009]).

52. http://english.bayynat.org.lb/jurisprudence/art.htm (accessed July 17, 2009).

53. http://arabic.bayynat.org.lb/mbayynat/nachatat/04-10-99.htm (accessed July 17, 2009).

54. This was not the first instance. The 1994 UN Conference on Population Control, held in Cairo, saw an unprecedented concordance of ideas, especially those pertaining to religious and moral issues, among the Vatican, Hizbullah, and the Islamic Republic of Iran.

55. See Lebanese daily newspapers of June 28–30 and the National News Agency (http://www.nna-leb.gov.lb/details.php?cat=searchba).

56. Hizbullah has no problem with al-Maleh's religious identity, but, from an ideological perspective, the party avoids any dealings with any Israeli citizen. Technically, since the armistice agreement of 1949, Lebanon and Israel are still at war. That is why Israeli citizens are not granted visas to Lebanon and vice versa. It is noteworthy that the Lebanese state issued al-Maleh a visa and did not revoke it after Hizbullah's allegations.

57. See Nasrallah's statement in the introduction of this chapter.

58. In its audiovisual media and press, Hizbullah displays caricatures of politicians and laymen, but never religious personalities.

59. Personal interviews conducted in August 2009.

60. Personal interview, August 3, 2009.

61. Personal interview with Muhammad Kawtharini, August 7, 2009.

62. This reflects the trend in Iran, where not all musiclike activities have been controversial. Since the music tradition has long been incorporated into the lives of Iranians, Persian traditional gymnastics (*zur khane*) seems like a particularly interesting point of intersection of art in the service of noble human goals (*al-fann al-hadif*). For instance, see http://www.youtube.com/watch?v=4QkVaaVwrkI (accessed March 24, 2010).

REFERENCES

Alagha, J. 2001. "Hizbullah's Gradual Integration in the Lebanese Public Sphere." In *Sharqiyyat: Journal of the Dutch Association for Middle Eastern and Islamic Studies* 13 (1): 34–59.

———. 2006. *The Shifts in Hizbullah's Ideology.* Amsterdam: Amsterdam University Press.

———. 2008. "Ahl Al-Dhimma in Hizbullah's Islamic State: Acceptance and Tolerance." *Shia Affairs Journal* 1 (Winter): 23–39.

Baig, K. 2008. *Slippery Stone: An Inquiry into Islam's Stance on Music.* Garden Grove, CA: Openmind Press.

Bayat, A. 1996. "The Coming of a Post-Islamist Society." *Critique: Critical Middle East Studies,* 9 (Fall): 43–52.

———. 2007a. "Islamism and the Politics of Fun." *Public Culture,* 19 (3): 433–460.

———. 2007b. *Making Islam Democratic: Social Movements and the Post-Islamist Turn.* Stanford, CA: Stanford University Press.

Bdir, F. B. 2008. "Legitimizing Haram in TV Series: Till When?" *Al-Intiqad* 1278 (August 5): 11.

Boubekeur, A. 2007. "Post-Islamist Culture: A New Form of Mobilization?" *History of Religions* 47 (1): 75–94.

Bourdieu, P. 1990. *In Other Words: Essays towards a Reflexive Sociology.* Cambridge: Polity Press.

Cultural Islamic Al-Ma'arif Association. 2007. *Majalis Al-Afrah [Celebration of Feasts].* Beirut: Cultural Islamic Al-Ma'arif Association.

Fadlallah, M. H. 2009. *Al-Ijtihad Byna Asr Al-Madi wa Afaq Al-Mustaqbal [Jurisprudence between the Shackles of the Past and the Horizons of the Future].* Beirut: Al-Markaz Al-Thaqafi Al-'Arabi.

Freemuse. 2006. *All That Is Banned Is Desired: Conference on Freedom of Expression in Music* (October 2005). ISSN: 1601-2127. Copenhagen: Freemuse.

Hamidi, S. H. 1994. *Al-Ghina' wa Alat Al-Tarab [Singing and the Instruments of Enchantment].* Tehran: Markaz Nashr Jami'at Al-'Ilm wa Al-Sun'a fi Iran.

Hammud, A. 2008. "A Person Can Be Duped with Two Things: Idleness Is More Tiring Than Work." *Al-Intiqad* 1288 (August 8): 12.

Hammud, M. A. 2005. *Al-Qawl al-Fasl bi Hurmat al-Ghina' fi al-'Urs [The Final Word on Prohibiting Singing in Weddings].* Beirut: Dar al-Manhal al-Lubnani.

Harb, M. 2006. "Pious Entertainment: Al-Saha Traditional Village." *ISIM Review,* no. 17, 10–11.

Kepel, G. 2002. *Jihad: The Trial of Political Islam.* Translated by Anthony F. Roberts. London: I. B. Tauris Publishers.

———. 2008. *Beyond Terror and Martyrdom: The Future of the Middle East.* Translated by Pascale Ghazaleh. Cambridge, MA: Belknap Press of Harvard University Press.

Khamina'i, A. 2009. *Al-Fann Al-Islami ʿinda Al-Imam Al-Qaʾid [Islamic Art According to Imam Khamina'i].* Compiled by Muhammad Salar, the cultural attaché of the Islamic Republic in Lebanon. Beirut: Dar Al-Mahajja al-Bayda'.

Khosrokhavar, F. 2002. "Le Hezbollah, de la Société Révolutionnaire a la Société Post-Islamiste [The Hizbullah: From a Revolutionary Society to a Post-Islamist Society]." In *Passions et sciences humaines,* ed. Claude Gautier and Olivier Le Cour Grandmaison, pp. 129–144. Paris: Centre Universitaire de Recherches sur l'Action Publique et le Politique (CURAPP).

Khu'i, A. 1990. *Mihaj Al-Salihin [The Curriculum of the Righteous].* Qumm: Madinat Al-ʿIlm.

Korpe, M., ed. 2004. *Shoot the Singer! Music Censorship Today.* London: Zed Books

Maʿhad Al-Imam Al-Mahdi li Al-ʿUlum Al-Islamiyya. 2006. *Thalathun Adaban li Al-Muta ʿalim [Thirty Religious Rulings for the Educated].* Beirut: Jamʿiyyat Al-Maʿarif Al-Islamiyya Al-Thaqafiyya.

Mandaville, P. 2007. *Global Political Islam.* New York: Routledge.

Murtada, B. 2002. *Al-Islam wa Al-Taswir. Al-Fann Al-Muqawim [Islam and the Plastic and Performing Arts. The Art of Resistance].* Beirut: Dar Al-Hadi.

Rayya, M. 2008. "The Villages' Children in the Summer: A Dire Need for Purposeful Activities." *Al-Intiqad* 1288 (August 8): 14.

Roy, O. 2004. *Globalized Islam: The Search for a New Ummah.* Rev. and updated ed. London: Hurst and Company.

———, ed. 1999. *Le Post-Islamisme.* Revue du Monde Musulmans et de la Méditerannée. Aix-en-Provence: Édisud.

CHAPTER 6

OF MORALS, MISSIONS, AND THE MARKET: NEW RELIGIOSITY AND "ART WITH A MISSION" IN EGYPT

KARIN VAN NIEUWKERK

ISLAMISM AND POPULAR ARTS seem to be an unlikely pair. Egyptian Islamists, with whom this chapter is concerned, have strongly condemned vulgarity in films, the obscenity of dancing, the dangerous hold of music on youth, and the laxity of performers' morality. Performing artists have been attacked, and female performers in particular have been heavily criticized for the exposure of their bodies. Religious fervor and fundamentalism seem to be incompatible with art and playfulness. In an inspiring article, the sociologist Asef Bayat wonders why puritan Islamists express hostility toward fun and joy (2007, 433). He argues that "anti-fun-damentalism" is not restricted to Islamists, or even to religious fundamentalists, but extends to all rigid one-dimensional discourses and authorities. According to Bayat, purists do not reject pleasure as long as it is rationalized and controlled (ibid., 437). It is particularly the spontaneous, uncontrolled character of fun and relaxation that worries the puritans, because it not only disrupts the moral order, but more importantly, the doctrinal paradigm on which their power and authority are based.

As several anthropologists and sociologists of performance (Schechner 2002; Carlson 2004; see also Karin van Nieuwkerk, Introduction, this volume) also have argued, ritual and cultural performances have a potential for disrupting social configurations. Although scholars diverge in their ideas about whether performances ultimately reinforce or subvert social order, they have pointed to performances' potential unsettling character. Adding to their disconcerting capability is the centrality of the body in performing arts. The body is often perceived as a microcosm for "the social" in general. The body is inscribed by social norms and cultural frames, including gender scripts (Blackman 2008; see also Van Nieuwkerk, Introduction, this volume). Yet in performing arts, the body is not only matter to be disciplined, but also live material that embodies and produces norms and values. Moreover, piety and pious productions are potentially subversive for the secularized regime in Egypt. Hirschkind (2006) in particular has drawn attention to the pious counterpublic in Egypt. (Pious) performing arts are thus a potentially unsettling, as well as productive, field that is regarded with ambivalence by one-dimensional secular and religious authorities.

Since the 1980s, Islamist preachers in Egypt—such as Sheikh al-Shaʿarawi and Dr. ʿUmar ʿAbd al-Kafi—have persuaded a number of artists, mainly women, to quit the scene and to veil. These former performers publicly denounced their former artistic activities as "sinful" and devoted themselves to religious studies, preaching, and charity (Van Nieuwkerk 2008b). Due to many factors—that will be explained in the next section—parts of the Islamist movement turned into what Bayat (2005) calls a "post-Islamist" movement. Since the middle of the 1990s, a wave of "new religiosity"—particularly among the middle and higher classes—has come to the fore. The new religious style of these classes can be characterized as a moderate consumerist combination of piety and modern lifestyles. It is mockingly called "air-conditioned Islam" and "casual Islam" (Tammam and Haenni 2003). In the "lite" version of Islamism, or post-Islamism, art became an important topic. Engaging with art became a salient way to distance the "modern" Islamist thinking from the previous "hard-liners' intolerant Islamism." According to the moderate "*wasatiyya*" discourse, Islam and arts are compatible if they are performed in a religiously correct, *multazim*, way. Preachers such as ʿAmr Khalid went beyond this discourse and asked for the artists' return so that they could produce art in service to the Islamic Revival. Several of the retired performers decided to make a comeback and produce pious art. These productions aim at supporting a pious lifestyle and providing an alternative to "lowbrow" art. Female performers experimented with acting veiled roles.

In this chapter I will deal with the development toward pious performing arts and the discourse backing the preaching–performing art project. This Islamist art project has several labels, such as Islamic (*islami*), licit (*halal*), and clean (*nidif*), but the most often used generic label is *al-fann al-hadif,* "art with a mission" or "purposeful art." Since the most important aim of these productions—in accordance with the goals of the piety movement more generally (Mahmood 2005; Hirschkind 2006)—is to inspire audiences to live a pious lifestyle, I will also refer to these productions as pious art. The pious art productions have fans and critics. Based on fieldwork in 2005, 2006, and 2008 among retired performers and artists who returned to produce pious art, as well as a number of journalists, producers, and artists with Islamist and non-Islamist leanings, I will analyze the present discourse on *al-fann al-hadif.*[1] What exactly is the mission of "art with a mission"? Should we analyze the present upsurge of pious pleasure, *halal* songs, clean films, and religious wedding bands as the result of a relaxation on the part of Islamist puritans? Or are they advocating a controlled form of pleasure and entertainment? Is piety balanced by pleasure in these productions? How do those involved deal with the exposure of female bodies in pious production? How is *fann al-hadif* received by the consumers? And are these pious performances unsettling for the (secular) social order?

In this article, I will analyze the emergence of new ways of thinking on Islam and the performing arts, and more specifically elaborate the ideas behind art with a mission. I will describe the developments toward *fann al-hadif* in two fields of performing arts. First, I will look into the productions made by pious actors and actresses who decided to return to the screen or stage in order to produce pious performing arts. I will particularly deal with the religious soaps that overflowed Egypt during Ramadan 2006. Second, I will go into the development of the successful religious market for Islamic weddings and the production of songs catering to this field of popular art. In the conclusion, I will look into the relationships among pious art, its moral mission, and the religious market.

POST-ISLAMISM, *WASATIYYA*, AND NEW RELIGIOSITY

In order to understand the changing discourse with regard to arts, we have to understand recent developments in Egypt that are described under different labels such as "post-Islamism," "new religiosity," and "moderate Islamist discourse" (*wasatiyya*). These terms describe related processes but are not completely equivalent.

Post-Islamism is a term used by Roy (2004), Bayat (2002, 2005), Kepel (2000), and Stacher (2002) to denote slightly different but interlinked developments in the Islamist movements. Bayat and Kepel relate it to the moderate turn of Islamist movements away from violence or rigid doctrinal views toward a fusion of "religion with democracy." Post-Islamism does not mean the end of Islamism, but a reformulation of Islamist discourse from within the Islamist movement. Bayat describes post-Islamism as a condition and a project. Among the social and political conditions that gave rise to post-Islamism is a period of trial and error that induced Islamists to reformulate views. As a project, it aims to reconcile "religiosity and rights, faith and freedom" (2005, 5). This view of post-Islamism directs attention to intellectual movements such as the *wasatiyya* movement and political platforms or parties such as al-Wasat, which emerged in 1996.

Roy links post-Islamism to the individualization and privatization of Islam (2004, 97–99). Post-Islamism is not directed at reconstructing the state, but at the re-Islamization of individual practices. This view stresses the turn from "religion" into "religiosity" and focuses on the development of new forms of piety and religiosity in countries such as Egypt. This take on post-Islamism is related to the above-mentioned post-Islamist conditions. Due to the politicization of Islam, those with religious sentiments seek different ways of expression. These conditions have led to a fragmentation of religious identity and authority and a blossoming of new and different forms of religiosity and religious movements (2004, 3). In Roy's description of post-Islamism, religious lifestyle, rather than the political aspirations, are emphasized.

I will use the term "post-Islamism" to indicate the sociopolitical conditions and project leading to a more open, moderate reformulation of Islam in the contemporary era. It has given rise to such intellectual movements as, in the Egyptian context, *al-wasatiyya* or political projects such as al-Wasat. These are specific post-Islamist intellectual and political trends within the Islamist movements. Post-Islamist trends can also evolve into lifestyles induced by preachers endorsing moderate discourses such as *al-wasatiyya*. These preachers promote new forms of religiosity. When discussing the intellectual currents I will specify them as *al-wasatiyya*; when discussing the ensuing lifestyle by pious Muslims I will use the term "new religiosity." The new religious lifestyles are influenced by the new discourses and vice versa. I will not go into the general post-Islamist conditions leading to the reformulation of Islamism but restrict myself to the field of art. I will first discuss the post-Islamist discourse on art of "moderate Islamist" intellectuals and next the pious lifestyle, or new religiosity, insofar as it pertains to producing and consuming pious art.

The Egyptian *wasatiyya* movement is a centrist Islamist intellectual trend. Baker (2003) situates the movement between the "quietist pietistic" trend, which focuses on individual belief and ritual, and "extremists" who seek to remake society by means of violence. It emerged from the mainstream Muslim Brotherhood, but has become an independent trend. Scholars, journalists, and intellectuals such as Yusif al-Qaradawi, Muhammad al-Ghazali, Fahmi Huwayda, and Muhammad 'Imara are important thinkers of the *wasatiyya*. They have reformulated Islamist positions on social, cultural, and political issues. Gender and art are prime topics with which they demarcate their moderate ideas from those of "hard-core Islamists." They reject those Islamists who denigrate the arts, condemn singing, and declare a woman's voice '*awra*, a source of shame (Baker 2003, 56). The *wasatiyya* movement has put art back on the Islamist agenda. Art, instead of being reviled, has become a focal theme to position the movement's centrist views.

Of the *wasatiyya* intellectuals, particularly al-Qaradawi (1997, 2001) and Muhammad 'Imara (1991) have written extensively on art. They developed positive ideas about arts in general that paved the way for the specific discourse on art with a mission. First, they firmly state that there is no conflict between piety and moderate entertainment and systematically refute the sources used by opponents of music, singing, and diversion by demonstrating that the quoted *hadith* is either weak, interrupted, or inauthentic. Second, they refer to the general rule that everything is permissible except if the sources clearly state that something is *haram*, deducing that art is *mubah*, permitted. Third, they argue that "diversion" is essential to recreation. A community without arts is unimaginable, and creativity is an essential part of human nature. The beauty of creation is God's gift to humanity, and artists must use their God-given talents. Finally, the *wasatiyya* intellectuals argue for authentic arts, or an "aesthetic of belonging," that expresses the cherished values of society, yet warn against an unlimited freedom of expression, or an "aesthetic of abstract rights" (Baker 2003, 57–63). There are conditions for the lawfulness of music, singing, and listening to them related to the content of the production and the comportment of the performers. The audience should also find a sensible middle point, a balance between religious obligation and a need for diversion (al-Qaradawi 2001, 287–302). So the *wasatiyya* thinkers advocate a moderate and controlled form of relaxation.

The trend of new religiosity and the emergence of a generation of new preachers are influenced by the *wasatiyya* intellectuals. 'Amr Khalid is the most popular of these new lay preachers, alongside Khalid al-Guindi and Habib 'Ali (Wise 2003; Bayat 2002; Haenni 2002). They are neither religious scholars nor intellectuals, but young lay preachers who hold degrees from the Cairo University or the American University in Cairo. They dress in a modern-looking outfit and lecture at middle-class homes and clubs. Besides their use of new electronic technology for reaching out to youth, their perceived independence from both "extremists" and al-Azhar's "official orthodoxy" adds to their popularity.

Several of these preachers, most importantly 'Amr Khalid and recently the rising star Mo'ez Mas'ud, stress art's importance for society (Khalid 2005; Winegar 2008). 'Amr Khalid's seventh lecture in the TV series *Life Makers* addressed the topic of culture and art. He emphasized the immense importance of art and culture in representing the characteristics of any community. If the young generation does not commit itself to producing art and culture out of fear of it being *haram*, the community will turn into a featureless face. The Prophet enjoyed beauty and art. He turned it into a tool to build the new community and strengthen the stage of revival in which the community was finding itself. This is, according to 'Amr Khalid, exactly what needs to be repeated in our time. He called upon all artists to use their

God-given talents to support the *nahda*, the revival. They should turn art into a tool to create pious subjects and support the *umma*.

In order to understand the new preachers' influence we have to take into account the emergent new religiosity among the well-to-do. These new preachers directed their message no longer solely at the lower middle classes, but mainly at the affluent classes who had become Islamized. Particularly, middle- and upper-middle-class women and youth who have become pious are an important niche for the new preachers. Many factors—which are beyond the scope of this chapter—are influential in the Islamization of the privileged classes since the mid-1990s. The general Islamic revival movement laid the foundation for this process. The flow of wealthy returnees from Saudi Arabia also brought an affluent religious lifestyle back to Egypt. They mingled in the expensive clubs and posh neighborhoods that were previously restricted to the secularized upper-middle classes or members of privileged groups who showed a more passive religious attachment. Several role models, such as famous actors and actresses who turned devout, helped to move piety into the wealthy classes as well (Van Nieuwkerk 2008b). The new preachers addressed these well-to-do classes with an attractive message: piety and prestige can go hand in hand, and wealth is no obstacle to reaching paradise (Wise 2003). They preached a pious lifestyle and developed an attractive and easygoing style of religiosity (*al-din al-laziz*).

Besides declaring as fact that faith and fortune can be coupled, the message contended that faith and fun can be united (Bayat 2002). As wealth and fun are not unrelated, it was particularly the potent mixture of wealth and religiosity that created the call for pious art and entertainment. The wealthy classes—used to recreational activities—asked for art and entertainment in accordance with their new religious sensibilities. They not only sought after a discourse that legitimized recreation, but also a form compatible with a pious lifestyle. Several singers, actresses, and actors who had retired for religious reasons returned to produce *halal* forms of art. They responded not only to calls of preachers such as ʿAmr Khalid to support the Islamic Revival by producing pious art, but also to an emergent market for religious productions (Van Nieuwkerk 2007). I will describe some of these productions in more detail below.

Besides the new discourse about pious art and the new religiosity among different classes, another influential factor in the expansion of pious art merits attention: the changes in the mediascape. Especially with the advance of satellite TV and the Internet, new opportunities for religious programs and instruction became available. The state-controlled media in Egypt offered hardly any space for religious programming except by state-approved religious scholars. The state media policy was inconsistent and counterproductive. While intending to fend off Islamist influences, the state actually increased the amount of religious programming and aired conservative sheikhs such as al-Shaʿarawi (Van Nieuwkerk 2008c). Veils were banned from the Egyptian channels, thus blocking the religious productions of veiled female actresses. Satellite TV, and particularly the booming religious channels—mostly owned by Saudi or Qatar businessmen or members of the royal family—offered the veiled actresses an alternative route to reach Egyptian homes. Since the late 1990s, religious TV has grown in number and diversity. The first Islamic channel, Iqra, was launched in 1998, and by 2008 there were about 21 Islamic and 11 Christian Arabic satellite channels. Also the 350 secular Arab satellite channels broadcast religious programs (Galal 2008). Many veiled actresses who returned to acting pious roles made their comeback through al-Risala, which is part of the Rotana Channel network and owned by the Saudi multimillionaire al-Walid bin Talal. At present there are thus favorable conditions for the production of pious art: a market, the means, the media, and a discourse backing art with a faithful mission.

AL-FANN AL-HADIF

The generally positive views on art among new preachers and *wasatiyya* thinkers paved the way for the discourse on *fann al-hadif*. Moderate Islamist thinking formed the condition for the *fann al-hadif* ideologues' project. Art was transformed into a project to mould society and individuals in accordance with the Islamic Revival. In order to analyze the discourse on *al-fann al-hadif*, I have used interviews with performing artists, producers, and journalists engaged in or critical toward pious art.[2] In addition, I have used visual material provided by the editor-in-chief of the Islamic magazine *al-Zuhur*, who organized a conference on *fann al-hadif* in April 2007.[3] At this meeting ten speakers and short interviews with invited guests highlighted the theme.

    Fann al-hadif is not the only term used to convey the idea behind art with a mission, or purposeful art. Also *fann al-nadif* (clean art), *fann al-multazim* (pious art), *fann raqiʿ* (uplifting art), *fann al-mabadiʾ* (art based on principles), *fann al-badil* (alternative art), and finally *al-fann al-islami* are current. It is in clear opposition to *fann al-habit* (lowbrow art). *Al-fann al-islami* as a label is becoming obsolete. It was used by the first generation of Islamists pioneering the field of pious art such as the group around Masrah il-Qima (Theatre of Values), which started in 1991.[4] Many committed artists at present either avoid the term or stress that by Islam they mean a nonexclusive notion pertaining to Muslim civilization, including religious minorities.[5] In order to avoid misunderstanding, most people I spoke to refrained from the adjective "Islamic" and emphasized the overarching morals and values of religious traditions that should be represented in art. Islamic art can be without a purpose, whereas purposeful art is not necessarily Islamic, according to the editor-in-chief of *al-Zuhur* magazine.[6]

Purposeful art is considered to be a neutral and thus more attractive label because it avoids association with "overpoliticized" or "extremist" Islamists. The renowned actor Wagdi al-'Arabi—also connected to Masrah al-Qima and leading actor in its 2008 production *al-Shifra (The Code)*—rejected all these labels. In his view, art should always be based on principles, values, and beauty. To include these qualifications in the label would mark the art production as exceptional, and thus be counterproductive. He prefers to call *al-Shifra* a "comedy" in order not to frighten the audience. The public could associate "Islamic" theater with being boring, austere, and in contradistinction to fun.[7] Other artists use the label *fann al-hadif* to avoid the image of the pulpit while still being able to express their moral message. This clearly indicates the awareness of these Islamist artists of the need to balance morals, mission, and merriment.

The reasons why its advocates deem art with a mission important are various. First, they realize the great importance of art in molding society and individuals. Second, if they would leave such a critical field to the artists presently enjoying popularity, it would destroy the "moral fiber of society," "sell the souls of youth," and "corrupt women and the family." Third, the pressing need to develop an alternative is not only in critical opposition to the reigning "*fann al-habit*," with its "indecencies" and "obscenities," "*fawahish*," but also to combat misguided views on Islam. An effort equal to that to combat secular artists, who "cherish absolute freedom of expression," is directed at "religious bigots" who distort Islamic views on beauty and art. Religious scholars who "blast art without distinguishing between *fann al-habit* and *fann al-hadif*" are regarded as just as dangerous.[8] "Backward thinking" contending that Islam and Muslims have nothing to do with beauty should be uprooted.[9] *Fann al-hadif* advocates thus spend much energy in explaining the positive relationships among Islam, creativity, and art.

This discourse builds upon the *wasatiyya* discourse. Yet the *fann al-hadif* missionaries argue beyond simply refuting the notion that Islam and art are incompatible, holding instead that Islam and art are organically linked. Several examples highlight this argument. First, they point to the imperative to beautify the mosque, by which devotion is directly connected to beauty. Second, the Qur'an is the clearest example of beauty, which makes experiencing beauty a religious practice. Third, they argue that God knows the basic constituents of man, that is, reason, body, feeling, and conscience.

Nothing that benefits the human being is prohibited in Islam. Islam cannot prohibit creativity or beauty, because they nurture human feeling and conscience.[10] Lastly, the *hadith* "God is beauty and He loves beauty" is another indication of enjoying beauty as devotional practice. The idea is that God created beauty, and in order to thank God for this blessing it is incumbent upon men to enjoy this beauty.[11] A person cannot be devoted to God and at the same time be incapable of sensing the beauty in this universe. Art and enjoying God's beauty are a devotional practice, and *fann al-hadif* becomes a means to implant pious dispositions into present and future generations.

Fann al-hadif thus has a strong (religious) pedagogical goal. Most speakers and interviewees pointed to the power of art to rectify, uplift, and reform individuals and society. Purposeful art is a "source of noble values" that supports "the didactic role of the family," "enhances people's morality," "inculcates good values in youth and society at large," and rectifies the image of Islam. All creative persons are influenced by the epistemological paradigm surrounding them. If this paradigm is Islamic, or one of cherishing values and morals in accordance with the *shari'a*, the creative person under its influence will never create anything that contradicts *shari'a* or its ethics.[12] In the event that the field of art is left to nonreligious people, all existing creativity will violate the *shari'a*, whereas by using the power of art to Islamize society, all individuals will develop pious dispositions. *Fann al-hadif* thus encourages devotion, raises pious individuals, and helps to realize an alternative to the prevailing art. This pedagogical view on *fann al-hadif* explains its importance and makes it into a critical project. Or in the words of actor Ahmed Mursi, "Participating in the work of *al-fann al-hadif* is a vital choice for our community. If *al-fann al-hadif* does not prevail in our community, then it will be lost."[13] *Fann al-hadif* is vital for creating pious subjects.

Several speakers emphasized the religious aspect of *fann al-hadif* by defining it as "art that makes the human being thank God for His blessings of beauty in this universe"[14] or as "virtuous art that makes the believer God-fearing (*yittaqi bi Allah*)."[15] Actor Samih al-Sariti gave an example from the *hadith* of how art was already used in the time of the Prophet to instruct people in a subtle and nice way. He described how Hassan and Hussein witnessed a recent convert to Islam doing the ritual ablution in the wrong way. Instead of directly approaching the man and correcting his mistake, they staged their ablution as a performance to be witnessed and followed without offending the man.[16]

Pleasure and enjoyment are not totally neglected though. Art should provide "high pleasure"—that is, it should motivate people to perform good deeds. Or in the words of actor 'Abd al-'Aziz Makhyun: "*Al-fann al-hadif* is neither depressing nor somber. Art should be cheerful; *al-fann al-hadif* should motivate people to excel and use their positive energy in a good way rather than wasting it on sensual pleasures that are invoked by *al-fann al-habit.*"[17] Fun and faith can thus only be united in "high forms of pleasure" through their moral purpose and content. Before looking into several examples of pious art that try to balance pleasure and high standards of morality, I will briefly describe some views of those against this socioreligious reform project.

I discussed the term "art with a mission" with the film director Dawud 'Abd al-Sayyid.[18] According to him this label was also used to denote the new realist genre during Nasser's reign. Realist productions at the time had the goal of raising people's consciousness and reforming society. The crucial difference between new realist films and the present pious project is that the former aimed at national or social reform and the latter at moral reform. According to Dawud 'Abd al-Sayyid, art is neither a tool to promote morality nor against morality, but should be outside the scope of morals completely. The *fann al-hadif* project is *tablighi*, missionizing, whereas art's mission should be to provide enjoyment because of its creativity and good quality. There should be total freedom of creativity and no limiting frame or purpose. Most secular artists and producers agreed with his point of view. For instance, *al-Fajr* journalist Muhammed al-Baz argued that art is neither related to morals nor to preaching, so purposeful art is bound to fail.[19] Like several other secular art directors, Dawud 'Abd al-Sayyid mentioned that there is only one measure to evaluate art: its quality. In short, they strongly criticized the present forms of art that were produced under the banner "art with a mission" for their lack of creativity and poor quality. They also attacked *fann al-hadif* present productions for being imitative and in need of refinement and professionalism. I will now discuss some of these productions and analyze whether they were successful in accomplishing the mission to produce pious pleasure.

RAMADAN SOAPS AND CLEAN CINEMA

The moderate discourse on Islam and art and the growing demand for pious productions stimulated the production of several forms of "religious" plays, films, and serials. First, an already existent genre of religious and historical plays of an explicitly religious nature, for instance about the Prophet or important imams, or glorifying historical battles, were given a boost. Some of these themes were also adapted to the soap genre, such as the serial about Sheikh al-Sha'arawi entitled *Imam al-Du'a* (Van Nieuwkerk 2007). Second, several actors insisted on working in contemporary social soaps instead of religious-historical drama in order to show the importance of moral and religious values for today's world. They felt that the historic costume productions represented Islam as bygone history and folklore (see Van Nieuwkerk 2008a; Salamandra 2008). Several social soaps "with a mission" were released during Ramadan 2006. Last, there is a genre labeled "*sinima nidifa*." Strictly speaking, it does not belong to art with a mission, but rather caters to morally conservative audiences and their religious sensibilities. I will particularly deal with the last two trends.

In 2006, several veiled actresses returned to the stage or screen and produced Ramadan soaps. For a whole month, the public could gaze at the familiar, but now veiled, faces of comedienne Soheir al-Babli, old star Soheir Ramzi, Sabrin, well known for her role as Umm Kulthum, and young star Hanan Turk, who quite recently donned the veil and continued her career as a veiled actress.[20] The veiled actresses had stipulated conditions upon their return to the screen and stage. The veil was one of the obvious conditions, just like no kissing, no embracing, and no "hot scenes." They were also much concerned about the text and the topic raised in the play or film. They insisted on its usefulness for society. So, for instance, *Awlad Shawari'* addresses the topic of street children and all the abuses they are exposed to. The veiled leading character, though, played by Hanan Turk, despite living in the street remains remarkably well on the right path. In the image of most Egyptian soaps, the family is central, such as in *Qalb Habiba*, depicting a well-to-do Upper Egyptian family of farmers. The family is headed by the widow Habiba, played by veiled actress Soheir al-Babli, who admonishes her wayward eldest son. He fell prey to the materialist seductions of the financial gains that became available to some after Sadat's open-door policy. Waiting for the repentance of her son, Habiba is supported by her lenient, moderate brother, who is the sheikh of the village.

Religious morals and family values are central and expressed by several means without turning the soap into a religious story. Not only the way of dressing and behaving, but also the abundant use of religious expressions and religious home decorations, and the positive representation of moderate Islam, tend to Islamize the soap. Bad and good characters are clearly separable along indicators of religious, moral, and family values such as filial love, modesty, patience in the face of bad luck, striving for the good, and warding off evil (see also Ahu Yiğit, this volume). So these productions are not simply pious performances, but also performing piety. Also, the body is not simply a chaste body, but foremost a pious body. The bodily comportment, way of dressing, and the way the body is moving enact piety (see Zeinab Stellar, this volume; Van Nieuwkerk, Introduction, this volume). Particularly the soap *Qalb Habiba* (see figure 6.1) shows lengthy shots of a mo-

FIGURE 6.1. Soaps of the veiled actresses: DVD cover of the soap *Qalb Habiba* (screened Ramadan 2006)

tionless mother, mumbling Qur'anic expressions and moving serenely when in action. Whether performing the daily prayers or a supplicatory prayer, holding and reading the Qur'an, or consoling and advising women to be patient and obedient with gestures of submission and patience, her body avoids restlessness and agitation. This pious body embodies religious values of calmness, *sakina*, and patience, *sabr*.

Despite their announcement of future plans, most veiled actresses have not yet reappeared in new productions as the main character.[21] Most people I interviewed agreed that the soap productions more or less failed. Particularly the exposure of the female body was a difficult issue. It was not allowed to provide pleasure and was accordingly strictly bounded by rules of comportment and covering. We can analyze this conveniently by looking into my informants' discussions about the veiling of actresses. Several artists and journalists belonging to the secularist fold stressed that there is no problem with veiling as such. Wearing *hijab* is an individual decision and belongs to the realm of personal freedom. Yet the problem emerges when the "rules" of the veil are enforced on art. My secular informants clearly distinguished between a veiled character and a veiled actress. The first is possible, the second not. They pointed at the many unnatural scenes that resulted from using a veiled actress: she cannot kiss or embrace her own "son" or "husband." Even when sitting at home with her "relatives" around her or alone in her bedroom, she is still unable to unveil. Soheir al-Babli was ridiculed because she refused to kiss her "son" when he returned from a long journey. This criticism needs qualification, though, as she allowed for kisses, but only on her hand, forehead, or shoulder. Soheir al-Babli explained, however, that she insisted on her "husband" being written out of the script and accepted only the role of a widow in order to avoid compromising scenes.[22] 'Afaf Sho'ib allegedly refused to look her "husband," the religiously committed actor Hasan Yusif, in the eyes during the series about Sheikh al-Sha'arawi. Eye contact was deemed improper and against Islam.[23]

The secular producers I interviewed refused to work with veiled actresses, although they did not mind occasionally producing films in which a veiled character is portrayed. In their view, this role should be played by a nonveiled actress. The producer 'Imad al-Bahad provoked tension when his veiled character had her—realistic—periods of doubts and unveiled.[24] Other secular critics argued that the problem is not the veil, but the veiled actresses' position on art. They had first declared art *haram* and now only permit a restricted form of art. It is this limited and restricted vision of art's permissibility that makes their art so poor.[25] Secular producers also blamed the productions for their "commanding good and forbidding wrong" style.[26] "If we like sermons we watch religious programs, not soaps," several producers and journalists said. They considered these productions unrealistic, boring, and preachy.

Criticism did not only come from the secular adversaries of *fann al-hadif*. Also within the circles of pious producers, journalists, and fans, I heard critical voices. Several veiled fans had set their hopes high with regard to the return of the veiled actresses, but were disappointed by the result. First, like the secular critics, they disapproved of the unnatural situations—actresses who remained veiled while resting in their bedroom—for not reflecting their own reality at all. Second, they criticized the image of the veiled character as a flawless creature for its lack of representativeness. In the soap *Habib al-Ruh* (*Sweetheart*) (see Figure 6.2), veiled actress Soheir Ramzi starred as a morally upright character enacting with her veil all the goodness and beauty of Islam. She acted the role of a virtuous wife who provided a strong moral alternative to her husband's devious lifestyle, at home and in public. This flawless, angelic representation of the veiled character was felt to impede the development of a natural image of veiled women and girls in Egypt. Finally, they also blamed the veiled actresses for using too much makeup, wearing very expensive accessories, and putting on ridiculous numbers and layers of veils. They did not feel represented at all as normally veiled Egyptian girls. Only Hanan Turk, who played the role of a street girl, was liked for her so-

FIGURE 6.2. Soaps of the veiled actresses: DVD cover of the soap *Habib al-Ruh* (screened Ramadan 2006)

ber outfit and simple makeup and was considered to be connected to the "normal life" or even to the poor strata of Egyptian society.

The veiled actresses thus embodied piety and the "moral good" of Islam, which restricted their possibilities for creative freedom. The way the fans wanted to deal with the artistic obstacles differed. Most did not have clear solutions for the unnatural situations except for shooting almost all scenes outside the home so that veiling is required and realistic. There were suggestions of wearing light shawls inside the house. Fans thought the veiled character should be allowed to make some mistakes. The editor-in-chief of *al-Zuhur* maintained that the veiled character can make mistakes as long as she immediately repents. In this way she remains a role model without becoming an unrealistic character.[27] The stricter religious critics preferred that the veiled actresses stay away from the screen and preferred that they appear in children's programs. Actor Wagdi al-'Arabi doubted whether the presentations of the veiled actresses, with their makeup, accessories, and shiny, colorful dresses, had done any good for the veiled girls and women in

Egypt. Although he acknowledged each individual's freedom to veil or not to veil, once veiled one has a great responsibility to spread the right image of Islam.[28]

The soaps were thus generally seen as a flop, and this probably explains the lack of a follow-up. This does not mean that the veiled actresses have had no influence. They have been influential in making veiling fashionable. Although they were heavily criticized for the layers of shawls, excessive accessories, and makeup, they were also admired for the way they have made veiling chic and stylish. They have also been successful in conveying the message that the veil is a common sight in the Egyptian streets and that this should be reflected in soaps and cinema. The number of films with a veiled character played by a nonveiled actress is increasing. The veil is transplanted outside the *fann al-hadif* context. Yet the way of veiling tends to become increasingly an object of fashion instead of piety. Stylish *"muhajababes"* (Stratton 2006; LeVine 2008) are no longer excluded from the screen. This "diluted" version of veiling and the "watered-down" mission of art were not originally envisaged by the *fann al-hadif* project. The pulpit-style *fann al-hadif,* though, was not successful in transmitting its message to the general public.

The second genre I would like to discuss briefly is the "clean cinema." Not only the veiled actresses and retired actors had fulminated against "immoral art." Many young actors and actresses, too, started to experiment with *sinima nidifa.* No veils and no religious expressions or imagery are used in this genre, but they refuse to commit "indecencies." The trend started with the box-office hit *Ismaeliyya Rayih Gayy* in 1997 (Tartoussieh 2007). The production team did not expect any success at all and were overwhelmed when the response from the public proved them wrong. The assistant director of the film explained that he and his colleagues started to be fed up with the 'Adil Imam type of film with "hot kisses." He related the embarrassment he felt when he had to shoot a film with 'Adil Imam and his female counterpart more or less "doing it" on the beach amidst a curious crowd.[29] Clean cinema erased hot scenes, kisses, embraces, and any scenes that could insult moral sensibilities. Hot scenes were replaced by a light genre of jokes and satire. It could contain wordplays with a sexual overtone or other kind of sexual jokes, but no direct depiction of sex. A romance is not shown, but made clear in indirect ways. Director Dawud 'Abd al-Sayyid called this *"hubb bil yafta"* ("love by signboard"). He ridiculed the clean cinema's avoidance of romantic scenes or its passionless way of imagining romance. "You better put a signpost on their breast 'I love you' than showing any signs of tenderness," he said mockingly. Many people criticized the "clean actors" in the "love scenes" for acting like brother and sister rather than lovers. Yet the light comical genre of clean cinema set off a whole trend of similar productions that started to saturate the market.

It was not purely a matter of morals, but more of the market. Clean cinema is a commercial genre for a specific prudish market that has grown with the return of migrants from Saudi Arabia. They have become accustomed to a conservative style of entertainment. A large part of the clean cinema is catering to the market in the Gulf and thus has to adapt to the conservative morality of these societies. This light, comical, and clean genre, although related to the morally conservative climate and growing religious sensibility, is not seen as *fann al-hadif*. According to many people I interviewed, it is to be characterized as empty and without any purpose other than superficial momentary entertainment. There are no messages involved, let alone religious messages. It is just meant as innocent and floating moments of laughter. The genre is reflecting the changing sensibilities among the public and actors, but has no clear purpose. It is not ideologically motivated or art with a mission, but rather a commercial genre. Yet it is considered more respectable than the usual "indecent" productions. It has morals, but no mission, and is highly marketable.

HALAL SONGS AND ISLAMIC WEDDINGS

Islamic weddings started around the 1980s as a sober celebration consisting of a short religious ceremony attended by male guests, after which the male and female guests divided into two separate parties. They sang *anashid* songs or other lyrics praising the Prophet and played the *duff,* the tambourine, amongst themselves. After eating some snacks or having dinner, the party was over. The present form, in which the amount of entertainment and festivity is more elaborate, is a recent phenomenon. The general opening up of the Islamist discourse toward art, as well as the growing number of devout, well-to-do people, created favorable conditions for the flourishing of Islamic wedding bands.

The bands started at the universities at the end of the 1980s and beginning of the 1990s. The bandleaders I interviewed[30] related that they started as students at the university. They were more or less involved in the Islamist student movement, the *gama'iyya islamiyya.* They performed sketches, sang, and played music for their colleagues at their wedding ceremonies. As with other people in Egypt generally, they felt that weddings are such an important occasion that they needed more attention and festivity than what was given in Islamist circles. The usual way with musicians, singers, and dancers from Muhammad 'Alistreet, the center for lower-class wedding entertainment, was considered "vulgar" (Van Nieuwkerk 1995), so they performed among themselves. This wedding style was very much appreciated by the guests, and the student-artists were accordingly asked to perform at the weddings of the guests of their colleagues. One of the first Islamic wedding bands, Al-Hada, started this way in 1989 (Tammam and Haenni 2005). They were followed by many others, including Basmit Andalus in 1994[31] and al-Wa'd around 1996.[32] The all-female band Sondos started in 1995[33] and was one of the first female bands, followed by, amongst others, Banat Basmit Andalus, led by the wife of the bandleader of Basmit Andalus.[34] Al-Wa'd leader Mustafa Mahmud had performed at around 1,000 Islamic wedding processions by 2004.[35] The bandleader of Basmit Andalus calculated that in 1994 and 1995 he had about 30 or 40 weddings a year. By 2005, he had 150 weddings. Estimating that there are probably about 100 to 150 Islamic bands performing at weddings, each having around 100 weddings annually—which in his opinion was on the conservative side—he calculated that about 2 percent of all weddings—in 2004, 500,000 marriage contracts were registered—are performed in Islamic fashion.[36]

Discussing what made a wedding "Islamic" provoked different answers by my informants. First, the Islamic label had to do with the level of commitment of the wedding couple and their guests. For instance, the bride and female guests are usually veiled—either wearing *hijab* or *niqab*. Yet not all veiled brides opt for Islamic weddings, so other features are also important in creating an Islamic ambience. Most important, a degree of gender segregation between the male and female guests is implemented. Third, it was strongly related to the style of entertainment. No belly dancers or female singers and the common "indecencies" going on at popular weddings, but respectable artists who stay within the religious confines with regard to the kind of music and songs they perform, the instruments they use, and the lyrics of their songs. I will mostly deal with the last two characteristics.

Gender segregation can take many forms. The most obvious is two separate parties. Segregated parties created a demand for female bands. Separate entertainment for women increases the costs of weddings, and the Islamization of the upper-middle classes has accordingly been important in the further development of the female bands. Yet some female bands also perform with a small group of young women doing simple forms of entertainment to keep the cost low. For instance, I visited a wedding where the male guests were entertained with a band, but the female guests—separated by a brightly colored cloth—had a DJ installation and danced among themselves. At the upper-class separate parties I visited in the luxurious suburb Dreamland, the male and female guests had separate *sala's*, and both parties had bands of entertainers with extensive shows. The female guests could remove their veils, exhibit their fancy dresses, and dance freely among themselves.

Yet not all Islamic weddings are celebrated in two physically separated spaces. Mixed weddings can still be labeled Islamic if the female guests are veiled and share the table with their male and female relatives and avoid mixing with unrelated men. At mixed parties women usually refrain from dancing, although I witnessed an Islamic wedding where women danced. I was told, though, that it was uncommon and only elder women who are directly related to the bride and groom are allowed to dance at mixed parties.[37] At these mixed parties the Islamic character is primarily defined by the style of entertainment that is performed. If the songs are "proper" and performed by an "Islamic" band that plays "suitable" music or performs "decent" shows, it is defined as *zaffa islamiyya*, an Islamic wedding procession, or *farah islami*, an Islamic wedding. Yet what counts as decent and Islamic has changed over time.

The bands, starting as small groups with only *"halal"* instruments, began to experiment with instruments and a more extensive repertoire. Which musical instruments are permitted is still under discussion. Most bands added drums to the *duff*, and some also *urg*, synthesizer, and violins. Most bandleaders I interviewed take a practical stance toward this matter. It is up to the "owner of the wedding" to decide the range of musical instruments. The flute, however, is rarely added, as this is considered *haram*.[38] The permissibility of the female voice is also under debate. But as far as live performances are concerned, this is not an issue, because women only perform in front of women. At mixed parties there are only male performers. This discussion is thus directed at the cassettes that are produced by several of the Islamic wedding bands.

The repertoire evolved as well. From the religious genre of the *anashid* it developed into a specific genre catering to the occasion—that is, mostly weddings, but increasingly also to other familial occasions such as the *subu'*, the party for a seven-day-old baby, the *hijab* party,[39] or people returning from *hajj*, and graduation parties. According to the lead singer of al-Wa'd, Mustafa Mahmud, the *anashid* songs were highly popular within the circles of students of the *gama'iyya islamiyya*. He became acquainted with *anashid* during his studies and initially sang them at parties. He quit the genre, however, because of its politicized content about struggle, as well as its foreign character. The songs were mainly imported from Palestine, Jordan, and Syria and sung by Egyptian singers with un-Egyptian names like "Abu Kaza," and also sung in another dialect. It was "not done" to sing *anashid* in colloquial Egyptian, use your own name, and diverge from themes such as the Islamic cause. He was, moreover, not impressed by the artistic level of the *anashid* and looked for a vernacular form of songs that suited the happy occasion of a wedding. Singers like Mustafa Mahmud thus started the "*halal* song movement"—a label he himself dislikes because it is not up to him to decide what is *halal* or *haram*.

Islamic wedding bands, looking for songs to entertain the guests without offending them with "indecent" texts, initially started to rework existing songs. They took songs of famous singers, and well-known melodies, and restyled them to the Islamic context. Making songs *halal* could mean not only adding a few words or cutting out sentences that were not deemed proper, but also writing a new song to suit the occasion. A song about separation from a beloved girlfriend became one about love for the parents or the husband. The importance of marriage was emphasized in preference to lamenting divorce. "Going to the *mulid*," literally a saint's day celebration, but also used to mean a chaotic place, was rephrased into "going to Paradise." The band Sondos restyled Sayyid Darwish's song in which improvident spending was encouraged into one praising generosity. They also revised a song for children from Sabaah and a song by Fayruz, which were already *halal*, to specifically address the topic of marriage and the bride. These songs were liked among the guests because they were entertaining, well known, beloved, and now guaranteed *halal*. Several bands started to record their songs and Sondos, Basmit Andalus, and al-Wa'd produced several cassettes. Al-Hayah Company is specialized in this type of tapes and has produced them since 2002.[40] It makes the tapes in three different casts: voice only, voice with *duff*, and voice with full complement of instruments. The "moderate" version, that is, voice and *duff*, is the most popular. In the meantime, the bands have become more professionalized and create their own songs. They earn enough money to ask renowned songwriters to write suitable songs, or they compose their own lyrics.

The bands did not restrict themselves to music and songs only. They also added sketches and folkloric dance to their repertoire. They were looking for new ways of diversion in order to satisfy their publics. They had to renew their shows and keep on developing their repertoire, because the guests demanded constant change in style and appearance. The band Basmit Andalus in particular now provides extensive male folklore dance repertoires similar to the regular folklore dance companies such as Firqit Qawmiyya, presenting the Upper Egyptian stick dance, the Suez fishermen dance, Nubian dance, and the whirling dance called *tannura* (see Figures 6.3 and 6.4). These male folklore dancers are professional dancers hired by the band for the wedding. Also members of the bands Sondos and Banat Basmit Andalus provide dances for female guests, with nice costumes and fitting veils, and do comedy sketches. Yet they are not professional dancers and actresses.

FIGURE 6.3. Islamic wedding: male folklore dance

FIGURE 6.4. Islamic wedding: male folklore dance

Islamic weddings have increasingly become a successful market, which also attracts people from outside the religious realm. According to Mustafa Mahmud, it has led to a host of singers who added a religious song to their repertoire. It was already fashionable, due to the growing pietization also among artists, to sing a religious song in Ramadan. Now many singers who perform at weddings, whether pious or otherwise, sing religious songs. Mahmud, of the band al-Waʿd, described the two-sided encroachment upon the Islamic wedding bands. Several singers who usually sang nonreligious songs, or even "vulgar" songs, started to perform a few religious songs. The public became less strict with regard to the style of entertainment at their "Islamic" weddings. With the Islamization of the upper classes, a nice, open, slightly watered-down version of Islam is gaining prominence. People feel that they can invite famous singers who have gained respectability and a religious image through an occasional Ramadan song. To show one's religious commitment, *iltizam*, one does not necessarily have to invite an Islamic band. As with all successful hypes, *halal* songs invite imitation that can lead to a diluted version. Whereas Mahmud is still in demand among the pious clientele, he has noticed transformations in the Islamic wedding scene. Due to their success, Islamic weddings have gained a wider popularity. Yet the style of entertainment in demand is increasingly of a pleasant and less clearly religious form. This form of entertainment is also performed by people at the margins of or outside the *fann al-hadif* project.

CONCLUSION

The instrumentalization of art for an ideological purpose is not a new phenomenon, as producer Dawud ʿAbd al-Sayyid noted. Art and television have been key institutions for the production of national culture in Egypt. The Egyptian state used the media to produce "the nation" through its discourse of national development and the genre of "development realism" (Abu Lughod 2005). The secularist and Islamist approaches toward cultural life are often understood in a contrasting and competing light (Zubaida 2002). Yet the revivalist and nationalist projects regarding art and entertainment converge in their claim that artistic expression and diversion should have a purpose. *Al-fann al-hadif*, art with a mission, can serve a nationalist and an Islamist purpose. The Islamist ideas differ from those behind the secular project of developmentalist nationalism mainly in that the former's goal for art and entertainment is moral improvement and the pietization of the believers' lifestyle (see also Schielke 2008). They share the purposefulness of art, yet the Islamist art project tries to create pious subjects instead of national subjects. The mission of *fann al-hadif* artists is to inculcate religious values and create space for pious subjectivities.

Coming back to Asef Bayat's ideas about the purists' rejection of non-controlled forms of arts, we can partly agree with this. *Fann al-hadif* is clearly a project that aims at controlling the form and message of art, to rationalize it into a format that is useful for promoting its mission. The rationalization of form and message was clearly noticeable, for instance, in sticking to the rules of the veil and the concern with the propriety of utterances and morally exemplary excellence of conduct. Particularly, the female body was to be managed, as veiled actresses were to embody the ideals of piety and morality. A large part of the moral mission was expressed through female bodily comportment.

Moral art seems to be inversely related to fun: the more missionizing, the less fun. Yet the less fun, the smaller the audience. Islamists felt the limits of an austere strategy and noticed they lost audiences, except for the most devout. For that reason the Theatre of Values preferred to promote its play as "comedy." The *fann al-hadif* artists felt the need to balance fun and faith, morals and merriment, without losing their mission. Yet this has appeared to be a difficult project to control. The various forces impinging on the project resulted in different forms of art that can be seen as a dynamic interplay between two scalable entities, that is, piety and pleasure. These scales do not necessarily contradict each other, but can vary in intensity. We can position the mixtures on a continuum, the left pole of which is occupied by artists who remain on the safe side of the religious discourse on the permissibility of art. They produce art that is overtly religious in content and missionary in purpose. They intend to rectify the audience rather than amuse them. The middle part is the heart of the *fann al-hadif* project, trying to produce moral art, yet within the fashionable formats such as soaps and contemporary songs. At the other extreme we can group popular art productions that have superficial references to religion and morality, such as clean cinema, or have moved beyond the scope of art with a mission. They are particularly meant to please a mass audience.

The need to balance morals and the market has thus led to ambiguous results for the *fann al-hadif* project. It has partly changed its formerly explicit Islamic content and frame of reference into a post-Islamist *al-din al-laziz* format, a nice and pleasurable form. We thus see a relaxation on the part of several Islamist artists. This relaxation is also visible in transforming the label from "Islamic art" into *fann al-hadif*. The gap that had existed between strict Islamists and the general public was somewhat closed up. The religious message was packaged in an enjoyable form by preachers and performers. It was successful in its aim to reach out to more people. It also addressed upper-class people, who were pleased by the message of *al-din al-laziz*. The new religiosity among the upper classes was an important condition for the further development of Islamist art into *fann al-hadif.* The eventual success of purposeful art, however, had a price. The more success it had, the more it lost its original message. It was copied, imitated, and transplanted outside its original frame and purpose. It spilled over to the non-*hadif* field of art production. It could "halalify" ordinary productions, and a diluted version came into being that was seen as an alternative to *fann al-hadif* productions that was even more enjoyable. The pious upper class increasingly tends to prefer listening to the famous, prestigious singers who have gained respectability through an occasional religious song, or watching a clean production without a clear religious mission.⁴¹

In a way, art with a mission thus seems to be buried by its own success. But this observation needs qualification, as it worked out differently for the songs and the soaps. *Fann al-hadif* in its original packaging was criticized for its lack of novelty and for its pulpit style. It was perceived as being boring, noncreative, and unimaginative art. Yet the songs have apparently been more successful in bridging the gap between fun and faith. When they experimented beyond the strict religious *anashid*, singers of *halal* songs began by cutting words and replacing them with clean alternatives, similar to the clean cinema strategy. Yet with this further development, the songs have become successful in attracting a large following, along with imitation. They were admired for quality and piety. There was a spillover that led to religious songs by performers with a normally "not-so-Islamic repertoire." This development is related to market forces, outside the control of Islamists circles, that also affected the soaps, but Islamists have been able to bring the songs and their religious content into the popular art scene. They have thus popularized piety and moved it into the secular art field.

The soaps were less successful in bridging faith and fun. They stuck to the message and could not that easily shake off the image of a sermon. The Islamist message remained visible in the form, for instance, of the veil and apparently imposed limitations on creative forms. The soaps were generally regarded as either a limited success or a complete fiasco. The soaps and historical productions that remained "truthful to the original message" were seen as unrealistic and preachy. Also the "comedy," or theatrical play, *al-Shifra (The Code)* was said to be only successful within the parochial circles of the Muslim Brothers.⁴² The packaging hindered the deliverance of the message. The soaps by the veiled actresses have not seen a new flow of productions, but there has been a spillover outside the *fann al-hadif* context that created veiled characters in the *muhajababe* style. These productions could be successful, or not, but were largely outside the scope of *fann al-hadif.* They are mainstream productions that are evaluated by the usual criteria for assessing art: their quality, story line, reflection of reality, etc., and not by their pious nature. These productions lost their pious frame of reference, while moving outside the scope of the *fann al-hadif*, instead of moving piety into the popular realm. Why have the songs done better than soaps in bridging fun and faith, while retaining the religious message?

First, it is remarkable that the success in the field of music is mainly achieved by male singers, whereas the failure of the television dramas is related, in large part, to veiled actresses. Gender is thus an important dimension, as has already been touched upon in the case studies. In performing arts, whether on the stage, small screen, or large screen, the body is focal. The body is a highly gender-sensitive issue. The female body on stage in particular remains a difficult issue (Van Nieuwkerk 1993, 1995). At weddings women sing in front of a gender-segregated audience. The market of religious songs as live performances is mainly dominated by men, although women, too, have entered the recording market. Actors and actresses heavily rely on a physical appearance that appeals to a general audience. The clean cinema, which counts as "morals without a mission," is mainly dominated by male actors. For a pleasing female body on stage, it is difficult to avoid sexual connotations whilst performing in front of the male gaze. The sexual dimension of the female body is contained by veiling and other forms of pietization. Religious comportment, as well as covering the female body in several layers of veiling, has the intent of changing the sexualized body into a religious body. Yet this neutralizing strategy does not produce a balanced form of pious pleasure. Maybe it counts as "high pleasure" for the *fann al-hadif* ideologues; most audiences apparently prefer less moralizing forms of enjoyment. The controlled or rationalized form, by emphasizing message rather than merriment, is considered boring and counterproductive. Exposing "pleasing" female bodies on stage is apparently difficult to combine with the piety of the project. It seems to be nearly impossible for "enjoyable female bodies" to escape connotations of "sensual pleasure." The range of male behavior between piety and pleasure is much larger than for women. The formats for pleasant forms of pious performances by female bodies are still not well developed.

Second, it is interesting to link the divergent success of the songs versus the soaps to a difference in the sensorium related to the genre. Using Charles Hirschkind's ideas (2006) on the location of the Islamist counterpublic in its alternative soundscape, it could be argued or imagined that the aural is a more fruitful foundation for an alternative, yet Islamic, message. Listening to cassettes has been an oppositional activity within the Islamic Revival. This could have led to a better adaptability of the aural to the Islamist project of *fann al-hadif*. Songs and cassettes have a strong base in the Islamic counterpublic and could lend themselves more easily to Islamist artistic production without losing the sting—that is, the message. The visual media to which the soaps belong have been largely dominated by the state and the secular field of art. For that reason, these media might less easily adapt themselves to alternative pious art, and visual productions of originally pious intent easily lose their sting and become mainstream. I discussed this theory with some of my informants, who pointed to the different material structure of the aural versus the visual media. The soundscape is more accessible and cheaper, in a sense more democratic, than the visual media. The latter need a lot of money and are dominated by market forces outside the scope and intentions of the actors, actresses, and producers involved. The visual media thus need a completely committed pious team from the level of the investor right down to the cameraman, and no less a committed pious public willing to pay for tickets for pious productions. These conditions are not met in Egypt, with its dominance by secularist ideas within the field of visual art. These remarks by my informants thus affirm the counterpublic status of the aural and the hegemonic character of the visual, not so much at the level of the sensorium, but rather at the level of the market.

We can infer from these remarks that the pious productions are, to a certain extent, subversive, inasmuch as they provide alternatives to the largely secularized field of art. By showcasing virtuous lifestyles, catering to religious sensibilities, and enabling pious subjectivities, they challenge the secularist project of the state. They particularly do so by reinforcing gender scripts and morality. Yet moral missions are shaped not only by intentional actions of its missionaries, but also by outside forces such as the market. Moral art has become a marketable genre, which is accordingly subject to the rules of the market. It has partly been buried by its own success and has almost lost its sting, that is, the moral message. As we have seen, the missionizing forms of *fann al-hadif* have remained contained within a small parochial market. Those forms that balanced morals, mission, and the market have been rather successful as far as male singers are concerned. With regard to male acting, the market forces allowed for morals but skipped the mission. Successful formats for pious, pleasurable art by female artists have yet to be developed further, as the demand for female artistic expression tends to be located either in the large sensual markets or the limited moral-religious souks, that is, either losing morals or the market.

NOTES

1. I interviewed twenty-five artists who either retired from art for religious reasons or returned to produce pious art. I also interviewed twelve producers and artists who are critical of pious art and eight journalists or reporters who critically follow developments in the art scene in Egypt.

2. See Endnote 1.

3. I would like to thank Joseph Alagha for translating the transcript from this conference.

4. *Al-Zuhur* conference, actor Ahmed Mursi.

5. *Al-Zuhur* conference, actor ʿAbd al-ʿAziz Makhyun.

6. Author interview of Nur al-Hoda Saʿd, editor-in-chief, *al-Zuhur* magazine, February 7, 2008.

7. Author interview of actor Wagdi al-ʿArabi, February 26, 2008.

8. *Al-Zuhur* conference, ʿAbd al-ʿAziz Makhyun.

9. *Al-Zuhur* conference, *wasatiyya* intellectual Muhammed ʿImara.

10. *Al-Zuhur* conference, preacher Muhammad Hamid. See also Alagha (this volume) on *maslaha* for similar ideas in Shiʿa discourse.

11. *Al-Zuhur* conference, Muhammad ʿImara.

12. *Al-Zuhur* conference, Muhammad Hamid.

13. *Al-Zuhur* conference, Ahmed Mursi.

14. *Al-Zuhur* conference, Muhammed ʿImara.

15. *Al-Zuhur* conference, Ahmed Mursi.

16. Interview with author, February 10, 2008.

17. *Al-Zuhur* conference, ʿAbd al-ʿAziz Makhyun.

18. Interview with author, February 2, 2008.

19. Interview with author, February 12, 2008.

20. Soheir al-Babli returned in the Ramadan serial *Qalb Habiba* (*Habiba's Heart*), Soheir Ramzi appeared in *Habib al-Ruh* (*Sweetheart*), Hanan Turk appeared in *Awlad al-Shawariʿ* (*Children of the Street*), and Sabrin returned in *Kashkol likull Muwatin* (*A Notebook for Every Citizen*).

21. At least at the time of writing, that is, Summer 2009, only Hanan Turk has returned, in *Hanim Bint Basha.*

22. Interview on Dream TV, Yata Salon, online at YouTube (accessed July 20, 2009).

23. Link 007, December 24, 2006, available online at http://www.linko7777.com (accessed February 18, 2008).

24. Interview with author, February 11, 2008.

25. *Al-Ahali*, no. 1299, October 18, 2006, available online at http://www.al-ahaly .com (accessed February 18, 2008).

26. Ibid.

27. Interview with author, February 7, 2008.

28. Interview with author, February 26, 2008.

29. Interview with author, February 2, 2008.

30. I interviewed a total of three male and two female bandleaders, a manager of a club that hosts religious weddings, a producer of religious wedding music cassettes, and an impresario. In addition, I visited eight religious weddings and talked with band members, as well as with the wedding guests and the couple. I also discussed the phenomenon with several young Egyptians, among whom ten were raised in Saudi Arabia.

31. Interview with author, February 12, 2006.

32. Interview with author, February 13, 2008.

33. Interview with author, February 11, 2006.

34. Interview with author, February 12, 2006.

35. *Islam Online*, October 6, 2004, available online at http://islamonline.com (accessed February 15, 2006).

36. Interview with author, February 12, 2006.

37. It is a common idea that the mothers of the bride and groom should dance to show their happiness (Van Nieuwkerk 1995).

38. Author interview of the bandleader of Basmit Andalus, February 12, 2006.

39. *Islam Online*, February 9, 2004, available online at http://islamonline.com (accessed February 15, 2006).

40. Interview with employee of Al-Hayah Company, February 7, 2006.

41. Author interview of Mustafa Mahmud, February 13, 2008.

42. Author interview of journalists of *Islam Online*, February 5, 19, 2008.

REFERENCES

Abu Lughod, L. 2005. *Dramas of Nationhood: The Politics of Television in Egypt.* Cairo: American University in Cairo Press.

Baker, R. W. 2003. *Islam without Fear: Egypt and the New Islamists.* Cambridge, MA, and London: Harvard University Press.

Bayat, A. 2002. "Piety, Privilege and Egyptian Youth." *ISIM Review*, no. 10, 23.

———. 2005. "What Is Post-Islamism?" *ISIM Review*, no. 16, 5.

———. 2007. "Islamism and the Politics of Fun." *Public Culture* 19 (3): 433–460.

Blackman, L. 2008. *The Body: The Key Concepts.* Oxford and New York: Berg.

Carlson, M. 2004. *Performance: A Critical Introduction.* New York and London: Routledge.

Galal, E. 2008. "Magic Spells and Recitation Contests: The Quran as Entertainment on Arab Satellite Television." *Northern Lights* 6:165–179.

Haenni, P. 2002. "Au-delà du repli identitaire. Les nouveaux prêcheurs égyptiens et la modernisation paradoxale de l'islam." *Religioscope*, Novembre. http://www.religioscope .com/pdf/precheurs.pdf (accessed May 20, 2005).

Hirschkind, Ch. 2006. *The Ethical Soundscape: Cassette Sermons and Islamic Counterpublics.* New York: Columbia University Press.

'Imara, M. 1991. *Al-Islam wa al-Funun al-Jamila.* Cairo: Dar al-Shuruq.

Kepel, G. 2000. "Islamism Reconsidered: A Running Dialogue with Modernity." *Harvard International Review* 22 (2): 22.

Khalid, A. 2005. "Culture: The Distinguishing Feature of a People." *TBS* 1:30–33.

LeVine, M. 2008. "Heavy Metal Muslims: The Rise of a Post-Islamist Public Sphere." In "Creating an Islamic Cultural Sphere: Contested Notions of Art, Leisure and Entertainment," ed. Karin van Nieuwkerk, special issue, *Contemporary Islam* 2 (3): 229–251.

Mahmood, S. 2005. *Politics of Piety: The Islamic Revival and the Feminist Subject.* Princeton, NJ: Princeton University Press.

al-Qaradawi, Y. 1997. *Fiqh al-Ghina' wa al-Musiqa fi Dhu' al-Qur'an wa al-Sunna.* Cairo: Maktabit Wahbah.

———. 2001. *The Lawful and the Prohibited in Islam.* Cairo: El-Falah.

Roy, O. 2004. *Globalized Islam.* London: Hurst and Company.

Salamandra, C. 2008. "Creative Compromise: Syrian Television Makers between Secularism and Islamism." In "Creating an Islamic Cultural Sphere: Contested Notions of Art, Leisure and Entertainment," ed. Karin van Nieuwkerk, special issue, *Contemporary Islam* 2 (3): 177–191.

Schechner, R. 2002. *Performance Studies: An Introduction.* London and New York: Routledge.

Schielke, S. 2008. "Boredom and Despair in Rural Egypt." In "Creating an Islamic Cultural Sphere: Contested Notions of Art, Leisure and Entertainment," ed. Karin van Nieuwkerk, special issue, *Contemporary Islam* 2 (3): 251–271.

Stacher, J. A. 2002. "Post-Islamist Rumblings in Egypt: The Emergence of the Wasat Party." *Middle East Journal*, June 22, 2002.

Stratton, A. 2006. *Muhajababes.* London: Constable.

Tammam, H., and P. Haenni. 2003. "Chat Shows, Nashid Groups and Lite Preaching: Egypt's Air-Conditioned Islam." *Le Monde diplomatique*, September.

———. 2005. "Daqat al-duff al-Islamiyya." *Wajhat Nazr* 73:45–57.

Tartoussieh, K. 2007. "Pious Stardom: Cinema and the Islamic Revival in Egypt." *Arab Studies Journal* 17 (1): 30–44.

Van Nieuwkerk, K. 1993. "Entertainment, Sexuality and the Body: Female Singers and Dancers in Egyptian Society." *Vrije tijd en Samenleving* 11 (2/3): 69–83.

———. 1995. *"A Trade like Any Other": Female Singers and Dancers in Egypt.* Austin: University of Texas Press.

———. 2007. "From Repentance to Pious Performance." *ISIM Review*, no. 20, 54–56.

———. 2008a. "Creating an Islamic Cultural Sphere: Contested Notions of Art, Leisure and Entertainment. An Introduction." In "Creating an Islamic Cultural Sphere: Contested Notions of Art, Leisure and Entertainment," ed. Karin van Nieuwkerk, special issue, *Contemporary Islam* 2 (3): 169–176.

———. 2008b. "Piety, Repentance and Gender: Born-again Singers, Dancers and Actresses in Egypt." *Journal for Islamic Studies* 28: 37–65.

———. 2008c. "'Repentant' Artists in Egypt: Debating Gender, Performing Arts and Religion." In "Creating an Islamic Cultural Sphere: Contested Notions of Art, Leisure and Entertainment," ed. Karin van Nieuwkerk, special issue, *Contemporary Islam* 2 (3): 191–211.

Winegar, J. 2008. "Purposeful Art: Between Television Preachers and the State." *ISIM Review*, no. 22, 28–30.

Wise, L. 2003. "'Words from the Heart': New Forms of Islamic Preaching in Egypt." Master's thesis, Oxford University. http://users.ox.ac.uk/~metheses/Wise.html (accessed November 28, 2006).

Zubaida, S. 2002. "Religious Authority and Public Life." *ISIM Newsletter* 11 (December): 19.

PART THREE

STAGING THE BODY AND THE WORLD STAGE

CHAPTER 7

ISLAMIC MODERNITY AND THE
RE-ENCHANTING POWER OF SYMBOLS
IN ISLAMIC FANTASY SERIALS IN TURKEY

AHU YİĞİT

THROUGHOUT THE TURKISH MODERNIZATION EXPERIENCE, one thing has remained the same: modernization has been defined with reference to the West. This frame of reference has either taken the form of admiration or distaste. Modern Turkey has been seeking the affirmative gaze of the West: whenever a major event, disaster, or success takes place in Turkey, newspapers devote a section to its echoes in Europe. This can concern a sports event, such as a football match, a natural catastrophe, or a social and political disaster, such as the assassination of a Turkish journalist of Armenian origin, Hrant Dink. If the European gaze approves of Turkish behavior, Turks are supposed to be proud. If poor infrastructure or corruption leads to a catastrophic end, newspaper headlines mourn that Turkey has been disgraced in the eyes of Europe. I remember writing an essay at the age of eight on the comments published in the international press following the death of the founding father Mustafa Kemal Atatürk. Even in the realm of political history, the European opinion on Turkey is important.

In the writings of the late Ottoman intellectuals, such as Ahmed Midhat or Mahmud Esat, there was either a fear of "the corrupt aspects of European civilization" or an admiration for the "spiritual aspects of Western civilization" (Berkes 1964, 285, 287). Ziya Gökalp combined the two approaches and argued that civilization is a transferable intergroup achievement, whereas culture is specific to specific national groups (in Berkes 1936, 243). According to Gökalp, it was legitimate to borrow from European civilization, as long as the authentic Ottoman culture was preserved.

With first the establishment of the republic in 1923, and then subsequent steps designed to make Turkey a Western-style state and society, it was already apparent that Turkey opted for the West. Yet the Turkish Republic would continue to rely on symbols as the sole measure of change. In the course of the modernization process, "secularism *à la turca*" emerged. Instead of withdrawing from religious affairs, the state put all religious activities under direct control. In 1924, the Directorate of Religious Affairs was established as a state branch. Currently, this institution is responsible for "regulating all work related to the practice of Islam, managing the conduct of places of worship, and enlightening society about the issue of religion."[1] In 1928, the constitutional article proclaiming Islam the official religion was annulled, and in 1937, the concept of secularism was incorporated into the constitution (Sakallıoğlu 1996, 234).

As a result of this control over religion, two kinds of religious "reality" coexist in Turkey. On the one hand, there is the state, which, in theory, controls the religious behavior of people. On the other hand, in everyday life Islam constitutes an integral element of daily cultural practice—which does not always correspond to a fundamentalist mode of existence. While the state has mobilized certain symbols for its nation-building project and the republican cause, it has also tended to ignore or undermine the symbols that belong to the Ottoman past and traditional Islamic society. Whenever religious symbols become contentious, and gain "political" meaning, the state has shown itself to be alarmed that its own symbols and goals are threatened.

The headscarf issue has been one of the most notorious cases. Trouble began in 1969, when a student who wanted to wear her headscarf during lectures was expelled from university. The Council for Higher Education (Yükseköğretim Kurumu [YÖK]), banned the headscarf in universities in 1982. The Council lifted this ban in 1984. The headscarf was again banned in 1987, only to be officially allowed in 1990. In 1997, students with headscarves were banished once more.[2] On February 2008, the president of the republic, Abdullah Gül, approved a constitutional change allowing the headscarf in universities. Still, the legal status of the headscarf remains undecided.

Space is another tool used by the state for its nation-building goals. The new capital, Ankara, was established as the republican center and rebuilt in accordance with the new republic's political agenda. The streets of Ankara were named after the republican elite and in accordance with nationalist concepts. Scenes from the Independence War of 1919–1922 were kept alive by the various monuments erected all over the city. Ankara was regarded as a blank canvas where the new Turkish state could paint its history and construct its future. Istanbul, on the contrary, was ignored during these early years because it was considered a symbol of the unfavorable and preferably distant imperial past. However, in 1994 Istanbul reentered the clash of symbols through the May 29 celebrations commemorating the five hundredth anniversary of Istanbul's conquest by the Ottomans. Istanbul was appropriated by the Islamist majority and presented as one of the central constituents of Islamic culture (Çınar 2001, 383). The celebrations began after the election of the Islamist city administration from the Refah Partisi (Welfare Party) in 1994. Prayers followed theatrical demonstrations of Istanbul's conquest (Çınar 2001, 366).

As the case of the headscarf and the existence of state institutions such as the Directorate of Religious Affairs clearly demonstrate, state behavior in the realm of religion can be defined as a regulation of practices and the control exercised over symbols. Yet the state has not always been successful in eradicating traditional symbols and replacing them with its own. The headscarf ban in the public sphere did not result in a decrease in the number of women wearing headscarves. On the contrary, the fashion industry created new styles of headscarves for women, using lively colors and designs, with the result that the headscarf became even more visible.

Just like colorful headscarves have become favorite with the new Islamic classes in the cities, authentic Islamic television series have underlain the presence and popularity of Islamic television channels. Television serials form a very important part of entertainment on the screen, and more than a hundred serials are produced per annum. Some of them become popular, whereas those lacking such popularity are often discontinued after a few episodes. During the last eight years, serials promoting an Islamist morality have been among the most popular programs on Turkish television. Islamist channels produce a kind of fantasy serials deeply influenced by some Western productions, although they give an Islamic interpretation of the originals. These fantasy serials adopt magical plots such as time travel, angels disguised as ordinary people, and appearing or disappearing objects and people. Several serials are set in the afterlife, from which the main character looks back on his or her life on earth. The producers refrain from naming a specific genre for these serials, and simply say that "these are original formats never tried before."[3] However, I will refer to them as fantasy serials, because of the many magical and supernatural events that occur in them.

This chapter focuses on popular fantasy television serials produced by Islamic channels, in particular STV (Samanyolu TV). I explore plots and narrative styles, as well as the various meanings of the symbols that are used. Although the serials are apparently concerned with spreading Islamic morality, the question remains why they use "original formats never tried before" instead of the documentary genre. Also, is there really a contradiction involved in the Islamist adoption of Western genres and the reproduction of Western serials in terms of their own concepts? And what does this choice tell us about Turkish modernity in particular?

For some time now, variations of the original format have been produced by almost all secular and Islamist channels. The serials have been designed to appeal to both types of audience, and their popularity provides a good opportunity to take a fresh look at the labels "secularist" and "Islamist" in the Turkish context. Islam, or Islamist, channels will not be treated as an isolated object of study, but as one of the constituent elements of contemporary Turkish political culture. Thus, one can investigate how the Islamic moral message delivered through TV serials and the idea of reproducing Western serials come together and, in this case, why the labels "Islamist" and "secular" do not have to be mutually exclusive.

In order to deal with these questions, the place Islam presently occupies in Turkish television will be studied. The Islamist channels broadcasting the serials will be introduced. Next, the fantasy serials will be explored by means of different examples, and an analysis of their plots and characters will be given. Different variations of the original serials will be described. Although the examples will mostly concern Islamist programs, their secular counterparts—which are not produced anymore—will also be mentioned, so as to compare secular and Islamist versions. In the final section, the concept of re-enchantment will be suggested as an alternative framework for studying the emergence and popularity of fantasy television serials. Also, an interpretation of Turkish modernity will be offered.

THE REAPPEARANCE OF ISLAM
IN CULTURAL CONSUMPTION

Islam has become a component of everyday cultural and also commercial consumption in Turkey. Until recently, the representation of Islam and religion on television hardly attracted any attention. Basically, there were two types of coverage concerning Islam. First were the fifteen-minute talks delivered on the state television channel TRT every Friday. A short speech by the head of the Directorate of Religious Affairs covered the virtues of Islam and the qualities of a good Muslim. On religious holidays, scenes from mosques filled by praying crowds were shown, but other than that, mosques were simply considered part of the national cultural heritage, as if they only had architectural authenticity and were unrelated to Islamic belief itself (Öncü 1995, 56). The TRT channel still produces programs of this format. *Hayat ve Din* (*Life and Religion*), on Thursday mornings at 6 a.m., and *İslamın Aydınlığında* (*In the Brightness of Islam*), on Friday evenings before prime time at 6 p.m., are contemporary examples of religious programs. As their names suggest, these programs treat religion as part of life, amongst other things, and not as something that should predominate. In Turkish, the word *aydınlık*, translated here as brightness, also means enlightenment. The title of the latter program therefore implies that Islam brings enlightenment. In both of the programs, usually a professor of religion is interviewed on the history of Islam, and the interaction of Islam with other religions is explored. It is emphasized that during the reign of the Prophet, people of different religions were all treated equally.

The second type of Islamic representation developed with the emergence of privately owned television channels in the 1990s. In the reality shows and news programs of these channels, ridiculous and traditional practices of Islam are exposed by means of hidden cameras. Fake *hodjas*, claiming to heal illness, are favorite targets. The fake *hodjas*, usually recorded by hidden cameras, try to persuade women to have sexual intercourse, or they write Arabic script on the women's naked bodies. They present these methods as a cure for illness or infertility, and they ask for a large fee in return for their services. The popularity of such programs reached a peak when an attractive young woman, Fadime Şahin, confessed on camera that she had been subjected to sexual assault by a *hodja* named Ali Kalkancı. Soon a case was opened against Kalkancı. As the trial proceeded in 1997, the media exploited the case to the limit and made several programs revolving around the themes of sex, money, religious sects, and *hodjas* (Dole 2006, 40–41). In this case, such representations of *hodjas* serve as figures of Islamication in the sense referred to by Marshall Hodgson, rather than symbols of Islam itself. Viewed from this perspective, the representations of Islam in Islamic popular culture do not have to be in accordance with the belief itself (Hodgson 1975).

The two ways of representation described so far have one thing in common. They make a distinction between "good Islam," which corresponds to the enlightened and modern interpretation of religion, and "bad Islam," which is associated with superstition and perceived as a source of backwardness. The *hodjas* and related scandals are presented as examples of "bad Islam." After the hidden camera recordings are broadcast, university-trained theological scholars are consulted on the *hodjas'* methods. The experts interviewed always stress that none of the practices employed by the *hodjas* are Islamic, or consistent with the Koran. Giving the view of academics on religion underlines the definition of good Islam as compatible with contemporary science. Academics, rather than (fake) *hodjas*, are the authorities on Islam.

The types of coverage outlined have continued until today, although at present they are no longer the only representations of Islam, nor do they enjoy their earlier popularity. Things have changed with the start-up of other private television channels, such as Samanyolu TV (STV), Kanal 7, and TGRT, which together I will refer to in this chapter as the Islamist channels. These channels, which target a more conservative audience, represent Islam in a different manner. Of the channels mentioned, TGRT has moved closer to central politics, by recruiting popular television stars, but until it was taken over by the American Fox Broadcasting Company and transformed into Fox TV, "it was positioned somewhere between central and peripheral politics" (Binark and Celikcan 2000). Kanal 7, one of the Islamic channels that used to produce serials, has been going through some trouble recently. It has been claimed that this channel was established with the charity money collected from Islamist Euroturcs. The channel has close links with the charity foundation Deniz Feneri (Lighthouse), which faces several corruption charges in a German court. A similar case is also about to be opened in Turkey against the executives of the channel and the foundation. Probably due to financial difficulties, Kanal 7 does not produce these serials anymore and concentrates on broadcasting repeats. STV, which broadcasts the fantasy serials that are explored here, was launched in 1993. It is owned by the Gülen community, which is a branch of the Nurcu movement, a religious order based on the teachings of Said Nursi (1878–1960), and which is headed by the religious scholar Fethullah Gülen. The Gülen community has extensive networks in education. It owns one hundred schools in Turkey and over two hundred schools worldwide. In addition, it owns a media network of television channels, radio, newspapers, and journals (Aras and Caha 2000, 34). STV also broadcasts in the USA, where it is called Ebru TV.

At present, popular television serials form the backbone of STV. Besides serials, it broadcasts documentaries, movies, and children's programs during the morning hours, as well as news and a discussion program on religious issues. STV is notorious for dubbing documentaries and movies from English into Turkish in a rather freely interpretative way. In the dubbed versions of documentaries, comments are given on the role of God in the creation process, even though in the originals this subject is not mentioned at all. More recently, in the channel's cooking program, *Yeşil Elma* (*The Green Apple*), the cook suggested replacing the names of some dishes with less "dirty" ones, because he thought the originals were "morally inconvenient." He proposed to change *kadınbudu* (woman's buttock) into rice meatball and *dilber dudağı* (lips of the belle) into moon dessert. Although these "clean," inoffensive terms became popular with the program's audience, they raised huge criticism in other circles, including women's organizations and academia. The head of the prominent Turkish feminist organization Uçan Süpürge (Flying Broom), Halime Güner, protested against the alternative names by saying that women love their bodies and enjoy eating food inspired by it. Murat Belge, a political scientist who is also famous for his work on culture, derided the inventors of "clean" terms for their ignorance. In return, Filiz Aydoğan, the female producer of the cooking program, responded by saying that the original words were slang, and one of the concerns of the program was to use proper Turkish. Besides, she said, why was the dish called "woman's buttock," and not a man's?[4] By the way, the STV channel does not seem to have a problem with working women: women with and without headscarves are employed at various posts by the organization.

The example of the cooking program sheds light on an interesting moment of convergence between modern and traditional ways of life, where women can go out working but, at the same time, allow themselves to be offended by "dirty names" referring to femininity. It is impossible to miss the creative approach the channel and its employees take in replacing the culturally rooted improper with the proper, and the way they adopt the modern way of life whilst taking a conservative view. As will be elaborated on in the next section, the case described is characteristic of "Turkish modernism," where modern ways of life coexist with conservative attitudes within the same entities.

The fantasy serials with which this chapter is concerned have become extremely popular since 2000. The success of the original serials resulted in an overflow of variations and imitations by both secular and Islamist channels. A study conducted in the Konya province of Turkey revealed that 75 percent of the participants in the survey regularly watched at least one of these programs (Koçak, Çakır, and Gülnar 2006, 353).

The initial serial was *Sırlar Dünyası* (*World of Mysteries*) on STV. It has been described as "a legendary production based on true stories, which has left the high-budget productions behind on the rating scale."[5]

In the course of time, other, similar serials in content with different formats joined the bandwagon. *Büyük Buluşma* (*Final Glance*) and *Beşinci Boyut* (*Fifth Dimension*) are broadcast by STV, and *Kalp Gözü* (*Eye of the Hearth*) by Kanal 7. For some time, similar productions were also shown on more secular popular channels. The main examples are: *Gizli Dünyalar* (*Mysterious Worlds*) on Show TV, *Cüneyt Arkın'la Yaşanmış Hikayeler* (*True Stories with Cüneyt Arkın*) on Star TV, *Aşkın Mucizeleri* (*Miracles of Love*) on ATV, and *Sırlar Alemi* (*The Kingdom of Secrets*) on Flash TV. The secular versions are no longer in production, probably due to the rising popularity of competing programs based on dancing or singing contestants and the newly gained popularity of different types of series. As mentioned above, Kanal 7 also abandoned the productions, but continues to broadcast repeats. STV, however, still follows the same format for all serials and movies that they produce.

In the following section, examples from the different serials will be provided in order to explore the plots, narrative, and functions of this specific genre. The examples described, in sequence, are: *Sırlar Dünyası* (*World of Mysteries*), *Büyük Buluşma* (*Final Glance*), and *Beşinci Boyut* (*Fifth Dimension*), which are all broadcast by STV.

FANTASTIC VERSIONS OF ISLAMIC MORALITY

In the initial serial that started the trend eight years ago, *Sırlar Dünyası* (*World of Mysteries*), supernatural occurrences were not yet common. Of the three examples explored in this section, *Sırlar Dünyası* lies farthest from the fantasy genre. Miracles do take place, but although spiritual beings in human form appear, we do not see them in a special light or in unearthly places. Most of the time, the spiritual characters do favors or give advice to people before disappearing again, but they rarely constitute protagonists. A male narrator elaborates on the episodes shown, which are claimed to be based on true stories, inspired by letters from the audience. The narrator is the equivalent of the wise old storyteller in ancient Turkish myths, with a deep voice and a talent for eloquent expression (Tunç 2005, 28). In contrast to the mythical storyteller, however, the narrator of *World of Mysteries* is a young man. He explains the moral lesson of the episode: "No one can intervene in God's judgment, so people should not complain at all. It is our duty to work hard, and God will reward us for this. People should refrain from saying their rights are violated. If they behave according to this principle, they will find a solution or, more correctly, a solution will find them in even the most difficult circumstances." The narrator's role is limited to this brief introduction.

In one of the episodes of *World of Mysteries*, the main character is a primary-school teacher, who pursues his university studies to become a lecturer. Despite his low income, he supports his parents financially and is always nice and helpful to his fellow students. This conduct qualifies him as "the good person." One day he attends a meeting, where one of his professors gives a lecture on the negative role of religion in the development of science and literature. The teacher/student criticizes this argument, and in return the provoked professor replies, "I shall never allow you to become a lecturer in our department." The professor also despises the student because he has lost his left arm in an accident. "A cripple cannot work at our university." Soon it appears that in order to obtain his MA degree, the student has to give a presentation on a topic chosen by "the mean professor," who selects an irrelevant subject on which hardly any sources are available. The student turns for help to another professor, who promises to provide him with some material. However, he gives the material to "the mean professor," because he is leaving for a conference in another city and is in a hurry. As a result, the student never gets the necessary sources for his presentation. Whilst he is the department's corridors, not knowing what to do, an old man responsible for cleaning the building asks why he looks so sad. This old man is reminiscent of one of the most respected spiritual figures in Turkey, Saint Hızır. Saint Hızır always appears to humans in the shape of an aged dervish with a long, white beard. He is the last-minute rescuer when everything else fails. Although the cult of Hızır is originally pre-Islamic, eventually he came to be considered a part of the Islamic heritage (Walker and Uysal 1973). The old man takes the student to a third professor, who lends him some books and articles, and also gives a long lecture on the topic in question. He asks the student to bring back the books after his presentation. In the end, the student is able to deliver a good talk and is accepted as a lecturer at the university. When he wants to return the books, he finds the door of his benefactor's office locked. He asks the university security guards about the professor and the cleaner. To his surprise, there have never been any such people employed by the university. Following the last scene, the narrator explains that God helps the one who studies and struggles without complaining about the situation. If the teacher-student had complained and not pursued his studies because of the obstacles imposed upon him by "the mean professor," he would not have succeeded. He realized what his responsibilities were and performed his task. And, in the most desperate of moments, God helped him.

Endurance and patience are among the central themes of Islamic belief. The Koran and the words of the Prophet praise such behavior. In the Al-Baqara sura of the Koran, people are advised to seek Allah's help with patience and prayer, and ask God for the wisdom to have patience.[6] The same message is repeated several times in the text. The *hadith*, the sayings of Prophet Muhammed, also praise patience on various occasions. Patience is admired by the Prophet as "the first stroke of a calamity," and as the greatest blessing that God can give to a person.[7] Submission is also a central theme: patience brings submission to God. In Sura Al-Naml, submission is seen as the opposite of arrogance, and the faithful should come to God in submission.[8]

Similar moral lessons of patience and submission are also present in the following example taken from an episode of *Büyük Buluşma* (*Final Glance*; see Figure 7.1). A woman is sitting up in her hospital bed. A modest smile is fixed on her face as she ties her headscarf. The door opens and she is shot dead. When she wakes up on a platform floating in the sky, a man dressed in white gowns, Amil, tells her that she is dead. She initially refuses to believe this, until she sees her own funeral. Amil introduces himself as the mirror of consciousness, and describes the platform as the gate to the afterlife. He explains the reason for her presence in this place with the following verses: "As time goes by, suddenly everything stops: all lights fade away. The bright side of life turns pale. It is now time to confront the greatest reality." Her life on earth was a dream from which she has woken up, yet her earthly life still has to complete its mission. Following this brief opening, the generic message is shown on the screen. In the generics, people are shown at the moment of their deaths. When they die, they are transformed into light. In the background, we hear a combination of the spiritual sounds of the *nay*, a kind of flute characteristic of Middle Eastern music, and modern rock. The music is accompanied by the lyrics "You cannot escape from the final judgment, turn back and watch your life."

Then we watch the deceased woman's life story. She was engaged to a man from her village, whom she loved. She was happy and waiting for her wedding day, until her sister's husband raped her. She lost the zest for life and attempted suicide, but failed. She prayed to God, "God please help me to stay sane, show me the light." She did not take legal action against the brother-in-law, or inform anyone about what had happened. She saw herself as unfit to get married because she had been "stained." However, under the pressure exerted by her family, who considered an engagement not followed by marriage a threat to the family honor, she had to marry her fiancé. As soon as her husband found out that she was not a virgin, he dragged her back to her parents' house. Her father, thinking the woman had sullied the family name through a dishonorable act, told her brother to kill her. As a result of the brother's first attempt, her spine was severely wounded, and she was unable to walk for the rest of her life. When she lost all hope, her husband rushed to the hospital to apologize. They promised not to leave each other again; however, just when everything seemed to have ended well, the brother found her again, and this time, truly killed her.

The second part of the story, in which her life is judged, is basically a long conversation among Amil, the deceased woman, and other people who formed part of her life. Amil interrogates her about the motivations behind her actions. Once, while chatting with her fiancé, she spoke ill of another girl who committed suicide after being raped. She said that if the girl had not behaved in an inviting manner toward her attacker, such a thing would not have taken place. Amil asks her if she still thinks she was correct in blaming the other girl, now that she has experienced a similar tragedy herself. Her husband, the brother-in-law, and the brother enter the scene, to be questioned by Amil. They cannot lie because "burning scissors will appear if the tongue resorts to lies here." After they have left again, the woman anxiously asks what will happen to her. "First they will ask you whether you have performed your daily worship duties." She confirms she did this, but

Herkes için kaçınılmaz olan!

UMIT ACAR

BÜYÜK
BULUŞMA

FIGURE 7.1. Poster for *Final Glance* (*Büyük Buluşma*) on STV

what will happen to her if she failed to carry out her duties properly? "Then the good deeds you did will save you." When the moment of final judgment arrives, a book of light falls from the sky into her hands, and drops of light encircle her. She is walking toward a glowing door with an expression of peace on her face, and professes her thankfulness to God.

Büyük Buluşma (*Final Glance*) can be considered a first variation on the theme of the original format. The main character is awarded in the afterlife, but her mortal life has been full of agony. Other episodes of *Büyük Buluşma* feature similar stories, with victims in mortal life being awarded in the here-after. The bad characters, who are usually well off during life on earth, are punished by hell in the afterlife. The moral message is obvious. Although the moments of eternal justice and repayment are not always obvious and immediate, they are inevitable.

The second variation on the original format can be found in *Beşinci Boyut* (*Fifth Dimension*; see Figure 7.2). The plots are the same as in the previously discussed serial; however, the characters are different. While similar events take place, two "beings" help people. Although they have the appearance of humans during the episodes, they are transformed into doves and light in the generic. One of them, the master, is an elderly man; his younger apprentice is called Salih. As described on the STV website: "Salih guides people in order to help them make the right choices. When he is in doubt, his master opens the doors for him. Salih is one of those responsible for sowing hope into people's hearts and manifesting God's compassion for people."[9] In the first episode, Salih's background is described at length. He was a soldier during Turkey's involvement in Cyprus in 1974, where he was shot in the back by a Greek soldier. Salih was a virtuous man when he was still alive, and always expressed his yearning to serve God. This prayer was answered when he was chosen to work as an angel.

The similarities with the popular American serial *Touched by an Angel* are striking. *Touched by an Angel* enjoyed popularity on American television between 1994 and 2003. It tells the story of three angels, one of whom is a loving supervisor, whilst the other two are interns, who deliver the message of hope. The story is heavily dominated by Christian teaching, and the message throughout the serial is the presence of God as a source of hope.[10]

In a similar manner, Salih and his master also deliver the message of hope to the audience; and likewise, they refrain from bringing dramatic solutions to the problems raised: if people listen to their own conscience, they will make the right choices. Salih and his master just help people to do this. Sometimes, they perform small acts that make people's life easier, but they do not really interfere. For example, in one episode, Salih is a shepherd in a village. A woman whose husband is paralyzed suffers from sexual abuse by her neighbor. This neighbor, who intends to rape her, waits for the moment that she will have to go into the forest to gather wood. He even steals some wood from her wood repository, so that she will need to go there sooner. However, the woman's wood supply does not shrink at all, because Salih discreetly brings her wood at night. Whenever the woman complains about the hardships of carrying the responsibility for a paralyzed husband and little children, Salih advises her to think of those who are suffering from worse conditions. In another episode, which has almost the same plot, with

FIGURE 7.2. Poster for *Fifth Dimension (Beşinci Boyut)* on STV

a woman, a paralyzed husband, an abusive landlord, and a shepherd named Salih, the woman asks how much worse things could get. She has definitely surpassed the legitimate limits of complaint. And worse things do happen: she falls ill and is unable to work any longer.

The episodes of *Beşinci Boyut* are always opened by a dialogue between Salih and the master. Similar to the opening of *Sırlar Dünyası*, these dialogues contain short moral lessons. They revolve around the questions asked by the pupil, Salih, and answers given by the master. Salih asks the master, "My lord, what should be our attitude when faced with oppression?" His master answers with a quotation from the Prophet, "Oh God, I take shelter with you, in the face of all oppression." Salih finds these words virtuous, but still needs more instruction, and asks, "If oppression is the source of all destruction, then why do oppressors succeed?" According to the master, Salih is questioning eternal justice with his comment, and he replies, "Eternal justice is always active. Only there is an appropriate time for everything, and the merits of the people who seek justice also determine the extent to which that justice is implemented." Salih is still confused. "But if the people fail to practice some of the virtues commanded by God, then should they feel insecure?" The master confirms, but states, "Oppression is annihilated by oppression, so people can always refresh their belief." But what about the appropriate timing? According to the master, it is only when oppression reaches its highest limits that eternal justice can become effective. By now Salih has grasped the whole argument, and he understands that eternal justice is the best consolation. The master's last sentence summarizes the entire logical idea behind the serial: "If people complain at moments of grief and agony, they will commit further sins and eternal justice will not bring relief."

The examples described above are all shown on STV, the most popular of the Islamist channels. The secular counterparts of these serials were also broadcast for a while. *Gizli Dünyalar* (*Mysterious Worlds*) on Show TV is an example of the latter. The productions broadcast by the secular channels were praised by the Islamist conservative press. One of the Islamist newspapers, *Yeni Şafak*, wrote that the serials "have attracted great attention from the audience. Despite being a popular channel, dominated by commercial concerns, Show TV has started its own series and profited greatly from it. The program has managed to reach fifth place in the rating scale. It seems that this series will continue to leave lots of programs standing."[11]

Gizli Dünyalar has the same structure and plot as *Sırlar Dünyası*; even the titles of the serials are almost identical. The narrator in *Gizli Dünyalar* is even more reminiscent of the traditional storyteller, being older. He is filmed in the historic setting of Basilica Cistern, a 1,500-year-old underground waterworks built during the reign of the Byzantine Empire in Istanbul. After a brief moral lecture, the story starts. In one of the episodes, a young man and a woman are sitting in a restaurant. The man is a promising businessman, who is about to propose marriage to the woman. He gives her a diamond ring. She accepts, saying, "Even death cannot separate me from this ring." In the next scene, we see the couple after they have been married for five years. However, the man is cheating on his wife with another woman, the latter being presented as selfish and greedy. Although the man's friends warn him that he puts all his wealth at risk for this woman, he does not listen. Soon, his wife dies in a traffic accident; shortly afterwards, the man finds out that he has been deceived by the other woman, and is left penniless. To pay his debts to the bank, he decides to take the ring from his buried wife's finger. He digs up the grave but cannot pry off the ring and ends up cutting off the finger itself. From that moment on, the ghost of his wife haunts him in his life and his dreams. His troubles are exacerbated by his constant abuse of alcohol, and he ends up in a mental hospital.

In this episode, as well as in the other episodes of *Gizli Dünyalar*, the symbols of good and bad are the same as in the Islamist versions; however, the reference to religion is mostly lacking. Again, supernatural events occur, such as the appearance of a ghost. The most commonly shown supernatural event in the secular serials is people foreseeing the future in their dreams. Dreams act as early warning mechanisms.

THE ABSOLUTE REALITY OF REPRESENTATIONS

Despite the differences in format among the various serials, they share the same message. All describe a chain of events in which caricaturized representatives of "the good" and "the bad" play a role. The good party is rewarded, and bad people are punished, either on earth or in the afterlife. There is a clear message that everyone will be held accountable for their own deeds. In *Sırlar Dünyası* (*World of Mysteries*), the payoff takes place in this world: the guilty parties and their beloved find themselves in quandary similar to the one they have created for other people. In *Büyük Buluşma* (*Final Glance*), we see a reproduction of the religious theme of *ahiret* (the afterlife), with deceased people being subjected to an interrogation about their lives on earth. In *Beşinci Boyut* (*Fifth Dimension*), the events take place in this world, but two angels disguised as ordinary people assist the main characters.

It is also worth mentioning another serial, broadcast by Samanyolu TV. Entitled *Hakkını Helal Et* (*Redemption*), it employs a comedy format, but still deals with the question of people's accountability. It shows striking similarities to the popular American TV serial *My Name Is Earl*. After a prologue describing certain circumstances that have resulted in his being imprisoned, the former thief Murat becomes aware of the Islamic concept *kul hakkı*—that is to say, one is not only responsible to God for his sins, but also to other people. Murat wants to make up for his crimes, and prepares a list of people from his past to whom he should make amends—just like Earl in the American serial, who adopts the Karma philosophy and prepares a similar list.

The question of justice and repayment is also a central theme of Islam. Writing on the relation between law and religion, Turner places the concept of law at the center of ritual and religious practices in Islam. Justice is at the core of Islamic spirituality (Turner 2006, 453). The focus of the television serials on the realization of justice can be understood in light of the penetration of the Islamic concept of justice into public and private life. In contemporary Turkey, Islamic law does not have a role in the legal practice, and the Islamic concepts of justice and repayment are excluded from the public sphere because it is a secular system. The serials explore the realization of eternal justice in the private lives of people. The extent to which the private sphere and the public sphere can be analyzed as disconnected is presented as questionable. However, it is not the serials' intention to extend the central message to the functioning of the public sphere: everything takes place at the personal level. If someone is subject to oppression or injustice in the public sphere, or people face injustice in a state institution such as a courthouse or hospital, this is not the fault of the political system. Rather, the people working there as employees are to blame, and, in the end, they will be punished by God's eternal justice.

A most prominent characteristic of the serials is that they validate and promote a sharply defined set of morals. Most of the time, these are Islamic rules, overlapping with generally accepted good morals. A professor of Islam acts as advisor for the scripts of the serials. Not only Islamic values are promoted; other norms generally regarded as good in society are also touched upon. One of these is nationalism. As described above, Salih, one of the angels in *Beşinci Boyut* (*Fifth Dimension*), was killed by a Greek soldier in Cyprus. This soldier is presented as bad because he shot Salih in the back, even though earlier Salih had shared his supply of water with him. A general distaste toward the Greeks in Turkish nationalist discourse is voiced here. Also, when Salih was asked to fight as a soldier in the Cyprus war, he was proud to serve the national cause—which underlines one of the most prominent features of Turkish society, i.e., its military culture.

Stealing, lying, greed, and adultery are considered "bad morals" and sinful, whereas, amongst other things, generosity, praying, and obeying one's elders are regarded as "good." In drawing the map of good and bad, the representations in the serials do not leave any room for interpretation or flexibility. First, everything is considered to have a certain moral value. Every item or action has a symbolic meaning, and these symbolic meanings are not dependent upon the context—in other words, they are not relative. For instance, in the series drinking alcohol is always bad, and it does not matter if the person consuming alcohol is good in other respects. Even if he is good, drinking alcohol will corrupt him. Second, people or their actions are, symbolically speaking, either extremely bad or naïvely good. Everything is black or white, and never gray. For instance, "the mean professor" in the episode of *Sırlar Dünyası* we discussed earlier looks down on Islam, which is one of the gravest sins one can commit in the serials. However, this is not the only bad thing about him. He despises the student for his physical disability, which is not something to be expected from a person of his rank.

In general, the message is that if someone has "flawed" political views, then he or she cannot possibly be a good person. Even if the main characters change their views at one point, and accept the morals promoted in the serials, they do not necessarily end up good. For example, in one *Sırlar Dünyası* episode, an active feminist considers Islam an impediment to women's participation in social life. In the end, she recognizes her "mistake" of judging Islam negatively, but she still has to die for her past error.

The effectiveness of the symbols applied becomes clear in the representation of women. Women should obey their husbands or, if they are single, obey their fathers and brothers. In their turn, husbands and fathers are responsible for the welfare and conduct of women. Salih summarizes this guideline in the following sentence: "Everyone is a shepherd in his own sense; we are responsible for those we pasture." In some cases, women might reject the "shepherd's" orders, but only if these orders conflict with the idealized morals. However, women rarely become rebellious, or refuse instructions in order to go follow their own will: one's own wishes have to fall within the limits of good morals. When women go beyond these strictly defined borders, they enter the sphere of culpability and thus deserve to be punished. In the example given above, the feminist character decides to live her life according to her own wishes. Choosing her own husband despite her parents' warning is an example of such an independent decision. She has to pay a very high price, though, because she soon finds out that her husband is addicted to gambling. She once claimed that women should continue to work after marriage, even if they have children, yet she herself finds it very hard to continue working after giving birth to her son. However, she is forced to, because her husband has been sacked due to his gambling habit. She takes refuge in the house of a woman whom she used to despise for her headscarf and Islamic beliefs. The feminist woman is in deep trouble, and in the end her husband kills her when she refuses to give him the money he asks for.

Excess is also invariably considered to be bad in the serials. Heavy makeup or loud laughter is a sign of a woman's poor moral qualities. For example, in an episode of *Büyük Buluşma*, the women who go to hell wear heavy makeup, whereas the other women, who wear headscarves, use barely any makeup at all. Remarriage of a widow with children is considered bad, and in most cases such a remarriage creates problems. If a woman complains about her husband's or father's financial status, she is wrong and deserves to be punished. In another episode of *Büyük Buluşma*, entitled "Women Who Go to Hell," a woman finds fault with her husband because he does not notice her new hairdo and has failed to remember their wedding anniversary. She makes an issue out of this and decides to participate in a television program in which lower-class women discuss their marital problems. The talk show host, a young and attractive female, encourages her guests to criticize husbands who neglect their wives. The wife tells the host about when she was chatting online with another man and her husband thought she was cheating on him. The host suggests that married women can have male friends, as well as female ones, with whom they can share their problems. The husband sits watching all this at home, feeling extremely offended by the two women's comments. He breaks into the studio and kills them both. At the gate to the afterlife, Amil blames the wife for "making an assassin out of her husband." The issue between the husband and wife is presented in such a manner that it leads the audience to the conclusion women should submit to the will of men, or at least to the established norms of good conduct. If they fail to do this, and make their own choices, they will end up in trouble. In "Women Who Go to Hell," both the wife and the talk show host go, of course, to hell.

In the narratives of this and other episodes, every form of behavior becomes a symbolic action, because it has greater meaning than is immediately apparent. Behaving respectfully toward one's elders and avoiding sexual intimacy before marriage are symbolic of good behavior. Such symbols differ from state symbols; examples of state symbols could be the flag, Republican monuments, the headscarf as a sign of disliked political Islam, or the Latin alphabet that was introduced in 1928 to replace the Ottoman alphabet. However, in both cases symbols are instrumental in promoting the visions and morals of the parties involved. Most symbols of good behavior in the examples from the Islamist TV serials described refer to the Islamic concepts of submission and justice. Unfortunate events on earth are presented as tests set by God. Instead of complaining, people should try and pass these tests. Justice need not be meted out immediately, but sooner (on earth as in *Sırlar Dünyası* and *Beşinci Boyut*) or later (in the afterlife, such as in *Büyük Buluşma*), God's final judgment will come. Unlike temporal justice on earth, which is open to abuse by the powerful, God's judgment is accurate. As stressed several times, the reality on earth is not the reality of life. Interestingly enough, one can see a similar association between actions and symbols in some other Islamic societies—for instance, in Iran. Zeinab Stellar (this volume) shows how the meanings and representations of dance as a symbol have changed over the years, and through successive political regimes, in Iran, but in each of the episodes, dance could not be perceived as a neutral aesthetic form of art. It had always to be contained or rejected.

I have mentioned the secular counterparts of the Islamist fantasy serials, which are not produced anymore. These secular programs employed similar sets of symbols and morals. However, in their case, the moral messages were not necessarily presented as the teaching of Islam: they were simply good morals. Aytaç Yörükaslan, the narrator of *Gizli Dünyalar* (*Mysterious*

Worlds), hints in an interview with the *Yeni Şafak* newspaper at an understanding of morality based on traditional norms and values. He does not refer to Islam or religion at all, but, according to him, people struggle and have to make huge efforts to stay honest and kind. Incentives for doing bad abound, which is why there should be television programs aimed at guiding people toward good morals. All television channels, he says, should realize this duty and make programs based on this principle.[12]

CONCLUSION

In this chapter, the word "modern" has been used as the reverse of "traditional," in particular with regard to lifestyles. However, the concept "modern" might be viewed in a different sense, which provides an opportunity to look at the Islamic fantasy serials from another perspective. Weber defines modernity as the loss of incalculable and mysterious forces from the face of the earth. In the phase of modernity, everything can be explained by calculations, formulas, or in more general scientific terms (Weber 1918). With the disenchantment process, the legitimacy of magic erodes as well, and any knowledge or insight related to the magical realm becomes irrational and will retreat from public life (Lee 2008, 749). What was once considered God's wrath is now an explicable phenomenon, explicable through formulas, which create understanding of means and ends as breeding one another. It is not sins that cause hurricanes and earthquakes anymore, but global warming with its consequences or earthquake faults which can be seen all over the world. Even religions have been rationalized and bureaucratized, and lost their mystical appeal (Greisman 1973, 497). Modernity through disenchantment means a reinterpretation of human experience and knowledge through different lenses that are "less mysterious, knowable, predictable and manipulable by humans." Of course this reinterpretation of knowledge is not the only aspect of Weberian modernity; it is incorporated into a system of science and rational government. On the political level, secularization is the flip side of disenchantment (Jenkins 2000, 12).

However, Weber's notion of disenchantment has been challenged from different corners. One criticism is that the "enchanted world" was never as unified as Weber presumed. Skepticism, heresy, and pluralism were never absent. Also, the disenchanted world and the break with magic have never been as absolute as Weber professed. Jenkins mentions several challenges posed to orthodox science as signs of a growing re-enchantment. Popular distrust in modern medicine matched by an increased interest in alternative therapies, and the decline of Newtonian physics and the need for further interpretations, are two examples of, not necessarily a distrust of science, but new room for epistemological pluralism. New and modern ways of re-enchantment such as religious fundamentalism, alternative lifestyles geared at a return to nature, neopaganism, and even psychoanalysis and psychotherapy have come to coexist with established rational and disenchanted practices (Jenkins 2000, 17–18). Jane Bennett's two varieties of re-enchantment are "techno-chantment," which transforms typewriters into PCs, or alcoholism into an addiction rather than a sign of weak will and self-control, and, second, the "miracle of co-ordination," which refers to the miraculous realization of creative and harmonized thinking in an age where the grounds for doing so are "non-harmonious, non-designed and unnecessary," making creative and innovative thinking almost impossible (Bennett 2001, 17–20).

The worldwide popularity of television serials such as *The X-Files* and *Buffy the Vampire Slayer* and movies such as *Star Wars*, *X-Men*, and *Lord of the Rings*, the last an interpretation of J. R. R. Tolkien's trilogy of novels, also shows an interest in the enchanted side of storytelling. Jenkins treats this interest under the umbrella of romanticism, which yearns for a mythical premodern and unrationalized past. This feeling is effectively translated into commercial success (Jenkins 2000, 19). According to Saler, though, the popularity of these productions is owing to the greater acceptance and freer use of imagination, and is one of the signs of a reconciliation between modernity and enchantment. This does not necessarily mean more enchantment in a modern world inhabited by demons (Saler 2004, 146). It is just a function of mass culture.

The TV serials discussed in this article are not as fantastical as the examples just given. However, in these Islamic serials too, we see a strange combination of religion, magic, and unnatural occurrences in an age of modernity. Underlining the presence as well as the superiority of religion and religious morality is the ultimate aim of the scripts used. The supernatural incidents are tools to prove the reality of religion, rather than a legitimate part of the text. Although the Western fantasy products can also be inspired by biblical stories or creatures, this influence is limited: myths and characters have been borrowed from other sources and incorporated. For instance, in the *Superman* series, the father sends his son Kal-El to earth not only to save him, but also to make him guide people toward the good and virtuous. In the *Star Wars* series, Anakin Skywalker, who is expected to bring balance to the Force, is not born from a father. Both cases echo the story of Jesus Christ.

In the TV serials, Islam is praised as the most rational religion extant. Sorcery and magic are condemned throughout them. Yet, as shown in the examples discussed above, magical events do take place, and this kind of magic or miracles is presented as a reward for being a good Muslim. There is a strange parallel between the presentation of early science fiction in the West and Islamic fantasy series. Toward the end of the nineteenth century, imagination found its legitimate place in Western children's literature, which was formerly highly didactic. With authors observing this popularity and acceptance of science fiction themes, similar novels started to appear for adults too. However, the narratives of the latter were constructed in such a manner that scientific value, and at least the possibility of truth, could be attributed to the text. Writers such as Edgar Allan Poe, Jules Verne, Arthur Conan Doyle, H. Rider Haggard, Robert Louis Stevenson, and H. G. Wells wrote fantastical tales under a scientific guise; new printing techniques allowed them to use maps, realistic illustrations, and even footnotes to underline the reality, or rather the possibility of reality, of their texts (Saler 2004, 141). We see a very similar effort being made in the Islamic fantasy serials. The reality and rationality of the script and its contents are constantly emphasized, although what the audience witnesses on the screen is undoubtedly of a supernatural nature. As already mentioned, the scriptwriters are assisted by university scholars. Time and again Islam is mentioned as the religion of science and rationality, and practicing magic is depicted as an evil act to be punished by hell. Yet, despite all this background emphasis on science, the series do not refute the reality of practicing magic, most probably because the Koran itself professes magic to be evil, but still recognizes its reality.

The study conducted in the province of Konya revealed the basic motive for watching the serials as one of "experiencing or reinforcing religious beliefs [feelings]." It is connected to the "wish to see justice done and experience religious feelings" (Koçak, Çakır, and Gülnar 2006, 353). It can be claimed that the serials are alternative and modern ways of experiencing religion. They can be viewed as moments of re-enchantment, since they make the teachings of Islam a visual experience. Although they present the miracles that occur as the will of God, from another perspective these miracles are magic, and the characters in the serials are supernatural beings.

If the coexistence of modernity and (re-)enchantment is possible, then there exists room for religion. Rather than analyzing religion as a remnant of the traditional and antimodern past, it might be seen to fall within the confines of modernity and as partially constituting modernity. Disassociating the concepts "secular" and "modern" shows the possibility that modern culture has not necessarily cut all ties with religion (Bracke 2008, 58–59).

Besides those about the effect of re-enchantment, some final questions can be asked about the fantasy serials discussed. What does this network of symbols correspond to, and what do they tell us about Turkish politics and society? For one, it shows a great deal of interaction between Islamists and secularists in cultural terms. These two seemingly distinct positions influence and sometimes shape each other. In the present case, the Islamists have used the fantasy genre, which is unexpected, as fantasy stories are associated with Western culture. On the other hand, the secular channels did not hes-

itate to start their own serials inspired by the Islamic originals. Commodification, as a concept and activity, is shared by Islamists and secularists, rather
than being something that divides the two parties (Navaro-Yashin 2002,
222). Television channels are part of the commodification, so interaction can
be expected. The popular television serials try to attract the greatest number
of people with their programs. The fantasy serials have helped secular media owners pursue their goal, and by avoiding the religious tone of the Islamic originals, they can still claim to have followed a secularist broadcasting
policy. Conservative Islamist channels may also have a commercial interest,
but they also intend to promote Islamic morality. By employing the fantasy
genre, they have been able to gain wide popularity. If the ends justify the
means, in this case the end being popularity, but popularity for the sake of
religion, and the means the originally Western genre of fantasy, then the interaction between the modernist and religious methodologies and symbols
does not really create a conflict for the Islamist channels. The same conclusion applies to the secularist channels.

NOTES

1. http://www.diyanet.gov.tr/turkish/dy/Diyanet-Isleri-Baskanligi-Duyuru-8222
.aspx (accessed February 26, 2008).
2. http://www.taraf.com.tr/ayse-hur/makale-turbanin-60-yillik-seruveni.htm (accessed January 3, 2011).
3. http://www.stv.com.tr/ShowProgram.aspx?ContentId=11 (accessed January 3,
2008).
4. http://www.ntvmsnbc.com/news/438206.asp.
5. http://www.stv.com.tr (accessed January 3, 2008).
6. http://www.usc.edu/dept/MSA/quran/007.qmt.html#007.087 (accessed April 9,
2008).
7. http://www.usc.edu/dept/MSA/fundamentals/hadithsunnah/bukhari/023.sbt
.html#002.023.372 (accessed April 9, 2008).
8. http://www.usc.edu/schools/college/crcc/engagement/resources/texts
/muslim/quran/027.qmt.html (accessed April 9, 2008).
9. http://www.stv.com.tr/ShowProgram.aspx?ContentId=11 (accessed April 9,
2008).
10. http://www.imdb.com/title/tt0108968/plotsummary (accessed June 6, 2009.)
11. http://yenisafak.com.tr/arsiv/2004/agustos/06/televizyon.html (accessed April
9, 2008).
12. http://yenisafak.com.tr/arsiv/2004/temmuz/17/televizyon.html (accessed April
9, 2008).

REFERENCES

Aras, Bulent, and Omer Caha. 2000. "Fethullah Gulen and His Liberal Turkish Islam
Movement." *Middle East Review of International Affairs (MERIA)* 4, no. 4 (December): 30–42.

Bennett, Jane. 2001. *The Enchantment of Modern Life: Attachments, Crossings, and Ethics.* Princeton, NJ: Princeton University Press.

Berkes, Niyazi. 1936. "Sociology in Turkey." *American Journal of Sociology* 42 (2): 238–246.

———. 1964. *The Development of Secularism in Turkey.* Montreal: McGill University Press.

Binark, Mutlu, and Peyami Celikcan. 2000. "Border Crossings in Multi-Channel TV Environment: The Discourse of the Islamic Other in Turkey." *Iletisim* 5:71–92 (http://www.medyakronik.net/akademi/makaleler/makaleler21.htm).

Bracke, Sarah. 2008. "Conjugating the Modern/Religious, Conceptualizing Female Religious Agency: Contours of a 'Post-secular' Conjuncture." *Theory, Culture and Society* 25 (6): 51–67.

Çınar, Alev. 2001. "National History as a Contested Site: The Conquest of Istanbul and Islamist Negotiations of the Nation." *Comparative Studies in Society and History* 43 (2): 364–391.

Dole, Christopher. 2006. "Mass Media and the Repulsive Allure of Religious Healing: The Cinci Hoca in Turkish Modernity." *International Journal of Middle Eastern Studies* 38:31–54.

Greisman, H. C. 1973. "Disenchantment of the World: Romanticism, Aesthetics and Sociological Theory." *British Journal of Sociology* 27 (4): 459–507.

Hodgson, Marshall. 1975. *The Venture of Islam.* Vol. 1, *The Classical Age of Islam.* Chicago: University of Chicago Press.

Jenkins, Richard. 2000. "Disenchantment, Enchantment and Re-Enchantment: Max Weber at the Millennium." *Max Weber Studies* 1:11–32.

Koçak, Abdullah, Vedat Çakır, and Birol Gülnar. 2006. "Mystery Serials: The Relations between the Watching Motives and Religiousness." http://perweb.firat.edu.tr/personel/yayinlar/fua_1667/1667_52809.pdf (accessed November 24, 2010).

Lee, Raymond. 2008. "Modernity, Mortality and Re-enchantment: The Death Taboo Revisited." *Sociology* 42 (4): 745–759.

Navaro-Yashin, Yael. 2002. "The Market for Identities: Secularism, Islamism, Commodities." In *Fragments of Culture: Everyday Life in Turkey,* ed. Deniz Kandiyoti and Ayşe Saktanber, pp. 221–253. London: I. B. Tauris.

Öncü, Ayşe. 1995. "Packaging Islam: Cultural Politics on the Landscape of Turkish Commercial Television." *Public Culture,* no. 8, 51–71.

Sakallıoğlu, Umit Cizre. 1996. "Parameters and Strategies of Islam-State Interaction in Republican Turkey." *International Journal of Middle East Studies* 28 (2): 231–251.

Saler, Michael. 2004. "Modernity and Enchantment: A Historiographic Review." *American Historical Review* 111 (3): 692–716.

Tunç, Gökhan. 2005. "Kalp gözü, efsane ve ikincil sözlü kültür." *Milli Folklor* 10:23–29.

Turner, Brian. 2006. "Law and Religion." *Theory, Sociology and Culture* 23 (2–3): 452–454.

Walker, Warren S., and Ahmet E. Uysal. 1973. "An Ancient God in Modern Turkey: Some Aspects of the Cult of Hizir." *Journal of American Folklore* 86:286–289.

Weber, Max. "Science as Vocation." [1918]. http://www.ne.jp/asahi/moriyuki/abukuma/weber/lecture/science_frame.html (accessed May 3, 2008).

CHAPTER 8

FROM "EVIL-INCITING" DANCE TO CHASTE "RHYTHMIC MOVEMENTS": A GENEALOGY OF MODERN ISLAMIC DANCE-THEATRE IN IRAN

ZEINAB STELLAR

DESPITE ALL MORAL PROHIBITIONS, the genre of "rhythmic movements" (*harikat-i mawzun*) has brought dance to the service of Islamic theatrical culture in postrevolutionary Iran. Embodying chastity, modesty, and spirituality, *harikat-i mawzun* has sublimated the dancer from a religiously subaltern "evil-inciting self" (*nafs-i 'ammarah*) to a respectable "contented self" (*nafs-i mutma'innah*) in the Islamic mystical tradition. Offering a genealogy of this theatrical dance from the early twentieth century to the present, this chapter explores the postrevolutionary genre of rhythmic movements (*harikat-i mawzun*) and investigates its evolution and transformation from the prerevolutionary "national dance" (*raqs-i milli*), a "high art" theatrical genre created and promoted during the Pahlavi period as an authentic Iranian national art form.[1]

It was approximately a decade after "dance" (*raqs*) was banned as an immoral cultural practice that a new mode of performance appeared on the formal stage in Iran. Cast as rhythmic movements (*harikat-i mawzun*), this new genre soon became a vehicle embodying the Islamic government's religious and political ideology. Appropriated through a renaming and reshaping of the dancing subject, the genre of rhythmic movements was constructed to counter the previous associations of dance (*raqs*) with immorality, corruption, and "imitated modernity" (*tajaddud-i taqlidi*) largely instigated by the image of the unconstrained dancing subject of the popular entertainment scene of cabaret and European social dancing in the Pahlavi era, particularly the cabaret dancer. It is not solely the postrevolutionary rhythmic movements that distanced itself from the signifiers associated with the negative notions of dance; the Pahlavi era's high-art dancer of *raqs-i milli* (national dance) also defamiliarized the image of its contemporaneous dancing subject of the popular scene, *raqqas*, in her polite representation of Iranian culture.

This chapter traces the creation of the two artistic modes of Iranian theatrical dance in twentieth-century Iran, the Pahlavi-era Iranian national dance and the postrevolutionary rhythmic movements, and traces their dialogic relations to the press discourse of their times, as well as to the dances practiced in the popular urban entertainment scene prior to the Revolution. It explores the terminologies deployed to dissociate these artistic dance forms and their performers from those of popular dances, as well as the themes prevalent in these high-art theatrical dances. Focusing on the staged performing body as a physical site for theatrical representation, capable of manifesting the outward projections of constructed identities and ideal bodies and relations (Dolan 1992), this chapter examines the ways in which the appearance and actions of the dancing subjects in the artistic genres of national dance and rhythmic movements were constructed to defamiliarize the dancing body of the cabaret stage, associated with the "evil-inciting self." Finally, through analyzing the performers' bodily aesthetics, actions, ethics, and behaviors, and focusing on representations of gender performativity and relations on stage, this chapter examines the ways in which the performing body of the twentieth-century govermentalized Iranian theatrical space would relate to the regulatory social conventions of everyday life, and reflect the state's biopolitics.[2]

"INCITING DANCE" AND ITS COUNTERS

The negative view in Islam of dance as a manifestation of this-worldly pleasure (Hanna 1988), and the mere notion that dance falls in the category of "fun," as described by Bayat (2007), point out that dance is often considered as a subversive activity that can distract Muslim society from piety. In her 1949 article "The Theatre and Ballet Arts in Iran," Nilla Cram Cook, relating the prejudices against dance in the Middle East, asserted that "dance has degraded into a vulgar form of cabaret entertainment and has entirely lost its religious and national association" (Cram Cook 1949, 406). There are others who, like Cram Cook, presumed the high status of religious dances in pre-Islamic Iran (Ali-Akbari Baigi and Muhammadi 2000, 1326). The dance scholar Anthony Shay also recognizes the conflict over dance in most Muslim countries, asserting that within these societies, "the term dance can possibly bear powerfully negative or at least ambiguous connotations" (Shay 1995, 61). In his ethnographic study of the diasporic Iranian community in California, Shay coins the term "choreophobia" to refer specifically to the negative views of dance in the Iranian cultural sphere (Shay 1999).

The public (modern) dancing body was exposed in Iran in the first half of the twentieth century, when, with the development of urban public life, new hetero-social sites of sociability were created in large cities of Iran.

These included the theaters, cinemas, cabarets with live dance performances (*raqqas-khanah*), cafés and restaurants (with Western social dancing), wine houses (*may-khanah*), and gambling houses. Concurrently, and in response to this new lifestyle, social hygiene became an important concern for the state and intelligentsia, who targeted popular urban entertainment for their moral modernity. The immorality associated with the new forms of "cheap" urban popular entertainment made them a sphere blamed for the dissemination of the social maladies of corruption, venereal disease, and repression of the sexual drives of men, thus leading to shrinkage of the average family size (Schayegh 2009, 122).

The popularity of European social dancing in the nightlife of the larger cities, particularly Tehran in the 1940s–1960s, brought to the surface another transgressive behavior in urban life. This trend became very popular, especially during and after World War II, when American soldiers also joined the nightlife of the Westernized Tehrani upper middle class, who actively practiced social dances such as the tango, cha-cha, *pasodoble*, and waltz in public. The close public bodily proximity of men and women thoroughly incited the perception of dance as a means of social corruption, to which can be traced the stance of the Pahlavi government in banning rock 'n' roll dance from Tehran's nightlife in the 1950s (Ali-Akbari Baigi and Muhammadi 2000, 730).

While from the early 1900s cinema theaters screening foreign movies had been sites for gazing at exotic female bodies, the development of the widely viewed *filmfarsi* (a commercial genre of Iranian cinema) in the 1950s brought the Iranian cabaret dancer to the screen. The bold presence of the cabaret-dancing body in the films and sites of sociability such as cafés and cabarets, with seemingly uncontrolled sexuality, added to the already existing negative attitudes toward *raqs* (dance) and *raqqas* (dancer). The cabaret performer was convicted of arousing sexual excitement in her supposedly lower-class male audience, who would proceed to chase other women in public after watching her sexual dance (see Figure 8.1 for a photograph of a cabaret dancer).

The sensitivity toward the public dancing body has pervaded the modern Islamist discourse since the first half of the twentieth century, and is traceable in the periodicals of that era.[3] Associating all societal corruption and failures, including prostitution, gambling, alcohol consumption, materialism, and communism with *tajaddud* (modernity), these periodicals often identified *raqs* as an alien activity of the Western-driven modernized individual (*mutijaddid*) and a signifier of his or her blind imitation of the West.[4] Along with bearing all these stereotypical corrupted and anti-Islamic characteristics, the "unconstrained" body of a *mutijaddid* was presumed to publicly

FIGURE 8.1. The famed cabaret dancer Djamileh in the 1960s

engage in dance with a person of the opposite sex. *Raqqas* was often used as a negative metaphor and a swear word to describe a deviant person, a Westernized *mutijaddid*, or a male politician.[5] The rejection and the association with prostitution and sexual laxity were not limited to social dancing, but extended to all kinds of dancing, regardless of whether the performance was in a kindergarten class or a cabaret setting. These popular movement practices included cabaret, social dancing, ballet, and rural and urban dances, as well as group (*raqs-i ijtima'i*) and solo (*raqs-i infiradi*) dances (Bandari 1326/1947, 3). One of the chief reasons for this condemnation was the association of dance with the evil-inciting self (*nafs-i 'ammarah*).

Dance, one of the most corporeally rooted of individual physical activities, was seen as the worst possible behavior of an undisciplined body in public, and the symbol of all vice. It was described by these periodicals as a "religion-destroying and Islam-murdering performance" (*namayish-i din kharab kun va islam kush*), and was deemed a crime ("Hunaristan-i a'ali-yi" 1332/1953, 1). Dancing and the act of attending dance events were associated with incitement of evil and offending the divine and religion. Implying divine punishment, the periodical *Nida-yi Haq* warned people after an earthquake to stop dancing, so that the earth would not dance again ("Az raqs-i zamin" 1336/1957). The extent of the popular reception of dance at the time, and the ensuing religious dispute, can be inferred from a 1947 article in *Parcham-i Islam*, which claimed that dance and other forms of corruption had conquered Tehran's public life:

> We watch Tehran dancing in the fire of corruption, pleasure and crimes, not only Tehran, but Iran and the whole Muslim world are dancing in this fire . . . Tehran is dancing and burning. (Karbasi 1326/1947, 2)

Such discourses were found not only in the religious press; a critical stance toward dance was also reflected in the secular nationalist periodicals of various ideological persuasions. In a piece published in the weekly *Ashuftah* in 1949, dance was identified as a bodily action of a prostitute ("Raqs" 1328/1949). Young women were especially warned against the corrupt nature of Western partner-dancing, which could cause them to lose their virginity. For example, Surur Afkhami, in an article in *Taraqiq*, asked educated women to resist social corruptions and trendy activities such as Western social dancing, and instead, to invest their energy in acquiring their social rights (Afkhami 1329/1950). Zahra Azari, a member of the women's association linked with the weekly *Ittila'at-i Banuvan*, also criticized social dancing as a means for dissemination of societal corruptions. Warning about the spirit of family destruction lurking in dance, she advocated the removal of dance from Iranian society (Ibasalti 1340/1962). It is important to note that this attitude stands in contrast to some women's periodicals, including *Mihrigan*, which encouraged women to practice dance as a physical exercise.[6]

Another channel through which dance was attacked in these periodicals was fictional writing, mainly published in magazines that were read primarily by men. Appearing in increasing numbers into the 1950s, these

FIGURE 8.2. A scene from *Haft Paykar*, performed by the National Folklore
Organization, 1970s

erotic condemnations of eroticism often invoked provocative associations
by employing the word *raqs* in their titles, as in "Devil's Dance" (*shiytanak-
ha miraqsand*), "The Spy Dancer" (*raqqasah-yi jassus*), or the "Weeping
Dancer" (*raqqasah-yi giryian*). Most of these stories featured exotic female
dancers who were flirtatious, sensual, and conniving, and used their beauty
to charm and betray men.[7]

It was in reaction to these negative discursive constructions that the
comparatively chaste and virtuous female dancing subject of Iranian national dance was constructed. Being purged of all the negative characteristics linked to the supposedly undisciplined cabaret dancer, the national
dancer's ballet-trained, disciplined body was desexualized by her authentic-
looking clothing (see Figure 8.2 for an example of national dancers). Instead
of dancing in the cabaret, the national dancer appeared in polite gatherings.
This newly constructed national dancer acted as a muted means to convey
the glory of Iranian history and literature to the audience, which often included the Iranian elite, foreign guests, and dignitaries. In contrast to the
"evil-inciting" cabaret dancer, the dancing subject in national dance is associated with the corrective [conscious] self (*nafs-i lavvamah*) in the traditional Islamic definition of *nafs* (self). Seeking to reflect the modern Iranian
national identity, the self-reflexive national dancer responded to the rapid

social changes of the first half of twentieth-century Iran by constantly repositioning and reflecting upon itself (see Adams 2003 on self-reflexivity and social change).

The appropriation of the dancing subject, along with the Pahlavis' attempts to elevate dance to the level of a national high-art form, changed the status of dance to a certain extent in that era. The negative attitude toward dance persisted, however, as reported by dancers of various generations. For instance, in a 1954 interview, Sarkis Djanbazian, the pioneering figure of ballet in Iran, explained the difficulties he faced while starting his ballet company in Iran in the 1930s due to the cultural taboos against dance (Nabavi 1333/1954). In a 1972 interview with *Zan-i Ruz*, Farzaneh Kabuli, the lead dancer of the Iran National Folklore Organization, expressed the ways in which she and her colleagues suffered as dancers working in a society where dance was not respected as a profession (Pirnia 1967). To differentiate the high status of trained national dancers from that of those dancing cabaret-style, the term *raqsandah* was coined in the Pahlavi era to refer to the performers of high-art dance forms. This term was used in contrast to the term *raqqas*, which could carry derogatory meanings referencing the less-respected contemporaneous dancers of popular entertainment settings. Due to the negative connotations associated with the term "*raqs*," in 1970s, the directors of the Iran National Folklore Organization were debating its replacement with the term "*vashtan*," the Pahlavi word for dance, aiming to differentiate art-dance from the popular and provocative dance forms.[8]

While the 1979 revolution purged all types of dance from Iranian public life as symbols of the evil-inciting self, a new dancing body reappeared on the Iranian stage about a decade after the revolution. Defamiliarized through renaming to *harikat-i mawzun* and revived by relocation to the theatrical stage, the postrevolutionary dancing subject constructed herself as the other in opposition to the popular provocative image of *raqqas*. Desexualized and controlled, the performer of this genre embodied the virtues of an Iranian Muslim, conveying a message often related to God and revolutionary values. Through connecting to God and overcoming the evil-inciting self, as in the Sufi ritual of Sama, the performing subject in rhythmic movements correlated with the "contented self" (*nafs-i mutma'innah*).[9] Reinforcing the image of a proper Muslim through embodying the expressions of heaviness, chastity, purity, and spirituality, the purified body of this subject continues to enact the ideology of the government.

Despite having undergone the defamiliarization process, rhythmic movements continues to be positioned under the shadow of the immorality associated with the "evil-inciting" *raqs*, as evident in the tone of a major rhythmic movements choreographer, who called for a differentiation between the virtue-based (*khub*) and vice-based (*bad*) forms of *harikat-i mawzun* (Kabuli

1381/2002; Chaharduli 1380/2002). Referring to the diversity of Iran's time-honored regional folk dances and movement-based rituals that are popular among Iran's Muslim population, including the Sama and Zurkhanah, Jahansooz Fuladi, a former soloist of the Iran National Folklore Organization, emphasized the affinity of these performances with Islam ("Raqs dar chand qadami-i" 1380/2001).

The ongoing dispute over *harikat-i mawzun* and its association with *raqs* was manifested in the conflicts over the opening ceremony of the Fourth Women's Islamic Games in 2005. While its director had previously clarified that the ceremony included "only *harikat-i mawzun* and not *raqs*" ("Pasukh-hayi Fa'izah Hashimi" 1384/2005), the event was widely criticized by some factions of the society. Reflecting on the same event, the author of the weblog *Raz-i Khun* questioned *harikat-i mawzun*, calling it "*raqs* according to kindergarten artsy fartsies" (Sajjad 1384/2005). While the creation of an association for *harikat-i mawzun* in 2005 was a sign of its official acceptance, its renaming to the Association for Muted Performers (Anjuman-i Namayishgaran-i Bidun-i Kalam) in 2007 to imply mime rather than dance testifies to the uncertain situation of this genre. The genre is also being referred to with alternative terms including "structured movements" (*harikat-i furm*), "expressive movements" (*harikat-i bayani*), and "ritual movements" (*harikat a'ini*), and its performers are interchangeably referred to as "actors of form" (*bazigar-i furm*), "performer" (*namayishgar*), and "choir" (*hamsurayan*). All these attempts at terminological defamiliarization and rescripting of theatrical dance as a kind of narrative-based, muted physical theater can be seen as evidence of its dynamic presence in postrevolutionary theatrical culture.

THEMES, TERMS, AND PERFORMING SUBJECTS IN THE PRE- AND POSTREVOLUTIONARY IRANIAN THEATRICAL DANCE

During the early decades of the twentieth century, with the emergence of a politically conscious theater and music community, themes pertaining to the homeland (*vatan*) and the nation (*millat*) became prominently employed in various forms of performances, including the theatrical dance. Communicating the sociopolitical needs of the time, this relatively small community sought to employ the performing arts as a means to educate the public, transmit patriotic narratives, and elevate the Iranian national culture. The progovernmental nationalistic themes, however, were imposed on performing arts in the Reza Shah era (1925–1941), during which glorifying the nation and shah became a prerequisite for public permission for a theatrical performance (Mir-Ansari and Zia'i 2003). The imposition of the pro-Pahlavi nationalistic disposition onto dance is evident in some choreographic works of that era, which bear such titles as the *Iranian Flag Ballet* (*ballet-i bayraq-i iran*), *Rustam and Suhrab* (from the Iranian national epic poem *Shahnamah*), and *Crown Glory Ballet* (*ballet–i taj-i iftikhar*) (Mansouri and Shirvani 1975).

These nationalist themes were also traceable in the works of several dance artists who fled the Soviet Union after the Russian Revolution of 1917 and resettled in Iran. These newcomers expanded the European-influenced dance scene in Iran by holding performances and dance classes of various styles, including ballet, European folk dancing, and European partner dancing. The most important of these dance schools were Madame Cornelli's Ballet School (founded in 1930 in Tehran), the Tehran Ballet Academy of Sarkis Djanbazian (1940, Tehran), Yelena Ballet Academy (1950, Tehran), and the Lazarian Ballet Academy (1949, Tehran) ("Darichah-yi bah su-yi" 1333/1955; "Jashn-i hunaristan-i ballet-i Tehran" 1329/1950; "Hichgah faramush" 1340/1961; "Kilass-i khususi-yi" 1329/1950; "Dah sal talash" 1339/1960). Most of these private schools received financial support from the Ministry of Culture and Arts. Adapting to their new home, Iran, where the state and elite class were concerned with nation-building and developing national arts, and following the European trend of national dance in nineteenth-century Romantic Ballet, which fused stylized folk dances into ballet (Garafola 1997), these new immigrant dance artists also brought Iranian themes and movements into ballet (see, for example, Nabavi 1333/1954; "Ballet" 1328/1949; "Dah sal talash" 1339/1960), marking the invention of a genre often categorized as national dance (*raqs-i milli*).

The major Iranian national dance project of the first half of the twentieth century was initiated in 1946 by Nilla Cram Cook,[10] who founded the Studio of the Revival of the Iranian Classical Arts (*istudiyu-yi ihyia-yi hunarha-yi bastani-yi iran*), aiming to revive and restore the "forgotten" ancient Iranian performing arts (Nazimi 1327/1948). Having a background in dance and theater, Cram Cook sought to create ballet-based dances with various Iranian themes and motifs inspired by mythology, folklore, and Persian poetry, as well as religious processions and prayers of Zoroastrianism and Islam, including the Sama of the Mevlevi Dervish orders. Some of her works include *Gurd-Afarid*, inspired by a story of Shahnamah and movements of *zurkhanah* ("Gurd-Afarid" 1335/1957); *Majnun and the Tulip*, inspired by Nizami Ganjavi's *Leili and Majnun*; *Prayer of Darius*, inspired by a five-thousand-year-old Luristan goddess figurine and Magi, the fire priest; and the *Dance of the Rose and Nightingale*, inspired by a poem of Hafiz (Cram Cook 1949, 406; Ramazani 2002).

Besides "restoring Iranians' sense of pride in their own culture" (Ramazani 2008, 298), Cram Cook aimed to break the barrier set up between public dancing and women of "good families" (ibid., 301), a project planned to speed up the modernization process in Iran. Receiving support from the Pahlavi family, the Iranian government, and the US embassy, Cram Cook's group later performed in Turkey, Greece, Italy, Egypt, Iraq, Syria, India, and Lebanon (Mansouri and Shirvani 1975). She left a legacy to Iranian dance, as two of her protégés, Haideh Akhundzadeh and Nejad Ahmadzadeh, later started the National Ballet Company of Iran in 1956. The early repertoire of the Company in particular included Iranian national and folk dances.

Staging national dances was also on the agenda of the Iran National Folklore Organization (*sazman-i milli-yi fulklur*), a large state-funded company created in 1967. In the words of its British director, Robert de Warren, the Organization was founded "to safeguard the nation's treasures in ethnic dances, music and ceremonies" ("Mahalli Dancers" 1976). Besides staging folk dances, the company created and staged dances based on the Sufi ritual of Sama, a wide range of national dances, including the dances of the Safavid and Qajar court, as well as *Haft Paykar*, a full-length work based on the poetry of Nizami Ganjavi. It also performed balletic works such as *Simurgh*, inspired by seven Iranian love stories, including the *Candle and Butterfly* and *Rose and Nightingale* (Safa 1353/1975). This company regularly performed Iranian dance in the Rudaki Hall, Iran's most prestigious concert stage, founded in 1967, as well as at court, and sometimes displayed Iranian national art to various foreign politicians and dignitaries. The company also toured many foreign countries, such as England, Turkey, Pakistan, and the United States to showcase Iranian culture ("Antalya festivali" 1973; "Preserve Folklore" 1974; "Dirakhshish-i raqsandigan-i" 1351/1972).

In periodicals of the Pahlavi era, national dance (*raqs-i milli*) appears to have been used synonymously with the following terms: "ancient dance" (*raqs-i bastani*), "Iranian classical dance" (*raqs-i kilasik-i irani*), "Iranian ballet" (*ballah-yi irani*), "characteristic dance" (*raqs-i karaktiristik*), and sometimes, "Iranian traditional dance" (*raqs-i sunnati-yi irani*). The term "national" was applied to dances related to Iranian national identity, but in slightly different ways. "Ancient dance" could be related to a notion of Iran's glorious pre-Islamic past, promoted at the time as the true Iranian culture. Dances from more recent historical periods were also claimed as national dances; these were often reconstructions from miniature paintings of the Safavid period (1501–1736) and the Qajar era (1794–1925), whereas "ancient" pre-Islamic dances were based on descriptions or imagery from archeological sites and mythology. Traditional dances such as *mutribi*, *zarbi*, and other dances from the late Qajar period were sometimes also referred to as national dances.

The terms Iranian classical (*kilasik*) or characteristic (*karaktiristik*) dance indicated that the dance was European-influenced or imported by practitioners of some types of Western characteristic or classical dance who combined their own classical dances with Iranian movements and themes. Finally, Iranian ballet should be considered as European-style ballet with an Iranian theme.

Persian poetry offered some of the most important inspirational themes for the national dance, and was a topic of discussion for many scholars and choreographers who aimed to arrive at a high-art Iranian dance genre. Persian poetry and literature were repeatedly offered as the authentic Iranian source to draw upon in revitalizing Iranian dance. For example, in 1946, Nilla Cram Cook identified Persian poetry as the sacred content of Iranian dance. By linking dance to Persian poetry, Cram Cook believed this art form would re-ascend to its sacred level (Cram Cook 1325/1946, 33).

Viewing poetry as the foundation of the noble culture in Iran, Hassan Shirvani, a regular commentator on music and theater, and later the head of the Tehran Opera Bureau, suggested a combination of Persian poetry, music, and dance in lieu of a pure national performing art form (Shirvani 1336/1957, 38). Abdullah Nazemi, the founder of Pars National Ballet (*ballah-yi milli-yi pars*), contended in his 1966 interview with *Talash* that the only solution for elevating the art of dance in Iran was to pay attention to national dance and national ballet. Nazemi maintained that Iran's rich poetic narratives would be better suited for Iranian ballet productions than the content borrowed from Western countries (Shafi'ee 1350s/1970s, 77). In a more recent account, an informant of Anthony Shay identified the frequent use of literary and historical themes in Iranian dance productions as "a green card to dance" and "a legitimate way of validating dance" (Shay 2005).

Poetry and mythology remain prevalent themes for the theatrical dance of postrevolutionary Iran, for all its differences with prerevolutionary national dance. The theatrical productions *Simurgh* (2002) and *Haft-Iqlim* (2003) are examples of such full-length movement-based productions. However, the mystical themes, which also were employed in prerevolutionary national dance, are central in the postrevolutionary genre. As a midpoint between the worldly practice of dance for the single purpose of entertainment and the strict interpretations of Islam, which fully reject dance, the Sufi ritual of Sama has served to legitimize dance in Iran, often justifying *harikat-i mawzun* as a spiritual dance. In the early 2000s, when this performance genre was receiving more attention, several authors emphasized the significance of Sama as a performance for the divine, thereby rejecting worldly dances, which serve no purpose but pleasure (see, for example, As'adi 1382/2003; Sajjadifar 1381/2003, 1383/2004; "Raqs bara-yi" 1383/2004).

Concurrently, the producers of *harikat-i mawzun*, struggling to stage their work, widely related their dance to Sama and the philosophy behind it, or emphasized dance and other rituals as national art forms. For instance, in an interview about the *Amen Festival* (*Jashnvarah-yi Amin*)—a narrative-based full-length rhythmic movements production that featured several regional folk dances—the director described those dances as "a means for praying to God." Furthermore, she argued that the last scene of the work, in which diverse groups simultaneously perform various regional folk dances to the same music, represents the communal prayer of the nation of Iran, consisting of many ethnicities and cultures including the Kurdish, Turkish, Khorassani, and Gilaki (Babakhani 1381/2003). The attempt to associate all types of dance as mystical or religious was also evident in an article published in 2001 in the monthly *Hamshahri-yi Mah*. Interviewing several active dance artists, and reporting the present-day activities related to this art form in the society, the author emphasized the importance of "preservation of this religious-national art form [*raqs*]" ("Raqs dar chand qadami-i" 1380/2001).

While the Sama is invoked to legitimize rhythmic movements, the more conservative circles often disagree on the legitimacy of this mystical ritual itself. An example of this attitude can be found in an account by Hamidullah Rafi'i, a contributor to Andishah-yi Qom, in response to the Rumi scholar Seyyed Salman Safavi, who argues that Islam needs to be presented in ways appealing to youth, recommending Sama, the spiritual (*ma'navi*) dance, as an appropriate means to this end.[11] While emphasizing the prohibition of dance in Islam for arousing sexual and sensual passion, Rafi'i asserts that the only dance allowed in Islam is the dance of a wife for her husband. Rafi'i rejects Sama as a way to get closer to God, asserting that "dance is dance, and there is no such thing as spiritual (*ma'navi*) dance . . . dance distances the man from God, and, in particular, leads the youth to sensuality and sex" (Rafi'i n.d.).

Besides mystical themes, religious narratives have also been dominant in the rhythmic movement productions, to the extent that this genre has widely been used as a means to stage stories of Ashura, and those holy figures of Shi'a Islam such as Zeinab, Fatimih, Hussein, and Ali, as well as Muslim Ibn-i Aqil and Hurr. All of these productions have been categorized as "Religious Theatre" (*namayish-i mazhabi*).[12] Movement-based performances identified as "engagé art" (*hunar-i-muti'ahid*) have enacted narratives related to the Iran-Iraq war and become an element of the "Holy Defense Theatre" (*ti'atr-i difa'i muqaddas*). Produced in varying lengths, these performances have been regularly commissioned for different purposes by government organizations. In fact, the first full-length play of this genre, *The Epic of the Rock Revolution* (*himasah-yi inqilab-i-sang*), on the theme of the Intifada and Israeli-Palestine conflict, was commissioned by a sector of the government in 2000 (see Figure 8.3 and Figure 8.4). This work was referred to as the first Islamic ballet (Abulqasimi 1386/2007).

FIGURE 8.3. A scene from *The Epic of the Rock Revolution* (2000). Photo by Umid Salihi.

FIGURE 8.4. A scene from *The Epic of the Rock Revolution* (2000). Photo by Umid Salihi.

Recognizing the need for change in the presentation of these genres of theater, Hussein Mussafir-Astanah, a prolific director in the genres of Religious and Holy Defense Theatre, has been directing movement-based works. Aiming to make these themes more accessible to the general audience in Iran and abroad, and to attract the younger generations, his works often feature a contemporary combination of various theatrical elements, including movements, video projection, and sound effects (Biniyaz 1386/2008).

RHYTHMIC MOVEMENTS UNDER THE CORRECTIONAL GAZE

Although constructed to identify with the "contented self," in a manner similar to that of other theatrical performances, rhythmic movements productions must be previewed by an inspection and evaluation committee responsible for deciding whether a work is suitable for the public audience in Iran. This committee is charged with the task of ensuring that no component of a performance, including its theme, and performers' appearances and actions, is against the Islamic law and thus the government's policies. A main responsibility of this committee, however, is to verify that the performers' appearance and actions onstage do not provoke sexual desires in the audience.

With a limited number of performances, rhythmic movements productions have themes that are either religious or mystical. While regular plays could expose a wide range of Iranian and foreign narratives, the review process for these genres is much easier than the one contemplated for rhythmic movements. In fact, staging a short rhythmic movements piece in a long narrative-based play is much easier than staging a full-length rhythmic movements production.

The main rationale is that while renamed as *harikat-i mawzun*, a stage performance merely concerned with body movements still could be interpreted as dance (*raqs*). Often coming from a religious background, the inspection committee members are likely to have been exposed to the common prejudices against dance as a "sexual and cheap entertainment" and the "behavior of an unconstrained body," descriptions found in the early-twentieth-century Islamic discourse. Moreover, since the inspector's decision about the suitability of a particular public performance can be read as the government's statement on the performance, (I can hypothesize that) the inspector exercises a great deal of caution. Moreover, "the erotic pervasion of the theatrical space," and the interpretation of the staged body as a "commodity for strangers' gaze," as Senelick (1992, xii) notes, add to the critical situation of the preview session.

While a spectator's interpretation of a dance performance significantly relies on his or her own personal history, understanding, and knowledge, as Carter (1998, 250) suggests, "the interpretation of dance is also necessarily contingent upon the recognition of common cultural meanings ascribed to signs, symbols, patterns, structures, etc." In the subjective process of inspection, movements and other visual aspects of stage that could possibly signify unacceptable semiotic meanings and aesthetics or bear a sexual undertone may get eliminated or cause elimination of a work. Movements that are not considered expressions of a proper Muslim, and resemble lightness, carefreeness, and spontaneity (Bayat 2007), also might be red flags. More importantly, movements that signify *raqs* for the public can doom a work.

Drawing upon Foucault's concept of the correctional gaze (Foucault 1980), I argue that the inspection committee members are part of a network of power that regulates the theatrical space. These individuals not only gaze at a theatrical work for the purpose of surveillance, but also have the power to decide whether it is suitable for the public to watch. Moreover, because of the importance of the committee's decision, its eye of power functions effectively in its absence—its corrective gaze subjugates the performers, in an internalized manner, to constant self-monitoring before the preview session (see McLaren 2002 for mechanisms of the correctional gaze).

THE STAGED BODY'S APPEARANCE AND ACTIONS

The performing body on the stage is a physical symbol, reflecting various complex meanings through both its appearance and actions, as well as interaction with various stage signifiers such as costume and, more importantly, with the audience (Gilbert and Tompkins 1996). This section is a survey of the transformation of the three different dancing subjects of twentieth-century Iran—the evil-inciting *raqqas* of cabaret dancing, the self-reflexive national dancer (*raqsandah*), and the contented performer of rhythmic movements (*namayishgar-i bidun-i kalam*). This analysis proceeds through an examination of the performers' costuming, behavior, performance space, music, style of movements, and use of space, as well as the performers' relations to each other.

A performance costume is the most obvious signifier for framing the performing body. In prerevolutionary Iran, the "contaminated body" of a seminaked female cabaret dancer, who dressed to expose and accentuate her hips and breasts, looked distinctly different from the body of a national dancer.[13] The asexual performer of *raqs-i milli* was often fully covered with vivid clothing inspired mostly by Persian miniature paintings, in which the curves of her body were apparent. In contrast, the costumes used in performances of rhythmic movements today are mostly black, white, or other muted colors, and are loosely fitted so as to obscure the shape of the body. Sometimes, in mixed performances, both men and women have similar costuming, which occasionally also covers the face, a strategy of degendering that reduces sensitivity toward the female public dancing body.[14]

As Gilbert and Tompkins assert (1996, 244), the "paradox of the costume's simultaneous specificity and versatility makes it an unstable sign/site of power," which can be deployed to "(mis)identify race, gender, class and creed, and make visible the status associated with such markers of difference." This is especially evident in the postrevolutionary theatrical dance costumes in Iran, which play an important role in representing the newly constructed gender identities on stage. These loosely fitted costumes of both male and female performers in the rhythmic movements often do not represent any regional culture of Iran or any traditional Iranian clothing, but follow a style developed for this particular performance genre. They also provide much more covering than the regular clothing one would wear in public in postrevolutionary Iran. Arguably, this kind of costuming not only aims at preventing sexual connotations of performing body on stage, but also reinforces the Islamic bio-ideology.

Behavior of the performers is another area of contrast between prerevolutionary and postrevolutionary dance. The confident performance of sexuality expressed by a cabaret dancer was intolerable both for the Pahlavi government and the majority of the Iranian society. While the image of both men and women presented on stage in *raqs-i milli* was asexual, physically fit, healthy, confident, joyful, and active, displaying a sense of pride in behavior, men showed more masculinity in their moves, whereas women's movements had traces of femininity and charm. The dominant characteristic of the performer of *harikat-i mawzun*, however, is to embody and perform the expressions of heaviness, modesty, chastity, and austerity. The representation of women is seemingly more "passive, invisible, and unspoken," contrasting with men's more active and strong roles.

Another important transformation placed upon the dancing body in the twentieth century was through a change of the performance venue: a departure from the traditional stage of *hawz* and popular cabaret stage to the Western-style proscenium theatrical space elevated Iranian dance to a high-art form (Safavi 1339/1960).[15] The transition from the prerevolutionary national dance to the postrevolutionary rhythmic movements genre, however, did not come about merely through relocation, but also through conversion of the secular theatrical space, charged with the "erotic pervasion" associated with the stage, into an Islamic sphere (Senelick 1992, xii), and the sublimation of its performing subject.

The urban popular folk music of Tehran, often bearing explicit lyrics played in cabarets, never accompanied the elite national dancers. Instead, these dancers performed to traditional Persian music, regional folk music, and sometimes contemporary and classical Western art music. While the goblet drum *zarb* was often dominant in the music used for national dance, the circular drum *daf*, which is usually associated with mystical music, is more dominant in postrevolutionary dance. In general, to keep these performances from becoming celebratory and therefore inappropriate, both musical rhythms and movements are slowed down.

While the nature of the worldly pleasure depicted in the sensual dance of a cabaret dancer is very different from the relatively asexual celebratory national dance, the staged presentation of festive scenes has been completely transformed in postrevolutionary performances through the implementation of mystical elements. This often creates a contradiction between the theme and style of these dances. An example of this can be seen in the depiction of love scenes, where the dancers also communicate with God by performing movements of the Sufi mystic dance Sama. In addition, in the postrevolutionary productions of secular celebratory scenes, where one would expect to see Persian classical dance, there is, instead, dance that has elements of the Sama.

Cabaret dancers were usually confident in crossing their stage. This certainty and freedom were also evident in national dancers, who traveled freely across the stage. This self-assurance and liberty in movement, however, are not evident in all the postrevolutionary dance productions. The cabaret dancer moved in proximity to the musicians on stage, and directly asked audiences to adore her sexuality. The female dancer of the national dance was relatively free in communicating with her male partners: she often acted playfully, teased the men on stage, and unreservedly communicated with them. Societal restriction on gender relations is manifested and rather exaggerated in the postrevolutionary theatrical performances. In particular, depicting a love relationship between a husband and a wife is quite challenging, as both performers are mute and sometimes it is impossible to see the facial expressions of a female dancer's covered face. In this situation, the pauses between movements to express doubt or affection become a key channel of communication for the dancers in depicting love. The exchange of props such as books, flowers, or a piece of fabric is also metaphorically employed to depict the love relation, since the performers are not allowed to touch each other.

Altering the movements of a dance perceptibly affects the style and character of the performance. The choreographers in both prerevolutionary and postrevolutionary Iran have endeavored to adapt dances to the sociopolitical milieu through adjustment and modification of movements. The Iranian solo improvised dance adapted to a cabaret situation stands in contrast to the more stylized version of this dance employed in national dance or Persian classical dance. Although appropriated to fit the biopolitics of the time, movement is still the most obvious element shared by the dancing body of both prerevolutionary and postrevolutionary dances. A main reason for *harikat-i mawzun*'s deep reliance on the prerevolutionary national dance is the latter's corporeal transmission through the embodied knowledge of the former's main choreographers and instructors, most of whom were once dancers with the prerevolutionary dance companies.

In the creation of national dances, choreographic units of the popular dance form known as solo improvised dance had been widely used. This theatrical genre also borrowed from the movement vocabulary of Iranian regional folk dances and rituals. This included the rotation of wrists, triplet steps, some movements of arms and shoulders, and, occasionally, minor hip movements. Depending on the proficiency of the performers and choreographers, as well as their background, the movements could be more polished or influenced by ballet.

One movement that plays a crucial role in characterizing the Iranian dance styles is *qir*, which involves the movement of hips from side to side, or their rotation. Both the *qir* and the shimmylike movements of shoulders are commonly used in the Iranian solo improvised dance, while exaggerated adaptations of them were widely used in cabaret styles to highlight the sexuality. These movements, however, were not absorbed into the national dance, perhaps for their sexual resemblance and presumed connection to cabaret-style dances. The choreographer and director of the company Pars National Ballet, Abdullah Nazemi, interprets this alteration and elimination of the *qir* in dances of this genre as leaving out the essence of Persian dance (Friend 1997). The sensitivity toward these movements can also be noticed in postrevolutionary productions, in which these parts of the body remain almost inert.

While wrist rotations similar to those of the Iranian solo improvised dance are an important element of national dances, the arms in this genre are further extended. A major distinction between the prerevolutionary and postrevolutionary genres is the absence in the latter of movements that signify the solo improvised dance, perhaps because these would connote *raqs* for the public. This is also evident in the performances of the Khorassani folk dance, in which the *bishkan* have been replaced by clapping.[16] Moreover, to distance women's movements in *harikat-i mawzun* from *raqs*, the free-flowing rotation of the wrists, triplet steps, and delicate shoulder movements borrowed from the Iranian solo improvised dance are either less emphasized or completely removed. Instead, in *harikat-i mawzun*, women mostly move their arms for a defined purpose in a way that resembles prayer or for the carrying of props such as books, candleholders, flowers, and fabrics. The movements of *harikat-i mawzun* are often a theatrical blend of ballet, stylized folk dances mainly from men's Bauluchi and Khorassani dances, the Sufi ritual of Sama (including the movements of swaying, swiveling, and whirling), the Shi'a ritual of *ta'ziah*, and the mourning for Imam Hussein (including the *sinah-zani* [beating the chest], *zanjir-zani* [beating oneself with chains], and *qamah-zani* [self-flagellation with swords]).

The movements of the female dancers in national dance are indirect, light, sustained, floating, free, and expanding, while the movements of rhythmic movements are indirect, bound, and shrinking toward the center. The spatial stress in national dance is more sagittal, as the dancers use their trunk in shoulder-opposite-hip relationships, whereas in rhythmic movements, the dancer's stress is on remaining neutral and erect, as the head, neck, and trunk are fairly fixed around the vertical midline of the body.

For men, there are fewer limitations, but not a total freedom in movements and costuming. For instance, men do not use feminine movements in their dances, or incorporate the angular shoulder and neck movements from Tehrani dances such as *baba-karam*. Occasionally, during the preview sessions by an inspection committee from the Ministry of Islamic Culture and Guidance, some movements of the male performers might also be identified as suggestive and hence have to be eliminated. For instance, in an all-male commissioned work in 2006, the inspection committee requested the elimination of a balletic *step-jeté* movement from the choreography, perhaps because it identified the movement as inappropriate.

THE DANCING BODY ON THE THEATRICAL STAGE AND IN SOCIETY

The connection between gender performativity on stage and in society has been a topic of discussion among scholars. Judith Butler finds the link between a theatrical role and a social role rather more complex, and posits that "gender performances in non-theatrical contexts are governed by more clearly punitive and regulatory social conventions" (Butler 1990, 278). Another group of scholars recognizes performance as a space for tracing the gender relations in society. Both Desmond and Carter perceive theatrical dance as a site for observing "related systems of gender performativity" as the dancers "crystallize, exaggerate, abstract and otherwise intensify the enactment of the gender system as it operates in non-theatrical everyday arenas" (Desmond 1999, 318; see also Carter 1998). Dolan also maintains that "most performances employ culturally determined gender codes that reinforce cultural conditioning" (Dolan 1998, 289).

Butler's assessment of the complex relationship between real life and staged performance is evident in case of prerevolutionary national dance. During the last decades of the Pahlavi era, the range of Iranian society included both highly Westernized and more traditional Muslim sections of the population, each practicing its own cultural ideology. This situation presented obstacles to finding a direct link between gender performativity on stage and in the society. Even in the fairly open society under the Pahlavis, regulatory social conventions may have controlled the dancing bodies, especially given the negative associations of dance. This sentiment was expressed by two renowned dancers of different generations, who explained the difficulties of working in a society where dancing is a cultural taboo (Nabavi 1333/1954; Pirnia 1967). These societal pressures have certainly affected the life and works of these dancers, who always sought to find ways to legitimize their careers to the public.

In the case of postrevolutionary Iran, however, the viewpoints of Dolan, Desmond, and Carter, who regard the stage as a site for tracing gender performativity and relations, are more pertinent. According to Shahshahani's general observations of bodily behaviors and appearances in Iranian society, women have a more restricted range of bodily movements than men (Shahshahani 2004), and this can also be observed in theatrical dance. Shahshahani, however, sees facial expressions and clothing as domains for the self-expression of women. In the case of postrevolutionary *harikat-i mawzun*, given the significance of the staged body and sensitivities toward dancing, the facial expressions and costuming of women are even more restricted than in everyday social situations. In addition, I believe that the postrevolutionary regulations on the theatrical space, reinforced by the inspection committee and seen in the limited interaction between performers of the opposite sex in rhythmic movements, are far more advanced in restricting gender relations than the "regulatory social conventions" imposed on the public sphere by societal pressures.

Furthermore, since the government seeks to condition gender roles and relations in society, the bodily representation of dancing women on stage as rather "passive, invisible, and unspoken" in comparison to the men's more active and strong roles can be seen as a reflection of the state's biopolitics. This is in line with Senelick (1992), who perceives the possible role of the performing arts, including dance, in reinforcing the status quo, especially in the case of gender, and reproducing gender power relations within society (Senelick 1992). Furthermore, the female body's appearance on stage in full *hijab*, embodying the characteristics of chastity, modesty, and spirituality, highlights the image of a "proper" Muslim woman on the official Iranian stage.

Accordingly, what Butler fails to spot in her above-mentioned argument is that for a country like Iran, nothing appears on the formal stage without being fully compatible with the very tight regulations on gender relationships and movements. For that reason, by the time a performance appears on stage in Iran, it has already been heavily regulated, allowing even less space for audience reading and evaluation. While the restrictions on performers' appearance and actions may vary depending on the policy of the government of the time, the performing bodies of women in rhythmic movements productions can be seen as reflecting the ideology and biopolitics of the government.

The restrictions especially imposed on the female dancing subject consign her to being passive and undermine her agency to move with freedom on stage. However, considering the societal pressures on women in a society such as Iran's, where the performing arts, and particularly dance, are considered as transgressive, the female presence on stage is itself an evidence of the agency of the performers. The postrevolutionary dancing subject, regulated to appear on the govermentalized Islamic stage, has been continuously reshaping itself while pushing the limits. Being agents of change, these dissident performers employ their heritage of the Iranian vocabulary of movement to adapt to the ever-changing performing situation of the Iranian public stage.

CONCLUSION

"Dance" (*raqs*) seems to have held an ambiguous position in Iranian culture, and the "controversial" public dancing subject of the cabaret and the popular social dancing scene in the twentieth century, associated with evilinciting self (*nafs-i 'ammarah*) and loaded with sexual laxity, nudity, and corruption, has furthered the strong and largely negative reactions in the society. The introduction of European artistic theatrical dance culture, along with the rise of nationalism in Iran and the support of the Pahlavi government, led to the invention of the genre of "national dance," in which the dancing body's appearance and actions defamiliarized all the negative signifiers and characteristics associated with the "corrupt" entertainment dance scene. Corresponding to the notion of the "corrective self" (*nafs-i lavvamah*) in the Islamic mystical tradition, and embodying the glory of the Iranian nation, the progressive outlook of modern Iran, and its ideal healthy, educated subject, the self-reflexive national dancer acted as a metonym for the national body, and manifested the Pahlavis' bio-ideology. About a decade after the Iranian Revolution of 1979, when the public presentation of dance was aborted, the genre rhythmic movements (*harikat-i mawzun*) brought the dancing subject back on stage. Appropriated and reshaped from, and deeply rooted in, the prerevolutionary national dance (*raqs-i-milli*), the movements of rhythmic movements do not signify the evil-inciting "*raqs*." Instead, its dancing subject is sublimated to correspond to a contented self (*nafs-i mutma'inah*), who embodies the qualities of chastity, purity, and spirituality, and moves to narrate the stories of Islam, the Revolution, and the "holy defense."

Through a transformation of form, theme, content, and even name, dance has become a physical medium for enacting the Islamic ideology of the government and reflecting its biopolitics on the stage, reinforcing the image of a "proper" Muslim. The process of defamiliarization, sublimation, and reinvention of "*raqs*" is not painless; it is a constant battle between a dissident performing self and numerous technologies of domination that govern the body on stage, and in everyday life.

NOTES

1. This discussion is limited to the public domain and the official theatrical stage, and does not deal with the private dance spheres. My sources for this article primarily include Persian periodicals, published both in pre- and postrevolutionary Iran, as well as published government documents of the Pahlavi era and visual materials, including pictures and videos of dance.

2. Biopolitics is a Foucauldian term that refers to the ways modern states control the population through subjugating their bodies in everyday life. See Foucault (1984).

3. "Modernity" (*tajaddud*) was one of the focal issues discussed in the Islamist magazines of the 1930s–1950s, including *A'in-i Islam, Parcham-i Islam, Dunya-yi Islam,* and *Nida-yi Haq.* It was viewed as a product of Iran's encounter with the West and as a social malady from which Islamic society needed to recover.

4. For an article on the association of *tajaddud* with the imitation of the West, see Niyazmand-i Shirazi 1326/1947.

5. The term *khush-raqsi* was mostly used to insult politicians. See Yaraqchi 1326/1948, quotation on p. 2; "Shab-i nur-afshani-i Islam" 1325/1947, quotation on p. 4.

6. For examples of such articles, see "The Need for Women's Sports," *Mihrigan,* 23 Murdad 1316 (August 1937), 4; "Raqs nu'i varzish ast [Dance Is a Type of Sport]," *Mihrigan,* Azar 1318 (November 1939), 13; Safavi 1339/1960; "Kumpani-yi raqs [Dance Company]," *Ittila'at-i Banuvan,* 14 Farvardin 1340 (3 April 1961), 4+.

7. Examples of such writing can be seen in "Raqasah-yi sirk [The Circus Dancer]," trans. Esmaeil Riahi, *Rushanfikr,* 11 Mihr 1336 (20 September 1957), 15; "In raqqasah-yi ziba" 1329/1950; Pejhman 1337/1958; "Avalin raqs" 1336/1957.

8. Personal communication with a former dancer of the Iran National Folklore Organization.

9. Through Sama, the Sufis are believed to overcome their evil-inciting selves and unite with God.

10. Nilla Cram Cook was an employee of the US embassy in Iran who also served as the head of theater and cinema censorship under the Pahlavi government. In 1946, Cram Cook quit both her posts to start a major dance project in Iran.

11. Andishah-yi Qom is the website of the Center for Religious Studies and Research in Qom (*markaz-i mutali'at va pajuhish-hayi dini huzah-'i ilmiyah-'i qum*), dedicated to answering questions regarding religious matters.

12. *Mir-i Ishq* (2001, on Imam Ali), *Rasul-i Ishq* (2007, on Prophet Muhammad), *Ghazal-i Kufr* (2006, on Imam Hussein), and *Dar Qab-i Mah* (2008, on Zeinab) are some of the theatrical works with religious narratives.

13. Regarding the public dancing body in newly developed urban sites of sociability such as cabarets and cafés, to better elucidate the social context, I refer to the terminology used in the Pahlavi-era periodicals, in which the dancing body was associated with societal corruptions. The term "contaminated" is an example of such terminology.

14. This is especially evident in *Rastakhiz-i Ishq* (2006), directed by Hussein Mussafir Astaneh.

15. *Hawz* is a small pool, usually built above the ground and common in traditional homes. It was transformed to a traditional stage by setting wooden planks over it for traditional performers, *mutribs*.

16. Persian-style snapping employing both hands.

REFERENCES

Abulqasimi, M. 1386/2007. "Goftigu ba Hadi Marzban, Farzaneh Kabuli va Sa'id Nikpur [A Conversation with Hadi Marzban, Farzaneh Kabuli, and Sa'id Nikpur]." *I'tmad-i Milli*, 10 Murdad 1386 (1 August 2007), 7.

Adams, M. 2003. "The Reflexive Self and Culture: A Critique." *British Journal of Sociology* 54 (2): 221–238.

Afkhami, S. 1329/1950. "Man bara-yi swing mimiram, shuma chitur? [I'd Die for the Swing, How about You?]." *Taraqiq*, 28 Shahrivar 1329 (8 September 1950), 11.

Ali-Akbari Baigi, A., and I. Muhammadi, eds. 2000. *Documents on Music, Cinema and Theatre in Iran, 1300–1357*. Vols. 1–3. Tehran: Sazman-i chap va intisharat-i vizarat-i farhang va irshad-i islami.

As'adi, A. R. 1382/2003. "Raqs-i jan [The Dance of the Soul]." *Maqam-i Musiqa'i* 8: 144–145.

Babakhani, N. 1381/2003. "Zani kah az ghurub amad [The Woman Who Came from the Sunset]." *Hambastigi*, 8 Bahman 1381 (31 January 2003).

Bandari, S. A. 1326/1947. "Tarfdaran-i qat'namah-i dukhtaran-i danish-amuz bikhanand [The Advocates of Schoolgirls' Statement Must Read This]." *Dunya-yi Islam*, 14 Azar 1326 (6 December 1947), 1, 3.

Bayat, A. 2007. "Islamism and the Politics of Fun." *Public Culture* 19 (3): 433–459.

Biniyaz, O. 1386/2008. "Hussein Musafir-i Astanah." *Iran* 3844 (3 Bahman 1386 [23 January 2008]).

Butler, J. 1990. "Performative Acts and Gender Constitution: An Essay on Phenomenology and Feminist Theory." In *Performing Feminisms: Feminist Critical Theory and Theatre*, ed. S. E. Case, pp. 270–282. Baltimore: Johns Hopkins University Press.

Carter, A. 1998. "Feminist Strategies for the Study of Dance." In *The Routledge Reader in Gender and Performance*, ed. L. Goodman and J. De Gay, pp. 247–250. London: Routledge.

Chaharduli, M. 1380/2002. "Ta'sir-i harikat dar namayish-i simurgh [The Effect of Movement in the Play Simurgh]." *Abrar*, 26 Isfand 1380 (17 March 2002).

Cram Cook, N. 1325/1946. "Raqs dar iran [Dance in Iran]." Translated by Hussein Ali Sultanzadeh Pessiyan. *Iran va Amrika*, Azar 1325 (December 1946), 33+.

———. 1949. "The Theatre and Ballet Arts of Iran." *Middle East Journal*, October, 406–420.

Desmond, J. C. 1999. "Engendering Dance: Feminist Inquiry and Dance Research." In *Researching Dance: Evolving Modes of Inquiry*, ed. S. H. Fraleigh and P. Hanstein, pp. 309–333. Pittsburgh: University of Pittsburgh Press.

Dolan, J. 1992. "Gender Impersonations on Stage: Destroying or Maintaining the Mirror of Gender Roles." In *Gender in Performance: The Presentation of Difference in the Performing Arts*, ed. L. Senelick, pp. 3–13. Hanover, NH: University Press of New England.

———. 1998. "The Discourse of Feminisms: The Spectator and Representation." In *The Routledge Reader in Gender and Performance*, ed. L. Goodman and J. De Gay, pp. 288–294. London: Routledge.

Foucault, M. 1980. "The Eye of Power." In *Power/Knowledge: Selected Interviews and Other Writings, 1972–1977*, ed. C. Gordon, pp. 146–165. New York: Pantheon.

———. 1984. "Bio-Power." In *The Foucault Reader*, ed. M. Foucault and P. Rabinow, pp. 257–289. New York: Pantheon Books.

Friend, R. C. 1997. "Status and Preservation of Iranian Dance: Cultural Factors Influencing the Iranian Attitude Concerning Dance." Paper presented at the 1st International Conference on Middle Eastern Dance, Orange Coast College, Costa Mesa, California. http://home.earthlink.net/~rcfriend/Hojb--1997.htm (accessed 2 October 2007).

Garafola, L. 1997. *Rethinking the Sylph: New Perspectives on the Romantic Ballet*. Hanover, NH: University Press of New England.

Gilbert, H., and J. Tompkins. 1996. *Post-Colonial Drama: Theory, Practice, Politics*. London: Routledge.

Hanna, J. L. 1988. *Dance, Sex, and Gender: Signs of Identity, Dominance, Defiance, and Desire*. Chicago: University of Chicago Press.

Ibasalti, P. 1340/1962. "Raqs, balah ya na? [Dance, Yes or No?]." *Ittilaʿat-i Banuvan*, 23 Bahman 1340 (12 February 1962), 11.

Kabuli, F. 1381/2002. "Ja-yi khali-yi harikat [The Empty Space of Movement]." *Iran*, 18 Khurdad 1381 (8 June 2002).

Karbasi, H. 1326/1947. "Tihran dar atash-i fisad misuzad [Tehran Is Burning in the Fire of Corruption]." *Parcham-i-Islam*, 12 Azar 1326 (4 December 1947), 1–2.

McLaren, M. 2002. *Feminism, Foucault, and Embodied Subjectivity*. Albany, NY: SUNY Press.

Mansouri, P., and H. Shirvani. 1975. *Faʿaliyat-ha-yi Hunari dar Panjah Sal Shahanshahi Pahlavi [Artistic Activities in the Fifty Years of Pahlavi Dynasty: Theatre, Music, Opera and Dance]*. Tehran: Ministry of Culture and Arts Publication.

Mir-Ansari, A., and S. M. Zia'i. 2003. *Selected Records of Drama in Iran, 1926–1941*. Vol. 2. Tehran: Iran National Archive.

Nabavi, I. 1333/1954. "Ustad Djanbazian [Master Djanbazian]." *Afarin*, 5 Aban 1333 (27 October 1954).

Nazimi, F. 1327/1948. "Namayish-hayi istudio-ye ihyia-yi hunar-hayi bastani-yi iran [Performances of the Studio of Revival of Ancient Arts of Iran]." *Jahan-i-Naw*, Tir 1327 (June 1948), 169–170.

Niyazmand-i Shirazi, Y. 1326/1947. "Zan dar ijtimaʿi diruz va imruz,4 [Women in Society, from Yesterday to Today]." *Nur-i-Danish*, 12 Azar 1326 (4 December 1947, 289–290.

Pejhman, H. 1337/1958. "Raqqasah-yi giriyan [The Weeping Dancer]." *Ittilaʿat-i Mah*, 11 Farvardin 1337 (31 March 1958), 12.

Pirnia, M. 1967. "Raqs-hayi Irani, muhimtarin ruydad-i hunari-yi fasl dar landan [Iranian Dances, the Most Important Artistic Incident of the Season in London]." *Zan-i-Ruz* (1967): 56+.

Rafiʿi, H. n.d. "Islam, din-i shariʿat va maʿnaviyat [Islam Is the Religion of Shariʿa and Spirituality]." Andishah Qom. http://www.andisheqom.com/Files/shobheinternet .php?idVeiw=30514&level=4&subid=30514 (accessed 31 August 2009).

Ramazani, N. 2002. *The Dance of the Rose and the Nightingale*. Syracuse, NY: Syracuse University Press.

———. 2008. "A Meeting of Cultures: Writing My Memoir." *Middle East Critique* 17 (3): 293–308.

Safa, P. 1353/1975. "Saz-ha-yi irani ba zaban-i jahani sukhan miguyand [Iranian Musical Instruments Speak Global Language]." *Rudaki*, Isfand 1353 (February 1975), 8.

Safavi, F. 1339/1960. "Raqs dar jamiʿah-yi ma [Dance in Our Society]." *Iran-i Abad*, Azar 1339 (November 1960), 69–72.

Sajjad. 1384/2005. "Varzish-hayi banuvan-i kishvar-hayi Islami [The Sports of the Women of Islamic Countries]." *Raz-i Khun*, 4 Mihr 1384 (26 September 2005), http://razekhoon .parsiblog.com/-25541.htm (accessed 30 January 2009).

Sajjadifar, L. 1381/2003. "Paykubi va sama [Dance and Sama]." *Hunar-pu*, Zimistan 1381 (Winter 2003), 9.

———. 1383/2004. "Sama-i-Daravish [Sama of Dervishes]." *Hunar-pu*, Bahahr 1383 (Spring 2004), 12.

Schayegh, C. 2009. *Who Is Knowledgeable Is Strong*. Berkeley: University of California Press.

Senelick, L. 1992. *Gender in Performance: The Presentation of Difference in the Performing Arts*. Hanover, NH: University Press of New England.

Shafiʿee, K. 1350s/1970s. "Guftigu-yi ba Abdullah Nazemi piramun-i raqs dar Iran [A Discussion with Abdullah Nazemi on Dance in Iran]." *Talash* 6:77.

Shahshahani, S. 2004. "Body as a Means of Non-Verbal Communication in Iran." In *Body as Medium of Meaning*, ed. S. Shahshahani, pp. 57–71. Piscataway, NJ: Transaction Publishers.

Shay, A. 1995. "Dance and Non-Dance: Patterned Movement in Iran and Islam." *Iranian Studies* (Winter–Spring): 61–78.

———. 1999. *Choreophobia: Solo Improvised Dance in the Iranian World*. Costa Mesa, CA: Mazda Publishers.

———. 2005. "Choreographing Persia." Middle Eastern Forum. http://www.artira.com /danceforum/articles/shay_choreopersia.html (accessed 29 April 2009).

Shirvani, H. 1336/1957. "Hunar-hayi milli [National Arts]." *Namayish*, Urdibihisht 1336 (May 1957), 36–38.

Yaraqchi, M. 1326/1948. "Azadi-i zanan, 4 [Women's Freedom]." *Dunya-yi Islam*, 8 Isfand 1326 (28 February 1948), 1–2.

ANONYMOUS ARTICLES IN PERIODICALS

"Antalya festivali yarin başliyor." 1973. *Takvim*, 31 May.

"Avalin raqs [The First Dance]." 1336/1957. *Ittila'at-i Mah*, Day 1336 (December 1957), 31.

"Az raqs-i zamin bitarsid [Be Scared of the Earth's Dance]." 1336/1957. *Nida-yi Haq*, 19 Tir 1336 (10 July 1957), 1–2.

"Ballet." 1328/1949. *Saba*, 4 Khurdad 1328 (25 May 1949), 11.

"Dah sal talash bara-yi hunar [Ten Years of Effort for the Arts]." 1339/1960. *Ittila'at-i Banuvan*, 9 Khurdad 1339 (30 May 1960), 29+.

"Darichah-yi bah su-yi ayandah [Windows to the Future]." 1333/1955. *Rushanfikr*, 19 Isfand 1333 (10 March 1955).

"Dirakhshish-i raqsandigan-i mahalli dar landan [Mahalli Dancers Shone in London]." 1351/1972. *Ayandigan*, 21 Aban 1351 (12 November 1972), 6.

"Guftugu ba Hussein Musafir-i Astanah, kargardan-i ghazal-i kufr [A Conversation with Hussein Musafir Astanah, the Director of Ode to Blasphemy]." 1384/2006. *Hamvatan*, 29 Bahman 1384, (18 February 2006).

"Gurd-Afarid." 1335/1957. *Ittila'at-i Mah*, Day 1335 (January 1957), 35.

"Hich-gah faramush nimikunam [I Will Never Forget]." 1340/1961. *Ittila'at-i Banuvan*, 11 Urdibihisht 1340 (1 May 1961), 4.

"Hunaristan-i a'ali-yi ballet, tarbiyat-i atfal bah raqs va fisad-i akhalq [The Ballet School, Training Dance and Corrupted Behavior for Children]." 1332/1953. *Nida-yi Haq*, 2 Tir 1332 (23 June 1953), 1, 3.

"In raqqasah-yi ziba asrar-i khalifah ra ifsha mikard [This Beautiful Dancer Used to Reveal Qalif's Secrets]." 1329/1950. *Saba*, 13 Urdibihisht 1329 (20 April 1950), 24.

"Jashn-i hunaristan-i ballet-i Tehran [Tehran Ballet School Recital]." 1329/1950. *Saba*, 17 Khurdad 1329 (7 June 1950), 21.

"Kilass-i khususi-yi ballet-i Lili Lazarian [Lili Lazarian's Private Ballet Class]." 1329/1950. *Saba*, 29 Azar 1329 (20 December 1950), 23.

"Mahalli Dancers of Iran." 1976. Souvenir Program.

"Pasukh-hayi Fa'izah Hashimi bah su'alat-i bishumar-i khabarnigaran [Fa'izah Hashimi's Response to Numerous Questions Posed by the Journalists]." 1384/2005. *Baztab*, 26 Shahrivar 1384 (17 September 2005]), http://www.baztab.com/news/29121.php (accessed 30 January 2009).

"Preserve Folklore before It Is Lost." 1974. *Pakistan Times*, 14 April.

"Qabil-i tavajuh-i aqay-i Ja'fari, vazir-i farhang [Worthy of Note for Mr. Ja'fari, the Minister of Culture]." 1333/1955. *Nida-yi Haq*, 4 Isfand 1333 (23 February 1955), 1, 3.

"Raqs [Dance]." 1328/1949. *Ashuftah*, 5 Aban 1328 (3 October 1949), 17.

"Raqs bara-yi khuda [Dancing for the God]." 1383/2004. Translated by Mas'ud Faryamanish. *Iran*, 10 Day 1383 (30 December 2004).

"Raqs dar chand qadami-i marg [Dancing a Few Steps from the Grave]." 1380/2001. *Hamshahri-yi Mah*, Khurdad 1380 (May–June 2001), 22–23.

"Shab-i nur-afshani-i Islam [The Night of Islam's Luminance]." 1325/1947. *Dunya-yi Islam*, 19 Bahman 1325 (8 February 1947), 1, 4.

"Tasvib-i asasnamah-yi anjuman harikat-i mawzun [Ratification of the Rhythmic Movements Association's Constitution]." 1385/2006. *Sharif-News*, 20 Tir 1385 (11 July 2006), http://www.sharifnews.com/?19645 (accessed 2 August 2009).

CHAPTER 9

SUFICIZED MUSICS OF SYRIA AT THE INTERSECTION OF HERITAGE AND THE WAR ON TERROR; OR "A RUMI WITH A VIEW"

JONATHAN H. SHANNON

AS IS WELL KNOWN AMONG scholars and the faithful, Syria has been home to vibrant traditions of mystical Islam, or Sufism, for centuries. Many of the great Sufi luminaries either came from Syria or settled and taught there for periods of their lives—perhaps the most important being Muhi al-Din Ibn al-ʿArabi (1165–1240) and his near contemporary Jalal al-Din Rumi (1207–1273). Today there are important mosques in Aleppo and Damascus named after these individuals and animated by weekly séances of *dhikr*—i.e., ritual invocations of God that are usually accompanied by chanting and bodily movements collectively termed *samaʿ*. Sufi devotional practices have remained living traditions in Syria and remain so today, as is the case elsewhere in the Arab world. Yet the public performance of Sufi-related song forms in Syria—something more readily identified with the Turkish *mevlevi* or "whirling dervish" ensembles—is of relatively recent provenance. Although Syrian groups have performed and in some cases even recorded song repertoires taken from the *dhikr* for many decades, since the 1990s Syrian ensembles have increasingly promoted their recordings and performances of these repertoires as examples of "Sufi music," partly to meet domestic needs but also to meet the growing demand of international audiences for sacred music worldwide, primarily at festivals and concerts devoted to sacred or spiritual musical traditions.

The increase in the performance of repertoires based in the *dhikr* and the practice of marketing this as "Sufi" music raise for me the following questions: What can account for the relatively recent rise and proliferation of so-called Sufi and Sufi-inspired musics from Syria? What happens to ritual performance genres when they become repackaged for consumption in global circuits of performance and commoditization? Perhaps more prosaically, what is "Sufi" about "Sufi music"?

This chapter offers an interpretation of recent Sufi music production in

Syria and on the World Stage as a response to two interrelated phenomena: transnational discourses of heritage production and preservation, and transnational representations of Islam, Islamic resurgence, and what we call the "War on Terror," though it's not understood that way in Syria, to be certain. In light of these mutually constitutive discourses, Sufi music in Syria has to be understood as part of a larger process of creating a style of music known as "Sufi music." Artists create this musical genre, as I have argued elsewhere (Shannon 2003), *expressly*—with an emphasis on the notion of speed contained therein—for performance on the World Stage, that is, for international audiences tuned to the sounds of World Music, and retuned to what, following Kapchan (2008), we can call a "fluency" in sacred music listening. While many of the song repertoires have their basis in ritual practices that themselves are linked to Sufism (even if not all participants would describe themselves as Sufis), I propose that we need to understand these musics as "Suficized"—that is, constructed for a transnational category of not only sound, but of being in the world, called Sufism that may bear only a passing relationship to practices associated with mystical Islam, or *tasawwuf.* Indeed, it is through the performance of "Suficized" musics that artists (many of them devout, some members of Sufi orders) aim to capitalize on new markets while sounding forms of Muslim spirituality that reconfigure current debates about Islam, spirituality, and the politics of performance.

"SUFI MUSIC" AND SUFICIZED MUSICS TODAY

There are two main problems with the term "Sufi music." First, few musicians who perform the song repertoires of the *dhikr* describe themselves as Sufis or describe the music as "Sufi" music (see Shannon 2006). They tend to use the label "religious song" (*al-inshad* or *al-ghina' al-dini*) or merely refer to it as "songs from the *dhikr*" (*aghani al-dhikr*). While certainly many participants in the *dhikr* are members of specific orders (for example, the Qadiriyya and Rifaʿiyya) and would describe themselves as devoted to a Sufi path, the majority of musicians I've known, and many nonmusician participants, describe themselves as "Muslims" and don't see much that is mystical in their lives: *dhikr* is a command, *'udhkuru allaha dhikran kathiran,* says the Qur'an (i.e., do *dhikr* frequently). Second, the songs performed during *dhikr* are not confined to the *dhikr*, but rather may also be performed, with some alterations, on "secular" stages (*masarih*), in concerts (*haflat*), evening musical gatherings (*saharat*), and at home and abroad at festivals (*mihrajanat*). Thus the label "Sufi" carries a certain semiotic instability or polyvocality and does not refer to a clear-cut genre of song forms among traditional Syrian music makers (I am restricting my remarks primarily to artists in Aleppo). I won't rehearse the debates about whether this is or is not "music"; suffice it to say that vocal forms predominate, hence "song" is a more appropriate label.[1]

By pointing out the constructed nature of the category of "Sufi music," I do not wish to deny the existence of communities who label their practices as "Sufi" or even "Sufi music." For example, in Turkey, Pakistan, and India there are vibrant popular traditions whose practitioners may indeed consider themselves to be "Sufis" and their music to be "Sufi" music, as analyzed in the work of Irene Markoff (1995), Regula Qureshi (1986), and Richard Wolf (2006), among others. My concern here is not with the music per se, but with the rise of "Sufi Music" as a *style* of music, and how this new "style" resonates with new times, that is, neoliberal times. In what I am calling "Suficized" musics, a wide range of practices, some clearly related to practices of Sufi orders, others less often associated with forms of spiritual practice commonly called Sufi, come together under the marketing label of Sufi or Sufi music. An earlier study (Shannon 2003) reported on the rise in World Music marketing of Sufi and sacred musics as "styles" and "genres" distinct from other styles and genres (the terms are used interchangeably) such as Middle Eastern, and so on. By way of updating some of the information reported in the earlier study (collected in 2001 and published in 2003), here is a quick glance at some facts and figures pulled from some recent online catalogues and searches:[2]

Google search for Sufi music = 182,000 hits
Google search for music Sufi = 2,200,000 hits
Google search for Sufism music = 520,000 hits

There also exists a website devoted to "Sufi" musics of South Asia: www .sufimusic.org, as well as numerous online purveyors, such as MondoMix (formerly Calabash Music; mp3.mondomix.com). MondoMix currently has twelve titles under what it calls the "subgenre" of "Sufism" within the broader genre of "Sacred"; the Sufism subgenre, distinct from "Qawwali," consists of a mix of Turkish, Arab, Persian, South Asian, and fusion groups. The regional genre "Oriental" includes the subgenres "Arabic World," "Arabo-Andalusian," and also Sufism.

The World Music Institute (www.heartheworld.org) online catalogue features buttons where you can purchase music according to region, style, artist, or title. In 2001, twenty-eight titles were in the "Sufi" style category, whereas eighty-five were labeled "Sacred." As of March 2009, the WMI catalogue showed the following:

Style = SUFI: 49 titles (growth of 75% since 2001)
Style = SACRED: 79 (decline of about 7% since 2001)

Now, I take this "data" as suggestive and not definitive (I am far from advocating what we might call "Google-ethnography"). However, as a sort of meta-analysis it indicates the development in recent years of a very loosely organized system of "styles" and "genres" within the World Music industry—a looseness that serves, I would suggest, the function of flexible cultural specialization to cater to consumer behavior: one can search and find these musics in a number of boxes, under different stylistic and generic labels. The relatively large growth of titles in the Sufi Music stylistic bin (75 percent) compared to the Sacred (-7 percent) reflects the increased purchase of Sufism in the contemporary world and World Music market.

My interest in tracing these contours is to investigate how the category of "Sufi Music" has taken on a life of its own (as a "style" or "genre") in association with the increased presence internationally of performers of ritual traditions from the Islamic, or, to borrow from Marshall Hodgson (1975), the "Islamicate," world. What happens when these sounds are divorced from their origins in what Feld (1996) has termed, for recorded sounds, *schizophonia*? Indeed, how do we understand this question when the *origin* of these song forms *is* in fact the World Stage—that is, their production is intended for performance outside a presumed originary ritual context?

As I have suggested, the World Stage is a discursive arena for representational practices and strategies for cultural production that give the effect of an origin when in fact, à la Derrida, the practices rehearsed there are their own origin. That is, when we see and hear Sufi Music on the World Stage (in festivals, recordings, and other performances, loosely understood), we are actually experiencing *Suficized* musics—those that are created expressly for the stage and that bear sometimes only a passing relationship to their reputed referents.

Why is this an important distinction? As scholars such as Timothy Taylor (1997) have pointed out, the World Music phenomenon trades in the twin currencies of hybridity and authenticity. Some performances are celebrated as interesting fusions of different traditions, for example, the various incarnations of Celtic music (see Stokes and Bohlman 2003), whereas others are lauded for their bringing authentic sounds and sights to a wider (i.e., Western) audience (see Shannon 2003). It is the consumption habits of the implied transnational audiences that create "authenticity" in the music to begin with. As Taylor notes (1997, 23–26), whereas World Music and World Beat are generally associated with globalization and transnational cultural economies, "sacred music" is the domain of the spiritually authentic and the local. The efforts of the Syrian ensembles (such as the Ensemble al-Kindi, which is my case study here) to record and promote Sufi music reveal how spiritual traditions are in fact produced and authenticated within the same sets of discourses and representational practices as the World Music market. In the rush to perform on the World Stage (again, this can include recording projects as well as actual concerts), artists and managers also participate in the *Suficization* of their performance repertoires.

SUFICIZATION AND "FAST MUSIC"

By using the term *Suficize* I am deliberately playing with the notion of super-sizing food items at fast food restaurants, as depicted in Morgan Spurlock's movie *Super Size Me!* (Spurlock 2004). In the context of this chapter, Suficized musics are those that are produced for global consumption with the same attention to form and presentation as fast food: Sufi music and dance may be slow and ecstatic (think of the whirling dervishes doing their slow turns), but the aesthetic regimes of value that create them are very much fast.

To extend the culinary metaphor,[3] I consider Suficized musics to be a variety of what I call "fast music"—fast, that is, in terms of its production and marketing. Some might argue that Sufi, or Suficized, musics are "slow," along the lines of slow food: wholesome, local, slowly and carefully produced and consumed by aficionados, and so forth. Are Sufi musics slow music, or fast? It is important to note that we should understand slow ideologies—such as slow food, slow sex, slow cities, slow schooling, and so on (Honoré 2004)—as not only responses to (or resistance to) globalizing fast cultures, but as part and parcel of globalization itself. In other words, if we take seriously the proposition, advanced by Appadurai (1996) among others, that globalization implies not a unilinear model of change, but fractal, at times chaotic, and ultimately heterodoxic (heterotopic?) developments, then slow and fast culture—and slow and fast musics—can be considered to be two sides of the same coin. Or to borrow from the symbol of slow food—the snail, with its gender-amorphous properties—the slow movement advocates slowness within the global. Just as we cannot understand musical or other forms of authenticity apart from processes of commoditization, we cannot understand the movement toward slow apart from the fast versions that spin off it. The Sufi musics I am talking about—that is, *Suficized* musics—are "fast" (*commoditized*) spins of "slow" (*ritual*) practices.

It is important to note here that I am decidedly *not* referring to musical tempo by referring to this or any other style of music as "fast" or "slow." Rather, I use these terms to reference the patterns of creation, presentation, and consumption that characterize these styles of music today. Both highly commoditized ("fast") and ritual ("slow") forms of "Sufi" musics contain slow and fast tempos, simple and complex metrical and tonal structures, and intricate webs of associations with classical and popular texts, ideologies, and practices. In Syrian "Sufi" musics, the ritual and stage-presented commodity forms of the music generally follow a highly structured progression from complex rhythms at slower tempos to simpler rhythms at faster tempos, usually understood by participants as corresponding with the achievement of ecstatic states (see Shannon 2004). For the purposes of this chapter, "fast" and "slow" refer to points on a continuum of representational and consumption practices, and not actual musical tempo. Increasingly it is difficult to determine the difference between "fast" and "slow" varieties, as the slow ones themselves only come to be recognized as legitimate "musical" practices (as opposed to spiritual or devotional practices) in the context of the world of the fast—of World Music, for example. This relates to what I have elsewhere described (Shannon 2003) as the representational practices of World Music whereby the world as exhibitionary stage becomes, in the realm of sound and music, the world as soundstage, and the sounds as made for a world of staging, of performing.

The transformation from "slow" to "fast" music is facilitated by three processes that are central to musical globalization everywhere:

1. the construction of musical and cultural "authenticity" in the market;
2. the use of niche marketing by ensembles following an implicit model of what we might term "flexible musical specialization," drawing on the key feature of post-Fordist industrial production in neoliberal economics
3. the standardization of repertoires and their reification (or naturalization) as varieties of folk, ethnic, world, or, in these examples, "Sufi" music.

I. AUTHENTICITY AND RECENT SYRIAN SUFICIZED MUSICS

I wish to illustrate this argument with two examples of Suficized musics from Syria, focusing on recent recordings by the Aleppo-based Ensemble al-Kindi. This group, perhaps the best known from Syria after Sabah Fakhri's (if not better known in the West), has toured the world promoting varieties of Syrian music, from the traditional "salon" variety (*The Aleppian Music Room*, 1998) and musics of the Crusades (*The Crusades Seen through the Eyes of the Orient*, 2001) to different versions of ritual musics from Aleppo and Damascus. I focus on the latter.

The Ensemble al-Kindi was founded in 1983 by the Swiss-born and French *qanun* player Julien Weiss. Weiss has based himself in Aleppo for about the last fifteen years (though he now lives mostly in Istanbul), where he owns a mini-mansion festooned with inlaid boxes, brass platters, tapestries, and religious memorabilia: it constitutes a mini-museum of authenticity in the heart of the Old City, a UNESCO World Heritage site (this will become important later in our story). A convert to Islam, Weiss assumed the name of the most popular poet in America—that is, Jalal al-Din Rumi! Jalal Eddine Weiss serves, therefore, as a mediator, a cultural broker and translator, between the realms of Islam and those of the West, where he primarily performs; al-Kindi rarely if ever holds public performances in Syria. Like any cultural broker, Jalal Eddine Weiss projects an air of authenticity, in his musical programs as in his habit of wearing flowing gowns. He also has shown a keen business acumen and a concern for financial and political influence; for example, his performance fees are high and his invitations to politicos frequent. He is in many ways a "Rumi with a view"—a Jalal Eddine who has embraced a global vision of musical possibility in the worlds of Islam and the West, as evidenced in the multiple ensemble configurations of al-Kindi that have opened the World Stage to varieties of Syrian Arab music rarely heard in the West. Weiss has to a large extent created Syrian music for overseas audiences—and for lovers of Syrian music this is a positive phenomenon.

Let's take a brief look at two "Suficized" recordings by al-Kindi: The first is *The Whirling Dervishes of Damascus* (1999), with the late Shaykh Hamza Shakkur (1939–2009; see Figure 9.1). This album marked the entrance of al-Kindi into the "sacred music" domain, and this particular configuration (with Shakkur) has performed multiple times at the Fes Festival of World Sacred Music. In 2007, almost every advertised performance of al-Kindi abroad featured this ensemble, despite the group's other configurations; following their successful 2004 American tour they scheduled a second in January 2009.

The liner notes to this recording, prepared by a mix of religious authorities and well-known scholars of Sufism and ethnomusicology, accentuate the authenticity of both the performance practices and the al-Kindi performers (with special attention on Hamza Shakkur and of course Weiss himself on *qanun*). The notes outline the history of Sufism, the centrality of Damascus for certain branches of mystical Islam, the ritual of the whirling dervishes, and the CD's song selection. Information on the performers rounds things out. It is an impressive achievement and far surpasses in production quality other recordings by Syrian artists.

The second recording is *Aleppian Sufi Trance* (2003), featuring Shaykh Ahmad Habboush accompanied by some of the same musicians as performed on the first recording. The liner notes were prepared by Brazilian

FIGURE 9.1. The cover of the CD *Les Derviches Tourneurs de Damas* (*The Whirling Dervishes of Damascus*) (1999)

FIGURE 9.2. Ensemble al-Kindi with Shaykh Hamza Shakkur, New York City (2001).

anthropologist Paulo Pinto, a specialist in Syrian ecstatic Sufism. This grants them a quasi-academic air, and the photos (often striking) of such practices as *darb al-shish* (skewering the flesh—a practice rare in Syria today) add a sense of authenticity, as well as exoticism, to the notes. Like the notes for *The Whirling Dervishes of Damascus*, these outline the history of Sufism, but for Aleppo, not Damascus. The focus is not the whirling dervish ceremony, but the *dhikr*, and the role of *sama'* in mystical initiation to the Sufi order (both the Damascene and Aleppine are from the Qadiriyya and Rifa'iyya branches). Again, as with the first recording, the package is impressive.

Both recordings go to great pains to promote a concept of cultural and spiritual authenticity. The liner notes in both instances attempt to locate the songs in the context of Sufi practice in Syria, though aside from the brief scholarly introductions to Sufism, there is no attempt to link the songs on the CDs to the specific rites mentioned—the "whirling dervishes" and the *dhikr*, respectively. The effect, as I read it, is to displace attention from the music to the authentic environments of Damascus and Aleppo for the experience of *sama'*. The notes and photographs set the stage for an authentic encounter. However, there is almost no discussion of the decision to use musical instruments such as the *qanun*, *'ud*, and *nay* in the recordings, as these instruments are rarely if ever used in the context of the *dhikr* (some Sufi lodges, or *zawiya*-s, allow the *nay* but not the other instruments; all use various percussion instruments, including slapping the back of the hand as a sort of metronome).

2. NICHE MARKETING AND STANDARDIZATION OF REPERTOIRES IN SYRIAN SUFICIZED MUSIC

In addition to al-Kindi, there are other Syrian, mostly Aleppo-based, ensembles that now feature "Suficized" repertoires. These include the ensemble Urnina, founded and directed by Muhammad Qadri Dalal, the well-known *'ud* master and director of the Arab Music Institute in Aleppo, since June 2008 called the Sabah Fakhri Institute. This ensemble consists of leading members of Aleppo's traditional music scene and situates itself as a local version of the Ensemble al-Kindi; indeed, Dalal and others have performed extensively with Weiss's group. Named after Urnina, a third-millennium BC Babylonian female musician, the ensemble follows al-Kindi's model of flexible specialization and performs numerous repertoires, adding the *dhikr*, or "Sufi," tunes in recent years to appeal to local and international audiences of devotional musics; previously, it had devoted itself to the nonsacred repertoires, including the songs of important Syrian composers such as Bakri al-Kurdi.

A second ensemble is the Ensemble al-Turath (the Heritage Ensemble), founded by the late vocalist Sabri Moudallal and now directed by his nephew, Muhammad Hamadiyya. This group, once prominent on the Syrian and global music scene, declined as al-Kindi's star rose and Moudallal joined Weiss's ranks. In the aftermath of Moudallal's loss and more recently his death, the Heritage Ensemble now offers programs in various styles of Arab, Arab-Andalusian, and Islamic music and dance, including performance of the *dhikr* repertoire. Its effort to retool and reformat illustrates the ways in which Syrian groups desirous of accessing wider and diverse audiences propose different musical configurations along the lines of the Ensemble al-Kindi's mix of sacred and profane repertoires. Elsewhere I analyze this niche marketing as a kind of flexible musical specialization that draws implicitly on post-Fordist models of production to take advantage of, or in some cases to help promote, World Music marketing categories such as "Sufi" music (Shannon 2003, 272). The Heritage Ensemble was always keen to market itself as a do-all ensemble representing all that is Syrian in music and dance, but now has expanded to include pan-Arab and Arab-Andalusian repertoires to reach more diverse audiences.

There are other groups that perform and record repertoires from the *dhikr*, including many who do not engage in the type of flexible specialization and niche marketing discussed above. A number of well-known Aleppine and Damascene *munshid-s* lead troupes that perform at weddings and other local social events such as house warmings, graduation parties, and pilgrimage celebrations. Many of these groups issue recordings, and some have traveled abroad to perform religious songs on international stages, among the most famous being that of the renowned *munshid* Hasan al-Haffar. In addition, the *munshid-s* of the Hilaliyya *zawiya*, the oldest Sufi lodge in Aleppo, have produced a CD of the *dhikr*, recorded at a live performance in Paris and accompanied by scholarly liner notes that attempt to translate the experience of audition—*sama*'—to a Western audience. Their performances are arguably more authentic than those of the Ensemble Urnina and the Heritage Ensemble, since the "artists" are all avowed members of a well-established *zawiya*, and they do not perform other repertoires in Syria or abroad; most would not consider themselves to be artists or singers either. On the ritual-Suficized continuum they tend to reside more on the ritual end, as their recordings do not strive self-consciously to promote authenticity, and these ensembles typically do not perform other repertoires.[4]

In addition, a number of other well-known Syrian composers have composed, performed, and recorded specifically religious varieties of traditional Arab and Arab-Andalusian song forms, such as the *muwashshah*; these artists include Zuhayr Minini, Suhail 'Arafa, and others, usually of an older generation now in their seventies and eighties. They have for the most part remained outside the commercial spheres of music making and marketing in Syria, and hence I would refer to them as non-Suficized. Indeed, Minini, among the most famous composers of his generation, stopped performing and composing secular music over forty years ago and instead devoted himself to the study and composition of religious songs while earning his living as a calligrapher; in recent years he has also trained a younger generation of religious singers, but not for commercial aims. Moreover, in interviews, neither 'Arafa nor Minini ever referred to their compositions or performances as "Sufi music," but instead used the term *islami* (Islamic) or *dini* (religious). Their experiences mark a certain resistance to the globalizing forces that promote the Suficization of Syrian sacred repertoires, indexed by the use of the term "Sufi" to refer to these repertoires.

Similarly, the Ensembles Urnina and the Heritage Ensemble usually refer to their repertoire as "*dhikr*" and only rarely as "Sufi" (*sufiyya*). Nonetheless, no matter what they call the music, the groups mentioned above, including the non-Suficized ensembles and individuals, tend to draw on the same sets of songs from the *dhikr* repertoire in their recordings and performances. In doing so they contribute to what I sense is the growing standardization of the repertoire which is variously called "*dhikr*" or "Sufi" and is drawn from the larger corpus of song sequences performed in the *dhikr*. The ensembles are selective, and from their recent recordings it seems they are more often than not selecting many of the same song sequences, usually from the beginning portions of each of the six main sections of the *dhikr*. Their choices reflect several limitations, technological, financial, temporal, aesthetic, and perhaps moral. A complete *dhikr* lasts several hours, and thus a complete *dhikr* recording would require multiple CDs, stretching most recording project budgets. While several of the available *dhikr* recordings were registered in live concerts, in part to achieve a semblance of authenticity, a full-blown *dhikr* would tax the patience of noninitiated audiences, for whom a several-hour ceremony would in all likelihood be too lengthy. Moreover, the aesthetic and moral dimensions of the choice of repertoire for recording and live performance are not insignificant; the members of the Zawiya Hilaliyya and others with whom I spoke conveyed a desire to keep part of the *dhikr* experience, its core, in the *zawiya* and off the stage; they were wary of revealing what they thought to be the essence of the *dhikr*, including portions in which participants may experience ecstatic emotional states.[5] Commercialization may promote a certain standardization of the repertoire, but it also encounters aesthetic and moral limitations; the transformation from slow music to fast is incomplete, perhaps even self-limiting, so long as the criteria of spiritual authenticity remain important factors in choosing repertoire. It remains to be seen whether anyone, and if so who, will be the first to "sell out" and record and perform the sacred core of the ritual.

SPIRITUAL HERITAGE AND THE GENTLE FACE OF ISLAM

What accounts for the rise of "Suficized musics" and why the emphasis on authenticity, flexible musical specialization, and standardization? The short answer is that neoliberal times require neoliberal solutions and approaches in all domains of life. This may well be the case, but it is important to anchor these abstractions in concrete processes. I would point to two as critical in today's performance and marketing of Sufi music:

1. niche marketing capitalizes on foreign interest in *spiritual heritage*, promoted by UNESCO, EuroMed, and other intangible heritage programs, foreign direct investment and promotion of heritage, and state sponsorship (however limited) of heritage-inspired programs.
2. Sufi music is a response to the US-launched War on Terror and promotes a vision of "tolerant Islam" compared to the radical Islam occupying our headlines. In this context Suficized musics on the World Stage index a tolerant, kinder, and gentler face of Islam.

I. SUFICIZED MUSICS AND HERITAGE PRESERVATION AND PRODUCTION IN SYRIA

UNESCO and related heritage preservation and documentation programs (such as the MediMuses Project, funded by the EuroMed Heritage Project, and the Aga Khan Trust for Culture) are at once common in Syria and highly influential, not only on the state in its role as caretaker of the ancient cities, but also on a popular level, as artists, musicians, critics, and other cultural brokers (among them Weiss and his associates) assume the mantle of authority and authenticity for cultural preservation. As numerous scholars have pointed out (Kirshenblatt-Gimblett 2006; Kreps 2003; Scher 2002, among others), heritage preservation and documentation programs—for both tangible and intangible heritage—are part of a transnational movement of ideas and practices concerning human patrimony and cultural memory. Although architecture may be the most visible of these, music and song forms, as well as other intangible heritages, are gaining increased attention and funding. This means that major funding has been pouring into local NGOs and affiliated networks of patronage in places like Aleppo and Damascus for more than a decade, having important ramifications for national policy-making and local responses.

Transnational funding sources have promoted a variety of state-sponsored and independent efforts in Syria to raise awareness about cultural heritage and to document it and preserve it. While folkloric and other festivals have been common in Syria for decades, there is a notable increase in festivals in recent years, many driven by foreign cultural centers in conjunction with international agencies, such as UNESCO, the Aga Khan Trust for Culture, and EuroMed, as well as regional partners such as Egypt, Jordan, Iraq, Lebanon, Tunisia, Morocco, the United Arab Emirates, Turkey, and Iran. These festivals allow for the reimagining of the national space in terms of the older Orientalist models of Syria as a cultural mosaic and cultural crossroads (see Coon 1958). For example, in the last few years the Syrian Ministries of Tourism and Culture, which are working hand in hand to promote Syrian cultural and religious tourism on an unprecedented level, have sponsored several new festivals, including an international festival, a Silk Road festival, a Mediterranean cultures festival, and others. International investment in these cases has spurred local investment in cultural resources, including music.

The ways in which nationalist imaginings as well as new configurations of patron-clientage might be promoted through these programs are perhaps too obvious to mention. It is, however, important to note that in many ways the Syrian state is both a partner with, as well as a parasite on, private and international investment in its heritage, as state-sponsored programs are usually limited both by political ideologies (notably Baathist, pan-Arab ideologies) and by resources. Syrian artists, too, have often co-opted the same discourses in their attempts to integrate themselves in this new world of "fast" music. I have noted above the numerous Syrian ensembles that have adopted the flexible specialization approach to performance. Many now perform repertoire from the *dhikr* as a variety of Sufi music, even when the ensemble members are not members of particular Sufi orders. I often heard the sentiment "We can do Sufi music, too!" from my Syrian musician friends; others wanted to promote projects with me in North America, drawing on the preexisting models of the Ensemble al-Kindi and on their experiences at international music festivals in Europe, Asia, and North America. Others expressed skepticism toward the state-sponsored programs, and some of the more prominent artists have refused to perform for local festival audiences, citing low earnings, poor organization, and personal sensibilities as influencing their decisions. Few culture brokers are able to navigate with aplomb the two worlds of international festival stages and local performance circuits. The desire even among young artists is to learn the traditional repertoires (sacred and secular) and then use their experience to launch an international career, and not focus on performances in Syria. It is a continuing paradox that Syria's best artists rarely perform at home, particularly when compared to the number of performances they give abroad.

2. THE WAR ON TERROR

The second pillar of support for the Suficization of Syrian music is the so-called War on Terror. The links between the War on Terror and heritage preservation are tacit, but important to recognize. In furthering the idea of Syria and Syrians as on the right side in the War on Terror, Suficized musics help to promote awareness of an Islamic heritage that is peaceful and "good" (see also Ahu Yiğit's distinction in this volume between "good" and "bad" Islam in modern Turkish television productions). The Syrian state (usually) attempts to portray the nation as an ally in the War on Terror, and at the same time as a source of "good" Islam and "good" Muslims—Sufism and Sufis—versus the forms of "bad" Islam that lap at its borders. In this highly politicized context, Sufi-related expressive culture forms, usually *sama'*, are Suficized to meet the needs of Syrians and the state in promoting a message of tolerance to the world. We see this in the promotion of religious, or spiritual, tourism by the Syrian Ministry of Tourism in brochures that include descriptions of famous mosques and temples—but not, notably, synagogues—and in the increasing presence of Sufi or Sufism-inspired songs in the repertoires of local artists, as indicated above.

Perhaps it goes without saying that the primary motive for most musicians engaging in Suficized music performance today is financial: Suficized music facilitates the translation of cultural or spiritual capital—"real Sufism"—into monetary capital: heritage pays, and Sufi heritage pays especially well in the global marketplace of ideas today. A derivative but no less important idea is that the artists who perform the music at festivals such as the Fes Festival of World Sacred Music implicitly share a message of tolerance in the face of activist, radical, or militant ideologies of Islam such as those of al-Qaʿida. Indeed, Moroccan anthropologist Faouzi Skali founded the Fes Festival in the aftermath of the first Gulf War (1990–1991) to promote a message of peace and tolerance through music. In 2006 Skali launched the Festival of Sufi Music and Culture, which, like the Fes Festival, organizes a parallel colloquium series that takes as its motto "Giving a Soul to Globalization" (*Donner une âme à la mondialisation*). It is a soul or spirit of peace and tolerance deriving from the mystical traditions of Islam and reaching out to other cultures through musical performance; in these contexts music, especially Sufi or Suficized musics, plays a central role as mediators of cultural difference, and bridges between peoples.

Regardless of the motivations of the musicians, which are bound to be multiple and even contradictory at times, the sacred music festival attracts large audiences and in many cases significant funding sources because of what Kapchan (2008) calls the "promise of sonic translation" that lies at the heart of sacred music festivals. In the post-9/11 world, al-Kindi and other Syrian groups aim to participate in this promise of a new vision for the world through musical performance, and artists have been very forthright with me in their denouncing of narrow interpretations of Islam and in praising Syria's history of tolerance and openness, however romanticized that may be. While the notion of using music as a bridge among peoples is not as developed in Syria as it is in Morocco, for example (see Shannon forthcoming), there is a growing sense among artists of the potential use of musical performance, especially of Suficized song forms, to promote tolerance, or at a minimum to capitalize on the sentiments of those who believe it has the power to do so. Indeed, we might ask the question, Have these sacred music festivals created "Sufi" music and the ideology of "Sufi" music as a bridge among peoples? Along these lines, Kapchan (2008) explores how "Sufi tourism" at the Fes Festival and other related festivals has created new habits of listening among audience members, what she calls a World Music literacy or fluency of listening. International audiences have acquired an aesthetic sense of musical and spiritual authenticity in the context of these festivals and related recording and performance projects, and this in turn feeds back into the programming for the festivals and the selection of repertoire by ensembles who perform at them or wish to do so, contributing to the marketing and standardization of repertoires and experiences of "Sufi" music, that is, of Suficized musics.

CONCLUSION

To conclude, Suficized musics are a form of commercialized "fast music" that draws on transnational representational practices that, while not entirely removed from Muslim spiritual practices (themselves not always understood as "Sufi"), nonetheless have become important markers of contemporary ("neoliberal") cultural economies.[6] Suficized musics occupy an interzone between the ritual and the ritualized. The World Stage serves as a representational arena where musical practices associated with Sufi ritual become "Sufi" musics: that is, Suficized. In parallel with neoliberal economies and the niche marketing of flexible specialization, culture brokers may add the "Sufi" repertoire to their grab bag of performance set lists to increase their cultural and monetary capital. With their enhanced repertoires, these artists also promote a new vision of Sufism and of Sufi and sacred music as bridges of understanding among peoples, playing into new habits and desires among mostly Western or Westernized audiences attuned to the vibrations of the sacred. In the context of the War on Terror, Suficized musics assume an important political mantle, as they are charged with promoting peaceful coexistence and understanding among the world's peoples, while at the same time providing a groove for audiences seeking spiritual authenticity. We can see the same processes of legitimation, mixing, and presentation at work in the creation of the rhythmic movements (*harikat-i mawzun*) in contemporary Iran (Zeinab Stellar, this volume).

The move from slow to fast, from ritual to ritualized, and from Sufi to Suficized music is fraught with contradictions. Some Syrian performers eschew the World Stage, or modify their repertoires in order to shield from eager foreign ears and eyes what they feel to be the heart of their spiritual practices; others attempt to transcend the traditional boundaries in their performances and risk transgressing local moral and aesthetic codes. The road ahead is unclear, but there is a growing sense that a once emergent category is in the process of becoming fixed; it remains to be seen how artists adapt to the global scene and arrange their repertoires to better accommodate international festival programming and demand for sacred music. An important factor in promoting Suficization in Syria and elsewhere is the growing cachet of the spiritual, driven no doubt by pop-star spirituality—Madonna's involvement with the Kabbalah, for example, or Richard Gere's Buddhism, even perhaps Mel Gibson's Christianity. It's hip to be spiritual, to do yoga, read Rumi and Kabir, and to consume not only World Music—so '80s in a way—but World *Sacred* Music or Sufi Music—very twenty-first century! Fast, Suficized musics thus represent a vanguard of global change, and perhaps a harbinger of things to come.

NOTES

1. For an overview of Sufism, see Baldick 1989; Schimmel 1975. For an overview and analysis of the *dhikr* ritual in Syria, see Pinto 2002; Shannon 2004.

2. As of March 24, 2009. These numbers are to be taken as suggestive of the popularity on the Internet of such terms, and not as accurate representations of worldwide interest in Sufism, music, or "Sufi music."

3. For more on the links between the realms of musical and culinary metaphor, see Frith (2004, 129), Guo and Farrow (2005), and Guo (2006).

4. I would argue that the more a group touts the authenticity of its performances and recordings, the more its authenticity is a social construction that serves the interests of marketing.

5. Kapchan (2008) notes a similar reluctance on the part of Moroccan Gnawa musicians to perform all elements of the ritual *lila* on stages in Europe for fear of exposing audiences to the most powerful and sacred parts of their traditions.

6. I'm not too happy with the term "neoliberal," as it seems to have replaced "transnational" and "global" without too much critical rethinking.

REFERENCES

Appadurai, Arjun. 1996. *Modernity at Large*. Minneapolis: University of Minnesota Press.

Baldick, Julian. 1989. *Mystical Islam*. New York: New York University Press.

Chittick, William C. 1989. *The Sufi Path of Knowledge: Ibn al-ʿArabi's Metaphysics of Imagination*. Albany: State University of New York Press.

Coon, Carleton. 1958. *Caravan: The Story of the Middle East*. New York: Holt.

Danielson, Virginia. 1990/1991. "Min al-Mashâyikh: A View of Egyptian Musical Tradition." *Asian Music* 22 (1): 113–127.

al-Faruqi, Lois Ibsen. 1985. "Music, Musicians and Muslim Law." *Asian Music* 17 (1): 3–35.

Feld, Steven. 1996. "Pygmy POP: A Genealogy of Schizophonic Mimesis." *Yearbook for Traditional Music* 28:1–35.

Frith, Simon. 2004. *Popular Music*. London: Routledge.

Guo, Yue, and Clare Farrow. 2005. *Music, Food, and Love: A Memoir*. London: Portrait.

Hodgson, Marshall. 1975. *The Venture of Islam*. Vol. 1: *The Classical Age of Islam*. Chicago: University of Chicago Press.

Honoré, Carl. 2004. *In Praise of Slowness*. New York: HarperCollins.

Kapchan, Deborah. 2008. "The Promise of Sonic Translation: Performing the Festive Sacred in Morocco." *American Anthropologist* 110 (4): 467–483.

Kirshenblatt-Gimblett, Barbara. 2006. "World Heritage and Cultural Economics." In *Mu-

seum Frictions: Public Cultures/Global Transformations, ed. Ivan Karp, Corinne A. Kratz et al., pp. 161–202. Durham, NC: Duke University Press.

Kreps, Christina Faye. 2003. *Liberating Culture: Cross-cultural Perspectives on Museums, Curation, and Heritage Preservation*. New York and London: Routledge.

Markoff, Irene. 1995. "Introduction to Sufi Music and Ritual in Turkey." *Bulletin. Middle East Studies Association of North America* 29 (2): 157–160.

Mitchell, Timothy. 1991. *Colonising Egypt*. Berkeley and Los Angeles: University of California Press.

Pinto, Paulo. 2002. "Mystical Bodies: Ritual, Experience and the Embodiment of Sufism in Syria." PhD diss., Department of Anthropology, Boston University.

Qureshi, Regula. 1986. *Sufi Music of India and Pakistan: Sound, Context, and Meaning in Qawwali*. Cambridge: Cambridge University Press.

Scher, Philip. 2002. "Copyright Heritage: Preservation, Carnival, and the State in Trinidad." *Anthropological Quarterly* 75 (3): 453–484.

Schimmel, Anne Marie. 1975. *The Mystical Dimensions of Islam*. Chapel Hill: University of North Carolina Press.

Shannon, Jonathan H. 2003. "Sultans of Spin: Syrian Sacred Music on the World Stage." *American Anthropologist* 105 (June): 266–277.

———. 2004. "The Aesthetics of Spiritual Practice and the Creation of Moral and Musical Subjectivities in Aleppo, Syria." *Ethnology* 43 (4): 381–391.

———. 2006. *Among the Jasmine Trees: Music and Modernity in Contemporary Syria*. Middletown, CT: Wesleyan University Press.

———. 2007. "Performing al-Andalus, Remembering al-Andalus: Mediterranean Soundings from *Mashriq* to *Maghrib*." *Journal of American Folklore* 120 (477): 308–334.

———. forthcoming. "Andalusian Music, Cultures of Tolerance, and the Negotiation of Collective Memories: Deep Listening in the Mediterranean." *Cuadernos de Etnomusicología*.

Stokes, Martin, and Philip Bohlman, eds. 2003. *Celtic Modern: Music at the Global Fringe*. Lanham, MD: Scarecrow.

Taylor, Timothy. 1997. *Global Pop: World Music, World Markets*. New York: Routledge Press.

Wolf, Richard. 2006. "The Poetics of 'Sufi' Practice: Drumming, Dancing, and Complex Agency at Madho Lal Husain (and Beyond)." *American Ethnologist* 33 (2): 246–268.

DISCOGRAPHY AND VIDEOGRAPHY

Ensemble al-Kindi. 1998. *The Aleppian Music Room*. With Sabri Moudallal and Omar Sarmini. Le Audio CD. Chant du Monde CML 574 1108.09.

———. 1999. *The Whirling Dervishes of Damascus*. With Sheikh Hamza Shakkur. Le Audio CD. Chant du Monde CMT 574 1123.24.

———. 2001. *The Crusades Seen through the Eyes of the Orient*. With Omar Sarmini. Audio CD. Le Chant du Monde CMT 574 1118.

———. 2003. *Aleppian Sufi Trance*. With Sheikh Habboush. Audio CD. Le Chant du Monde CMT 5741251.52.

Guo, Yue. 2006. *Music, Food, and Love*. Audio CD. Real World B000DZV4J8.

Spurlock, Morgan, dir. 2004. *Super Size Me!* Documentary film. Showtime Networks.

Various artists. 1989 (1975). *Syria: Islamic Ritual Zikr in Aleppo*. Audio CD. UNESCO: D 8013.

Zawiya Hilaliya. 2002. *Chant soufi de Syria; Dhikr Qadiri Khalwati de la Zawiya Hilaliya, Alep/Sufi Chanting from Syria; Dhikr Qadiri Khalwati of the Zawiya Hilaliya, Aleppo*. Audio CD. Inedit W 260109.

AFTERWORD

MARTIN STOKES

MUSIC, COMEDY, SOAP OPERAS, DANCE, cultural festivals—the contemporary popular culture of the Muslim world discussed in these pages—are sites of cosmopolitanism and public self-fashioning, neither fully under the control of the state or of religious authority. In tune with broader ideological currents, they wear their religiosity lightly, self-consciously, reflexively. "Post-ness" is at play in all of these chapters: "post-Islam," Islam "air-conditioned" or "Lite." Elsewhere, Bayat (2007) has discussed the politics of "fun" in the new Islamist movements, Boubekeur the Islamic "society of spectacle," in which activist becomes "fan," and imam "celebrity" (2007). Such categories are ideologically rich and complex.

The popular cultural practices described in this book are not just "expressions" of an underlying transformation. The contributions to this volume would, rather, seem to underline Hirschkind's recent words about cassette sermonizing in Egypt. "The affects and sensibilities honed through popular media practice are as infrastructural to politics and public reason as are markets, associations, formal institutions and information networks," he remarks (Hirschkind 2006, 9). The ease with which this volume's authors move from popular culture to politics and back suggests we have traveled a long way from simplistic Marxian reflexes relegating "popular culture" to superstructure or false consciousness. They also suggest that we have traveled a long way from a time when reaction to such reflexes took the form of an equally problematic romance with "popular-culture-as-resistance." The essays in this volume explore an emerging theoretical space, whose broad coordinates might be signaled, telegraphically, by the word "publics" (Fraser 1990; Warner 2002), on the one hand, and by "expediency" (Yúdice 2003), on the other. I will return to the interesting dynamics of this theoretical space, and some of its problems, shortly.

The chapters in this volume also suggest the distance traveled from an earlier discussion of art and music in the Muslim world, which assumed a shared and highly normative core to aesthetic experience constituted by abstraction, arabesque, the primacy of the word and so forth. The complicity of such formulations with orientalism has been subject to much discussion (Stokes 2002). The contributors to this volume, most of them anthropologists and ethnomusicologists, share a commitment to ethnography, to local meanings and histories, to subjects in various senses "dialogued with" rather than "spoken for," to a popular cultural politics that is emergent rather than known in advance. They also share a commitment to attempting to see social and cultural worlds from the bottom up rather than the top down. The challenges such commitments involve, particularly when they are located in the Middle East, or in Middle Eastern migrant culture, are increasingly well known (see Armbrust 2000).

In a Middle Eastern context, the question of orientalism continues to raise its head. Along with all of the other things Muslims are deemed to lack, many in the West continue to believe they lack "popular culture." Like *Reading Lolita in Teheran*, news of *Afghan Star* or of heavy metal bands in Iraq relies on patronizing assumptions by the press that such places have never before enjoyed "real" popular culture. Now that they do, thanks in part to the Western military interventions of recent years, freedom of the media, freedom of women, freedom to embrace globalization, freedom to love and desire will surely, at last, be theirs. This, at least, is the implication (Varzi 2008).

It is important to remember that popular culture, defined in terms of mass-mediation technologies, has a long history in the Middle East. Film and recording technology took root quickly at the beginning of the twentieth century. The history of mass media in the Middle East is the history of women, of sexuality, of desire, of popular cultural cosmopolitanism, of cities, of migrancy, of political mobilizations and contestations, of publics. Such histories are at last beginning to make their presence felt in Middle East studies. Slowly, in academic circles at least, we are showing signs of moving away from the idea that the term "popular culture" in the Middle East is simply a way of registering—negatively or positively—the "impact of the West," that it will always refer to something somehow extraneous. Pierre Hecker's account of heavy metal fans and Islamists in Istanbul in this volume, for example, shows global cultural practices at play in distinctly local struggles.

As I noted above, the broader theoretical space articulated by this volume is framed by the idea of "publics" on the one hand and "expediency" on the other. Or, to put it another way, by a view of culture as an emergent form of participatory and more or less democratic social relations, on the one hand, and as a resource to be mobilized in the pursuit of influence and space by specific social groups, on the other. There is an important difference of emphasis here. On the one side we have a picture of culture as a kind of world-building project, constructing social solidarities and senses of ethical and aesthetic value through media-facilitated processes of exchange. In the Middle East such processes of exchange are not fully absorbed by the nation-state, whose media systems remain sclerotic, underfunded, over-bureaucratized, and usually exceedingly dull. The solidarities they constitute take shape both beyond and within the nation-state and its ideological categories, which fact alone marks them as a threat, at least from the point of view of those social groups whose fortunes are still bound up with the state. The notion of "counterpublics" has consequently been much debated. Counterpublics emerge from these debates not so much as a space of opposition to "publics" but, rather, an alternative way of *tracking* public formation. Alternative, that is, to Habermas's heavily normative account of eighteenth-century *Öffentlichkeit*. Habermas's account, as is well known, has been criticized for its exclusive emphasis on reading practices, and his tendency to ignore or downplay the social exclusions of the late-eighteenth-century public sphere.

For Hirschkind, modern public formation is reliant on mobile mass media. It engages the voice, the ear, and the sensorium. It engages public emotionality and affect. Counterpublics understood in this way often have an oppositional feel, but this fact alone does not define them. Cassette sermonizing in Egypt has, as Hirschkind has shown, shaped a space of opposition to the state. An equivalent practice in Turkey (I am thinking of the cassette sermonizing of Fethullah Gülen in the 1980s) has shaped a space of compliance with neoliberal programming and Islamist governmentality. The challenge, then, if we are to stick with this set of terms, is one of noting their social forms and processes without reading either opposition or some kind of Habermasian normativity into them from the outset. If this challenge can be met, we stand a chance of grasping the complex political dynamics of art, music, and other forms of expressive culture in the public sphere.

A different set of problems relates to cultural "expediency." Yúdice has noted the growing instrumentalization of culture, an issue he relates, broadly, to neoliberal transformation. The state withdraws from everyday life in this scenario. Banks, corporations, aid agencies, and private foundations take over. Culture assumes a particularly important role in mediating the relations between state and nonstate actors. "Multiculturalism," understood as a regulation of diversity, is thoroughly implicated in the process. This and other forms of expediency mark the emergence, for Yúdice, of a society of control, the ongoing erosion of civil society and the public sphere. Something of Yúdice's worldview is at play in Michael Frishkopf and Jonathan H.

Shannon's chapters in this volume. Frishkopf notes the ways in which Canadian multiculturalism instrumentalizes culture, "pushes minority groups toward closure, stifling internal diversity as a means of translating 'minority capital' into political capital." For Canadian Muslims, a small and vulnerable minority in that country, the idea that "music is forbidden" assumes a prominence and force it has seldom had in the Middle East. As it becomes a token of "cultural identity" in Canada's complex multicultural struggles, a spiritual legacy embracing music is neglected and eventually lost. Shannon observes the commodification of Sufism in somewhat similar terms. "Slow ritual" is only able to become a token of difference within the logic of a "fast" global capitalism, as he explains with enjoyable irony.

Instrumental attitudes toward popular culture in the Muslim world are described in many of the chapters of this book. Joseph Alagha's account of Shi'a clerics' and intellectuals' reconciliation with popular culture in Lebanon is particularly fascinating. Karin van Nieuwkerk and Zeinab Stellar also note the emergence of evaluative terms that relocate longer-standing concerns with artistic utility (some of them of secular provenance) in new and emerging "Islamic" media environments. Ahu Yiğit's account of Islamist soap operas illustrates the energetic pragmatism with which the Turkish Islamist movement colonized the newly deregulated media system in that country. These are rich and thought-provoking accounts, inviting further questions when considered collectively. What do artists have to say about these new demands and opportunities? How do they walk the line between expediency and aesthetic pleasure? What of those who find themselves marginalized or sidelined in these new dispensations? And pious artists might claim to be able to monitor their own intentions ("*niyya*"), but how do they ensure those of their listeners or viewers, on the other side of television screens or computer terminals? Are they responsible for them? Islamic mystical traditions, from the time of al-Ghazali, have stressed the legitimizing role of the *ikhwan* in regulating and controlling spiritual and aesthetic bliss. What kind, or sense, of community can be relied on to fulfill the same function in cyberspace, in packed concert halls, in art galleries, at home in front of the TV?

There is a tension in this volume, then, between an interest in "culture" as a space of public formation, forging new kinds of sociality, and an interest in culture as a space of expediency, discipline, and control. Questions accumulate, on the first side of this split, around the political optimism associated with the idea of the counterpublic. They accumulate, on the second, around the ungrounded assumptions of interest and agency in the "expediency" scenario. Are such calculations of political capital made, then, in a space of rationality somehow "outside" or "beyond" culture? How and where and in what kind of historical space are such agents and their interests formed? The core theoretical tension at play in this volume is an old one, and is not peculiar to the Muslim world.

One issue, though, has a more complex resonance in discussing the Muslim world. There have been particular and specific difficulties in discussing Islamic aesthetics that raise broader theoretical problems in interesting ways. Put crudely perhaps, but for the sake of argument: "aesthetics" emerged as a category of discourse in Western society at a particular moment for a particular set of social, political, and historical reasons. Aesthetics, thus understood, has contributed to the broader orientalist characterization of Islam in terms of its lacks and negativities. So Islamic aesthetics have habitually been construed in the West in terms of "rejecting representation," "preferring ornament to structure," "banning music," and so forth. Western aesthetic discourse has, over time, been appropriated by Muslims, often under colonial conditions, its critical values reversed, so an aesthetic vice, from a Western point of view, became a virtue.

There are strong and long-standing arguments that the term "aesthetics" is problematic (see, for example, Gell 1999). Applied to non-Western cultures, the argument goes, it fails to account for the pleasures and meanings of ways of seeing, moving, and listening where art objects don't exist, and where practices of solitary, disinterested contemplation are not the norm. Applied to Western culture, it fails to account for so much of the social function of art, for instance in establishing and shoring up social distinctions. Following such arguments, social scientific approaches to art, music, and other kinds of performance have tended to approach the values attached to them in terms that explain them away—as productive of social distinction, as hegemony, as weapons of the weak. And it is easier in the context of such approaches to focus on art, music, and other kinds of performance when they are being talked about—justified, rationalized, condemned—by people or groups in positions of power or influence. And yet, as all of the chapters in this volume recognize, "the performing arts" generate social affect and pleasure in ways that can't always simply be reduced to such explanatory schemes. Such things make a difference. They impel people to do or say things they otherwise would not do or say. They generate movement. Hence the anxiety that surrounds them.

It is one thing to note that anxiety, but another to analyze its causes, to ask what the difference *is* that makes the difference. The mainstream humanities (literature, music, history of art) have developed ways of talking about texts, art objects, and performing bodies that have strongly made their presence felt in the social sciences in recent years, and that have opened up aesthetic questions in social and historical terms. The aesthetic, we now know, has a social life, and vice versa. But tensions remain. It will be more than an individual volume such as this can do to resolve them. But exploring them in a context in which "the aesthetic" is a particularly complex and elusive category, subject to rather intense social, cultural, and political pressures, allows the authors here to raise them in fresh and productive ways.

REFERENCES

Armbrust, W. 2000. "Introduction: Anxieties of Scale." In *Mass Mediations: New Approaches to Popular Culture in the Middle East and Beyond*, ed. W. Armbrust, pp. 1–31. Berkeley: University of California Press.

Bayat, A. 2007. "Islamism and the Politics of Fun." *Public Culture* 19 (3): 433–460.

Boubekeur, A. 2007. "Post-Islamist Culture: A New Form of Mobilization?" *History of Religions* 47 (1): 75–95.

Fraser, N. 1990. "Rethinking the Public Sphere: A Contribution to the Critique of Actually Existing Democracy." *Social Text*, no. 25/26, 56–80.

Gell, A. 1999. "The Technology of Enchantment and the Enchantment of Technology." In *The Art of Anthropology*, ed. E. Hirsch, pp. 159–186. London: Athlone Press.

Hirschkind, C. 2006. *The Ethical Soundscape: Cassette Sermons and Islamic Counterpublics*. New York: Columbia University Press.

Stokes, M. 2002. "Silver Sounds in the Inner Citadel: Reflections on Islam and Musicology." In *Interpreting Islam*, ed. H. Donnan, pp. 167–189. London; Thousand Oaks, CA; New Delhi: Sage.

Varzi, R. 2008. "Miniskirt Democracy: Muslim Women's Memoires." *London Review of Books* 30, no. 15 (July 31): 25–26.

Warner, M. 2002. *Publics and Counterpublics*. New York: Zone Books.

Yúdice, G. 2003. *The Expediency of Culture: Uses of Culture in the Global Era*. Durham, NC: Duke University Press.

Joseph Alagha received his PhD in Middle Eastern and Islamic Studies from the Free University of Amsterdam. Alagha, a postdoctoral researcher at Radboud University Nijmegen, the Netherlands, is the author of *The Shifts in Hizbullah's Ideology* (2006) and *Hizbullah's Documents* (2010), both published by Amsterdam University Press. He has published widely on Islamic movements, Iran, Lebanon, Hizbullah, the Palestinian Intifada, *jihadi* Salafism, and political mobilization and performing arts in the Middle East.

Michael Frishkopf is an ethnomusicologist. He is an associate professor in the Department of Music, and associate director of the Canadian Centre for Ethnomusicology, at the University of Alberta (Canada). He specializes in sounds of Islamic ritual, the Arab world, and West Africa. His research interests also include social network analysis, action research, and digital multimedia technology. He has an edited collection entitled *Music and Media in the Arab World* in press (American University in Cairo Press), and two books in progress: *The Sounds of Islam* (Routledge), and *Sufism, Ritual and Modernity in Egypt: Language Performance as an Adaptive Strategy* (Brill).

Pierre Hecker is a visiting lecturer at the Institute of Oriental Studies at the University of Leipzig, Germany. His main research interests are youth and youth cultures in Muslim societies, as well as gender studies. He is the author of several articles on heavy metal in the Middle East and coeditor of the book *Muslimische Gesellschaften in der Moderne* (*Muslim Societies in Modernity*) (Wiener Studien Verlag, 2007).

Farzaneh Hemmasi is an ethnomusicologist and Visiting Assistant Professor of Ethnomusicology at Hunter College in New York. She recently completed her dissertation at Columbia University on Iranian exiles in North America, popular music, and transnational media production and circulation. She has been a fellow with Columbia's Middle East Institute and Institute for Social and Economic Policy, and her work has been published in the Iran-based journal *Mahoor Musical Quarterly*. Currently, she is working on a book manuscript that examines the intersection of music, technological mediation, and politics in Iran and its diasporas from the 1950s to the present. Her other interests include migration, dance and dance musics, and popular culture in the United States and Middle East.

Jonathan H. Shannon is an associate professor in the Department of Anthropology at Hunter College of the City University of New York (CUNY). He was a fellow of the John Simon Guggenheim Memorial Foundation for 2009–2010. His main research interests are music, aesthetics, ethnomusicology, modernity, and food in the Middle East and the Mediterranean. His main publications include "Sultans of Spin: Syrian Sacred Music on the World Stage," in *American Anthropologist*, and *Among the Jasmine Trees: Music and Modernity in Contemporary Syria* (Wesleyan University Press, 2006).

Thomas Solomon is an associate professor in the Grieg Academy–Department of Music at the University of Bergen, Norway. He has taught ethnomusicology and popular music studies at Istanbul Technical University, the University of Minnesota, and New York

University. He has conducted field research in Bolivia on musical imaginations of ecology, place, and identity; and in Istanbul on place and identity in Turkish hip-hop. He has also done research on Turkish video clips and on music in the Turkish diaspora in Europe. His publications include articles in the journals *Ethnomusicology, Popular Music, Yearbook for Traditional Music*, and *European Journal of Cultural Studies*, as well as papers in several edited volumes.

Zeinab Stellar is an independent scholar. Her research currently centers on performing arts in the Middle East, chiefly focusing on the interrelations of the performing body, biopolitics, gender performativity, and representation.

Martin Stokes is University Lecturer in Ethnomusicology at Oxford University, and a Fellow of St. John's College. He researches music with a particular interest in social and cultural theory. His publications include *The Arabesk Debate: Music and Musicians in Modern Turkey* (Clarendon Press, 1992) and *Ethnicity, Identity and Music: The Musical Construction of Place* (Berg, 1994). His most recent book is *The Republic of Love: Cultural Intimacy in Turkish Popular Music* (University of Chicago Press, 2010).

Karin van Nieuwkerk is an anthropologist and associate professor at the University of Nijmegen, the Netherlands, and coordinator of the NWO (Netherlands Organization for Scientific Research) research program Islam and the Performing Arts in Europe and the Middle East. Her main fields of interest are gender and conversion to Islam, Islam and migration in Europe, and performing arts and entertainment in Egypt. Her main publications include *"A Trade like Any Other": Female Singers and Dancers in Egypt* (University of Texas Press, 1995), as author, and *Women Embracing Islam: Gender and Conversion in the West* (University of Texas Press, 2006), as volume editor. She also guest-edited and wrote an introduction for "Creating an Islamic Cultural Sphere: Contested Notions of Art, Leisure and Entertainment," a special issue of *Contemporary Islam* issued in 2008.

Ahu Yiğit is a PhD candidate in political science at the Bilkent University (Turkey). Her main fields of interest are Turkish political history and Islam in popular culture. She has previously studied at Leiden University (the Netherlands), in the Turkish Studies Department, and at the Middle East Technical University (Turkey), in the International Relations Department.

Lightning Source UK Ltd.
Milton Keynes UK
UKOW05f1803300813

216237UK00002B/33/P